PIRO AND THE GULABDASIS

PIRO AND THE GULABDASIS

GENDER, SECT, AND SOCIETY IN PUNJAB

With Best Compliments
from
Oxford University Press, India

ANSHU MALHOTRA

OXFORD
UNIVERSITY PRESS

OXFORD
UNIVERSITY PRESS

Oxford University Press is a department of the University of Oxford.
It furthers the University's objective of excellence in research, scholarship,
and education by publishing worldwide. Oxford is a registered trademark of
Oxford University Press in the UK and in certain other countries.

Published in India by
Oxford University Press
YMCA Library Building, 1 Jai Singh Road, New Delhi 110 001, India

© Oxford University Press 2017

The moral rights of the author have been asserted.

First Edition published in 2017

ISBN-13: 978-0-19-946818-8
ISBN-10: 0-19-946818-4

Typeset in ScalaPro 9.5/12.5
by Tranistics Data Technologies, Kolkata 700 091
Printed in India by Replika Press Pvt. Ltd.

Every effort has been made to trace the copyright holder of Figure 4.2.
The publisher would be pleased to hear from the copyright owner so that
proper acknowledgement can be made in future editions.

Contents

Figures

Abbreviations

GC	:	*Gulāb Chaman*
160 Kafis	:	*Ik Sau Saṭh Kāfiāṅ*
S1	:	*Siharfī 1*
S2	:	*Siharfī 2*
S3	:	*Siharfī 3*
SS	:	*Saṅjhī Siharfī*
RS	:	*Rāg Sāgar*

Note on Transliteration and Diacritical Marks

The book has many Punjabi, Hindi, and Urdu words. The first usage of Indian-language words and terms is in italics and appear in roman subsequently. Diacritical marks are avoided in the body of the text and only used for quotations and words from primary texts, conversations, and interviews, and for the first mention of titles of primary texts. Names of people and places do not have diacritics. Thus, 'Gulabdas' and not 'Gulābdās', 'Piro' and not 'Pīro', 'Chathianwala' and not 'Chaṭhiānwālā', and so on. Words that appear in the body of the text repeatedly also do not carry diacritics. Thus, *dera* and not *ḍerā*, *varnashramadharma* and not *varṇāshramādharmā*, *qissa* and not *qissā*, and so on. Since the language of quotations is a mix of Punjabi, Urdu, and Hindi (Braj and Khari boli) and both Gurmukhi and Devanagari scripts have been used, I have attempted a simplified scheme of easy comprehension, at the same time giving a sense of pronunciation to the interested. Thus, throughout I use 'ch' for 'च' and 'छ' sounds, not 'c'. Similarly 'sh' for 'श', 'ष', and 'स' sounds, and not 'ś' or 'ṣ'. 'ṛ' is used for 'ੜ' and 'ड़' sounds. All nasalization is marked as 'ṅ' for Gurmukhi 'ਂ', 'ਁ' sounds. All translations from Punjabi, Hindi, and Urdu are mine.

Acknowledgements

This work has taken a long time to complete, and I have over these years acquired many debts, which I happily acknowledge with a sense of appreciation and gratitude. A chance reading of an article on Piro written by Gurpreet Bal initiated this project. This took me to Amritsar on many occasions, where Piro's manuscript was available at the library of Guru Nanak Dev University (GNDU), Amritsar, India. Each time I relied on Gurpreet's hospitality. She not only ensured accommodation at GNDU's guesthouse, but also that I got to see various aspects of the lovely city of Amritsar. Shahryar sahib, then a librarian at GNDU's Bhai Gurdas Library, and a scholar and playwright, took keen interest in my work, helping me identify the scholarship in Punjabi on Piro and the Gulabdasis, including his own. This work would neither have been initiated nor completed without their selfless generosity. I am also thankful to H.S. Chopra, the university librarian, who facilitated the work. I also wish to thank Manjit Kaur of the manuscripts section for her help.

This work would also not have taken the shape it did if Shahryar sahib had not passed on my contact to Vijender*ji*, the head of the Gulabdasi *dera* (sect) at Hansi, a person who is a part of this study and who gave his benediction to it as well. He and his wife Saroj*ji* have over the years welcomed me to their home, festivals, and melas. Vijenderji has been generous both with his time and his own archive on the Gulabdasis. His infectious enthusiasm for my work on his guru Gulabdas and his 'mother' Piro has been a source of strength, and I thank him for it.

This study, embarked on earlier, gained its present shape during my fellowship at the Nehru Memorial Museum and Library (NMML), New Delhi. The then director of this remarkable institution, the energetic Mahesh Rangarajan, ensured a conducive academic environment to pursue research and to share it with fellow academics. His warm concern for the progress of my research and my well-being has meant that I will always remain nostalgic about my unfettered time there.

The University of Delhi, where I teach, granted me leave to join the NMML and also an earlier study leave that allowed the initiation of this project. I thank the institution where I have spent more years than I care to remember! I also received research and development grants from the university, which facilitated my archival work. My colleagues at the Department of History have stood by me with steadfast support and I take this opportunity to thank them. My particular thanks to Upinder Singh, Nayanjot Lahiri, Seema Alavi, Farhat Hasan, Bhairabi Prasad Sahu, Sunil Kumar, and Kesavan Veluthat; and also to Shahid Amin, Razi Aquil, Aparna Balachandran, Charu Gupta, Biswamoy Pati, and Anirudh Deshpande for being there.

Siobhan Lambert-Hurley initiated and helmed one of the most wonderful and rewarding collaborative projects that I have been a part of—Women's Autobiography in Islamic Societies. Coming together after our days at SOAS, University of London, UK, when we pursued our doctorates, this project allowed us to think together and share research and ideas as we met over many conferences (University of Texas at Austin, USA, in 2010; India International Centre at New Delhi in 2010; and American University, Sharjah, UAE, in 2011), or jointly convened panels in some (European Conference of Modern South Asian Studies, Bonn, Germany, in 2010; Berks Conference, Toronto, Canada, in 2014; and European Conference of South Asian Studies, Zurich, Switzerland, in 2014, which Siobhan could not attend). In 2011, Loughborough University, Leicestershire, UK, which she was then a part of, hosted me for three weeks, and we used this time to plan the volume that we edited together on women's autobiographies in South Asia. These conferences also facilitated interaction with a remarkable set of scholars. I thank Marilyn Booth for her erudite papers and her warm interest in my work. Farzaneh Milani, a scholar of Iranian women's autobiographies, organized a conference on women's autobiographies in the Middle East and South Asia at the University of Virginia, USA, in 2012 that showcased some exceptional work in the field. I thank her for her invitation.

A six-week Hughes Fellowship at the Center of South Asian Studies, University of Michigan at Ann Arbor, USA, in 2008 was the time when I first seriously thought about this work. The lasting academic engagement with and friendship of Farina Mir and Will Glover is what I have brought back from there.

I have visited the Punjabi University at Patiala, Punjab, India, with its treasure trove of archives on more than one occasion. I wish to thank Professor Jaspal Kaur for her hospitality in Patiala. Professor Birinder Pal Singh went out of his way to help locate some material that I urgently required and I remain grateful to him. The librarian, Saroj Bala, helped in accessing the library and Ichhya Kaur assisted in locating materials.

The invitation of Lahore University of Management Sciences, Pakistan, in the summer of 2008 was a boon that allowed me a glimpse of the Gulabdasi establishment at Chathianwala, Lahore, Pakistan, or what is left of it. This would not have been possible without the warm hospitality of Furrukh Khan, and the Head of Humanities, Ali Khan. The scholar at large Iqbal Qaiser's knowledge of all things Punjabi, particularly its geography, ensured not only a visit to Chathianwala, but also to my father Sat Pal Malhotra's *qasba* (town) of Chunian, which the family left around the time of the Partition. Iqbal sahib's enthusiasm for research on Punjab is remarkable and I thank him and his research centre, Khoj Garh, for their work.

I have participated in many conferences and workshops over the years this work has been in the making. The comments of many scholars, friends, and colleagues who took interest in my work and pushed me to think through issues are gratefully acknowledged. I wish to thank Avril Powell, Gerry Forbes, Barbara Ramusack, Antoinette Burton, Barbara Metcalf, Kathy Hansen, Carla Petievich, Jack Hawley, Tyler Williams, Gail Minault, Radhika Chopra, Ravinder Kaur, Shubhra Ray, Anne Murphy, Yogesh Snehi, Milind Wakankar, Hephzibah Israel, Gurinder Singh Mann, Indu Banga, Srilata Raman, Francesca Orsini, Martin Fuchs, Ratna Raman, and Malavika Kasturi. My conversations with Timothy Dobe were insightful as we shared our mutual interest in the religious history of Punjab. Vasudha Dalmia's warm encouragement has been much appreciated as I struggled to bring this book to an end.

Many students have over the years heard my ideas and have been an exciting presence in class and other fora. I wish to thank Samiksha Sehrawat for believing. Also Mahima Manchanda, Devyani Gupta, and Shilpi Rajpal for providing intellectual curiosity; so also Saurabh Vatsa, Emi Aikawa, Sunita Kumari, Vijjika Singh, Anisha Srivastava, and Serohi Nandan.

I wish to acknowledge that earlier versions of some of the chapters in this book were published in *Indian Economic and Social History Review* (vol. 46, no. 4, 2009); *Modern Asian Studies* (vol. 46, no. 6, 2012); *Journal of Women's History* (vol. 25, no. 2, 2013); *Journal of Punjab Studies* (vol. 20, nos 1 and 2, Spring–Fall 2013); and *NMML Occasional Paper* (new series, no. 55, 2014).

The editors at Oxford University Press have tracked this project for the last two years and I thank them for their support and encouragement in bringing it to completion.

My large and wonderful family is the constant support I need, and this acknowledgement is to tell them how much they mean to me. My mother Swaran Malhotra is the reason I have researched on Punjab. My siblings, their spouses, and children are the madness I love being surrounded by: Hemant, Nita, Poonam, Manoj, Sharad, Ina, Karan, Aditi, Devika, Madhav, Tarini, and little Saina, thanks for being there. To my delight, my talented niece, Aditi Kodesia, lent me her drawing skills in map-making. My partner Satyajit has been with me through it all. My sons Mihiraan and Milind make life worthwhile. This work is dedicated to them all.

Self, Sect, and Society
An Introduction

Almost ten years ago, when I came upon Piro's voice, recondite and elliptical in its allegorical, allusive language, yet forthright and scathing in its
condemnation of societal codes of caste, gender, and religious behaviour,
I was startled. In my earlier research on the reconstituting of gendered
cultural norms for high-caste women among Hindus and Sikhs from the
late nineteenth century to the first two decades of the twentieth century,
I had struggled to hear women's voices. The famed fertile land of Punjab
had proven to be singularly barren in fructifying its women's expressions
in written and published forms, and I had to strain my senses to read a
few discordant notes. And here was Piro (d. 1872); though not prolific
or garrulous and not published till very recently, not quiet or restrained
either, and determined to tell 'her' story, 'a' story, in her cryptic, oblique
way, preserved in written manuscripts.

Piro, a Muslim prostitute/courtesan of Lahore, narrated the saga, 'the
event', of her apparently wilful flight, kidnapping, escape, and obsequious
asylum in the Gulabdasi dera of Guru Gulabdas. Gulabdas (1809–1873)
was a dissentient *advaitin* (monist) guru from a 'Sikh' sectarian background, living with his disciples in the socially heterodox and literarily
efflorescent environs of Chathianwala village, Kasur, defiantly close
to Maharaja Ranjit Singh's centre of power in Lahore.[1] The pages

---

[1] The reasons why this can be interpreted as defiant are discussed in Chapters 1
and 2.

that follow endeavour to make sense of the fragmentary, versified tale Piro unfolds in her 'autobiographical' *Ik Sau Saṭh Kāfiāṅ* (One Hundred and Sixty Kafis, henceforth *160 Kafis*) and her other writings as well, including her *siharfīs* or acrostic verses.[2] This work also attempts to give a glimpse of the Gulabdasi dera, a small sect shrouded till recently in anonymity, grappling nonetheless with their importance, showing what made them significant from their time through to their afterlife in ours. This book can thus be seen to be an elaborate analysis of a 'micronarrative': the telling of a story of an event in her life by a woman who may be called 'the exceptional normal', in the sense that she was not a 'woman worthy', nor yet an 'everywoman'.[3] She was 'exceptional' in her agential command over her life as in recording aspects of it for posterity, not to speak of the various boundaries she crossed, including the religious. At the same time, through her narrative Piro gives us a sense of her time and its culture, significantly allowing us to see how a woman could speak and what she could speak of. Though Piro's deviance can shed light on what may have comprised 'normal' in her time, significant too are the attempts at erasing her, or 'normalizing' her through maternal metaphors by some contemporary Gulabdasis.

The book is also a 'microhistory' of the Gulabdasis as constructed with the help of three moments in time. It initiates from Gulabdas's and Piro's unconventional life as they began their journey together during Ranjit Singh's rule (1799–1839), their partnership coming to an end with Piro's death a little over two decades after the British had established firm control over Punjab (1849)—their story woven together from their writings and other contemporary and later sources. It moves forward by examining

---

[2] *Ik Sau Sath Kafian*, ms. 888, Bhai Gurdas Library, Guru Nanak Dev University (GNDU), Amritsar. In this study, three of Piro's siharfis are studied. Of these, *Siharfī3* (*S3*) is available in the same document listed earlier and is used in preference of other sources. *Siharfī1* (*S1*) and *Siharfī2* (*S2*), along with a *Saṅjhī Siharfī* (*SS*), or joint verses with her guru Gulabdas, are available in Sant Vijender Das's compilation of her writings. Piro's *Rāg Sāgar* (*RS*) is also sourced from this compilation. (Vijender Das, *Sant Kavyitri Ma Piro* [Mohali: Satluj Prakashan, 2011].)

[3] Eric R. Dursteler discusses the concept of 'the exceptional normal' in his description of the women under his lens in his *Renegade Women: Gender, Identity, and Boundaries in the Early Modern Mediterranean* (Baltimore: The Johns Hopkins University Press, 2011), pp. 107 and 117. The concept is also discussed by Carlo Ginzburg in 'Microhistory: Two or Three Things That I Know About It', in his *Threads and Traces: True, False, Fictive* translated by Anne C. Tedeschi and John Tedeschi (Berkeley: University of California Press, 2012), pp. 193–214.

the interventions in the colonialist public sphere through Gulabdasi Ditta Ram/Ditt Singh as he cogitated over new understandings of caste and religious identity, turning his back on his Gulabdasi antecedents. It finally proceeds through the contemporary imaginings of Piro's life, and the reimaginings of Gulabdas's life and legacy by some of his successors. We thus get glimpses of Punjab's social and cultural life through stories of the self and of the sect that begin sometime in the latter part of Ranjit Singh's rule; cast a fugacious glance at the colonial era through the public life of one man; and try and unravel Punjabi disposition for social change as well as for replenishing cultural habits by looking at aspects of the Gulabdasi dera in our own time.

ON MICRONARRATIVE AND MICROHISTORY

The historian Peter Burke describes 'micronarrative' as the 'telling of a story about ordinary people in their local setting', and so discusses it as a narrative and stylistic innovation adopted by historians experimenting with 'fictional techniques' for their 'factual works'.[4] However, the manner in which the term is used here is to indicate Piro's own autobiographical narration, her 'micro' or 'small' story, centre-staging her remote life with its local events by writing about it. More interestingly, it points to the scrambling of the fictional and the factual—what some scholars call 'faction', which is the nature of the autobiographical oeuvre itself— adopted by Piro.[5] The performative rehearsing of aspects and events of one's life, seen from the presentist perspective through the prism of memory, is a necessary ingredient of the autobiographical; it is what goes into making the autobiographical a montage of fact and fiction.[6]

---

[4] Peter Burke, 'History of Events and the Revival of Narrative', in *The History and Narrative Reader*, edited by Geoffrey Roberts (London: Routledge, 2001), pp. 305–17.

[5] Sidonie Smith and Julia Watson speak about 'faction' or 'autofiction' as techniques adopted by contemporary writers. However, what I emphasize here is the nature of autobiographical writing. See their *Reading Autobiography: A Guide for Interpreting Life Narratives* (Minneapolis: Minnesota University Press, 2000), p. 10.

[6] For a discussion on the performative aspects of the autobiographical, see Anshu Malhotra and Siobhan Lambert-Hurley, 'Introduction: Gender, Performance and Autobiography in South Asia', in *Speaking of the Self: Gender, Performance and Autobiography in South Asia*, edited by Anshu Malhotra and Siobhan Lambert-Hurley (Durham: Duke University Press, 2015), pp. 1–30.

To the historian, Piro's micronarrative provides the cue and the reason to thicken the discussion by highlighting the social and cultural structures of her society and, moreover, posits and shows how the mentalities of an early modern denizen, particularly a woman who broke the varied disciplining codes imposed by her culture, were deeply moulded by a bhakti imaginary and its affect. Thus the 'event' that Piro came to write about with reference to its specific locales—of first hearing Gulabdas's discourse at Moti Bazaar of the Lahore city (*sahar*), of abandoning the brothel in Lahore, of abduction and incarceration in Gujranwala, and the escape (via the River Ravi?) to Chathianwala in Kasur—was not a 'creative event' in the sense in which it may have changed the structures of the society; far from it. It was 'creative' insofar as it unspooled the creativity of a woman, leaving a record of the 'constraints and possibilities' that a woman's life on the margins may hold.[7] Instead, in this context, it was a creativity which was the genesis of action, of doing, and, in the long run, of change.

The question of talking from the margins is an important one; the margins here are defined not in spatial terms, but in social and cultural ones. Spatially speaking, Piro lived and constructed her story in the very heart of the Sikh empire, perhaps one of the reasons why she gained notoriety. Piro's person, however, inhabited multiple marginalities: a professional prostitute/courtesan, she was deemed to be low caste, with Piro designating herself a *sūdar vesvā* (a low-caste prostitute), a term indicative of both figurative and real constraints on her life. She was a woman in a society that extolled sharp gender hierarchies. Moreover, she went into a monastic establishment where women may have been unwelcome, though were not completely absent. She was a Muslim among the Gulabdasis, a sect seen as occupying interstices between being Hindu and Sikh. She was thus profoundly conscious of her religious crossing over and the ambivalence of status that the situation generated. The historian Natalie Davis asked of her three 'women on the margins' what advantages they had by being situated there? And indeed which novel ways of living did they carve out by that placement

---

[7] For a discussion on events and structures, see Burke, 'History of Events'. The expression 'constraints and possibilities' is the manner in which Natalie Z. Davis speaks of how her sixteenth-century peasant couple in France, the impersonator Martin Guerre and his wife Bertrande de Rols, experienced life and their fashioning of it. See her *The Return of Martin Guerre* (Cambridge: Harvard University Press, 1983).

on what one may call the cultural borderlands?[8] For Piro, apart from the novelty of her chosen soteriological path, these borderlands became her domicile and engendered her liminal status. They encompassed her positioning between social respectability and unacceptability; sexual promiscuity as a prostitute and sexual containment as a 'mother' to the Gulabdasi disciples; between Hinduness (and Sikhness) and Muslimness. Such tenuous dwelling gave her a unique perspective to see, as she repeatedly affirmed, the vacuity of upholders of morality as well as of ritualistic religious practice. Further, and on a more positive note, her training as a courtesan likely gave her musical and poetical skills, and maybe even basic literacy, which she developed and honed under the Gulabdasis, equipping her to engage with literariness, a hallmark of the Gulabdasis. Most of all, her marginality rent a frisson of desperation in her life, making her seek new paths of living and being, for which she had to rely on her own instincts and careful calibrations, her agency, and the quality of self-possession and confidence that she was keenly aware of.

Despite some perspectival sharpness that her abode at the margins may have bestowed on Piro besides its many shortcomings, and in spite of the force of her oftentimes blunt manner adopted in writing, her voice may be located amongst the 'small voices' of history. Against the univocal statist discourse—the authoritative commanding from a place of power—Ranajit Guha draws attention to a certain 'disorderliness' of small voices. He speculates on their form, which may 'force the narrative to stutter in its articulation instead of delivering in an even flow of words; perhaps the linearity of its progress will dissolve in loops and tangles; perhaps chronology itself ... will be sacrificed at the altar of the capricious, quasi-Pauranic time, which is not ashamed of its cyclicity'.[9] While Piro did not stutter, she did speak in loops and tangles of Pauranic cyclicity, for as A.K. Ramanujan noted, the premodern peoples were neither pressured by the desire for novelty or autonomy, nor that of originality.[10] Mythic time and

[8] Natalie Z. Davis, *Women on the Margins: Three Seventeenth Century Lives* (Cambridge: Harvard University Press, 1995), pp. 203–10.

[9] Ranajit Guha, 'The Small Voice of History', in his *The Small Voice of History: Collected Essays*, edited by Partha Chatterjee (Ranikhet: Permanent Black, 2009), pp. 304–17.

[10] A.K. Ramanujan, 'Where Mirrors are Windows: Towards an Anthology of Reflections', in *The Collected Essays of A.K. Ramanujan*, edited by Vinay Dharwadker (New Delhi: Oxford University Press, 1999), pp. 6–33.

miraculous deeds interceded in the human condition, and people, even if living in distinct circumstances, imagined themselves as re-enacting or connecting with lives lived earlier. Piro, temporally lodged on the brink of colonial modernity, delivered an autobiographical fragment—indeed a fragile fragment of her life—which did not adhere to a 'modern' autobiography of the kind that men were beginning to write in India in which they observed what seemed to them cataclysmic public events through the prism of their lives;[11] nor yet did Piro's work conform to a premodern genre—in which too men wrote, fashioning selves in ingenious ways.[12] Piro's disorderly small voice, uncaring of sophisticated formal forms and literary polish of complex metres and genres (though sensitive to the poetical aesthetic), can be seen to be a determined lament, a cataloguing of grievances, barely concealed by an albeit sincere carapace of respect for the guru and his monist doctrinal position.

The fragmentary nature of Piro's utterance, or rather Piro's life in a fragment, leaves the historian impeded, a professional frustration eloquently described by Guha who comments on the historian's voracious 'urge for plenitude'—'an insatiated, indeed insatiable urge for more and more linkages to work into the torn fabric of the past and restore it to an ideal called the full story'. Piro's incomplete though eventful story can then be seen as Guha's 'untamed fragment' that 'stalls a plot in its drive for denouement'.[13] So instead of a 'before' and an 'after' of 'the' event—the chronological method dear to historians—the intention in this study is to not try too hard to fill the gaps of her life as much as try to comprehend it by attempting to apprehend the processes around her.

---

[11] Udaya Kumar, 'Autobiography as a Way of Writing History: Personal Narratives from Kerala and the Inhabitation of Modernity', in *History in the Vernacular*, edited by Raziuddin Aquil and Partha Chatterjee (New Delhi: Permanent Black, 2008), pp. 418–48; Sudipto Kaviraj, 'The Invention of Private Life: A Reading of Sibnath Sastri's "Autobiography"', in *Telling Lives in India: Biography, Autobiography and Life History in India*, edited by David Arnold and Stuart Blackburn (Ranikhet: Permanent Black, 2004), pp. 83–115; A.R. Venkatachalapathy, 'Making a Modern Self in Colonial Tamil Nadu', in *Biography as History: Indian Perspectives*, edited by Vijaya Ramaswamy and Yogesh Sharma (Hyderabad: Orient BlackSwan, 2009), pp. 30–52.

[12] See Chapter 2.

[13] Ranajit Guha, 'Chandra's Death', in his *The Small Voice of History*, pp. 271–303.

Piro's guru, Gulabdas, and the sect she belonged to, the Gulabdasis, are thus investigated: Gulabdas's ideas are discussed at some length, and why they were considered radical, even libertine, in their time is brought out through significant contemporary and later accounts. A quick view of Punjab on the cusp of colonialism is made, of the Anglo-Sikh wars and their effect on society and the soldiery, some of whom turned to the *bhekh*, the garb of the mendicant (see Chapter 1). Attention is given to Piro's catastrophic event and her life thereafter through her autobiographical and other writings, a hybrid of the spiritual and the autobiographical, where her bhakti devotional make-up and the deployment of its tropes, and her complex subject positions are explored (Chapters 2, 3, 4, and 5). This combination of the spiritual and the autobiographical—though not 'autohagiographical' in the sense of how one may wish to be renowned as a spiritually advanced being—does, however, perform the self in anticipation of how one would wish to be remembered.[14] Further, attention is given to what some today make of her life, and the cultural tropes through which they approach her (Chapter 7). The performance that Piro gave of the transformative moment in her life through her autobiographical recall of it is set in a couple of plays by Punjabi litterateurs; the dramatic events she describes are played out in dramas overlaid by gendered norms of Punjabi society and cultural topoi, for example, of the romantic *qissa* (story) tradition. A detour through the colonial period in Punjab is made by delineating the career and writings of Ditt Singh, a Gulabdasi, Arya Samaji, and Singh Sabhiya at subsequent junctures in his life, and through it all his endeavours to understand and re-conceptualize caste and religion (Chapter 6). The *varnashramadharma* that Gulabdas repudiated through the logic of advaita monism and which Piro castigated through recourse to a bhakti imaginary was discussed as caste in discourses in the colonial public sphere. What were seen as the depredations of caste, and by way of its tentative questioning, Singh sought to recast it towards the end of the nineteenth century through a reimagined Sikh religion and history. A survey is also made of the attempts at a new rehabilitation of Gulabdas's life, his afterlife insofar as how some of his legatees today understand and construct him, celebrating what in their estimation is his exemplary life (Chapter 8). If cultural memory requires spatial reference

---

[14] For the autohagiographical, see the discussion on 'Vernacular Vedanta', in *Hindu Christian Faqir: Modern Monks, Global Christianity and Indian Sainthood* by Timothy Dobe (New York: Oxford University Press, 2015), pp. 182–3.

and temporal recall, then these elements are seen at play in the manner in which Gulabdas's life is remembered and celebrated.[15] In sum, here is an attempt at presenting a sort of a microhistory of a sect and some of its acolytes, not with the intensity of a gaze that unravels its condition in all its complexity at a given time, but rather, a longer panoramic view to understand what makes a relatively small sect come into being, flourish, experience attrition, amplify again, and through it all remain meaningful for its votaries.

The prefix 'micro' in microhistory indexes a smallness of scale, which has been interpreted by individual scholars in a variety of ways: a minute analysis of a single, perhaps structurally speaking significant event; a *longue duree* analysis of an obscure village; a serializing of recurring patterns in non-eventful lives; or as Carlo Ginzburg said of his project on the miller Mennochio, of focusing on the 'anomalous, not the analogous'.[16] Piro's *160 Kafis* may be taken as anomalous in that a rare woman wrote in her time, and rarer still it was that she did so about her own life or experience. One may also regard as aberrant to an extent the Gulabdasis with their ostensibly libertine proclivities, but just barely so. For such 'sects', *sāmpradāys*, *paṅths*, or deras, that is, the groupings of people sutured together on the basis of specific doctrinal and philosophical inclinations and oftentimes ritual and cultic practices, were surely available in numbers in India signalling perhaps a pattern rather than a deviation from it. Aware that the term 'sect' emerges in the nineteenth century and in the colonial context, this study uses it interchangeably with the term 'dera', the nomenclature most commonly found in Punjab, and for the Gulabdasis, for convenience.[17]

The term 'dera' conjures encampment, it signals the spatiality of abode, the domicile of doctrinally like-minded peoples who are institutionally

---

[15] On cultural memory, see Jan Assman, *Cultural Memory and Early Civilization: Writing, Remembrance, and Political Imagination* (Cambridge: Cambridge University Press, 2011), p. 24.

[16] Ginzburg, 'Microhistory: Two or Three Things', p. 213. Also see Carlo Ginzburg, *The Cheese and the Worms*, translated by John and Anne Tedeschi (London: Routledge and Kegan Paul, 1980).

[17] Vasudha Dalmia discusses the use of the term 'sect' in the nineteenth century for *sampraday*. See her '"The Only Real Religion of the Hindus": Vaisnava Self-representation in the Late Nineteenth Century', in *Representing Hinduism: The Construction of Religious Traditions and National Identity*, edited by Vasudha Dalmia and H. Von Stietencron (New Delhi: SAGE Publications, 1995), pp. 176–210.

independent.[18] The term 'sect', on the other hand, derived from the Middle English *secte* or the Latin *secta*; it speaks of a smaller group that is part of a larger entity, perhaps with its Christian antecedents, even signifying a schismatic break. 'Sampraday' indexes both a doctrinal group and part of a larger grouping, while 'panth' connotes a particular way or path. The Gulabdasis, as these variegated usages suggest, may be seen to be doctrinally defined, while at the same time may be regarded as a part of a larger Hindu or a Sikh religious community. Their separate abode, dera, indicated their inclination for monastic dwelling. However, these different terminologies and their usage point to the complexity of the multitudinous 'sects' that were present on the Indian landscape, a complexity that is further explored later. While the ethnographic data of the colonial state attest to such cultic and doctrinal proliferation, what some scholars referred to as the 'obscure religious cults', the study here has no intention of obfuscating this complexity, though it will use the term 'sect' for its popularity in a commonsensical way.[19]

The term 'obscure' recurs in writings on microhistory as it does on Indic sects, pointing to their supposed distance from the 'mainstream', in the apparent abstruseness of their ideas and practices, as well as in the difficulty in accessing their voice and records. Burke, for example quotes a scholar's observations on a work on microhistory as 'the miserable chronicle of an obscure village'.[20] With reference to the present work, one may easily replace the word 'village' with 'sect', suggesting perhaps the esotericism of their ideas, what to their contemporaries had seemed the irregularities of their practice, and, of course, the difficulty in accessing records. Obscure may also suggest what was to the colonialists India's bewildering variety of practice and belief, a disorderliness that the Orientalists (in their search for textual and pristine forms) as much as the Anglicists/Utilitarians (in their dismissal of Hindu practice) found difficult to categorize as serious or true religion.

---

[18] 'Dera' may also signal temporary abode, indicating the need for an ascetic to be on the move. However, the manner in which the term is used for the Gulabdasis, and indeed the way it is deployed in contemporary Punjab, it simply refers to the domicile of a sect. That gurus and sects often acquired and amassed property in these establishments has been shown by Daniel Gold. See his *The Lord as Guru: Hindi Sants in North Indian Tradition* (New York: Oxford University Press, 1987).

[19] Shashibhushan Dasgupta, *Obscure Religious Cults* (Calcutta: Firma KLM Pvt. Ltd, 1976).

[20] Burke, 'History of Events', p. 312.

However, the obscure and the arcane must not be overly emphasized. The training of the lens on the 'local' and the 'forgotten', as certainly the focus on Piro and the Gulabdasis suggests, must surely illuminate aspects that a culture gives valence to and what it considers is meaningful and valuable to its partisans. Piro's anomalous speech provides an inkling of how a woman may grasp an agential hold over her life, relying upon a deep, recurring, cultural resource that the empathetic bhakti devotion lent her. Her unique voice, sometimes seething with rage, may also be heard singing of the company of bhaktas, the imagined community of devotees to which Piro averred she too belonged. Thus, her anomaly yields a paradigm, of women's recurring resort to and solace in the path of bhakti, renewing it in their own light and circumstances, a phenomenon to which Ramanujan had made us aware.[21] On the other hand, the Gulabdasis' relatively analogous presence in the cultural landscape of Punjab, where many religious conglomerations flourished, suggests how more intimate sectional relationship with a guru and his ideas was an aspect of people's ethereal yet everyday quest. This was true not only of the guru's epigones who stayed within his dera, his establishment, but also of a number of other lay followers, who looked to him not so much for salvational options as for spiritual grace and consolation, and for meaningful piety. The fact that great inventiveness went into the fusing of complicated philosophical doctrines with accessible cultural spaces available to the acolyte and to the ordinary is a tribute to the many gurus who have dotted the Punjabi and Indian topography. It is precisely this creativity of the Indian saints, the polyvalence of their self-fashioned personas, and their performative synergies with changing times that Timothy Dobe has recently drawn attention to in his study of two Punjabi 'upstart' saints. The locus of the 'religious everyday' in such ascetic and saintly practices is important to bear in mind.[22] That the Gulabdasi ingenuity continues its creative journey in our times points to a deep-seated cultural habitus, adapted and constantly responding to changed times and disparate circumstances.

Piro's voice, particularly in her autobiographical oeuvre, remains sui generis: it is uncommon in north India before the intervention of

[21] A.K. Ramanujan, 'On Women Saints', in Dharwadker, *The Collected Essays of A.K. Ramanujan*, pp. 270–8.

[22] Dobe, *Hindu Christian Faqir*, p. 29.

colonial modernity to come across women specifically 'speaking of their selves', of fashioning themselves, though it is not entirely unknown.[23] This raises the issue of what Eric Dursteler calls 'exceptionality and representativity'.[24] Critiquing microhistory and specifically Ginzburg's study of the miller Mennochio in his famous book *The Cheese and the Worms*, a critic hinted at the impossibility of a singular individual helping to understand a paradigm, by asking if there were 'one, two, three, a thousand Mennochios?'[25] The same may be asked of Piro, if her voice, in fact, made a difference. I hope I have already answered this question by pointing to the indubitable exceptionality of her voice, but the recourse to her bhakti inheritance points to a cultural pattern resorted to by many a marginalized people. Moreover, the social and cultural constraints of which Piro speaks with acuity born of experience reveal the gendered social and cultural realities of her time, of religious tyrannies and authority figures, towards whom she is especially caustic. Further, a rare voice, by flagging and raising alarm about oppressions borne regularly, gives a glimpse of what a society considers as normal, the codes it lives by, and the repression that is part of the routine. Thus, the unveiling of normality that an anomalous voice like Piro's ushers can be seen as a gateway to the everyday, her extraordinariness allowing the viewing of the ordinary.

ON RELIGION

The complexity of religion as a category is understood by scholars today, sensitive as they are to local usages. The process of the universalization of religion under the ambit of Western enlightenment and later the evangelizing missionaries was seen as one embedded in power relations that rendered various peoples of the world as mired in practices (tribal, animalistic) that had no conception of the 'fundamental nature of reality'. In this view for those who did 'affirm something', their affirmation was seen

---

[23] 'Speaking of the Self' is taken from the title of the volume edited by Malhotra and Lambert-Hurley, *Speaking of the Self*. In some of it essays, the volume discusses how some premodern women fashioned their selves.

[24] Dursteler, *Renegade Women*, p. 116.

[25] Dursteler quoting the critique of Paola Zambelli, and asking the question about the women in his study, 'one, two, three, a thousand Fatimas?' (*Renegade Women*, pp. 116–17).

as shallow, or perverse, and so was to be dismissed.[26] However, religion remains a category of analysis, one that can be veered away from preoccupations with origins towards 'a focus on use and pragmatics, placing it as a deeply historical phenomenon that is particular to its core'.[27] Emphasizing the need for always 'locally' understanding the dynamics of what comprises the religious, Anne Murphy has pointed towards the manner in which one may look at the interactions between diverse traditions, and how these relationships and negotiations are implicated in producing notions of the 'secular' and the 'modern'.[28]

Sensitivity to colonial power relations and to the imbrication of the modern understanding of religions in the asymmetries of interaction between the colonialists and their native collaborators on the one hand and the colonized on the other, has given rise, among others, to a debate on the 'invention' of Hinduism.[29] Those seen on the side of Hinduism's invention have argued that the Orientalists, with their appreciation of the ancient Indian textual traditions, and the Anglicists, missionaries, and the Utilitarians, with their disparagement of the same, together constructed Hinduism from disparate and discrete traditions. Further, Hindu reformers and nationalists, in order to overcome the ostensible disabilities associated with a religion not seen to be evolved enough to take its place among world religions, also contributed towards giving it a coherence it lacked. Gauri Vishwanathan has spoken of the Hindu nationalists' 'will to monotheism' and their repulsion to idolatry and polytheism.[30] On the other side are scholars who, though aware of the changing dynamics that a textual and a public debate on the nature of Hinduism

---

[26] Talal Asad, 'The Construction of Religion as an Anthropological Category', in his *Genealogies of Religion: Discipline and Reasons of Power in Christianity and Islam* (Baltimore: The Johns Hopkins University Press, 1993), pp. 27–54.

[27] Anne Murphy, 'Introductory Essay', in *Time, History and the Religious Imaginary in South Asia*, edited by Anne Murphy (London: Routledge, 2011), pp. 1–11.

[28] Murphy, 'Introductory Essay', p. 4.

[29] There is vast literature on this debate. It has been usefully summarized by David Lorenzen in 'Who Invented Hinduism?', in his *Who Invented Hinduism: Essays on Religion in History* (New Delhi: Yoda Press, 2006), pp. 1–36. Also see Gauri Vishwanathan, 'Colonialism and the Construction of Hinduism', in *The Blackwell Companion to Hinduism*, edited by Gavin Flood (Malden: Blackwell Publishing, 2005), pp. 23–44.

[30] Vishwanathan, 'Colonialism and the Construction of Hinduism'.

entailed, insist that it is a travesty to speak of Hinduism's invention. Not only does this idea take away from the agency of the Hindus, it also does not take into account how the so-called metropolis and the periphery conjointly produced discourses on religions and Hinduism.[31] They posit that from at least the middle of the second millennium, if not earlier, of the Common Era, there was a distinct sense of who a Hindu was, particularly in relation to the Islamic presence and traditions in India.[32] Vishwanathan convincingly argues that 'the reluctance of many scholars to call Hinduism a religion because it incorporates many disparate practices suggests that the Judeo-Christian system remains the main reference point for defining religions'.[33]

This debate, vociferous and ongoing, is very briefly introduced here for two reasons. First, on whichever side of the debate one might be ranged, most scholars will concede the existence of 'strands', 'layers', or 'components' within Hinduism. Earlier scholars had spoken of 'great' and 'little' traditions, and the *mārga* or classical *dharma* and the *deshī* or the folkway. G.D. Sontheimer, to give one example, identified five 'components' of Hinduism, namely the work and the teaching of the Brahmans, asceticism and renunciation, tribal religion, folk religion, and bhakti.[34] Vasudha Dalmia speaks of the various 'strands' of religion that were subsumed in order to construct the 'collective category' of *sanātana dharma* (eternal religion).[35] The arguable point is about whether these layered religious practices cohered before or after the onset of colonialism and of modernity. Ramanujan's concept of 'reflexivity' among Hinduism's varied strands and their interactions, which could include 'encompassment, mimicry, criticism, and conflict, and other power relations', remains one of the most perspicacious ways to understand the awareness and entanglement of each strand with various religious others, which may be said to exist in a continuum with the self.[36]

---

[31] Brian K. Pennington, *Was Hinduism Invented? Britons, Indians, and the Colonial Construction of Religion* (Oxford: Oxford University Press, 2005).

[32] Lorenzen, 'Who Invented Hinduism?'

[33] Vishwanathan, 'Colonialism', p. 28.

[34] Gunther-Dietz Sontheimer, 'Hinduism: The Five Components and Their Interaction', in his *Essays on Religion, Literature and Law*, edited by Heidrun Bruckner, Anne Feldhaus, and Aditya Malik (New Delhi: Manohar, 2004), pp. 401–19.

[35] Dalmia, 'The Only Real Religion of the Hindus', p. 176.

[36] Ramanujan, 'Where Mirrors are Windows', p. 9.

In Piro's writing we see a sharp sense of larger conglomerations such as the Hindu and the Turak/Musalman, as well as loyalty to her sect and its guru expressed in a language of devotion, and mostly through Vaishnav mythology. Thus, varied levels of the religious—whether personal piety, devotion, particular identity of the self and of a larger community—exist simultaneously and in a continuum in her person. Piro's religiosity encompassed a theology that defined her soteriological aspirations; it included a sense of belonging to a community and a sect with which she could identify the self; it also bestowed upon her a community identity and a public persona with which people at large identified her; and saliently, it imparted to her devotional traditions within which she could situate herself. Thus at various times or simultaneously she could be seen as a Muslim, a Hindu (Sikh), a Gulabdasi, immersed in bhakti, and an advocate of advaita.

In the context of the debate here, however, and for someone whose cosmos did not much alter through the advent of colonial power and the changes it ushered—and to that extent occupied an early modern world—her sense of Hindu/Muslim as distinct, and indeed oppositional categories is noteworthy. The use of dialogue between two antagonistic figures to define and then reject the common-sense understanding of a Hindu and a Muslim was a common trope in bhakti literature, which pointed to turning to the interior as the unsullied space.[37] Such a stance negotiated difference, as Murphy has argued, but it also took into account what she calls 'commensurability', through a discussion on differences and similarities.[38] While one's other had commensurable qualities that refracted and opaquely reflected one's own, in Piro's case the oppositional stand also had palpability, for she tied her own autobiographical tale to its provenance. At the same time the Gulabdasis were inheritors of shared religious traditions, of religiosities expressed in idioms that were at once specific to their own theological orientation, but also reflected in the parallel and plural cultures

[37] In this context, see the discussion on Eknath's 'Hindu–Turk Samvad', in Lorenzen's 'Who Invented Hinduism?' For a similar dialogue on the question of caste, see the debate between Kabir and Raidas in Lorenzen, 'Sain's Kabir–Raidas Debate', in his *Praises to a Formless God: Nirguni Texts from North India* (Albany: SUNY Press, 1996), pp. 169–81.

[38] Anne Murphy, 'An Idea of Religion: Identity, Difference and Comparison in the Gurbilas', in *Punjab Reconsidered: History, Culture and Practice*, edited by Anshu Malhotra and Farina Mir (New Delhi: Oxford University Press, 2012), pp. 93–115.

of Punjab.[39] Thus, their advaitin beliefs found echoes in Sufi traditions of *tauhid*, the unity of being, and their use of Sufi vocabulary to express their own spiritual progress was common.[40] The esoteric, mystical, and even the mysterious aspects of such ontological knowledge was revealed to the knowers, the *ārif* (Gnostics), a title commonly assumed by Gulabdasi acolytes.

The second reason for introducing the debate on Hinduism is to factor in the Sikhs in Punjab, and to understand the extent to which we can speak, in the middle of the nineteenth century, of three distinct religious communities. Here too at least two positions are visible among scholars. Harjot Oberoi unleashed a storm of protest among practising Sikhs as well as scholarly circles when he discussed the idea of 'the construction of religious boundaries' among the 'diverse' ways of being a Sikh in nineteenth-century Punjab, and of 'sanatan Sikhism', which accepted its loose affiliation to Hindu ideals of caste, the Vedas, and so on.[41] In his estimation, it was the genius and the success from the late nineteenth century onwards of the 'Tat Khalsa' adherents among the Singh Sabhas that imparted a definitive Sikh identity to one that was more amorphous. Historians like W.H. McLeod agreed with Oberoi, linking the first Sikh guru, Nanak, with the north Indian *sant*/bhakti ideas, and speaking about the different positions that were found in the diverse *rahit* literature, which began to emerge towards the end of the eighteenth century, and which attempted to define correct conduct for Khalsa Sikhs.[42] More recently Arvind-Pal Mandair has spoken about the 'untranslatability' of the category 'religio', which was universalized as religion within the colonial imaginary. While European scholars like Ernest Trumpp linked Sikhism to Hinduism, those like M.A. Macauliffe, in collaboration with Sikh intellectuals of the Singh Sabhas, focused on the question of 'origins' of Sikhism, and looked at the 'bhakti movement' as the foundation of Sikh 'self-consciousness'.[43]

[39] Anna Bigelow, 'Post-Partition Pluralism: Placing Islam in Indian Punjab', in Malhotra and Mir, *Punjab Reconsidered*, pp. 409–34.

[40] Anshu Malhotra, 'Panths and Piety in the Nineteenth Century: The Gulabdasis of Punjab', in Malhotra and Mir, *Punjab Reconsidered*, pp. 189–220.

[41] Harjot Oberoi, *The Construction of Religious Boundaries: Diversity in the Sikh Tradition* (New Delhi: Oxford University Press, 1994).

[42] W.H. McLeod, *Guru Nanak and the Religion of the Sikhs* (New Delhi: Oxford University Press, 1996 [1968]); W.H. McLeod, *Sikhs of the Khalsa: A History of Khalsa Rahit* (New Delhi: Oxford University Press, 2003).

[43] Arvind-Pal S. Mandair, *Religion and the Specter of the West: Sikhism, India, Postcoloniality, and the Politics of Translation* (New York: Columbia University Press,

On the other hand, scholars like Gurinder S. Mann, in their revisionist stance and in reading the earliest available recensions of Sikh scriptures, are transforming the quietist image of Nanak, the first Sikh guru, to one of an energetic and self-conscious community builder. Mann is also pegging the entry of the Jats—normally seen to have come into Sikhism in the seventeenth century and to have imparted it with a more militaristic outlook—to Nanak's time in the late fifteenth and the early sixteenth centuries. In the process the development of Sikh self-consciousness, which also factors in their distinctiveness from Muslims and Hindus, is being pushed further back in time.[44] In this reading, the moment of epiphany is no longer that of the emergence of the Khalsa at the end of the seventeenth century and under the aegis of the tenth guru, Gobind Singh; nor that of the later rahit and *gurbilās* (play of the guru) literatures; or even that of the the Singh Sabhas' modernist project that contributed to a distinct Khalsa identity. Rather, in this construction, Sikhs were self-consciously so from their very genesis/origins; it is this question of origins that Mandair has shown to be so central to the colonial and modernist imaginaries.[45]

Like the debate on Hinduism, that on Sikhism is also an ongoing one, and neither are likely to end any time soon. However, more nuanced readings of a wide variety of sources pertaining to the eighteenth century—an ominous period in Singh Sabha histories, pregnant with a sharp sense of Khalsa identity in contestation with Islam—are beginning to appear (the Singh Sabhas were, of course, also simultaneously contesting a Hindu identity of Sikhs). The recent work of Purnima Dhavan on the development of a warrior tradition among the Sikhs shows both the emergence of distinct Khalsa institutions and the sharpening of Khalsa identity in relation to the 'othering' of Muslims. At the same time, she demonstrates how the realities of power politics and the manoeuvring for control in Punjab meant alliances of Sikh chiefs with all manner of Muslim religious and ethnic groups, and other power-seeking constellations of north India. Simultaneously, the rahit and gurbilas literatures, which were of great diversity, did create some

---

2009). Also see his 'Time and Religion-making in Modern Sikhism', in Murphy, *Time, History and the Religious Imaginary*, pp. 186–202.

[44] Gurinder Singh Mann, 'Guru Nanak's Life and Legacy: An Appraisal', in Malhotra and Mir, *Punjab Reconsidered*, pp. 116–60.

[45] The growth of a more muscular and militaristic tradition within Sikhism is also often pegged to the 'martyrdom' of the fifth guru, Arjan Dev, and to the bestowal of equal significance to the temporal as well spiritual power by the sixth guru, Hargobind.

sense of the Khalsa. However, in Dhavan's reading 'Khalsa' and 'Sikh' never became identical terms.[46] Focusing on the development of Sikh 'militancy' in the seventeenth century and on the 'type' of violence that the community came to adopt and justify, Hardip S. Syan shows the dialogical process taking place within the community on violence and on the ideals of 'householder sovereign' and 'householder ascetic'.[47]

Why do we need to discuss the Sikhs here? Colonial ethnographies and indigenous compendia of cultural traditions viewed the Gulabdasis as a part of a larger, looser Sikh tradition. More pertinently, the idea of a formless god (*nirguna*) and of repeating the Word (*nām*) were legacies for the Gulabdasis that were transmitted from Sikh and bhakti sources. The Udasi and the Nirmala orders that birthed and nurtured Gulabdas's ascetic inclinations were unambiguously Sikh—the Udasis tracking their inheritance to Nanak's son Sirichand, and the Nirmalas to the blessings of the tenth guru. The Nirmalas were instrumental in discoursing on advaita and Vedantin learning. More saliently still, being in Punjab— whether carrying a cultural memory of earlier, more turbulent times, or in settled circumstances under Ranjit Singh, or in the fractiousness of the closing years of the Sikh empire—Sikh history and culture left its imprimatur on the Gulabdasis in diverse ways.[48]

In Piro's writing, while 'Hindu' and 'Muslim' appear as sharply etched categories, there is ambivalence with regard to the Sikhs. She certainly distinguishes between the Sikhs and the Khalsas, without naming the latter. Instead she talks of 'Sikhi', the Sikh way, without defining what that was (and so assuming certain characteristics that would be familiar to most). She is harsh on, and juxtaposes this Sikhi against, those who have fashioned (read Khalsa) a new way (*banat*). Once again, she does not delve into any of Khalsa practices, except mentioning their wearing of drawers (*kachhā*), one among the ostensibly five symbols a Khalsa was enjoined to wear on his person.[49] This is because the focus for Piro was on her identity as a woman, and the manner of piety she could practise. She was bothered about the place she could occupy in a society that she

---

[46] Purnima Dhavan, *When Sparrows Became Hawks: The Making of Sikh Warrior Tradition, 1699–1799* (New York: Oxford University Press, 2011).

[47] Hardip S. Syan, *Sikh Militancy in the Seventeenth Century: Religious Violence in Mughal and Early Modern India* (London: I.B. Tauris, 2013).

[48] All these issues are discussed in detail in Chapter 1.

[49] The other four were *kes* (unshorn hair), *kanghā* (comb), *karā* (steel bangle), and *kirpān* (small sword). Exactly which five symbols were mandatory was not

claimed had sharp religious demarcations and shrill declamations and displays of public religiosities.

Piro's writing on these myriad religiosities can be understood in two ways. On the one hand, as already noted, we see a clear distinction that she makes between Hindus and Muslims, even emphasizing, as noted above, an agonistic relationship between the two. Sikhs and Khalsas, though identified, are implicitly placed by her within a wide 'Hindu' umbrella, which did not take away the varied ways in which Sikh distinctiveness could be defined. However, the point was that the notions of Sikhness were varied, and that these could be bracketed as Hindu in a non-specific, generalized way. At no time does Piro speak of her guru as a 'Sikh', or her sect as one within the Sikh tradition, though Gulabdas, as mentioned, received his early training under the auspices of the Udasis and Nirmalas. The competitors of the Gulabdasis were the ascetic orders, the Bairagis, Sanyasis, Madaris, Nirmalas, Udasis, and Akalis, who she explicitly mentions and puts down in her *160 Kafis*. Ditt Singh, on the other hand, as an early votary of the Singh Sabha, grappled with just the issue of defining Sikh distinction, particularly trying to work out its basis in attitudes towards caste. Whether he could altogether shed the plural Punjabi traditions of which he was an inheritor as a Gulabdasi is another matter.

The history of Punjab, including that of the conflict between 'Sikhs/ Khalsas' seeking political power and the 'Muslim' remnants of Mughal power, from the late seventeenth century onwards, and the religious idiom in which the conflict was occasionally presented, does impress itself on the manner in which Piro writes.[50] However, it was the evocative bhakti tradition, which often presented its interiorized piety by publicly invoking and ridiculing the external religious symbols and dogmas of the Hindu and Muslim paradigms, was the one Piro aligned with, and it was the bhakti idiom of devotion that she was most comfortable with. This language of devotion came to be transmitted to Piro through the existence of polysemous bhakti 'networks', significant among which was the Sikh tradition.[51]

---

clear through most of the late eighteenth and early nineteenth centuries, though there is clarity about keeping uncut hair. (W.H. McLeod, 'The Five Ks', in his *Essays in Sikh History, Tradition and Society* [New Delhi: Oxford University Press, 2007], pp. 115–23.)

[50] See Chapter 3.

[51] See Chapter 4. For a discussion on bhakti networks, see John Stratton Hawley, *A Storm of Songs: India and the Idea of Bhakti Movement* (Cambridge: Harvard University Press, 2015).

ON BHAKTI DEVOTION

Bhakti devotionalism, many scholars have noted, with its etymology in the word *bhaj*, invokes sharing, apportioning, participating, and partaking with a community of believers. In its wider semantics, it includes serving, honouring, revering, and adoring.[52] 'Bhakti is heart religion,' writes J.S. Hawley, 'the religion of participation, community, enthusiasm, song and often personal challenge.'[53] The bhakti 'movement', scholars have pointed out in increasing numbers, is a construction in its fully articulated form in the twentieth century, but created at many historical junctions, including the contributions from colonial enthusiasts and numerous literary nationalists.[54] The notion of bhakti 'networks' instead focuses attention on 'routes' of transmission rather than just the 'roots' of the bhakti tradition. This reveals how traditions are formed through multiple and layered accretions, speaking about the 'collective authorship' of bhakti poetry and songs, and the articulations of 'collective memory' rather than of individual authors.[55] The connections in the early modern period that ensued through growing economic and trading activity, and increased mobility of people, created and deepened webs of exchange, pivotal for the spread of bhakti. Thus, 'public' and 'performative' aspects of bhakti have come to be stressed; understanding bhakti then, is the unpacking of 'cultural memory'.[56] As the transfusion of bhakti through various communities of song and performance, and texts and scribes came to be, so its hagiographers 'assembled' lives of saints 'from the lives of all the others',[57] sometimes presenting them as saintly encounters and

---

[52] Christian Lee Novetzke, *History, Bhakti, and Public Memory: Namdev in Religious and Secular Traditions* (Ranikhet: Permanent Black, 2008), p. 9.

[53] Hawley, *A Storm of Songs*, p. 2.

[54] Hawley, *A Storm of Songs*; Novetzke, *History, Bhakti, and Public Memory*; Mandair, 'Time and Religion-making in Modern Sikhism', in Murphy, *Time, History and the Religious Imaginary*, pp. 186–202.

[55] Hawley, *A Storm of Songs*, pp. 296–7; Finbarr Flood draws attention to Clifford James' focus on 'routes' rather than 'roots' in his *Objects of Translation: Material Culture and Medieval "Hindu–Muslim" Encounter* (Ranikhet: Permanent Black, 2009), pp. 1–5. Also see the 'Introduction' in *Text and Tradition in North India*, edited by J.S. Hawley, Anshu Malhotra, and Tyler Williams (New Delhi: Oxford University Press, forthcoming).

[56] Novetzke, *History, Bhakti and Public Memory*, pp. 1–31; Assman, *Cultural Memory*.

[57] Hawley, *A Storm of Songs*, p. 297.

linkages, but also imagining the lives of the ordinary as living in rapprochement and fellowship with saints and believers.

This craving to be counted as one among other saints is an idea that Piro readily emulates, particularly the desire to intersect her life with that of the low-caste saintly community. Bhakti as a protest of the poor and the disenfranchised—the 'Dalit' among bhakti 'movements', understood in the plural—is important, giving it enabling symbolic possibilities and openings.[58] The idea that various saints achieved liberation despite a low caste (*jāt*) was a salient one for Piro, clearing the way for others like her, who may relive and re-embody the possibilities of others' lived lives. For Piro, as a low caste and as a woman, the question of embodiment is nodal, for those born within these confines can hardly hope to escape the strictures society places on their everyday somatic existence.

In this context, Karen Prentiss' explication of bhakti as a 'theology of embodiment', that is 'embedded in details of human life' is pertinent.[59] So is Karen Pechilis' notion that bhakti's thesis is that embodiment with all its challenges is the most efficacious approach to the divine, as is viewing the saints through their bodies and biographies.[60] Caste and gender are imbricated in the materiality of the body, in the reiterative disciplinary regimes that impel bodies to submission according to social conventions, as Judith Butler has highlighted in the context of gender, but whose logic can also be extended to that of caste.[61] In Piro we see a desire to recuperate a gendered and a caste-ridden body, an abject body, through spiritual knowledge gained through the blessing of the guru. Significantly, Piro did not wish to erase her body or deny its earthy materiality; rather she wished to recoup the subjected body by believing that liberation was inclusive, intended for all.

Prentiss links the idea of embodiment—insofar as god informs all the saints' worldly activities, and the saints engage in a variety of social and

[58] On plural bhakti movements, see Hawley, *A Storm of Songs*, p. 327. On Dalit recuperations of bhakti's radical potentialities, see Milind Wakankar, *Subalternity and Religion: The Pre-History of Dalit Empowerment in South Asia* (London: Routledge, 2010).

[59] Karen P. Prentiss, *The Embodiment of Bhakti* (New York: Oxford University Press, 1999), p. 6.

[60] Karen Pechilis, 'Bhakti Traditions', in *The Continuum Companion to Hindu Studies*, edited by Jessica Frazier (London: Continuum, 2011), pp. 107–22.

[61] Judith Butler, *Bodies That Matter: On the Discursive Limits of "Sex"* (New York: Routledge, 1993).

economic activity—to that of human agency in bhakti poets' appending their names to their poetry, and in describing human response to god.[62] Does this thesis, which assumes individual authorial voice, stand when we look at the question of 'authorship' as a collective one, with the accretion of scribal and performative memories over centuries? In this context, the idea of reliving saintly or even mythological lives, as in Piro's case, is significant as it is a reliance on cultural and mythological memory. It is by intermeshing the insignificant details of one's ordinary life with the extraordinary lives of the saints, or to put it another way, by appropriating magnificent lives of the saintly in the minutiae of one's own that these 'collective' lives were constructed, set in motion, and embraced. This did not make two lives or times identical. Rather, it set loose allegories and ideals primed for emulation and appropriation. It is in crafting empowerment from unpromising materials—whether gendered bodies, bodies stigmatized by caste, or unfavourable circumstances—that the question of human agency becomes important.

It was a long time ago that Ramanujan had pointed to the bhakti path as one that was especially amenable to women and their search for spirituality.[63] Though the challenges before women bhaktas were different, and manifested in familial and domestic situations, the bhakti way did make openings for them.[64] However, defiance of, rather than compliance to, these patriarchal norms was an aspect of the lives of women bhaktas. However, Kumkum Sangari, in her reading of the life and poetry of the fifteenth-century Rajput princess Mirabai as it has come to us, posits that a more ambiguous space is occupied by Mirabai and her poetry, and derivatively by what the bhakti path symbolized. There is a defiance and challenge to social, feudal, and patriarchal norms, but also an internalization of these, so that in her reading Mira represents 'a struggle, not a victory'.[65] While there is no denying that patriarchal norms remained difficult to dislodge—even more so than those of low (*nīch*) castes in some ways— and that patriarchy, even when defied, was reintroduced in constituting the relationship with god or guru, this is not the whole story, though an important aspect of it. The manner in which agency is established,

[62] Prentiss, *The Embodiment of Bhakti*, p. 6.

[63] Ramanujan, 'On Women Saints', pp. 270–8.

[64] A.K. Ramanujan, 'Men, Women and Saints', in Dharwadker, *The Collected Essays of A.K. Ramanujan*, pp. 279–308.

[65] Kumkum Sangari, 'Mirabai and the Spiritual Economy of Bhakti', *Economic and Political Weekly* 25, no. 27 and 28 (1990): 1464–75 and 1537–52.

not just by manoeuvring adverse situations to one's advantage, but also by grasping one's life in definitive ways, giving it particular direction is worth noting.

One way in which bhakti cleaved open women's spiritual potentialities was by women bhaktas' deployment of the topos of interiorized spirituality. Though the bhakti way was to be celebrated in community, what one may call the *communitas* of bhaktas and the devotees, it encouraged adherents to look inwards. The women bhaktas who walked naked, whether Mahadeviakka or Lalla, carried to the extreme the notion of the rejection of externalities, bodily difference and confinement, and worldly shame. The inward gaze that reached and composed the self in relation to god and guru did so by explicitly turning away from the externals of creed, caste, and worldly snares. Piro expressed this interiority first by rejecting externals of religious identity (circumcision, style of moustaches, top knot, sacred thread) and of adornment and wealth (*suinā, rūpā, līre, bhukkhaṇ*—gold, silver, fine clothes, ornaments). Second, she did this by announcing the desire to attain a state beyond limits (*had*), of Hindu and Muslim religious identities, as of a 'limitless' (*behadī*) state of spiritual knowledge like her guru had attained. And third, Piro speaks of an interiority that removes the veils of ignorance, opening the heart/liver to clarity of vision (*khole chasmā jikar kā*). In its variegated understanding of interiority, Piro strove to overcome limits imposed by gender and caste. It is a contention of this work that the bhakti path remained for a long time, from the early modern into that of colonial modernity, an enabling way for women. Subsequently, selfhoods could be fabricated through access to modern education and the public sphere, and the socially and politically enriching amenities that accompanied it. Piro's specific expostulations against the externalities of caste and faith have been commented upon extensively in this work, and her fashioning of the self through bhakti's metaphors, legends, and tales described in detail.

J.S. Hawley, in postulating the distinctiveness of Kabir's voice, even if it comes to us layered through the times, has commented on its 'modern' humanity, so that even contemporary interpreters discover their own selves in seeking him.[66] If the Kabirian voice encouraged self-reflection, I have tried to show here that the bhakti way itself held promise for women who turned to its empowering ideology time and again. It may be worth mentioning briefly here that in Tanika Sarkar's reading of the

---

[66] Hawley, *A Storm of Songs*, pp. 319–21.

life of the first modern woman autobiographer, Rassundari Debi, her Vaishnav bhakti, crafted in a secret and exhilarating relationship with words and god, allowed her to construct a self.[67] More recently Siobhan Lambert-Hurley has shown that Raihanna Tyabji, a Bohra Muslim singer and a Gandhian who secretly imagined herself as a *gopi*, an erotic play-mate and a devotee of the cowherd Krishna, constituted an inner life built on a well-loved myth, within an established bhakti paradigm.[68] Unlike Rassundari and Raihanna, whose personal piety was directed towards their gods, for Piro devotion was directed towards her guru—'the lord as guru' to which Daniel Gold drew our attention as a manifestation of late bhakti dynamics.[69] While her guru was an uncompromising advaita advocate, relying upon the path of knowledge to achieve his 'godhood' (he called himself *Brahm*)—a theology to which Piro acceded—it was in the emotional excess of bhakti devotionalism, in the supererogatory language vista it opened, that Piro could express her relationship with him and configure her own self.

ON GURUS AND SECTS

To pick up yet another strand of Indian religious experience, I attend briefly to the multiple gurus and their establishments that historically dotted the Indian and Punjabi landscape, and in fact proliferate in astonishing diversity today.[70] This will help us position the Gulabdasis historically and in the present time. From the earliest ascetics, the medi-eval Naths, the early modern sants, the Sikh gurus, to the later multiple guru and sant lineages of the seventeenth and eighteenth centuries that Gold has discussed, the gurus were multiple and multifarious, 'uncontainable' in their variegated manifestations, and 'expansible' in their

---

[67] Tanika Sarkar, *Words to Win: The Making of Amar Jiban—A Modern Autobiography* (New Delhi: Kali for Women, 1999).

[68] Siobhan Lambert-Hurley, 'The Heart of a Gopi: Raihanna Tyabji's Bhakti Devotionalism as Self-Representation', in Malhotra and Lambert-Hurley, *Speaking of the Self*, pp. 230–54.

[69] Gold, *The Lord as Guru*.

[70] Jacob Copeman studies one such contemporary contentious dera in his 'The Mimetic Guru: Tracing the Real in Sikh–Dera Sacha Sauda Relations', in *The Guru in South Asia: New Interdisciplinary Perspectives*, edited by Jacob Copeman and Aya Ikegame (London: Routledge, 2012), pp. 156–80. See Chapter 6 for further comments on contemporary sects.

manifold constructions, as a recent book describes them.[71] Guru (Sant) Gulabdas, Piro's guru, established his own dera, and his own lineage(s), and in following this path could probably lay claim to any or all of the above outlined legacies. Though apparently well defined—in the ten guruships within Sikhism, and thereafter in the shifting of guruship to the scripture, the *Adi Granth*, at the behest of the last Guru Gobind in 1708—guruship remained a contested domain within Sikhism throughout its history.[72] This is not to speak of the many Sikh sects that emerged as well, among them the Udasis and the Nirmalas with their gurus and *mahants* (monastic superiors), deras and *akhāṛās* (dwelling ground, groups), that were especially instrumental in shaping Gulabdas's early life as an ascetic.

The ubiquitous religious orders of Punjab and their wide reticulating ambit was one 'local' way in which religious experience was available to people. These sects could be the source of the most esoteric philosophies for those formally initiated into their fold, or they could be a mere presence in the mundane routines of life, or perhaps could be approached by the ordinary folk for succour and discourse. Though in the understanding of the Indic textual tradition the ascetics were meant to have opted out of prosaic life, and indeed scholars speak of opposition between the ascetics seeking individual liberation and the householder weighed down by worldly concerns, the reality was a little more complex than this binary suggests.[73] Instead of seeing the ascetic and the householder as oppositional entities, Sondra Hausner looks at these as collaborative categories, the two poles that hold each other in balance. Saying that true solitude was a rarity, Hausner shows various ways in which the ascetics' relationship with the laity may take place, including pilgrimage circuits and festival cycles, and in contemporary times a guru's following in the diaspora and in the bureaucratic dealing

---

[71] Jacob Copeman and Aye Ikegame, 'The Multifarious Guru: An Introduction', in Copeman and Ikegame, *The Guru in South Asia*, pp. 1–45. For an example of the colonialist enumeration of sects, see H.H. Wilson, *Hindu Religions: An Account of the Various Religious Sects of India*, reprint (New Delhi: Bharatiya Book Corporation, n.d.).

[72] Syan, *Sikh Militancy*.

[73] Sondra L. Hausner has discussed the binary between the ascetic and the householder that Louis Dumont made central to his understanding of Hindu society. See her 'Ascetic Traditions', in Frazier, *The Continuum Companion to Hindu Studies*, pp. 100–7.

with the state.[74] Within Sikhism itself, as Syan has noted, one could aspire to be a 'householder ascetic'.[75] Many ascetic orders had celibate and married followers, with the married disciples even succeeding to guruship, as with the Gulabdasis after the guru's death.

The use of the term 'dera' in Punjab is indicative of monastic dwelling, perhaps away from habitation, to encourage spiritual and intellectual insight, as with the Gulabdasis, but not so distant as to trammel interaction with people. Far from the otherworldly orientation, Dobe has emphasized the gurus' public and performative roles, and religion as *doing*.[76] One way in which the worldly aspects of various sects were visible was in the establishment of guru lineages and the bestowing of both the spiritual and the worldly mantle, including property and monastic authority, onto disciple(s), which could at times lead to conflict and rivalries.[77] Interaction with people could occur when preaching—the task of dissemination of ideas that formed an integral part of some sects—and as noted, on pilgrimages and special occasions like the annual observance of festivals. In the case of Gulabdasis, this had meant the celebration of the Holi festival spread over many days in Gulabdas's time; but now in one Gulabdasi lineage studied here, festivities revolve around newly fabricated and articulated traditions. As will be demonstrated, the ritual and performative fields, where interaction with the audience ensues, spectators who scatter from the sacred centre which holds acolytes to an ever widening arc of people in its fold, the scope of participation is dynamic and inclusive. While measurable influence of a sect's hold on people will be difficult to assess, suffice to say that there were manifold ways in which the demotic reach of sects worked.

The multiple roles that sects such as the Gulabdasis played can be understood by casting a quick glance at historically the most significant of these, the Naths. The Naths were a medieval sect found in all parts of India, with their imprimatur in Punjab being particularly impressive. Said to be a sect founded by Gorakhnath around the eleventh century,

---

[74] Hausner, 'Ascetic Traditions', pp. 100–7.

[75] Syan, *Sikh Militancy*.

[76] Dobe, *Hindu Christian Faqir*, p. 270.

[77] In *The Lord as Guru*, Gold studies the lineages and their conflicts. Also see his 'Continuities as Gurus Change', in Copeman and Ikegame, *The Guru in South Asia*, pp. 241–54.

they flourished and came into their own in the next two centuries.[78] Combining yogic and alchemical prowess with arcane rituals associated with tantra and Shaivism—the Siddhas or the realized and perfected ones, as they were called—the Naths had a series of gurus after Gorakh. Among the eleven major Nath jogis/yogis, six lived and settled in Punjab,[79] with Tilla Jogian in the mountains of the Salt Range in the Jhelum district of Punjab, now a part of Pakistan, as the oldest and perhaps the most important of their centres, which was associated in particular with Balnath.[80] Throughout their history in Punjab, they not only enjoyed extensive political patronage, and so exercised significant power, but also had a very strong hold on the social and cultural life of the people.[81] Even a relatively isolated establishment of the jogis in Jakhbar, in the Gurdaspur district of Punjab, whose preserved documents were perused and published by B.N. Goswamy and J.S. Grewal in 1967, received generous patronage. Among the Jakhbar jogis' political patrons and correspondents were virtually all the Mughal emperors starting from Akbar's time in the sixteenth century, and including Jahangir, Shah Jahan, and Aurangzeb, besides other officials and nobles. When in the 1960s the two scholars visited the area, they palpably felt the influence the jogis had on the locals. They reported, 'One gets the feeling that the mahants of Jakhbar had almost a controlling power over the local population.' This included not only their own agricultural tenants, but also the wider neighbourhood of Sherpur.[82]

Another way of appreciating the Naths' cultural influence on the Punjabi people is by taking a look at their qissa literature. In perhaps the most popular of Punjabi qissa romances, of Hir and Ranjha, so evocatively studied recently by Farina Mir who gives us a glimpse of its importance in the cultures of Punjab, Ranjha gets initiated into the Nath sect at Tilla

---

[78] David G. White, *The Alchemical Body: Siddha Traditions in Medieval India* (Chicago: University of Chicago Press, 1996).

[79] Quoted in Yogesh Snehi, 'Situating Popular Veneration', NMML occasional paper, *History and Society,* New Series 68 (New Delhi: Nehru Memorial Museum and Library, 2015), p. 14.

[80] George W. Briggs, *Gorakhnath and the Kanphata Jogis* (New Delhi: Motilal Banarsidass, 1973[1938]), pp. 101–2.

[81] B.N. Goswamy and J.S. Grewal, *The Mughals and Jogis of Jakhbar: Some Madad-i-Ma'ash and Other Documents* (Simla: Indian Institute of Advanced Study, 1967), pp. 1–46.

[82] Goswamy and Grewal, *The Mughals and Jogis of Jakhbar*, pp. 16–17.

Jogian. This occurs after the marriage of his lover Hir to Saido Khera against her wishes but in accordance with the caste status of her clan of the Sials.[83] In the guise of a jogi, Ranjha manages to regularly rendezvous with Hir in her marital village because of the tacit help of Hir's sister-in-law, until this idyll of theirs too gets shattered. Mir also draws our attention to both how well known this story of Hir and Ranjha's romance was by the late nineteenth century—that poets could compose texts that discussed only an episode of the longer tale as they could assume that all participants of the 'Punjabi literary formation' would be familiar with it—and that this was also an outcome of the flourishing print medium of this time.[84] Piro's 'Hir act', if we can call it that, in her interpretation of religion in imitation of Hir as in questioning the sophistry of religious authorities is discussed in this work.

Similarly, in another exceptionally popular qissa of Puran Bhagat, Puran is first rescued as a limbless young man from a well by none other than the mythical Gorakhnath himself, whose magical powers restore his limbs; Puran subsequently becoming a practicing Nath jogi, a central pivot around which Puran's saga develops.[85] This qissa, too, is discussed later in this work where episodes attributed as having occurred in Gulabdas's life are shown to mimic those of the mythical Puran. The fine intermeshing of the lives of the Punjabi people and the jogis can also be seen from the fact that the Bhartri yogis, known for their musicality, often sang to the people these very qissas, including the two mentioned above.[86] Thus the presence of the Naths, as of the numerous other sects in the Punjabi landscape, came to be knit into the very cultural fabric of Punjabi life.

Another way of commenting on the sects is to show their mutual awareness of and critique of the other, a world view that simultaneously encompasses the other even as it turns its back on them. The contexts of such acknowledgement of the other could be conflict-ridden, portraying oneself or one's tradition as more worthy than the other, as many scholars have commented, or the other could be referred to in order to appropriate their legacy, to enhance one's own. That Sufis and jogis often featured

---

[83] Farina Mir, *The Social Space of Language: Vernacular Culture in British Colonial Punjab* (Ranikhet: Permanent Black, 2010).

[84] Mir, *The Social Space of Language*, pp. 91–122.

[85] For a discussion on this qissa, see Chapter 8.

[86] Briggs, *Gorakhnath*, p. 24.

in contestations has been shown.[87] It is worth noting that such dissension that commented on the other and reflected on aspects of the self also occurred among many other groups that sought to win over novices, acolytes, and followers to their own sects in a situation of competing for attention. One may even speak about the establishment of a 'tradition' which required that the many others be run down (an auto-critique as it were) as false teachers and ascetic practitioners against the self as the exponent of the right path, so that the notion of various ascetics as charlatans was well-established among the different sects themselves. Guru Nanak (1469–1539) is said to have mocked the Naths or the Siddhas, in the *Siddh Gost*, a text on his dialogue with them, denying that renouncing the world and mundane existence is necessary for liberation, affirming instead his principle of 'living in this world' even as one withdraws from society, as a superior option.[88] This sentiment was captured in the *Adi Granth* in the words of the third Sikh guru, Amar Das (1552–1574), who commented on the futility of renunciation:

> Some sit in forest realms and do not answer any calls
> Some break ice in the cold [winter] and bathe in the freezing water
> Some rub ashes on their bodies and do not wash off the dirt
> With their hair matted some look wild and bring dishonor to their family lineage
> Some wander naked during the day and night and do not sleep
> Some burn their limbs with fire and damage themselves
> Without *nām*, the body is reduced to ashes.[89]

A similar sentiment is found in Gulabdas, who too critiques myriad ascetic practices:

> One heats up fires and burns his body but finds no peace in the forest
> One does not eat salt, spoiling his taste, but cannot resolve the mystery in this fashion.
> One wears a garb and calls himself a *sādh* and puts on a show for the people.[90]

[87] Carl W. Ernst, 'Situating Sufism and Yoga', *Journal of the Royal Asiatic Society*, 15, no. 1 (2005): 15–43; Simon Digby, trans., *Wonder-Tales of South Asia* (Jersey: Orient Monographs, 2000).

[88] Kamla E. Nayar and Jaswinder S. Sandhu, *Socially Involved Renunciate: Guru Nanak's Discourse to the Nath Yogis* (New York: SUNY Press, 2007).

[89] Nayar and Sandhu, *Socially Involved Renunciate*, pp. 15–16. 'Nam' refers to the repetition/chanting of god's name.

[90] Verse 286, *Pothī Gulāb Chaman* (hereinafter referred to as *GC*) (Lahore: Tajul Kutub, 1881).

And later Gulabdas affirms his monist conception of god:

Says Gulabdas he is not separate, Hari is everywhere.[91]

And a similar sentiment is echoed in Piro:

Piro says *satguru*, some have left the world
Wearing a garb they rob humanity
One becomes a *bairāgī* and shows the world
Donning a saffron garb they wear a necklace
Wearing a necklace of *rudrāksh* beads they call themselves *sanyāsī*.[92]

Naths were just one of the many sects of Punjab. Ganesh Das Badhera's *Char Bagh-i-Panjab*, a Persian text completed in 1849, recounts the variegated histories of Punjab in complex ways. Focused on the role of the Khatris, the service gentry of Punjab and their administrative skills and pious attitudes, it is also a biographical sketch of his own family laying down his lineage. Das also unravels a deep relationship with the localities and regions of Punjab, through his role as a raconteur of anecdotes, stories, and qissas of Punjab.[93] Discussing Punjabi regions through constructing Punjab's sacred topography, Das enumerates men (and occasionally women) of learning and piety. In his account he tells us of numerous *sādhs*, *faqīrs*, dervishes (mendicants), sanyasis, bairagis (Shaiva and Vaishnava renunciates), jogis, *pīrs*, and a rare *agāmī* (a follower of tantra). For Ganesh Das, every locality of Punjab is known through its stories and saintly lives, its sects and holy men, honoured by the rich and the respected elites.

At the turn of the century, J.C. Oman, a professor of Natural Science at the Government College at Lahore, also discussed 'sadhuism' of Punjab and India, giving copious accounts of its yogis, bairagis, and sanyasis, and 'other strange Hindu sectarians'.[94] If for Ganesh Das these holy

---

[91] Verse 289, *GC*.

[92] Verse 134, *Ik Sau Sath Kafian*.

[93] J.S. Grewal and Indu Banga, trans and eds, *Early Nineteenth Century Punjab: From Ganesh Das's Char Bagh-i-Panjab* (Amritsar: Guru Nanak Dev University, 1975).

[94] John Campbell Oman, *The Mystics, Ascetics, and Saints of India*, reprint (New Delhi. Oriental Publishers, 1973). Also see his *Cults, Customs and Superstitions of India*, reprint (New Delhi: Vishal Publishers, 1972). The influential presence of the bairagis in Punjab can be gauged from their Vaishnava establishment at Pindori, Gurdaspur, Punjab. (B.N. Goswamy and J.S. Grewal, *The Mughals and Sikh Rulers and the Vaishnavas of Pindori* [Simla: Indian Institute of Advanced Study, 1969].

entities of different hue were what made Punjab special, for Oman, it was their obscurantist superstitions that made Punjab a part of the essential East. His orientalist inquisitiveness took him to various parts of Punjab, where he particularly took pleasure in reporting stories of strange sects and their curiosities, among them discussing an *aghor panthī* (tantra follower) who survived by eating carrion; women *aghorinīs*; a bairagi who held a feast for five hundred unmarried girls, and a yogi who apparently protected Amritsar from the plague.[95]

Thus, through cultural embedment or through recursive reflexivity of the self, the multifarious sects of Punjab were a conspicuous presence in the lives of its people. From esoteric doctrines that could only be comprehended by their adherents and novices, they could in their relationship to laity be caught up in quotidian lives and represent approachable and personal religiosity that held traction. Their spectacular presence in Punjabi landscape, performed through peculiar costumes, inclusive festivities, discourse and preaching, refuge and rehabilitation, spiritual concern and intellectual activity, poetic and storied dissemination, and sometimes through sharp social critiques, as by the Gulabdasis, is a social phenomenon worth noting. By speaking of the Gulabdasis, this book will attempt to study this important strand of people's piety.

Chapter 1 examines how contradictory views on Guru Gulabdas have emerged—Gulabdas seen both as a learned man and as an independent-minded aberrant guru who broke rules of normal *sharā* (morality), including those of varnashramadharma. It closely looks at the sources available on the Gulabdasis, looking at how the dera came to prosper around the time of the fall of the Sikh empire. Gulabdas's philosophical and theological bent is discussed in some detail; the chapter thus sketches the background for understanding why Piro was drawn to this sect, and how she could live and flourish within its environs. Delineating Gulabdas's inclination towards advaita, the impress of bhakti, and his solipsistic belief in self-knowledge, the autochthonous understanding of individuation and its creative manifestation is shown.

The next four chapters (2–5) can be read conjointly as an exposition on Piro's life and writing, with particular emphasis on her autobiographical

---

[95] Oman, *The Mystics*, pp. 167, 214–17.

Ik Sau Sath Kafian (*160 Kafis*), but also her three siharfis. Chapter 2 looks at the autobiographical genre in premodern South Asia, sketches out Piro's story and self-fashioning, and goes on to uncover the meanings of her allegorical Ramayana-inspired narrative.

Chapter 3 attempts to unravel the necessary historical background and Piro's own reasons on why Hindu–Muslim antagonism plays such an important role in her autobiographical and other writings. By examining the cultural and social space that a woman like her, low-caste and formerly sexually available, occupied, and what possible manoeuvring she could manage in order to open or widen her options, the chapter looks at a woman's claim for autonomy. It also explores the semantics that terms such as 'Hindu', 'Muslim', or 'Sikh' carried in Piro's time, discussing these through her story of a thwarted 'reconversion' of her by her former Islamic community, as by her particular 'conversion narrative'. How we can understand 'conversion' in the first half of the nineteenth century in Punjab is developed through a historical view of religious dissension in Punjab.

Chapter 4 delineates Piro's inclination towards bhakti devotion and her attraction towards bhakti's legends and tales to make a case for the emancipation of a low-caste and former prostitute. By explicating the shaping of her cultural imaginary steeped in a bhakti ethos that became a source of strength, autonomy, and agency for her, the chapter argues for Piro's self-propelled effort to be empowered.

Chapter 5 begins by examining how we may comprehend notions of self and agency in contingent times and contexts. By studying the surrogate miracles that centrally define the life and choices of bhakti-inspired Piro and the Maharashtrian saint Bahinabai, the chapter discusses how these bhaktas asserted their agency even as they seemingly gave up formal power to gurus and others, and though they imbibed the nuances of their chosen devotional paths.

Chapter 6 delineates the polemics on caste in the Punjabi public sphere as it developed under colonialism. By looking at the life and career of the Rahtia Ditta Ram/Ditt Singh, formerly a Gulabdasi and latterly a Singh Sabhaite via the Arya Samaj, the chapter looks at the changing dynamics of anti-caste position from the mid-nineteenth to the late-nineteenth century. Ditta Ram's protean stands on caste, and what place it had in Sikh religion, culture, and social life, is a glimpse into both the persistence of the institution, and the difficulties in imagining a future sans this institution, even for a 'Dalit' Sikh. How community identities became implicated in the debate on caste is also shown.

Chapter 7 examines how the recent interest in Piro has manifested in a couple of plays written on hers and Gulabdas's life; and also the substantial introduction, a clue to reading their life, that a contemporary Gulabdasi guru of the Hansi dera has written in his compilation of mother' Piro's writings. Discussing the dialogical relationship between the past and the present, and memory that is mined from a presentist perspective, the chapter looks at the many who lay claim to interpreting the past. While the narrative of different literary genres follows certain 'cultural scripts'— whether the qissa romance, the trope of women in bhakti, the meanings of low casteness, the ambiguity of simultaneously embracing secularism and othering Islam, or the appeal of indigenousness in cultures—the chapter delineates the constraints and possibilities in the historian's craft, and that of the many others.

Chapter 8 looks at the Hansi dera's guru Vijenderji's attempts at reinventing Gulabdasi religiosity and relevance today. It argues that the Partition of India meant loss of sacred space and a continuity of tradition for the many Gulabdasi followers and branches. It also presented those keen on the sect's revival, and engaged in intra-sect rivalry, with new opportunity to do so in changed circumstances. By reworking themes around the birth and death of Gulabdas, the liminal but power-charged moments in the cycle of transmigration, the chapter looks at how certain Punjabi cultural traits are developed for new rituals and for the sacralizing of spaces. The chapter completes the circle traversed in the study, from Gulabdasi ideas and practice, to Gulabdas's renewed exemplarity as reworked by a young and dynamic guru. By showing the current understandings of piety, of the place of caste and women within the Hansi dera, and comparing it with what was the state in the nineteenth century, the chapter moves towards denouement, concluding the study by making observations on some Gulabdasis today.

Part I

1   Guru Gulabdas

A Savant Monist or a Deviant Maverick?

Sīs mahal ke kutte niṅdak kyoṅ kare bhoṅkeṅ nāhiṅ re
Apne rūp chuphere dīse...
Āge niṅdku chhuṭe nāhiṅ dozak mah jalāhī re
Dās Gulāb kahe phir nindak sukaru jūn pavāhī re.

Those insulting dogs of glass palaces, why should they not bark?
After all they see themselves on all four sides...
These offenders will not go free, they'll burn in the fires of hell
Says Das Gulab these insulters will be reborn as hogs.[1]

Kariye niṅd hamārī logoṅ niṅdyā hameṅ pyārī re
Niṅd hamārī behan bhāṅjī niṅd bāp mahī tārī re
Jahāṅ jahāṅ yahī niṅdā jāve tahāṅ tahāṅ ujyārī re....
Dās Gulāb na pahuṅch niṅdā saṅt janā avtārī re.

---

[1] GC: 300. *Pothī Gulāb Chaman* (Lahore: Tajul Kutub, 1881). This lithographed copy is available in Punjabi University, Patiala. It was copied for printing purposes by Krishan Das Ramli from an original handwritten manuscript, as the scribe notes: 'asl mutābak nakal karī haī'. According to Navratan Kapoor, *Gulab Chaman* was first published by the press of Haji Charag Din Siraj Din as *Kissa Gulab Chaman*, and then by Munshi Lal Din's Albion Press in Lahore, which had been copied by the scribe Ram Narayan of Amritsar from the original. (Navratan Kapoor, *Sadhu Gulab Das: Jivan te Rachna* [Patiala: Publications Bureau, Punjabi University, 2002], p. 20.) The multiple publications of this collection of spiritual verses indicate the popularity of Gulabdas and his panth in the second half of the

People insult me, these insults are dear to me
Insults are (like) my sister, niece; insults my father, mother,
Wherever these insults travel, so will my fair name...
Das Gulab is not touched by these insults for he is an incarnated saint.[2]

Merā nā hamre mānhī koī na bairī mītā re
Sājh na baran āsram kise samo bhekh na koī kītā re
Hamrā koī na hame kisī ke greha mahi atītā re
Fākē mahī saburī faqrāṅ masat pyālā pītā re
Hame kuchāhī kāfir bigre dhāī jagat kī rītā re
Dās Gulāb ajāt bhaye hau mil karī apne mītā re.

I alone, no one with me, none enemy or friend
Not in *baran asrama*, nor have (I) kept any garb
No one mine nor I of none, nor do I have a past
Hunger and patience in mendicancy, for faqirs supped the cup of unconcern
They may call me an unbeliever, for such are the customs of the world
Das Gulab is rendered casteless, after meeting his friend.[3]

Tū hī chain chainī tū hī rog rogī
Tū hī soch sochi tū hī jog jogī
Tū hī bhog bhogī tū hī rāg tānī
Tū hī chittī chetam tū hī budhīmānī.

You are calm and the calmer; you the disease and the diseased.
You the thought and the thinker; you the asceticism and the ascetic.
You the enjoyment and the enjoyer; you the singer and the song.
You the consciousness and the mind, you the intellect.[4]

This chapter investigates how we have come to receive two contradictory
views of Guru Gulabdas. According to the first, Gulabdas was a savant, a
learned man of his age with a prolific pen, who gathered around himself
lettered and literary disciples. The other view presents Gulabdas as a

---

nineteenth century in Punjab. (The verse numbers from *Gulab Chaman* will be
marked as: '*GC*: xx'.)

  [2] *GC*: 301.
  [3] *GC*: 319.
  [4] *GC*: 366.

FIGURE 1.1 Gulabdas as depicted on the title page of his book *Gulāb Chaman*. The title in *nastaliq* reads *Gulāb Chaman* and in Gurmukhi, *Pothī Gulāb Chaman Dī* published by Abdul Haq, Taj Kutub, Lahore, Bazaar Kashmiri. Gulabdas is shown sitting on his seat (*gaddī*) with cushions, a halo framing his head. One disciple stands in attendance before him while another, likely his successor Hargobind, holds the flywhisk. His shield and sword, aigrette and turban, all underline his majesty. In her descriptions of Gulabdas, Piro referred to him as adorned in *sastar* (weapons) and *bastar* (rich attire), exemplified here. (The work was published in 1881 in lithograph print.)
Source: Courtesy of the author.

fiercely independent maverick guru, condemned by many, perhaps the religiously orthodox elites and the arbiters of social propriety, not only for some of his ideas but also for the social composition, cultural makeup, and the running of his dera at Chathianwala village, in Kasur, near Lahore, now in Pakistan. This inquiry will give us a glimpse into the variegated nature of religious traditions in nineteenth-century Punjab, showing us how someone like Gulabdas, with his ideas that challenged dominant social and religious systems, and his disciple Piro, who was perceived to have transgressed multiple social norms, could live and flourish there.

Some of Gulabdas's verses, as the first two examples, and partly the third, in the epigraph, show him to be acutely aware of the insults of others directed at him, cursing them in turn for what he must have perceived as their unjustified vitriolic attacks. The second of the two verses display his deep engagement with the monist, non-dualist advaita philosophy, expressing his ideas in poetic compositions that give a glimmer of his erudition, spiritual progress, and command over prosody and poetics. He uses a curious mix of languages that strongly suggest Sadhukari,[5] or Sadhu Bhasha, the lingua franca of the northern sants, with inflections of Braj, Punjabi, and Urdu. Such language usage was a part of Sikh inheritance in the eighteenth and most of the nineteenth centuries; many Sufis, on the other hand, employed the western and central Punjabi dialects of Multani and Majhi.[6] Besides the common thread, particularly in syntax, of Punjabi in these parallel language traditions of Punjab, one sees many commonalities between the two, including of metaphors and genres, and as this work will show at various junctures, important themes indexing a vibrant exchange of ideas.[7]

Gulabdas is attributed more than twenty works, though his *Gulab Chaman* (Rose Garden/Garden of Gulab) and *Updesh Vilās* (Revelling in Teaching), also available as *Gulāb Sāgar* (Gulab's Ocean), were the most significant.[8] Such was his command over poetic composition that in

[5] Kapoor, *Sadhu Gulab Das*, p. 35.

[6] Denis Matringe, 'Hir Varis Shah, A Story Retold', in *Narrative Strategies: Essays on South Asian Literature and Film*, edited by Vasudha Dalmia and Theo Damsteegt (New Delhi: Oxford University Press, 1998), p. 19.

[7] Anshu Malhotra and Farina Mir, 'Punjab in History and Historiography: An Introduction', in *Punjab Reconsidered: History, Culture and Practice*, edited by Anshu Malhotra and Farina Mir (New Delhi: Oxford University Press, 2012), pp. xxviii–xix.

[8] Gian Inder Sewak, 'Gulabdasi Sampradya: Rachna Ate Vichar' (PhD diss., Guru Nanak Dev University, 1984), pp. 170–1. Scholars agree that Gulabdas's

Gulab Chaman alone he uses over twenty metres, including doha, chaupai, kabit, sortha, korda, jhulan, tribhangi, savaiyya, and davaiyya.[9] He also composed in the siharfi genre, literally thirty (*sī*) letters (*harf*), referring to the popular acrostic poetic form that followed the Indo-Persian alphabet, each verse beginning with the successive letter, the Gurmukhi variant of which was the *paintī*, following thirty-five alphabets of the script.[10] Scholarly himself, his disciples were also literary figures, many writing spiritual poetry (Bawa Desraj, Sant Bahadur Singh, Shamdas Arif, Piro, Muhammad Shah, Hira Singh), secular literature (Kishan Singh Arif, Sant Ditta Ram, Maiyya Das, Piro, Seth Vishan Das), or later reformist polemics (Giani Ditt Singh, Bhai Jawahir Singh Kapoor, Maiyya Das), and many others.

The juxtaposing verses that open this chapter portray Gulabdas's concern for being seen as a degenerate guru and display his knowledge steeped in a hoary monist tradition. Non-dualism for Gulabdas, as for many others, developed along with a bhakti ethos in a variegated Punjabi tradition that saw a close relation between the Creator and the Creation (Brahm and *Jīv* for Gulabdas), and included a strong strain of Sikh as well as Sufi literature. Such a diverse inheritance was not a peculiar repository

---

Gulāb Chaman is his most significant work. Navratan Kapoor has also studied his *Gulāb Sāgar*, which he considers the same as *Updesh Vilās* with an exegesis, and feels that it should be seen as a supplement to *Gulab Chaman*. *Gulab Sagar* is in prose in the form of a *samvad* or a conversation between Gulabdas and his adopted son/successor, Hargobind, who poses philosophical questions that are answered by Gulabdas and this acts as an exposition of Gulabdas's ideas. The compiling of *Gulab Sagar* seems like an effort of a strong following of the Gulabdasis in Haryana, post the Partition of India, published as it was in Rohtak in 1968 by the Sachdev family disciples—descendants of Nand Lal—Dr Parmanand and his son Devendra Kumar. It also attributes a very significant role to Sant Vishan Das and his wife, Jamna Devi, themselves in line from Gulabdas's disciple Seva Singh. (Kapoor, *Sadhu Gulab Das*, pp. 5, 24, 105–13.) On the latter two sants and the Hansi family *gaddi* (seat), see Chapter 8. Vijender Das, the present head of the Hansi seat, attributes more than fifty works to Gulabdas. See his *Sant Kavyitri Ma Piro* (Panchkula: Satluj Prakashan, 2011), pp. 39–40.

[9] Kapoor, *Sadhu Gulab Das*, pp. 44–6.

[10] The enormous popularity of the siharfi form in Punjab in the nineteenth century can be discerned by the fact that almost all notable poets of this period composed some of their poetry in this form. See Sant Singh Sekhon, *A History of Punjabi Literature*, vol. 2 (Patiala: Publications Bureau, Punjabi University, 1993), pp. 132–55.

of the Gulabdasis, and there were other similar groups in Punjab and elsewhere, for instance, the Sevapanthis.[11] Yet, as the opening verses indicate, there was something in his ideas and practice that made his contemporaries regard him as verging concurrently on the threshold of greatness and ignominy. How did this come to be? What were his philosophical inclinations and charismatic ways that made him such an attractive guru to follow, given that he counted several literary and intellectual figures of his time as his disciples? What were the beliefs, lifestyle choices, and the setting up and stewardship of his establishment, on the other hand, that so provoked the ire of some? This chapter will make an attempt to unravel the reasons he and his sect were regarded as alluring and abhorrent, reviled and revered in turns.

The chapter begins by scanning the various sources on the Gulabdasis that are available, examining them for the attitude they display towards the guru. The sectarian Sikh sources of scholars associated with the Nirmalas, which seemingly both owned and disowned Gulabdas will be examined in detail for their complexity. Ambivalent towards some of his ideas and the established praxis of his dera at Chathianwala, they nevertheless acknowledge his compelling intellection. A glimpse of the colonial accounts will be given, looking at sources that unambiguously condemn Gulabdas and his apparently epicurean ways. Gulabdas's disciples often came to the defence of their guru in their writings, and why they needed to do so and how they engaged with a putative public will be shown. This will be followed by a discussion on the more significant of Gulabdas's ideas that recur in his work, studying them for their erudition as for their radical tone, and tracing their importance in the context of his life within the dera. Finally, the moral ambiguity that his thought and actions provoked will be investigated through a discussion on the term *sharā*, consistently used by his critics, in the sense of violation of moral codes that required objurgation. Thus, how a conflicted 'public memory' of Gulabdas and the Gulabdasis, to use a

---

[11] A similar theological background has been shown by Monika Horstmann in her study of the Sevapanthis, a Sikh sect started in the seventeenth century, which showed the influence of advaita, bhakti, Sufi, and Sikh ideas. Since Sevapanthi texts are available in Rajasthan where they were preserved with the Dadupanthis, she speculates a larger north Indian sant tradition. See her 'Parasbhag: Bhai Addan's Translation of Al-Ghazali's Kimiya-yi sa'adat', in *Patronage and Popularisation, Pilgrimage and Procession: Channels of Transcultural Translation and Transmission*, edited by Heidi R.M. Pauwels (Wiesabden: Harrassowitz, 2009), pp. 9–22.

term employed by Christian Novetzke, came to be constructed and is with us today will be interrogated.[12]

Novetzke, in the context of the remembrance of the fourteenth-century Maharashtrian sant Namdev, discusses the public aspects of bhakti and of memory in a premodern context. He notes bhakti's performative predilection that addresses a community, imagining it into existence through practices of sharing, singing, and memory-making.[13] Other scholars of early modern religious histories too have drawn our attention to the complex relation between orality, performance, and the written word, emphasizing the manner in which networks of circulation and exchange were set afoot, wherein oral performers and scribal communities and their interaction played a significant role.[14] That such an interaction in time could occasionally transform what started out as oral and local into literary and cosmopolitan, accruing more prestige as scribal communities and higher castes became involved, shows the continually expanding scope of such exchanges.[15] The inter-animation of the oral, the performative, and the inscriptive is, therefore, instructive in understanding how cultural exchange occurred and connections were formed in early modern north India. In this context, it is important to remember that while society, as Christopher Bayly noted, was not a highly literate one, it valued literacy highly; and Sheldon Pollock commented on the significance of 'literization' and the written word in a society that is seen to 'hyper-value' the oral.[16] One can posit that the growth of an Indian 'ecumene' in the early modern period into the nineteenth century,

[12] Christian Lee Novetzke, *History, Bhakti, and Public Memory: Namdev in Religious and Secular Traditions* (Ranikhet: Permanent Black, 2008).

[13] Christian Lee Novetzke, 'Introduction', in his *History, Bhakti, and Public Memory*, pp. 1–31.

[14] Jaroslav Strnad, 'Searching for the Source or Mapping of the Stream: Some Text-Critical Issues in the Study of Medieval Bhakti', in *Text and Tradition in Early Modern North India*, edited by J.S. Hawley, Anshu Malhotra, and Tyler Williams (forthcoming).

[15] Tyler Williams, 'From Local to Trans-Regional Poets: Translating Texts and Traditions in the Niranjani Sampraday', in Hawley, Malhotra, and Williams, *Text and Tradition in Early Modern North India*.

[16] C.A. Bayly, *Empire and Information: Intelligence Gathering and Social Communication in India, 1780–1870* (New Delhi: Cambridge University Press, 2007 [reprint]), p. 13. Sheldon Pollock, *The Language of the Gods in the World of Men: Sanskrit, Culture and Power in Premodern India* (New Delhi: Permanent Black, 2007), p. 4.

connected through routes of transmission and exchange, both oral and written, produced a public. This was a public, as Michael Warner has noted, that comes into being by the 'reflexive circulation of discourse'.[17] Pollock points to something similar when he speaks of the 'sociotextual community', the 'community for which literature is produced, in which it circulates, and which derives a portion of its self-understanding as a community from the very act of hearing, reading, performing, reproducing, and circulating literary texts'.[18] Taking from Pollock the idea that such communities occur in history and are changed by temporality, and from Farina Mir the notion that such 'formations' are never complete and always processual, that is, in the process of becoming, we can begin to draw the changing, whether outwardly radiating or inwardly shrinking, contours of this public.[19]

In the early modern period and the period just prior to colonial modernity, this public participated in the circulation of certain ideas, within which intellectually stimulating, 'large tent' advaita polemics gained popularity.[20] Advaita intellectualism interacted with, and was impacted by the late bhakti ethos and the place of the guru within it,[21] as also by Sufi ideas and practice. The Gulabdasis, highly literate and participants in such a sociotextual community, eclectic in their philosophical choices that carried shades of advaita, bhakti, and Sufi ideas, must be seen to be actively a part of this north Indian public. It is important to emphasize how the act of disseminating ideas and poetry—most of Gulabdas and his followers' writings were in verse—was deployed by the Gulabdasis not only in oral narrations and performances but also in writing. The act of inscription on paper—when poetic compositions of poets and gurus elaborating theological and philosophical ideas were written by scribes—set into motion particular modes and routes, a public of the like-minded

[17] Michael Warner, 'Publics and Counter-Publics', *Public Culture* 14, no. 1 (2002): 49–90.

[18] Sheldon Pollock, ed., *Literary Cultures in History: Reconstructions from South Asia* (Berkeley: University of California Press, 2003), p. 27.

[19] Farina Mir, *The Social Space of Language: Vernacular Culture in British Colonial Punjab* (Ranikhet: Permanent Black, 2010), pp. 17–18, 97–103.

[20] Christopher Minkowski, 'Advaita Vedanta in Early Modern History', in *Religious Cultures in Early Modern India: New Perspectives*, eds Rosalind O'Hanlon and David Washbrook (New Delhi: Routledge, 2011), pp. 105–42.

[21] Daniel Gold, *The Lord as Guru: Hindi Sants in North Indian Tradition* (New York: Oxford University Press, 1989), p. 4.

and the interested was addressed through what Warner calls a 'poetic world-making'.[22] So too when Gulabdas responded through his poetry to the circulation of defamatory statements about him, or his disciples reacted to specific charges of calumny against their guru, an imagined public was invoked.

The nineteenth-century world in which the advaita, bhakti, and Sufi ideas floated was broad enough to be addressed as a public, but what about the putative audience for his defensive declamations, where he or his disciples explained his conduct or challenge to given morality? The address is, of course, to the same public, but it may take on the appearance of a counterpublic, one aware of its subordinate status in relation to the discourse of dominant morality.[23] The line between a broader public for advaita philosophies or bhakti poetics and a counter-public that defended the abandonment in practice of ordinary morality is surely a thin one. The Gulabdasis inhabited this social cleavage, a thin cleft between acceptable and unacceptable ethics, intellectual advaita and popular bhakti, the upkeep of shara and its thwarting. In other words, the Gulabdasis both tapped into a larger public built around certain discourses, and a counterpublic challenging some of the norms of even this order. The conundrum here of being on the margins, but also popular, needs to be understood, for this is the territory the Gulabdasis made their own.

Gulabdas's time, however, was on the cusp of colonial modernity in Punjab, when the associational politics and print medium of the 'public sphere' were beginning to make an appearance. Though the first printing press was set up in Punjab in 1836 by the American Presbyterian Mission in Ludhiana, the rest of Punjab began to be affected by the new technology only after all of Punjab came under the British Raj in 1849.[24] The term 'public sphere' is used here to draw attention to colonial modernity with its growth of print capitalism, associational and reformist politics, and elitist middle-class self-identity of its overwhelmingly male participants.[25] It created new discursive and institutional spaces and new norms—for instance

---

[22] Warner wishes to convey that every speech act or performance addressed to a public uses complex ways to specify in advance the world of its circulation, the character of its public. Warner, 'Publics and Counter-Publics': 82.

[23] Warner, 'Publics and Counter-Publics': 85.

[24] Mir, *The Social Space of Language*, pp. 32–3.

[25] Sanjay Joshi, *Fractured Modernity: Making a Middle Class in Colonial North India* (New Delhi: Oxford University Press, 2001), p. 24.

reasoned debate and activism—in its sweep.[26] The Gulabdasis, particularly
the guru and some of the first-generation disciples, remained aloof from
this world, though by the 1870s it was knocking on their doors and younger
disciples were beginning to participate in its various cultural forms,
including print. It is quite likely, for instance, that the lithographed print of
Gulab Chaman was not published during Gulabdas's lifetime, and the dera
of the guru at Chathianwala was not yet affected by the changes, though it
would soon be, as the likes of Kishan Singh Arif and Ditta Ram would enter
the 'Punjabi literary formation', that is, the shared practices of producing and
taking pleasure in Punjabi literatures through the print medium.[27] Thus,
the new public sphere congealing into being at least partially through print
capitalism was not yet the reason or the focus of Gulabdas's writing. When
he addresses an audience, he must be understood to speak to a public that
still relied upon older ways of transmission and engagement with varied
religious ideas, spread orally and through the written word, through networks of itinerant holy men, scribal communities, bazaar exchanges, and
public debates. These are variants of what Bayly called 'affective' and 'patrimonial' knowledge, 'knowledge gained through participation in communities of belief and marriage, through religious affiliation and association
with holy men, seers, astrologers, and physicians'.[28]

On the other hand, the sources on the Gulabdasis with which this
chapter commences were very much a product of the colonial print
culture and the public sphere in which it participated. The colonial
ethnographic accounts grew out of the need of the state to enumerate, catalogue, and mark the ruled in particular ways, as scholars have
shown.[29] The sectarian Sikh sources discussed below, however, responded
to the new ethnographic impulse as some native informants and social

---

[26] Francesca Orsini, *The Hindi Public Sphere 1920–1940: Language and Literature in
the Age of Nationalism* (New Delhi: Oxford University Press, 2002), pp. 11–16. Orsini
distinguishes between the Hindi public sphere she discusses from the Habermasian
bourgeois public sphere as it developed in Europe during modernity.

[27] On Punjabi literary formation—shared practices of producing, circulating,
performing, reading, and listening to Punjabi literary texts, *qisse* in particular—see
Mir, *The Social Space of Language*, pp. 17–18, 97–103.

[28] Bayly, *Empire and Information*, p. 16.

[29] Bernard Cohn, *Colonialism and Its Forms of Knowledge: The British in India*
(Princeton: Princeton University Press, 1996). Also see the essays in Carol A.
Breckenridge and Peter van der Veer, eds, *Orientalism and the Post-Colonial Predicament:
Perspectives on South Asia* (Philadelphia: University of Pennsylvania Press,
1993).

mediators began to compile their own compendia.[30] A modern historical consciousness developed out of the need to record 'appropriate' versions of events that increasingly came to be contested, but they also importantly maintained a link with the older networks of information gathering and exchange of gossip and news, all of which opens for us a window on the Gulabdasis. The Gulabdasis' time can be said to be the penumbral period when two distinct ways of being were staring each other in the face, though it was not plain to see for those who dwelled in it.

SOURCES ON THE GULABDASIS

The Sikh Accounts

There are three significant Sikh sources where the Gulabdasis are discussed: Giani Gian Singh's *Panth Prakāsh* (1880), Mahant Ganesha Singh's *Bhārat Mat Darpaṇ* (1926), and Kahn Singh Nabha's *Mahān Kosh* (1930)—all of these works are encyclopaedic in character.[31] The term 'encyclopaedic' is used here to describe the new impulse to organize and systemize knowledge in newer forms, the epistemological transformation initiated with colonialism.[32] These authors were concerned with what ought to be understood as falling within a Sikh tradition when the urge to outline such a tradition was emerging.[33] Gian Singh's *Panth Prakash* must be seen as an early attempt at catering to this urge. Though shaped by newer concerns, it did not shed its link with earlier knowledge forms, whether the hagiography or the genealogy, thus maintaining a link with

[30] On the appropriation of native scholarship by the colonial state, see Nicholas B. Dirks, 'The Textualization of Tradition: Biography of an Archive', in his *Castes of Mind: Colonialism and the Making of Modern India* (Princeton: Princeton University Press, 2001), pp. 81–106.

[31] Giani Gian Singh, *Sri Guru Panth Prakash* [hereinafter *PP*] (Patiala: Bhasha Vibhag, 1970, first published 1880), pp. 1292–5. Mahant Ganesha Singh, *Bharat Mat Darpan* [hereinafter *BMD*] (Amritsar: Vaidak Bhandar, 1926), pp. 127–30. Kahn Singh 'Nabha', *Gurushabad Ratnakar Mahan Kosh: Encyclopaedia of Sikh Literature* (Patiala: Bhasha Vibhag, 1981, first published 1930), p. 423.

[32] On the defining of such epistemological change see Robert Darnton, 'Philosophers Trim the Tree of Knowledge: The Epistemological Strategy of the Encyclopedie', in his *The Great Cat Massacre and Other Episodes in French Cultural History* (New York: Vintage Books, 1985), pp. 191–213.

[33] On the diversity of the Sikh tradition and the impulse to make it single, see Harjot Oberoi, *The Construction of Religious Boundaries: Culture, Identity and Diversity in the Sikh Tradition* (New Delhi: Oxford University Press, 1994). While

the well-established *tazkirah* biographical form, and creating a pastiche of forms. Published only seven years after the death of Gulabdas in 1873, *Panth Prakash* is a detailed history of the eighteenth century, along with narratives on the Sikh gurus, especially the first and the tenth. Towards the end of this massive history in Braj verse, intermingled with Punjabi and occasionally Urdu words, Singh gives accounts of Sikh sects, including the Nirmalas, Udasis, Nihangs, Kukas, and smaller ones like the Gulabdasis, Niranjanis, and the Hiradasis. The Gulabdasis in this work are, therefore, seen to be a part of this amorphous Sikh heritage. Gian Singh was a celebrated Sikh scholar and a historian, who had a varied career and education, but acknowledged the renowned Nirmala scholar Tara Singh Narottam as his mentor.[34] Mahant Ganesha Singh was a historian of the Nirmala order to which he belonged, hailing from its famous Panchaiti Akhara in Amritsar, where he served as its secretary at the time of compiling his philosophical bent of motley sects of north India.[35] Kahn Singh Nabha was a scholar of immense energy, constantly engaged with learned exegesis of different Sikh texts, including the *Adi Granth*.[36] He also became famous for his exposition of the Singh Sabha line when in 1898 he published *Ham Hindu Nahiṅ*, pushing forth the agenda of a separate identity of the Sikhs from the Hindus. His *Mahan Kosh* was a compendium of Sikh religious literature, and literary and historical figures, and he gives a brief account of Gulabdas's life and literature here in a serious mien, unlike the first two, who relate a fuller and more gossipy narrative of the Gulabdasis. Gian Singh's is by far the most significant

---

participating in defining Sikh culture and history, these authors, especially the first two, would not have passed muster with what eventually became the dominant tradition within reformed Sikhism. Even while defining Sikhism they were far more inclusive of Sikh diversity rather than being exclusively focused on Khalsa identity, as the more successful Lahore Singh Sabha.

[34] On Giani Gian Singh, see Harbans Singh, ed., *The Encyclopaedia of Sikhism*, vol. 2 (Patiala: Punjabi University, 1996), pp. 82–3.

[35] Ganesha Singh's important work *Nirmal Bhushan: Itihās Nirmal Bhekh* was a history of the Nirmala sect completed around 1937. The sect, with its emphasis on Vedic and Sanskrit learning, was meant to have started during Guru Gobind Singh's time, who is said to have sent three disciples to Benares for Sanskrit learning. They were distinguished by their celibate status, white or saffron garments, and uncut hair. See R.A. Rose, *A Glossary of the Tribes and Castes of the Punjab and the North West Frontier Province* (Patiala: Languages Department, 1970 [1883]).

[36] See H. Singh, ed., *The Encyclopaedia of Sikhism*, pp. 409–10.

of these accounts, closest as he was to the time of Gulabdas. He witnessed some of the events that he shows were formative in Gulabdas's life, for example, the fall of Sikh power after the two Anglo-Sikh wars were fought between 1845 and 1849, in the process giving us a peep into the twilight period between the two empires, the Sikh and the British. Ganesha Singh's prose largely follows the former's narrative, often even picking up Gian Singh's words and phrases. However, he supplies a few additional and important details, some of which we get only from Piro's autobiographical *Ik Sau Sath Kafian*, thus making his account an important supplement to Gian Singh's. Thus, by following these two authors in their yenta-like narrations, we get a fair idea of what the contemporary understanding of the Gulabdasis was during the guru's lifetime, as well as how they were perceived in the early twentieth century.

All Sikh accounts tell us that Gulabdas was born in 1809, in the village Ratol in the Tarn Taran district of Punjab, in a Jat family, to father Hamira and mother Deso. These authors also mention that he did service (*naukrī*) for a while, most likely as a soldier in the army, Ganesha Singh clarifying that he served the Pohuwind chiefs. Subsequently, his spiritual and philosophical journey initiated. The following is Gian Singh's sequence of teachers and fellow travellers of Gulabdas: Gulabdas became a disciple of one Brahm Das, stayed with some faqirs, then studied Vedanta with Deva Singh Nirmala, and kept the company of one Haridas Girdhar. Ganesha Singh reveals more details and differs slightly from Gian Singh. According to him, Gulabdas began his spiritual training with the Udasis (but does not mention the name of his guru), in particular their sub-branch of Sangat Sahibs, and like the *nāga*s or the naked sadhus among them, he smeared ashes on his body.[37] Later, he left the Udasis and went to Dhanaula village in the Malwa area to one Dhyandas to do his lexical and prosodic studies. Ganesha Singh further notes that being a restless character he then gave up rubbing ashes on himself, started wearing good clothes, and kept the company of Bulleh Shahi faqirs, when he apparently learnt to insult the ways of both the Hindus and the

---

[37] For a discussion on the Udasis and their sub-branches see James Hastings, ed., *Encyclopaedia of Religion and Ethics*, vol. 12 (New York: Charles Scribner's Sons, 1958), pp. 504–5. Sirichand, the eldest son of the first Sikh guru, Nanak, started the Udasi order, which has close resemblance to Hindu ascetic practices, including being celibate, and smearing ashes on the body, particularly their naga sadhus. They also recruited from all castes.

Muslims![38] Later, he studied Vedanta with Deva Singh of Kurukshetra, followed by an itinerant life with Haridas Girdhar. For Kahn Singh, after being in the service of some unspecified Sikhs, Gulabdas became a disciple of Hiradas Udasi of Kasur; then in Dhanuala village, near Nabha, he learnt prosody with Dhyandas; with Haridas Girdhar he began writing poetry; and studied Vedanta with Deva Singh Nirmala and became an atheist. While there is no agreement on the name of the Udasi preceptor of Gulabdas, the other two names of Deva Singh Nirmala and Haridas Girdhar do recur. Although Ganesha Singh adds details about the Udasis and the Bulleh Shahis, not mentioned by name by Gian Singh (though he may be pointing towards them) and Kahn Singh—limiting himself to writing of Gulabdas's learning—he is silent about the influence of any alleged faqirs. It is the first two narratives with their fuller treatment of the sect that are discussed here.

Both the narratives adopt a tone of disapproval in relation to the Gulabdasis almost from the word go, though Gian Singh's work appears more matter of fact in relating aspects of Gulabdasi thought and ways, and also in some points more appreciative of the intellectual prowess of Gulabdas. The fact that neither author could ignore the sect, both conceding that it attracted many followers at certain times, is a testimony to Gulabdas's eminence. At a point, Ganesha Singh also mentions that after efforts were made to put down the sect (more on that later) many Gulabdasis took to calling themselves Udasis and Nirmalas, indicating a closeness to his own sect which despite his disapproval he conceded.[39]

Gian Singh begins his narrative on the Gulabdasis by making a curious observation: *jaise bhaye varan ho taise nāstak ine lakhījo*—as is *varna*, so inscribe them *nastik*—to make a cryptic, literal translation. Brevity is, of course, a virtue in verse, but to understand this statement we need to unpack the semantics of both *varan* (varna) and *nastak* (nastik). 'Varan',

---

[38] Bulleh Shah (1680–1752) was the famous Qadiri-Shattari Sufi of Punjab, whose *kafis* or verses that challenged established religious authorities and accepted social norms have continued to be popular in contemporary Punjab, both Indian and Pakistani. His establishment was also in Kasur, where Gulabdas made his base.

[39] Ganesha Singh, *BMD*, p. 129. Sant Singh Sekhon, while discussing the Gulabdasi poet Kishan Singh Arif in his history of Punjabi literature, refers to his guru as Gulab Singh Nirmala. While this is the only place where I have come across the use of this name, it does confirm a close relationship of the Gulabdasis with the Nirmalas. Sekhon, *A History of Punjabi Literature*, vol. 2, p. 136.

literally colour and used to broadly catalogue the fourfold caste hierarchy, in this specific case refers to neither the Dumontian purity/pollution universalist binary nor to the understanding of caste as a species (*jāti*), or an essence or substance, attached to the body.[40] It may rather be seen as a system of classification, helping the reader place the sect in a category that disassociates it with the regular and the normal, those outside the varnashramadharma, perhaps indicating the astounding excoriation of the varna–caste nexus by the Gulabdasis. In this context, one may go back to the third verse in the epigraph, where Gulabdas describes himself as *ajāt*, a word that has connotations of being casteless, or having lost caste. Gulabdas may be said to have declared himself without caste from his own viewpoint, but also may be considered to have lost caste based on the strictures of society, through degenerate practices. Additionally, the word implies one who is not born, or unborn—an aspiration for those seeking emancipation from the cycle of birth and death. Gulabdas's identification with Brahm, or the Supreme Being, is discussed later, which may even place him as the unborn, being born like a godly incarnation (*avtār*) for the benefit of humanity.

The philosopher Judith Butler has argued that power is produced through naturalizing discourses, through a 'ritualized repetition of norms'.[41] It is by the reiteration of caste as normal that society produces consent to its inequalities. The disturbing denunciation of caste norms, in theory as in practice by challenging its normative status, therefore, made the Gulabdasis anomalous, creating categorizing problems for Gian Singh. Interestingly, the same classificatory term—'varan'—is used in Singh's statement to emphasize Gulabdasi existence outside its norms.

'Nastik', with its larger connotations ranging from atheism, unbelief, apostasy, to godlessness, pointed to Singh's ambiguity regarding the Gulabdasi beliefs, while underscoring their heterodoxy. He uses the term 'nastak' twice more in his description of the sect, once referring to their theology as 'dry Vedanta nastak' (*khushak bidāntī nāstak*) and at another time comparing Gulabdas to other renegade men who initiated *maujī panths*, hinting at ostensibly unrestrained sensual hedonism of some

[40] On the discussion on ascriptions of caste, see Partha Chatterjee, 'The Nation and its Outcasts', in his *The Nation and its Fragments: Colonial and Postcolonial Histories* (Princeton: Princeton University Press, 1993), pp. 173–99.

[41] Judith Butler, *Bodies That Matter: On the Discursive Limits of 'Sex'* (New York: Routledge, 1993), p. x. Also see Samuel A. Chambers and Terrell Carver, *Judith Butler and Political Theory: Troubling Politics* (London: Routledge, 2008), p. 34.

sects, which purportedly propagated atheism (*nastāk mat parchāriyo*).[42] Thus, it was the very fundamental beliefs of the Gulabdasis that put them on the margins of acceptability and respectability, identifying them in common parlance with perhaps the left-handed, tantra-like sects, or the materialist *Chārvāk* type.[43] Thus, nastak rather than connoting atheism as such, must be seen to be a euphemism for what were regarded as the disreputable traits of the Gulabdasis.

In this context, it is important to note that Navratan Kapoor in his study of Gulabdas's life and writing traces the influence of the Sarbhangi sect on him, which he understands as Aghori.[44] Literally, *aghori* means foul, unclean, and refers to a Shaiva community; while Sarbhangi ascetics are supposed to reject caste and pollution taboos.[45] The rejection of caste and its praxis lead to the charge of being unclean. Kapoor specifically traces the influence of Sarbhangis through Gulabdas's association with Haridas Girdhar and the chant of *soham* (also sometimes called *sohaṅg*), the mantra apparently explicated by an important Sarbhangi called Kina Ram and his disciple Gulab Chand 'Anand'.[46] While the significance of 'soham' (I am He) in Gulabdas's writing is discussed below, it is worth pointing out that the chant was apparently part of the spiritual repertoire of later bhakti sants like Paltu Das.[47] The embossing

[42] Gian Singh specifically mentions two sybarite gurus: Maghi Shah of Mansurpura and Man Shah of Rameshwarpuri. It is difficult to say whether these places or people existed. The reference to Maghi Shah is interesting because Kapoor mentions that towards the end of *Gulab Sagar*, wherein some of his disciples' verses are included, Gulabdas is also called Maghi: *Gulābdās pyāre, Māghī tin kā nām* (beloved Gulabdas, whose name is Maghi). (Kapoor, *Sadhu Gulab Das*, p. 7.) Significantly, one of the texts attributed to Gulabdas is *Mauj Vilas*, literally 'Sensuous Surge'. See Vijender Das, *Sant Kavyitri Ma Piro*, p. 39.

[43] Shaharyar, a scholar who has studied Piro's verses, calls Gulabdasis as *Charvakis*. See his 'Kalaam Mata Piro ka', *Hun* (January–April 2009): 166.

[44] Kapoor, *Sadhu Gulab Das*, pp. 13–16.

[45] R.S. McGregor, *Oxford Hindi–English Dictionary* (New Delhi: Oxford University Press, 1993).

[46] Kapoor does not give us their historical time though it seems to be the eighteenth century. The Baba Kinaram Aghorpith Ramshala in Ramgarh, district Chandauli, Varanasi, Uttar Pradesh, gives Kinaram's dates as 1601–1771, said to have lived for 177 years! I owe this reference to Anil Nauriya, a lawyer for the marginal farmers given land from the Ramshala under land ceiling laws, which the Ramshala is contesting.

[47] Kapoor, *Sadhu Gulab Das*, p. 14.

of bhakti ethos on Gulabdas, and more particularly on his disciple Piro, was very significant indeed, shaping their poetic personalities, as this work will show.

Gian Singh further refers to Gulabdas as identifying himself with the Supreme Being, calling himself Brahm (*brahm āp ko bhāse*) and imparting to his followers the mantra of soham. This was the elaboration of the advaita belief of the unity of Brahman and Jiv, and for the Gulabdasis, a solipsistic stress on locating the divine within the self. Christopher Minkowski has recently commented on the early modern period in India, noting that the view that 'it was possible to become liberated while still alive and embodied' had gained currency and that the unworldly Upanishadic philosophy of the Undivided Being had been socially adapted to ordinary life.[48] Moreover, Singh underlines that Gulabdas did not maintain differences between Hindus and Muslims (*Turak*), or between sin and meritorious act (*pāp* and *punya*), or heaven and hell (*narak* and *swarag*).[49] He gave his followers freedom to dress as they pleased, allowing them to sport uncut hair or the shorn, shaven look (*kes or muṇḍ*), maintaining no sectarian garb or distinction (bhekh or abhekh). Thus, a range of Gulabdasi ideas and practices were found to be questionable by Singh, for they were seen to carry to a radical extreme (or from Gulabdasi perspective, logical conclusion) the implications of their monist thought. These include, for example, Gulabdas's identification with the divine—not just the locating of the divine within the self, but also to go on to call himself divine (Brahm)—Singh calling him the exponent of *brahm gyān* (knowledge of the Brahman). Similarly, if god was within all, then theoretically caste or creed, and even gender differences amounted to little (though gender always proved to be a greater hurdle), along with popular understandings of heaven, hell, or sin. Furthermore, the Gulabdasis were seen to break norms of monastic self-discipline by shunning bhekh or sectarian distinctive garb, accoutrements, and praxis, an intrinsic aspect of ascetic orders like the Udasis or the Nirmalas, which may be identified with a range of objects, dresses, ornaments, and practices, from the ashes of the former to the white garments of the latter or celibacy for monks of both the orders. Ganesha Singh's tone of disapproval is palpable, even as he paraphrases

---

[48] Minkowski, 'Advaita Vedanta', p. 132.

[49] Though hell (*dozakh*) features in one of the verses with which this chapter has opened.

Gian Singh: *Na hī koī bhekh da chin ... apnī marjī te kes, apnī marjī te rod bhod raho ... khāna pīnā apne man bhonda karo ... chetan brahm khud khudā ih sarīr ya man hī haī* (Neither a mark of garb ... uncut hair if you so wish or clean shaven ... eat according to one's desire ... conscious supreme god is self, this body or the mind).[50]

Gian Singh also reports on Gulabdas's penchant for sensuous pleasures by clubbing together his relationship with a prostitute (*randī*) that he ostensibly came across on his travels, and his unearned wealth. He apparently travelled to Dwarka, where, in a place called Mashka Mandi, a beautiful (*nūr shahūr rūp*, literally a bright, famous beauty) prostitute fell for his charms (in the colourful language of Singh, *āshak is par thaī*). Singh also describes Gulabdas as charismatic—good looking, at the peak of youth, with an inconstant heart/mind (*chanchal chit*)—and, moreover, gifted with sweet speech and poetic delivery (*shirī sukhan, mohit bāk bakhāne*). Later, after settling in Chathianwala village in the Kasur district of Punjab, according to Singh, he cut quite a figure; often on a horseback, was addressed by his followers with the honorific '*sahib log*' (master), and his poetic renditions in various metres won him many disciples. At other times, he sat on a nice seat (*sundar palagh*) fanned by his disciples (*chaur karvāve*), wearing weapons and costumes (*shastar bastar*), his turban topped with an aigrette (*kalgī*). The randi of Mandi, to whom Singh had made a reference, then fell ill and died on the way (back to Punjab?) leaving behind considerable wealth, which he brought back to this village. The other sources of his wealth were rich disciples, and the wealth that many a Sikh soldier deposited with him (for safekeeping?) while they went and fought in the Anglo-Sikh war of 1845–6, referred to as the *Satluj bajang* by Singh. This indicated the war fought on the shores of the southernmost of Punjab's rivers, the Satluj, which was the border between the Sikh state and the British-controlled

---

[50] Ganesha Singh, *BMD*, pp. 128–9. Gian Singh wrote: *Guru pīr nij isht dev lo sharan ko rakhvāye; apnī marjī kes rakh ke chāho mund mundāo; khān pān man bhāvat khāve bhakh abhakh na koī; muljam jo na bane sarkārī besak kījo soī.* (The self was guru and pir, keeping disciples at his feet; they kept uncut hair if so wished or a clean shaven head; they ate as they pleased, keeping no garb; like a criminal cannot be of the government, they did as they pleased.) Singh's last line accused Gulabdasis as reprobate criminals, who cannot become 'legal,' or of the *shari'ah/sharā* in their behaviour. He calls them '*muljam-mulzim*'—a criminal/ accused—as against *sarkārī* or a '*mulāzim*', a government employee. Gian Singh, *PP*, p. 1294.

territories or those princely states under their protection to the south of the river since the Treaty of Amritsar in 1809.[51]

This specific historical information given as an aside by Gian Singh is rather significant, and one may take a little detour here to flesh out the historical background when the Gulabdasis flourished. Singh refers to Gulabdas and Piro as already settled in Chathe *graj* (village) before the Satluj war; the war itself signalled chaos and loss of further control by the Sikh state, which was relentlessly headed on a path of sanguinary and fratricidal politics since the demise of Ranjit Singh in 1839. This interregnum, between a powerful Punjabi state under Ranjit Singh (1799–1839), and the establishment of the British Raj proper in 1849, was when the Gulabdasis became ever more popular, gaining both followers and wealth in the unsettled conditions in Singh's estimation.

It seems the Gulabdasis were not recipients in any form of the Ranjit Singh state's largesse to religious institutions. The state by the end of the Maharaja's reign alienated a very substantial seven per cent of the revenue in *dharmārth* grants or endowments to religious institutions, the unprecedented growth of the Udasis being a case in point, but the Gulabdasis were outside this reticulate field.[52] This probably points to the disapprobation in which they were regarded, despite an initial affinity with the Udasis. The reason why the Gulabdasis may have also been kept at an arm's length was because an important general of Ranjit Singh's army, the gunner Ilahi Bakhsh, probably clashed with Gulabdas over the custody of Piro whom he evidently coveted for himself, making her move to Gulabdas's establishment, a contentious affair that took place during Ranjit Singh's time.[53] According to Ganesha Singh, Gulabdas's men clashed with those of Bakhsh's in Lahore near the tomb of Mian Mir, and the conflict was resolved only with the intervention of Ranjit Singh himself. Subsequently, Gulabdas and Piro settled in Chathianwala.[54]

---

[51] J.S. Grewal, *The Sikhs of the Punjab* (New Delhi: Cambridge University Press, 2002 [reprint]), p. 101.

[52] Grewal, *The Sikhs of the Punjab*, pp. 108–9. On Udasis as recipients of almost 10 per cent of dharmarth grants, see Grewal, *The Sikhs of the Punjab*, pp. 116–17. On dharmarth grants also see Ian Kerr, 'Sikhs and State: Troublesome Relationships and a Fundamental Continuity with Particular Reference to the Period 1849–1919', in *Sikh Identity: Continuity and Change*, edited by Pashaura Singh and N.G. Barrier (New Delhi: Manohar, 1999), pp. 147–74.

[53] See Chapter 3.

[54] Ganesha Singh, *BMD*, p. 128.

Gulabdas recorded his discord with Ranjit Singh in some of his works, including the *Gulāb Chhaṭi*.[55] Here he made reference to two blameless disciples, Deva Singh and Gulab Singh, being killed in the skirmish, ostensibly with Bakhsh's men. Indeed, Gulabdas exercised his saintly prerogative and cursed Ranjit Singh. Gulabdas noted that Ranjit's clan was finished, referring to the expiration of Ranjit Singh's empire along with the unnatural deaths of many of his sons and nobles by 1849, because of the ruler having attracted the saint's curse: *kāṇā saṅt sarāpe saṛiyā* (the one-eyed putrefied because of the sant's curse).[56] At another place, he apportioned the blame on Ranjit Singh's ministers who gave him wrong advice, saying that though the king was soft-hearted his ministers were bad company.[57] However, despite the history of such a discord, and though not officially favoured, the fact remains that Ranjit Singh's state tolerated the Gulabdasi establishment quite close to its centre of power, even if Gulabdas had to vacate Lahore. This speaks volumes for a society where multifarious sects and ideas could flourish, as long as they did not disturb the peace and acceptable societal norms, and the Gulabdasis did stretch social ethics to the limits.

The army, efficient and large (85,000 men), was the pride of Ranjit Singh's state,[58] though it became larger (120,000 men), unruly, and lawless after his death.[59] Gian Singh's account shows that many religious gurus had access to the army and preached within its ranks. He tells us, for example, that Gulabdas, a soldier to begin with, made his spiritual career preaching in the army (*fauj*) of the state, as did many others. The persistent nexus between monks and soldiers through the early modern period to the early nineteenth century has been established by many historians. William Pinch, for instance, has drawn attention to the role of the 'warrior ascetics' throughout this period, showing them as important components of the military labour market.[60] Though Gulabdas ended up being an ascetic

[55] Sewak, 'Gulabdasi Sampradaye', pp. 98–9. Sewak mentions such autobiographical references in Gulabdas's *Gulab Chhati, Anubhav Khanda,* and *Mauj Bilas.*

[56] Ranjit Singh was one-eyed, having lost an eye to small pox.

[57] *Kāṇā nrip ride kā komal ... Kāg mantra mile kusaṅgī* (One-eyed king was soft-hearted ... his crow ministers were bad company). Sewak, 'Gulabdasi Sampradaye', pp. 98–9.

[58] Grewal, *The Sikhs of the Punjab*, pp. 103–6.

[59] Khushwant Singh, *A History of the Sikhs,* vol. 2, *1839–2004* (New Delhi: Oxford University Press, 2008 [first edition 1963]), p. 6.

[60] William R. Pinch, *Warrior Ascetics and Indian Empires* (New Delhi: Cambridge University Press, 2006).

rather than a soldier, even as he attired himself in weapons, it is important to remember the easy traffic between the two institutions of asceticism and soldiery. The implication of Singh's statement in our context clearly is that many disbanded soldiers joined the Gulabdasi sect after the war. Those who survived may have either found it convenient to join ascetics like Gulabdas or were genuinely attracted to his monist tenets, while the fortune of the dead that was deposited with him inflated his coffers.

Interestingly, Gian Singh makes a similar statement regarding the Hiradasis, another sect connected to the Udasis in his estimation, which he describes immediately after the Gulabdasis in his work. Again, he asserts that even when the Sikh state of Lahore was powerful, many monks preached in the army (*rahite sādhū anak fauj maiṅ*—many sadhus stayed with the fauj), and that *satsaṅgs* (communal religious singing) were quite the norm within the army. He goes on to again make a reference to the Anglo-Sikh war of 1845–6 in the manner he does with reference to the Gulabdasis:

> When the fight began on the banks of the Satluj
> In the year 1903 [Bikrami, that corresponds to c. 1846]
> Those who went to fight
> The Sikhs leaving their wealth behind
> Many died, only few survived
> They too sacrificed wealth to become sadhus.[61]

Thus, the Hiradasi sect too gained a following around this disturbed time.

Another contemporary, Nurang Devi, a companion and disciple of Wazir Singh, a low-caste guru with strikingly similar ideas to those of Gulabdas, who settled in the village Lahuke, near Patti, in central Punjab, also made a reference to the Anglo-Sikh war, referring to it as the war with the *firaṅgī*.[62] She too drew the same conclusion, that the war drove many into *faqīrī*, or mendicancy:

> *Bahute faqīr hoye han Singhjī, firaṅgī dī vekhī laṛaī jī*
> *Kahe Nuraṅg Devī bahu hoye faqīr, hun giṇtī giṇī na jāye jī.*[63]

[61] Gian Singh, *PP*, pp. 1295–6.

[62] On Wazir Singh, see Raj Kumar Hans, 'Devotion and Dissent of Punjabi Dalit Sant Poets', in *Devotion and Dissent in Indian History*, edited by Vijaya Ramaswamy (New Delhi: Foundation Books, 2014), pp. 188–215.

[63] *Siharfī Satarvīṅ* (*Kafiaṅ Sant Wazīr Singh te Nuraṅg Devī diaṅ Sanjhiaṅ*) in Shamsher Singh Ashok, *Siharfian Sadhu Wazir Singh Kian* (Patiala: Publications Bureau, 1988), p. 72.

Many Singhs [Khalsa] became faqirs, Many saw the fight with the firangi
Says Nurang Devi, many became faqirs, now difficult to count how many.

Having had opportunities to interact with ascetics in Ranjit Singh's
time, many soldiers, in the ensuing chaos after his death, more so after
the Sikh defeat in the first Anglo-Sikh war, found asceticism with its
promise of refuge from worldly cares, or as a temporary shelter, an
attractive option.

To go back to the reportage of the randi episode in Gian Singh's
account, one can also interpret it as giving a clue to Gulabdas's sensuous
character in Singh's estimation, his penchant for relations with prostitutes, for soon Singh introduces Piro, a Muslim prostitute (*musāli, kasbī*),
with a reputation as a desirable beauty (*pekh arūj namūj rūp baḍh*). He
informs that she too fell for Gulabdas's charms, the two subsequently living together in intimacy (*abhed*) in Chathe village for the rest of their lives.
Ganesha Singh reports the same in a more prosaic language, noting the
two believed that both *jog* (asceticism) and *bhog* (sensory pleasure) were
good.[64] Further, as Gian Singh's narrative tells us, because of Piro's influence, other prostitutes (*besya*) became his disciples, and in his establishment spiritual singing and stories (*kirtan, kathā*) gave way to the *mujrā*,
a dance form associated with dancing girls, performed in an appropriate
mood (*samā*). Even after the death of Gulabdas and Piro, Singh further
relates, during the spring festival of Holi, such performances continued
over a number of days. Ganesha Singh relates the same information,
evidently picked up from Gian Singh.

The greatest deprecation in Gian Singh's account is reserved for the
many followers that Gulabdas was ostensibly able to assemble around
him, attracted as they were to the libertine lifestyle promoted by him,
indexed through Singh's use of terms like *khulāsā* (open, free living),
and Gulabdas stepping out of shara (literally, the shari'ah, Islamic
canonical law, but here used figuratively as acceptable moral/ethical
behaviour). While I will say more on the use of these terms later, it
may be mentioned that Singh interpreted the dissolute conduct of
Gulabdas's followers as breaking the bounds (*had*) of morality of both
Hindus and Muslims, and so was condemnable. He also apportions the
blame for such immorality on Gulabdas, whom he accuses of spoiling
(*bigāṛe*) young men and well-dressed dandies (*baṅke*) through his teachings and books: *rachi Gulābdās jo pothī so paṛh hot khulāse* (after reading

---

[64] Ganesha Singh, *BMD*, p. 129.

the books written by Gulabdas, libertinism spread). At the same time, he accuses decadent characters (thieves, and good-for-nothings—*chor, lavār*) masquerading as disciples, who took advantage of Gulabdas's liberality to have fun and muddied his name. Again, paraphrasing Gian Singh that these disciples went about singing and playing music in the villages of Punjab, Ganesha Singh adds a further explanatory note making the cause of his disapproval plain: 'Women and men having stripped themselves of shame went about free and without a care.'[65] For Ganesha Singh, such behaviour was inexcusable and symptomatic of shamelessness. For Gian Singh, on the other hand, we see in this context also a glimmer of admiration for Gulabdas: *jadpi sahī gian updesiyo, par chelion ne tānkī; ramaj na samjhī unkī gehrī anjan kīno fākī* (though he preached right knowledge, the disciples did not understand its depth and the sophists spread fraud).[66]

Thus, Gian Singh lets off Gulabdas, praising his teachings in a backhanded compliment, even as he accuses him of nurturing decadent conduct on the part of his disciples. This hesitation in an outright condemnation of Gulabdas can be interpreted as an appreciation of his intellectual acuity, the quality of his philosophical peroration, and his poetical talent. This too must be seen to be the reason why Ganesha Singh associates Gulabdas with many Nirmala preachers (his sect) along with whom Gulabdas sermonized in the Sikh army; these names were mentioned by Gian Singh, but not as specifically Nirmala.[67] Gulabdas, it seems, was too important to be ignored completely, but too dicey to be appropriated. Both historians, however, do report that the behaviour of Gulabdas's followers became too risqué to be tolerated, Gian Singh noting that the prince of Patiala, Narinder, and that of Faridkot, Wazir Singh, caught hold of Gulabdasis, making them bow to acceptable morality (*shara manā ke chhore*). Ganesha Singh adding that the British too started arresting them and that this occurred in the years 1855–7. He further adds that subsequently the Gulabdasis' egoistical and arrogant attitude dissolved and they straightened out (*nek chāl chalan*) and started calling themselves Udasis and Nirmalas, returning to a spiritual life.

---

[65] Ganesha Singh, *BMD*, p. 129.

[66] Gian Singh, *PP*, pp. 1294.

[67] These are Girdhar, Mal Singh, Singh Achhra, and Sarbag Singh. Gian Singh, *PP*, p. 1293.

Colonial Sources

Unlike the complex understanding of the Gulabdasis in the Sikh sources
and their sects' own tangled relationship with them, the colonial sources
are more unidimensional. They mark the Gulabdasis as epicurean, the
term that came to define them, describing them in a conceptual language
of Christian and European provenance that made the Gulabdasis
comprehensible to the colonialists.

The earliest mention of the Gulabdasis is in the Revised Revenue
Settlement of the Lahore district that was compiled by Leslie Saunders
between 1865 and 1869, when Gulabdas was still alive, as explicitly stated
in the report and which places the date of the compilation of this report
and source even earlier than the *Panth Prakash*.[68] Saunders describes
them as Deists, interpreting this as the Gulabdasis' belief in the immortality of man, and that man will be absorbed in the Deity, being of the
same substance as Him, and that they did not believe in a future state
(after life?). He described *Updes Bilas* as their chief work, which they
apparently venerated. Anyone from any caste could become a member of the sect, according to Saunders, if he carried some sweetmeats
to Gulabdas, prayed for the knowledge of the 'right faith', declared a
belief in immortality, and repeated 'sohang'. Saunders notes that
they had 'no peculiarity of dress', but were very clean in appearance,
and styled themselves *sains* (masters). He calls them great disputants,
eager to prove the immortality of man, but not strict in abstaining from
tobacco (banned to the Khalsa). Nor were they averse to 'immorality' as
their guru, Saunders asserts, was living in open 'adultery' without causing any scandal among his followers, who were most numerous in the
Kasur *parganah* (district). Saunders adds two further curiosities about
the Gulabdasis—though they admitted people of all castes, they did not
eat or intermarry among them, and that they saw no harm in incest.
Elsewhere, he mentions that Sikhs and Gulabdasis permitted marriage
of widows.[69]

Notions like deism, right faith, immortality of man, and substance
of man and deity emerged from Protestantism and eighteenth-century
European ideas of nature worship, and were seemingly used to explicate the advaita moorings of the Gulabdasis. The choice of the term

[68] Leslie S. Saunders, *Report on the Revised Land Revenue Settlement of the Lahore
District of the Panjab 1865–69* (Lahore: Central Jail Press, 1873), pp. 53–4.
[69] Saunders, *Report on the Revised Land Revenue Settlement*, p. 59.

'adultery' to define the relation between Gulabdas and assumedly Piro was strange as in the minimum it should have involved the marriage of one of them, which was not the case, as no Sikh or Gulabdasi source mentions marriage between the two, though they all acknowledge intimate relations between them. The reference to incest is stranger still as, once again, none of the Sikh sources mention it, something that would hardly have escaped their notice or condemnation. Again, the claim that different castes were admitted but neither inter-dined nor intermarried would perhaps defeat the very purpose of speaking against varnashramadharma, as Gulabdasis did vociferously. In any case, as Gian Singh made it very clear in his exposition of the sect, Gulabdas chose as his successor the son of Sahib Singh *Ghumār* (potter), Hari Gobind, and had him marry into a Jat family.[70] Thus, besides using lexical references with unfamiliar semantics in the Indian context, Saunders probably sought to convey the oddity of Gulabdasi beliefs even within Punjabi society, though neither adultery nor restrictions on caste intermixing quite carried the Gulabdasi sui generis status. Significantly, some of Saunders' formulations with regard to the Gulabdasis came to be enduring, repeated in every ethnographic compendium produced by the colonialists, and even by modern historians, though new details emerged as well.

The most comprehensive account on the Gulabdasis appeared in the *Glossary* compiled by H.A. Rose, the superintendent of the census in Punjab in 1901, based on notes made by earlier census officers and ethnographers, D.C.J. Ibbetson (1881) and E.D. Maclagan (1891).[71] A.H. Bingley's *Sikhs* (1899), a handbook of the Indian Army, had a succinct account on the Gulabdasis, mostly carrying the flavour of Saunders' report, but looking at the Gulabdasis as a form of modern dissenting Sikh sect along with the Nirankaris and the Kukas.[72] It is clear that by the time of the compilation of the *Glossary*, many elements seen in Gian Singh's account were also incorporated, but so were others that were absent there, and some that patently seemed to be misinformation.

Rose describes Gulabdas of Chattha village as originally an Udasi, giving up that affiliation about seventy years ago when he fell under

---

[70] Gian Singh, *PP*, p. 1295.

[71] Rose, *Glossary*, pp. 319–20.

[72] A.H. Bingley, *Sikhs* (Patiala: Languages Department, 1970 [first published 1899]), p. 91.

the influence of one Hiradas.[73] Haridas Girdhar of the Sikh accounts is transformed into Hiradas in colonial ones, who encouraged Gulabdas to give up nudity and accept ordinary attire. Moreover, the sect is supposed to have been started by an Udasi called Pritam Das, whose disciple was Gulabdas. Pritam Das ostensibly started a new sect because he suffered a slight at a Kumbh fair on the Ganges. The unlikelihood of this story is underlined by the name of the sect, Gulabdasi, for one does not come across a sect named after a disciple. Furthermore, the Udasi Pritam Das who did in fact get into a conflict with the Gosains at a Kumbh fair on the Ganges in the last quarter of the eighteenth century (a date that would not fit with Gulabdas's time), was an important leader of the sect, credited with changing many practices along with the garb of the Udasis, and Gulabdas is not mentioned as a disciple.[74] Evidently, a mixing up of different stories seems to have occurred here. Bingley and Rose also state that Gulabdas was a trooper (*ghorcharā*) in the army of Maharaja Sher Singh, and joined the new sect on the collapse of the Sikh monarchy.[75] This would make Gulabdas an Udasi right until 1849, whereas all our Sikh accounts, and information from Gulabdas's disciples, make it apparent that Gulabdas had settled at Chathianwala in Ranjit Singh's time itself.

Bingley and Rose also call the Gulabdasis 'epicurean' as noted, a term not found in Saunders, but repeated ad nauseam later. Rose credits him with having had a 'vision' that convinced him that he had no superior, and that pilgrimages and temples had no sanctity. Rose also wavers between calling Gulabdas an atheist and one who declared himself god (Brahm), believed as he did that 'man is of the same substance as the deity'. Bingley and Rose both quote from Maclagan underlining the hedonism of the Gulabdasis:

> Pleasure alone is their aim; and renouncing all higher objects they seek only for the gratification of senses, for costly dresses and tobacco, wine and

---

[73] The reference to seventy years is interesting. If Maclagan's account of the early 1890s was the basis of this statement, then it shows Gulabdas turning away from Udasis in the late 1820s. This fits well with his birth in 1809, if one assumes that by his early teens he had already been a soldier and had had a stint with the Udasis.

[74] Ganesha Singh, *BMD*, pp. 3–5.

[75] Sher Singh was a son of Ranjit Singh who succeeded to his throne after the death in November 1840 of his stepbrother Kharak Singh. He ruled till September 1843 when he was killed in ongoing court intrigues. Grewal, *The Sikhs of Punjab*, pp. 120–2.

women, the lust of the eyes, and the pride of life. They are scrupulously neat in their attire and engage in all worldly pursuits, some of them being men of considerable wealth.

These words, one may add, appear without, or with minor changes, in the accounts of later historians, G.S. Chhabra and Niharranjan Ray.[76] While hints of arrogance and pride and a predilection for breaking societal norms were indicated in the Sikh sources, nowhere do we come across 'pleasure alone' as the aim of the Gulabdasis, as more complex theological ideas were attributed to them. The discomfiture with some of the tenets and practices that we see in Sikh sources is here translated into disgust for sensuous pleasures in the midst of an ascetic sect, though Rose does not mention incest, which Bingley does. The debauchery of the Gulabdasis is underlined by saying that their co-religionists distrusted and despised them, though that hardly seemed to be the case. Rose further observed that the Gulabdasi attire could vary from the Nirmala to the Udasi, that they were clean-shaven, and that, moreover, it was a sect that held lying in special abhorrence with no hypocrisy in their principles. While Lahore and Jullundur were where they were found according to the censuses (the 1891 census reporting their number as 482), they were also present in Amritsar, Ferozepur, Ambala, and Karnal.[77] Rose again quotes Saunders when he notes that 'they admit any caste to the sect, but the different castes admitted do not eat with each other or intermarry'.[78]

Besides telling us that Gulabdas authored the *Updes Bilas*, two further observations of Rose pertain to describing the six-day fair held

---

[76] Historians writing of various Sikh sects in the third quarter of the twentieth century also quoted Rose's words verbatim, including the charge of epicureanism and incest. See G.S. Chhabra, *Social and Economic History of the Panjab* (New Delhi: Sterling Publishers, 1962), p. 128; Niharranjan Ray, *The Sikh Gurus and the Sikh Society: A Study in Social Analysis* (Patiala: Punjabi University, 1970), p. 168. Ray's own contribution to the understanding of the Gulabdasis was that they resembled the Young Bengal of Derozio, which does hint at the popularity of the Gulabdasis among the youth for a time between the two empires, Sikh and British.

[77] Bingley reported them as declining in number, with only 300 followers. As discussed in the Introduction, one could be a member of a sect and also be counted as Hindu, Sikh, or Muslim. Thus, relying on census figures for Gulabdasi numbers would be inadequate. It is evident that they were a popular sect between the empires and at least into the 1870s in Punjab.

[78] Rose, *Glossary*, pp. 319–20.

by the sect during Holi, and the tomb of Gulabdas at Chathianwala, where his followers gathered. The information regarding the fair and the tomb was available in Gian Singh's *Panth Prakash*, and it is possible that it was gathered from there, or that the fair was large enough to be recorded.

It might be appropriate here to introduce Mufti Ghulam Sarwar Qureshi Lahori's *Tarīkh Makhzān-i-Punjāb* (1877) on the history and records of Punjab, which too mentions the Gulabdasis when it discusses religious sects.[79] Also encyclopaedic in its scope, the *Tarikh* is an early formulation in Urdu, and once again mentions the waywardness of the Gulabdasis, that was beginning to be remarked upon in the colonial accounts, but also gives interesting asides that add to our information on them. Calling it a modern religion, initiated under the British (which was incorrect), Qureshi suggests that the Gulabdasis followed their own heart as a guide in everything, not afraid of anyone.[80] They did not distinguish between *halāl* (lawful) and *harām* (forbidden) in food or drink, or indeed in discerning the women they can have sexual relations with. Based in Chathianwala, Sarwar mentions that their guru died only a few years ago. Significantly, Sarwar describes their thought as monotheistic, in the Sufi language of tauhid (saying that the unity of god is always on their tongue), and that they are pantheistic in belief (*hama aust ke mukārhin*), pantheism having been noted by Rose as well as being the opinion of some others on the Gulabdasis. Sarwar also importantly gives information on a Sayyid Shia Muslim, Shah Mohammad, who became so impressed with the written book of Gulabdas that he read it all the time, keeping it closer to him than the Quran, so that his family broke off all relations with him, and he with them.[81]

Though we know of Piro, a Muslim woman who became a Gulabdasi, here is another example of Gulabdas's openness to all creeds and castes. Sarwar's brief account is also another telling of the Gulabdasis' loose morals, as of the Gulabdasis' apparently dissipate attitude.

---

[79] Mufti Ghulam Sarwar Qureshi 'Lahori', *Tarikh Makhzan-i-Punjab* (Lahore: Dost Associates, 1996 [first published in 1877]), p. 568.

[80] Sarwar describes them as *āg mukhī se dareṅ aur jo jī chāhe so kareṅ*, that is, their motto was 'be careful of fire and the government, otherwise do as you please' (Sarwar, *Tarikh Makhzan-i-Punjab*).

[81] On Shah Mohammad, see Chapter 8.

GULABDAS'S DISCIPLES AND THEIR CONCERNS

The compendiums discussed thus far, whether the Sikh or the colonial, introduce the Gulabdasis in the context of other Sikh sects, and so a comparative perspective informs them, wherein the Gulabdasis emerge as somewhat peculiar, if not bizarre, unique in their arrogant disregard for social niceties, and carrying to the extreme their monist theological logic. We now turn to the writings of some of the disciples of Gulabdas, where they either consciously acknowledge and praise their guru or make stray references to others' opinion of him, often vigorously defending his conduct. A few examples will suffice to get a flavour of their defence, which gives an inkling of what they thought provoked the anger of his critics. Another controversy about the birth and longevity of Gulabdas will also be introduced, for this gives a sense of how some, in his time and now, hoped to raise his status, placing him in the saintly world of the great, the miraculous, and the extraordinary. Such an attitude is, of course, a product of deep reverence, and gives a counter-perspective to the disparaging ones discussed above. However, we will begin with a disciple who, on the face of it, seemingly criticizes Gulabdas.

Gulabdasi thought, with its solipsistic monism—which brought in the charge of atheism—good living, a disregard for caste and bhekh or ascetic markers, an arrogant and discordant attitude, a youthful following, and a free mixing of genders, was seen to be condemnable in the eyes of those observing them. Interestingly, a particular controversial verse of a younger disciple of Gulabdas, Sant Ditta Ram (later Ditt Singh, as a Singh Sabha ideologue),[82] perhaps uncovers what his disciples thought was a reason for the critique of Gulabdas, taking us away from the more generalized all encompassing criticisms of the Gulabdasis to a more specific one—Gulabdas's relationship with Piro. In a set of verses published in 1876 called *Ablā Niṅd* (*Women's Wiles/Humiliation*), a genre that warns men of being ensnared by women and the disaster that awaits them, Ditta Ram penned a verse that seems to point an accusing finger at Gulabdas for his relationship with a prostitute.[83] In disparaging tones Ditta Ram

[82] See Chapter 6.

[83] 'Wiles of Women' was an established genre in Punjab and as the print medium grew towards the end of the nineteenth century, such verses emerged in cheaply produced chap-book style pamphlets. See Anshu Malhotra, 'Print and Bazaari Literature: Jhagrras/Kissas and Gendered Reform in Early Twentieth Century

ridicules an ascetic who succumbs to the charms of a prostitute and
destroys the accumulated advantages of the practice of celibacy:

> *Raṇḍī aur faqīr kā sadā anādī vair*
> *Jab ghar āye sādh ke kahāṅ gujāre khair;*
> *Kahāṅ gujāre khair, tej ko turat miṭāve*
> *Kahuṅ na hov satkār nirādar jahī tahī pāve;*
> *Kahe Ditt hari yār jagat meṅ baje pakhandī*
> *Rahe na tis dī tāb sādh ho rākhe raṇḍī.*[84]

A prostitute and a faqir are enemies forever
When she comes to the house of an ascetic where could there be well-being
Where could there be well-being, his ascetic radiance is lost
No one respects him and dishonour greets him everywhere
Says Ditt, friend of Hari, the world exposes such charlatans
There is no honour for the ascetic who keeps a prostitute.

It is important to bear in mind that Ditta Ram would probably not have
been in direct contact with Gulabdas, or if so then only for a short time,
as he was born in or after 1850, and came to Chathianwala only towards
the end of Gulabdas's time, when any controversy around his choices in
life seems to have settled down. Also, such a verse would not have been
out of place in a text purportedly enumerating women's wiles, for the
accent there was to show how women, and particularly their dangerous
sexuality, became a cause for the downfall of men. Nevertheless, the
content of the verse is too close to home to not have been some kind
of a reference to Gulabdas, perhaps a flaw that the disciple saw in the
guru. Or more likely, a flaw he perceived after the death of Gulabdas,
when Ditta Ram was beginning to be attracted to modern associational
politics. However, in some of his other writings before he became an
ideologue for the Singh Sabha, Ditta Ram acknowledges Gulabdas as his
guru, giving him respect. In *Kissā Shirīn Farhād*, probably his first piece
of writing, he praises Gulabdas as his guru, dedicating a long invocatory
verse in his eminence (*Pīr Murshīd Gulābdās kī Upmā*).

> *Awal hamad janāb Gulāb taiṅ, jinā tāraiyā kul Punjāb āhā*
> *Sāre jag de vich chā nashar hoye, goyā hor dūjā āftāb āhā.*[85]

Punjab', in *Gendering Colonial India: Reforms, Print, Caste and Communalism*, edited
by Charu Gupta (Hyderabad: Orient Black Swan, 2012), pp. 159–87.

[84] Quoted in Sewak, 'Gulabdasi Sampradaye', pp. 102–3.

[85] Sant Ditta Ram, *Shirin Farhad*, edited by Shamsher Singh Ashok (Ludhiana:
Punjabi Sahit Academy, n.d.), p. 17. According to the information given in Ashok's

First in praise of honourable Gulab, who delivered the whole of Punjab
He became famous in the world as a second sun.

Another disciple of Gulabdas, Kishan Singh Arif, who became famous
as a writer of popular qissas and verses, also hinted at Gulabdas being
stigmatized for his relations with Piro. In a verse clearly explicatory of
his guru's behaviour, he justifies his relationship with Piro by elevating
Gulabdas to the level of godly avatars who all had consorts. Arif writes:

Sant istrī chāh jo rākhe mat ko burā chitāre re
Ih bhī nahiṅ acharaj nayā ko rakhde āye sāre re;
Shiv Gorī ar Kishan Rādh ke, Sītā Rām pyāre re
Bhagat Kabīr ke ghar Loī, sabh saṅtan rākhī nāre re.[86]

A sant can keep a woman if he so pleases no one should think badly of him
This is not a new wonder it is quite the norm;
Shiv had Gori, Krishna Radha, and Sita was beloved of Ram
Bhagat Kabir had Loi in his home, all sants kept a woman.

In her *Ik Sau Sath Kafian* (*160 Kafis*), Piro also repeatedly raises the
issue of her guru bearing humiliation, and once broaches the topic in
exactly the same manner as Arif, or rather, Arif later virtually rephrases
her lines.[87] Piro iterates that her guru was not the only one to have done
something extraordinary by associating with a woman, a verse clearly
in explanatory mode: *charchā arath ajog bahu santan kar diyā, yāroṅ Dās
Gulāb hī acharaj na kiyā* (unseemly rumours were spread about holy
men, friends Das Gulab is not the only one to have done something
wonderful).[88] In a set of three *kafis* (157–9) towards the end of her
text, she brings the question of his bearing the insults of the world,

---

'Introduction', Ditta Ram wrote this kissa in 1872 and it was his first work, which
is preserved in a handwritten manuscript. *Abla Nind* was written in 1876, when he
may have begun to be more critical of Gulabdas. Sant Ditta Ram, *Shirin Farhad*,
p. 8.

[86] This verse from Kishan Singh Arif's *Kotre Khatpade* is quoted in Sewak,
'Gulabdasi Sampradaye', p. 104. Sewak also tells us that another poet, Kahn Singh,
in his *Hir Kahn Singh*, advises the hero of the kissa, Ranjha, to join the Gulabdasis
instead of the Nath Jogis, as he does in the narrative, for thanks to their guru he
would be united with his beloved Hir instead of facing tragedy. (Sewak, 'Gulabdasi
Sampradaye', p. 103.)

[87] Piro, *Ik Sau Sath Kafian* (*160 Kafis*), ms. 888 (Amritsar: Bhai Gurdas Library,
GNDU). Kafi numbers from this text are marked as '160: xx'.

[88] 160: 77.

presumably on her behalf, and hearing the accusations of those who had a wicked outlook. On the one hand, she expresses her gratefulness towards him by stating that he 'purified' (*pāk*) a 'fallen' (*palit*) woman like her, and on the other she accuses others of looking at a pure and blameless relationship from a polluted viewpoint. She also speaks about her guru allowing this manner of rumour-mongering (*charchā karvāī*) to highlight his good deeds in the manner of godly avatars who live out their human lives in order to restore dharma and defeat evil. She accuses people of looking at things from the outside like seeing the tusks of the elephant rather than the teeth it uses to eat, the real deeds of her guru hidden from their limited visions. Only those who had the ability to go beyond the facade and recognize real actions would know the true worth of the holy man. Her unrestrained expression of gratefulness towards the guru was expressed thus:

> *Ghol ghumaī satguraṅ houṅ vāram vāre*
> *Ham se jīv anek gur bhav pār utāre*
> *Yeh guṇ hamko kahāṅ houṅ sūdar nārī*
> *Niṅd sahārī jagat kī gur parupkārī.*

> Beholden to satguru I'm enamoured of him
> Many like me the guru has ferried across
> Where do I have any virtues being a sudra woman
> He bore the humiliation of the world the benevolent guru.[89]

That to most disciples Gulabdas's relationship with Piro was, or came to be in time, wholly acceptable, and that they came to look upon her as particularly reverential being his consort is plain to see from a number of examples. Shamdas Arif's following verse makes the point.[90] After paying respect to Gulabdas, calling him an avatar, sun, and the destroyer of ignorance, enlightening all with knowledge, he pays respect to *Māi sāhib* (respected mother):

> I bow before Māi sāhib now with my heart
> That she may bless Shamdas' intellect.[91]

---

[89] 160: 157.

[90] See Chapter 4 for Piro's own struggle to be accepted as a consort.

[91] Shamdasji, *Chaupat Granth*, pp. 23–4. This manuscript was in possession of Ram Kumarji, a Gulabdasi from Tigrana, Haryana, whom I met on 27 August 2013 in Ratol, the birth village of Gulabdas, where I went to attend a Gulabdasi function. See Chapter 8.

What this defence of their guru on the part of the disciples reveals is that Gulabdas's intimate relations with Piro was one of the reasons that the Gulabdasis were riled in their time, though as the other sources show, this was not the only reason. Thus, the insults (ninda) that Gulabdas and his disciples refer to were a belittling a learned man felt subjected to by ignorant and foolish people. The recurring references to ninda, whether Gulabdas's or his disciples', were neither in the mode of self-deprecation— a trope in some Indic genres that spoke of one's own insignificance—nor an invocation to god to rescue his disciple from humiliation, but were in fact anger at an impossible situation he faced, to offer refuge to Piro or renege it. He, of course, chose to keep his promise of asylum to her.[92] If we see the parallel sect of Wazir Singh, with close theological, philosophical, and lifestyle resemblance to the Gulabdasis, with a strong possibility that the two sects were in touch, we see that similar accusations of misconduct were made against them. Wazir Singh, like Gulabdas, also refers to facing the humiliation of the world, and not only because he too had a woman, the widow Nurang Devi, who lived in his establishment.[93] It was the social challenge that radical caste-denying sects, with their praxis that probably attempted to reframe gender relations as well threw up, which rankled among the orthodox and the custodians of the status quo, that led to their denunciation.

At this stage the controversy around Gulabdas's birth and age is introduced to get a sense of the reverence with which he was and is held by some of his followers, which gives us an alternate perspective on this reviled guru. Seth Vishandas (1843–1929) was a rich Sindhi follower of Gulabdas, and his biography, *Ratanjot*, was compiled by members of his family, perhaps when he was still alive.[94] Vishandas, of Manjho, Kotri, in Sindh, who later settled in Karachi, traced his Gulabdasi antecedents

---

[92] For *nindastuti* as a trope of self-deprecation or the lambasting of the Deity, see J.S. Hawley, *The Storm of Songs: India and the Idea of Bhakti Movement* (Cambridge: Harvard University Press, 2015), p. 301.

[93] See Raj Kumar Hans, 'Sant Poet Wazir Singh: A Window to Reimagining Nineteenth Century Punjab', *Journal of Punjab Studies* 20, nos 1 and 2 (2013): 135–58. Also see Ashok, *Siharfian*, p. 94. According to Ashok, another widow, Jai Devi, also lived in Wazir Singh's establishment. Ashok, *Siharfian*, p. xiii.

[94] *Seth Vishandas: A Great Philanthropist*, compiled by Khadim Hussain Soomro, translated by Zafar Iqbal Mirza (Sehwan Sharif: Sain Publishers, 1997). The information that this book was based on an abridged biography of Vishandas' *Ratanjot* is given in the book, p. 22.

to his father, Nehalchand (b. 1798), who became a follower of Gulabdas in 1837. Nehalchand's guru was Sant Permahans (Permahence), a disciple of Gulabdas who settled in Sindh, upon whose death in 1857, Nehalchand built a *samādhī*, a platform at the place he was cremated.[95] Vishandas' biography, *Ratanjot*, on which Khadim Soomro's abridged compilation is based, is a combination of genealogy and hagiography that charts the exceptionally fulfilling life he led. Hailing from the Bharvani Sanwalani family of Sindh, Vishandas became a trader, industrialist, and landlord of Sindh, who in his lifetime accumulated 8,000 acres of land. He dabbled in politics through an early membership of the Indian National Congress, attended its first session, and was also a member (and president) of the Sindh Hindu Panchayat, and given the title of Rai Bahadur by the British.[96] He was a connoisseur of the arts, establishing the Vishan Sabha in Karachi, where he patronized singers, dancers, and actors.[97] In this hagiographic account of Vishandas, a goodly space is given to the life of Gulabdas, and to Vishandas' journey of almost 320 kilometres at the age of nineteen in 1863 from Kotri to Chathianwala, which he undertook on boat and then on foot to spend six and a half months with Gulabdas. On the way, he collected two more devotees, and they would chant as they travelled *Chalo chalo ab darshan karen Satguru Gulābdev walī kā* (Let us go to pay respects to the saint Gulabdev).[98] It was an important time for Vishandas, and so given a pride of place in his biography, and subsequently it became the stuff of myth. It was a time when Vishandas grew spiritually, learnt the intricacies of music and singing, and the value of labour. Apparently, while physically carrying bricks on his head in Chathianwala, he developed a festering sore, but did not stop the gruelling physical labour. When Gulabdas noticed his wound because of its foul smell, he lavished praise on Vishandas, impressed by his devotion.[99] This story, amazingly, is still known in Chathianwala, and was related to me by an old man in the village in 2008, one of the few older residents in a village now mostly populated by Meos who migrated here from India in 1947.[100] It is a story

---

[95] Soomro, *Seth Vishandas*, pp. 21–2, 29, 33.

[96] Soomro, *Seth Vishandas*, p. 26.

[97] Soomro, *Seth Vishandas*, p. 51–8.

[98] Soomro, *Seth Vishandas*, p. 37.

[99] Soomro, *Seth Vishandas*, p. 38.

[100] This story was related to me when I visited Chathianwala on 25 May 2008 by the elderly Mohammad Shafi Ansari, the only resident who remembered the

that eulogizes Vishandas' dedication to his guru, as it does his generosity, for according to the *buzurg* (respected elderly) Mohammad Shafi Ansari, Vishandas from that year on came annually on foot to celebrate the great Holi festival that lasted many days and bore all the expenses towards it.

Vishandas' account gives Gulabdas a long life of a hundred and fifty-one years. According to Vishandas, he was born in 1723 and died in 1874, though the name of his village and district remain identical to Sikh narratives.[101] Gulabdas's birth in 1723 is also inscribed in the wok of Bir Singh, a disciple of Gulabdas.[102] The guru is said to have left his home at the age of eleven to wander, as many a holy man did, pilgrimage sites and to converse with men of wisdom. In this account, Gulabdas set up in Chathianwala in 1814. The salience of a long life here can be read as establishing the miraculous and mythical powers of the guru, his stature above that of mere mortals. More significantly, the long span allows the guru's interlocution with a variety of mystics of the past, including the eminent Sindhi Sufi, Shah Abdul Latif Bhitai (1689–1752), whose spiritual verses inscribed in the *Risālo* still echo in Sindh.[103] Not only does the guru glow in association with the charisma of one such as Abdul Latif, but Vishandas also establishes a special relationship of Gulabdas with the land of Sindh, from which he hailed. Accordingly, the guru's interaction with other Sindhi personalities is mentioned—Sri Bankhandi, Rohal Faqir (who it seems went to Chathianwala to learn poetics with Gulabdas) along with a number of disciples from this region who are not mentioned in other sources. Among the prominent disciples who are spoken of besides Permahans and the successors to Gulabdas's seat in Chathianwala,[104] were Sant Tara Chand (described as a *harijan* or an 'outcaste'), Syed Mohammad Shah (also mentioned by Sarwar, here described

---

Gulabdasis, as the demography of the village has changed dramatically after the Partition in 1947. Ansari told me that the wound on the man's head festered and had insects crawling in it (*vich kīṛe pai gaye*). He remembered that Vishandas was from Sindh, and that he became a very rich man there.

[101] Soomro, *Seth Vishandas*, pp. 31–9.

[102] Bir Singh's work, *Sri Sahaj Bilas*, gives this information. Sewak, 'Gulabdasi Sampradayc', p. 70.

[103] Annemarie Schimmel, *Mystical Dimensions of Islam* (New Delhi: Yoda Press, 2007 [1975]), pp. 390–3.

[104] These were through his adopted son, Hargobind, who succeeded Gulabdas, followed by his son, Tegh Bahdur. See Chapter 8.

as a hakim or a Unani practitioner from Mochidarwaza in Lahore), and *Mātā* (mother) Piro.[105]

Vijender Das of Hansi's account too gives Gulabdas a life of one hundred and fifty years (1723–1873), though he acknowledges that most narratives fix his birth year as 1809.[106] Vijender Das heads the Gulabdasi dera in Hansi, Haryana, and is an energetic guru, keen on expanding the base and activities of the Gulabdasis in contemporary north India.[107] Interested in academic and archival activity in relation to his sect, as much as in ritualistic and spiritual matters, Vijenderji expends enormous energy in collecting old manuscripts of former Guladasis, and establishing contact with other Gulabdasi deras. He has collected and published all of 'Mata' Piro's writings, with an introduction that, among other things, also tells us about Guru Gulabdas's life and writing. Shri Vijender's introduction to Piro's oeuvre is partially driven by the urge to establish the fantastical power of the guru, as by refurbishing the image of Piro as a spiritually inclined person from early life. Shri Vijender sketches Gulabdas as an independent-minded person, who never became a part of any sect, neither Udasi nor Nirmala. On the other hand, having left home at the age of eleven, and spent forty years in contemplation and austerities, including a period of staying naked, he tried to imbibe the best from all sects and saints he came across. Thus, like Vishandas, he too speaks of the guru's interlocutions with Shah Abdul Latif in Sindh, and also with one Meghraj Brahman. Moreover, returning to Kasur after his extensive travels in 1814 (Bikrami 1871), he met with Bulleh Shah (1680–1752), the famous Qadiri–Shattari Sufi from Kasur (temporally an impossibility), the district where Chathianwala is, and whose faqirs even the Sikh sources disapprovingly noted as having influenced Gulabdas. In this account Gulabdas is said to have travelled to religious places in

---

[105] Soomro, *Seth Vishandas*, p. 37. Ansari in his recollections mentioned other Muslim followers of Gulabdas. He said there was a small *samadh* (memorial platform) of one Sipaye Shah, a Muslim from a village near Amritsar, either Ghariala or Valtoha. He also mentioned Baba Sher Shah Wali, whose memorial was partly a dargah (a Sufi shrine) and partly a gurudwara (Sikh temple). I have not come across these names earlier, but Sher Shah Wali's dargah/gurdwara must refer to Shah Muhammad's tomb shrine—along with that of one of his disciples—which I saw in 2013 in the village of Lakhna, very close to Ratol. See Chapter 8.

[106] Sant Vijender Das, ed., *Sant Kavyitri Ma Piro* (Panchkula: Satluj Prakashan), pp. 35–6.

[107] I have been in touch with Vijenderji and his family since 2006. See Chapter 8.

India and Europe, besides Islam's sacred sites of Mecca and Medina, making his journey there via sea, but returning through the land route. In Vijender Das' estimation, the miracle-working Gulabdas must be considered among the best of Indian sages.[108]

This second perspective from another set of Gulabdas's disciples, including an active sant within the tradition, gives a glance of how well he was and continues to be regarded among them. Though many aspects of this second tradition are mythological rather than historical, it is important to remember that mythology is built around persons who touch and change the lives of those around them, if not a wider populace. Was it Gulabdas's charisma and his sweet speech, to paraphrase Gian Singh, which attracted people to him? Was there something in Gulabdasi thought, the elaboration of its guru's philosophical ideas, and the mystical hold of the guru on his flock that inspired people and brought them to him? A brief look at Gulabdasi thought as seen in his writings, primarily the *Gulab Chaman*, will help us grasp this complex personality.

GULABDASI THEOLOGY AND THOUGHT

As the discussion so far shows, the Gulabdasis were variously described as nastak (atheists), mauji (pleasure-seeking), Charvaki (materialists), Sarbhangi (against caste and pollution), aghori (tantra-inspired sect), and even Sufi. While these different assessments of the Gulabdasis may be correct or coloured by the observers' biases, there is no doubt that most commentators were impressed by Gulabdas's philosophical sophistication and poetic capability. In this section, some of the salient and recurring ideas in his *Gulab Chaman* and other writings will be highlighted to give a glimpse into this erudite scholar's mind.

Gulabdas's advaita monism, with its emphasis on the unity of Brahman and Jiv, to be located and developed within the Self has already been alluded to in the opening verses of this chapter. In a favourite metaphor used throughout his works, Gulabdas speaks of god as a being attached to one or as an intrinsic part of the self, and so an organic extension of the self—as limbs are to the body.

Ang anak sarīr jyoṅ, nikaṭ dūr nahiṅ koī
Aise isaru sarab meiṅ, neru dūr ka hoī.

---

[108] Das, *Sant Kavyitri Ma Piro*, pp. 37–42

Like many limbs of the body, what to speak of being close or far
So god is in all, what to say of near or far.[109]

That his philosophical inspiration was the Vedas and Vedanta is visible
in the following verse, where he sees for himself a role in liberating man-
kind by propagating the Vedas:

Janam liyo purkhārat ke hit, ichhā aur na kāī re
Sūdhā rastā bed banāyo, paṛh, sun bhav tar jāye re.

Having taken birth for the sake of welfare [of others], I have no other desire
The straight path are the Vedas, reading and listening to them one is
emancipated.[110]

It was the path of knowledge that Gulabdas favoured, his writing lit-
tered with appreciation of knowledge, the knowledgeable, and the discerning, as against the foolish. Assuming the significance of knowledge
(*gyān*), he speaks of science (*bigyān*) as even more important, as against
ignorance (*agyān*),[111] and the knowledgeable then, wise to everything,
stays quiet not uttering a word (*Dās Gulāb gyān jise yahī maun gahe phir
bolat nāhiṅ*),[112] presumably after experiencing the ultimate truth in the
knowledge of the Brahman.

It is in his dismissal of the ignorant that one perceives the haughtiness
of Gulabdas, pride that was seen as a hallmark of him and his sect; to sing
before a deaf person, he notes, was to be foolish (*mūrakh*);[113] like a blind
man cannot distinguish colour, so a donkey cannot become knowledgeable just because he is loaded with books. To teach an idiot, according to
Gulabdas, will make no difference,[114] as the company of the good does
not change a foolish person.[115] Indeed, so strong is Gulabdas's running
down of the undeserving that he seems to look at stupidity as a kind of
baseness that is essentially unchangeable (*nīch ūch na hot*)[116], seemingly
making foolishness an inherent quality.

However relentless he is in dismissing the foolish, Gulabdas does not
associate an essential or intrinsic nature with caste, as he seems to do

---

[109] *GC*: 223.

[110] Sewak quotes Gulabdas's *Mauj Bilas*. See his 'Gulabdasi Sampradaye', p. 148.

[111] *GC*: 257.

[112] *GC*: 263.

[113] *GC*: 265.

[114] *GC*: 266.

[115] *GC*: 272.

[116] *GC*: 270.

with foolishness, and speaks against varnashramadharma, the normative fourfold caste hierarchy and the notion of the stages of life. Gulabdas shared this radical aspect of his philosophy and social practice with sects like that of Wazir Singh. Some of Gulabdas's disciples, Piro in particular, took up this liberating ideology with great enthusiasm, underlining its significance in all her works. Gulabdas notes that the sants, the truly holy, are above considerations of caste and the worldly norms of society. He underscores that the sants are beyond garb, varnashrama, and the shame of family, world, and the Vedas (*santan ke bhekh pachh baran āsram nahiṅ kul haī na lok lāj bed lāj pare haī*),[117] an indictment of worldly interest on the part of a holy man. Indeed, the sage is one beyond artificial differences, including religious distinctions: *Turak Hiṅd kā bād na hamre baran āsram na kaī re* (no difference between Turk and Hindu, nor that of varnashrama).[118] Gulabdas lays stress on rising above and beyond what the ordinary people perceived as differences between Hindus and the Muslims. Sants, in his understanding, did not care for these differences, and offered a path distinct from ordinary religious considerations and their carefully drawn boundaries, which keep the faithful away from true liberation:

Gor masītan musle pūje, jabā Rahīm uchāre haī
Maṛī māṭ ko Hiṅdū pūje rasnā Rām pukāre haī
Gaṅgā ko sab Hiṅdū jae haī Makke Turak padhāre haī
Ek nainu te kāṇe Musle, Hiṅdū andhe sāre re
Gyanuvān na anke kāṇe Turuk Hiṅdū te nyāre re
Dās Gulāb bihad bhaye vahu hadaṅ mahī nakāre re.

Graves and mosques are revered by Muslims and they call out Rahim
Cremation platforms are worshipped by Hindus and they say Ram
All Hindus go to Ganga, and Turaks go to Mecca
Muslims are one-eyed and all Hindus blind
The truly knowledgeable are neither one-eyed nor blind, they are unlike Turaks and Hindus
Says Das Gulab they are limitless, who reject being within limits.[119]

It is here that we see a definitive influence of later bhakti thought on Gulabdas. As Daniel Gold has shown for the later bhakti sants, they defined their path as outside and distinct from the ways of Hindus and

117 GC: 275.
118 GC: 313.
119 GC: 312.

Turaks, where the guru became the conduit for reaching the divine.[120]
The guru himself was concurrently both human and divine, the accessible
and immanent aspect of the transcendent, more so a guru like Gulabdas
who claimed to be Brahm.[121] The scholars of Gulabdasi thought have
traced the influence of bhakti ideas on them, particularly the influence
of Kabir, Paltu Das, and the Dadupanthi Rajab.[122] On the salience of
the guru, the source of true knowledge, the vessel of mystical glory through
whom the disciple can hope for salvific emancipation, Gulabdas writes:
Gur hī charan saran pag hī janam maran bharam har hī (On the feet of the
guru and in his shelter; on his feet one is born and dies, he the remover
of doubts).[123] Elsewhere, Gulabdas speaks of a disciple's voice remaining
uncooked or raw (*kachī*) without the teaching of the guru.[124] Again, the
fulsome praise of the guru will manifest itself in the writings of Piro,
who looks upon the guru as an avatar, a source of material and mystical
redemption, describing herself as his slave.[125]

In his understanding of the composition of the universe and the
human body—the former made of twenty-five *prakritiāṅ* (natures), and
the latter of five elements—scholars have traced the influence of Sankhya
philosophy on Gulabdas.[126] His notion of birth and the process of reproduction is Brahminical. The coming together of female blood and male
semen creates life; cereal provides nourishment, the source of all energy,
and of human life:

Jananī khāve nāj ko tab rakte āve
Narū nāj ke khāt haī phir biṅd upāve
Rakt biṅd ke mel te yahī bane sarīrā
Chhit jal tej ākās ko pun mile samīrā.

---

[120] Gold, *The Lord as Guru*, p. 4.

[121] I have discussed the importance of the guru in Gulabdasi thought in Anshu
Malhotra, 'Panths and Piety in the Nineteenth Century: The Gulabdasis of Punjab',
in Malhotra and Mir, *Punjab Reconsidered: History, Culture and Practice*,
pp. 189–220.

[122] Kapoor, *Sadhu Gulabdas*, pp. 86, 98. Also see Anshu Malhotra, 'Bhakti and
the Gendered Self: A Courtesan and a Consort in Mid-Nineteenth Century Punjab',
Modern Asian Studies 46, no. 6 (2012): 1503–39.

[123] GC: 276.

[124] This is discussed by Kapoor in *Gulāb Sāgar*. Kapoor, *Sadhu Gulabdas*,
p. 31.

[125] Malhotra, 'Bhakti and the Gendered Self'.

[126] Kapoor, *Sadhu Gulabdas*, p. 21.

Mother eats cereal and produces blood
Man on eating cereal produces semen
The mixing of blood and semen creates the body
Earth, water, fire, space then meet with wind.[127]

Human birth was a polluting affair, the foetus in the womb suffered confinement and was nurtured in 'dirt', the only escape from human suffering was the ability to break the cycle of birth and death. The Gulabdasi Bahadar Singh's verse makes this plain:

Mal mūt aur lahu pāk maiṅ māt garabh maiṅ āvat haī
Nau mahīne kumbhī vāsā puṭhā hoī tangāvat haī
Mal mūt jhar mukh maiṅ par haī nis din aehi khāvat haī...
Janam maran kat sādh saṅg mil Bahādar Singh sachu gāvat haī.

Excrement and urine and in pure blood you come in the womb of the mother
For nine months you stay in the womb hanging upside down
Excrement and urine fall into your mouth and this is what you eat ...
Bahadar Singh sings the truth, to break the cycle of birth and death keep the company of the virtuous.[128]

Bahadar Singh uses words similar to Gulabdas's in describing the nurturing of the body in its own waste and blood.[129] In this understanding of human birth, the womb represents *kumbhī naraka*, the hell of being confined to the pot.[130] However, these Brahminical ideas are also overlaid with notions that have a bhakti orientation, so that sometimes it is difficult to disaggregate the varied sources of his thought. Gulabdas, like the foremost *nirguṇī* (advocating the formless god) sant Kabir, also depicts the body as a cage of bones, filled with dirt (*'mail-mūt'*), that one may adorn with sandalwood and good clothes, but only the foolish take pride in it: *dehī gumān kare nar mūrakh saṅjh saver nirodh pehchānī* (only the foolish take pride in the body, one should mourn and even recognize

---

[127] GC: 55.
[128] Sant Bahadar Singh Ji, *Amritras Granth* (Amritsar: Yantralaya Chasmanur, 1898), verse 7.
[129] GC: 4.
[130] Veena Das discusses the male legal discourse that sees foetal confinement in the womb as hell and the female discourse that presents it as a privileged guest in mother's womb. See her 'On Female Body and Sexuality', *Contributions to Indian Sociology* 21, no. 1, new series (1987): 57–66.

it as a constraint).[131] Keeping the company of the good and holy as the path to bliss and happiness is emphasized in the writing of Gulabdas, who uses the paradoxical language of bhakti sants to allude to the experience: *jo sukh hai satsaṅg meiṅ sukh te kahiyo na jāye; goongā gur ko khāye kar kyā svād batlāye* (the happiness of the company of the holy cannot be described, like a mute cannot tell the taste of jaggery).[132] Thus, good company was the way to ineffable happiness.

Like bhakti sants too, particularly Kabir for whom death is at the core of his thought, the immanence of death—referred to as *Kāl*, both Time and Yama, the messenger of Death—appears with poignancy in the poetry of Gulabdas.[133] He emphasizes the certainty of death, which no one can escape. It inevitably destroys the body that in one's lifetime one looks after and decorates with immense care. In a series of verses, Gulabdas speaks of the body destroyed in the fire of cremation; of the momentariness of this life, an illusion like the reflection of the moon in water; and dust as the final destination of all. The equality achieved by death, for king and beggar alike, is spoken of:

Jo Rām Rasūl kahāye haī
Jag te bhī rehan na pāye haī
Jag jo upjā so marā re
Tum kis par pāṅv pasāre re.

Even Ram and Rasul
Were unable to stay in the world
Whoever sprouts in this world dies
What are you proud of?[134]

Significantly, the notion that life is momentary and must be optimally used also makes Gulabdas express disdain for falling under the influence of sexual desire, variously referred to as *kām*, *isaq*, and 'bhog'. Beautiful

---

[131] *GC*: 5. On Kabir, see Charlotte Vaudeville, *A Weaver Named Kabir: Selected Verses with a Detailed Biographical and Historical Introduction* (New Delhi: Oxford University Press, 2005 [1993]), p. 107.

[132] *GC*: 405. The expression of 'sugar to the mute' was an expression used by Kabir, inherited from tantra yoga. '*Ultibamsa*', or upside-down language, was used by Kabir. This paradoxical language was used by many sants, and both Gulabdas and Piro deployed it. Vaudeville, *A Weaver Named Kabir*, p. 103.

[133] For the centrality of death in Kabir's thought, see Vaudeville, *A Weaver Named Kabir*, pp. 106–7.

[134] *GC*: 126.

women were a distraction, alluring in their appeal.[135] That the indication is also towards the physical aspect of love, the sexual act, is made clear in the following lines where he evokes the image of a saddened Ram looking for Sita and Lord Vishnu lusting after Lakshmi:

Rovte Rām udās phire ban sundar nārī pīchhe lalchāyo
Dās Gulāb pīchhe Lachhmī Hari kāḍ ke liṅg phire laṭkāyo.

Grieving Ram roams forests tempted by the beautiful woman
Says Das Gulab Hari trails Lakhsmi taking out and dangling his penis.[136]

Gulabdas advocates *birāg* (non-attachment) and *bibek* (discernment) as essential for conquering *indrī* (desires). In a surprising moment of self-reflection, or a slippage from the lofty tone of the guru, however one may read it, Gulabdas reveals an autobiographical insight into the effect of isaq, which makes one forget all the niceties of clan and custom (*kul kī sabho rītī*): *Dās Gulāb na jhūṭh kahuṅ ... āp su ūpar bītī* (Das Gulab doesn't lie ... it has happened to him).[137] Perhaps, this is the closest Gulabdas comes to acknowledging a relationship he had with Piro; it is clearly an autobiographical statement that he makes. Was this remorse? Or was it an iteration of the standard and acceptable ways in which women were held in society? It is difficult to say, though nothing in his practice suggests that. Nor should one look for consistency, for clearly there was a gap between theoretical stance and practice. Though he does not refer in any of his works to Piro entering the dera, he did write *Sanjhi Siharfi*, or joint verses, with her, indicating her as an important disciple.[138] In other places, he reiterates, as noted above that a sant is always aloof from

---

[135] Verse 11 begins by referring to women as distractions: *kām kharāb kare bāmā dikū rūp sutā tahi dekh lubhāyo* (women spoil things, luring with their beautiful looks).

[136] *GC*: 11.

[137] *GC*: 13. It may be noted that in Hindustani an autobiography is often called *Āp Bītī*. According to Metcalf, it has connotations of an account of one's sorrows. This suggests some regret on the part of Gulabdas. See Barbara Metcalf, 'The Past in the Present: Instruction, Pleasure, and Blessing in Maulana Muhammad Zakariyya's Aap Biitii', in *Telling Lives in India: Biography, Autobiography and Life History*, edited by David Arnold and Stuart Blackburn (Ranikhet: Permanent Black, 2004), p. 134.

[138] Sewak notes that Gulabdas's poetry makes no mention of the coming of Piro to the dera. Sewak, 'Gulabdasi Sampradaye', p. 93.

the norms of the clan, world, and the Veda, that is, normative social and religious practice.

Like the bhakti sants' emphasis on the repetition of name, *nām simraṇ*, a practice quite close to the Sufis' *dhikr*, Gulabdasis repeated 'soham' (I am He) both as a chant and a mantra.[139] Gulabdas speaks of both the importance of singing the praise of god (*hari bhajan*) and the repetition of the name, *binā nām ek phire haī udāse* (without name one roams morose).[140] But, it was the repetition of 'soham' that elevates one to the level of Brahm, the identification with the god within one-self: *pachhāno soī soham Brahm kahe kī hoī* (he who recognizes soham, understands Brahm).[141] The closing verses of *Gulab Chaman* are an exposition on the significance of Brahm, the recognition of its salience, making the person free from all attachment and happy in all circum-stances: *sarbe āpu pachhān kar rahe divānā hoī* (seeing self in all one stays carefree).[142] Elsewhere, Gulabdas explicates the significance of 'soham', the one who understands it stays intoxicated—*har hāl maiṅ mast bhayo haī.*[143]

This state of being *divānā* or *mast*—intoxicated on god within and so nonchalant—was not easily reached. In an alliterative passage, Gulabdas speaks of the tortuous path of faqīrī (mendicancy): *faqraṅ hoī faqīrī aukhī karnī paī saburī re; jaise tāṛ ūchte te ūchī sarab birakh te dūrī re* (mendicants find mendicancy tough, it requires patience; like the tall-est of the palm trees, far from everything).[144] However, to achieve it, Gulabdas asserts, does not require either adopting a sectarian garb (bhekh) or giving up the world. He ridicules those who torture the body in different ways to achieve asceticism as discussed earlier in the Introduction. Such effort, however, ends up in nothing—*bhekh anek kar kar hāre*—defeated even after multiple garbs, for all that a distinct garb does is to give one pride in its wearing.[145] Was this then a clue to the unusual path that he chose, an extraordinary sect that he started, based on breaking acceptable rules, the normative paths that the ordinary and the less accomplished plied?

---

[139] Malhotra, 'Panths and Piety'.

[140] *GC*: 280.

[141] *GC*: 399.

[142] *GC*: 404.

[143] *Gulab Sagar* quoted in Kapoor, *Sadhu Gulabdas*, p. 32.

[144] *GC*: 284.

[145] *GC*: 287.

GULABDASIS AND *SHARA* (MORALITY)

As the discussion so far reveals, the Gulabdasi panth displayed a schizo-phrenic doubleness: The guru steeped in the best traditions of Vedantic thought and bhakti ideas, and his practice smacking of individualistic idiosyncrasies, a nonconformist insistence on doing his own thing. In his writing Gulabdas warned against the pride of the body and bhekh, speaking against the foolishness of decorating the body or the haughtiness a sectarian garb bestowed. In practice, though he did not adopt a sectarian garb and allowed disciples to dress as they pleased, he did adorn himself with the best of clothes and weapons, sitting regally or riding a horse, getting fanned by sundry disciples—surely a dissenting bhekh that he made his hallmark? He wrote against the pull of desire and warned against falling under the spell of sexual need, yet he openly lived with a woman, a former prostitute, despite the contentiousness this relationship brought into his life. The two—Gulabdas and Piro—shared intimate relations, combining jog and bhog, as Ganesha Singh said. Discernment was a quality he appreciated, writing against fools and the non-discriminating, singing panegyrics to the company of the good and the virtuous. He, however, came to be accused of nurturing all manner of unsavoury characters that took refuge under his banner, muddying his name. He spoke about remaining nonchalant and non-attached in all circumstances, but created lasting attachments and relationships—with Piro, other disciples, and adopting an heir, Hargobind, to his gaddi or seat. How does one reconcile a carefree attitude that encouraged one to stay mast in all situations, with the vitriolic response to his humiliation and insults, the ninda of others that riled him? Was he a maverick, dissenting, heterodox guru, determined to throw a challenge to the world, or a sagacious savant, preaching the wisdom of advaita Vedanta?

Our Sikh historians, Gian and Ganesha Singh, repeatedly accuse Gulabdas of flouting the norms of shara, among other misdemeanours that they lay at his door. Gian Singh writes of Gulabdas that he sacrificed normative morality (*tajī sharā sab kerī*); and Ganesha Singh notes that Gulabdas scoffed at others, ridiculing them for being tied to ethics and religion while he projected himself as above such norms (*hornaṅ nuṅ sharā mazab de bajhe hoye kahe, āpnuṅ sharā toṅ pār daske uchā janāve*).[146] The term 'shara' referred loosely to the *shari'at*, the Quranic or Islamic law. Historians of South Asia have debated the ambiguity that may arise

---

[146] Gian Singh, *PP*, p. 1293; Ganesha Singh, *BMD*, p. 128.

among a Muslim populace when authority might be claimed from customs or laws other than that of the shari'at.[147] However, few have discussed
the ambiguity that may accrue around a word incorporated in a language—Punjabi—used daily by people from all religious communities.
In its everyday usage, the word 'shara' seemed to connote a moral law
applicable to Hindus and Muslims throughout the Mughal and Sikh rule
in Punjab as the historian J.S. Grewal has shown.[148] Grewal quotes the
British author Neil Baillie writing in the mid-nineteenth century that
except for matters pertaining to marriage, adoption, and inheritance,
the shari'at was applicable to Hindus in 'matters of contract and ordinary dealings of men with each other'.[149] Perhaps from such a general
applicability of the shari'at, one may speculate that the word 'shara'
came to acquire its ethical meaning for a general populace. That society
functions smoothly when denizens follow norms acceptable to all is
embedded in the usage of the term by our two Singhs; the term 'shara'
carrying accumulated semantics that connoted not only legal, but also
cultural and social ethos of a people. That this acceptable morality was
applicable to all is made clear by Gian Singh and Ganesha Singh when
they note that Gulabdas thwarted the shara of Hindus and Muslims both
by his conduct—*Hindū Turak dī sharā had jo sou ghol pilāve* (the limits
of ethics of Hindus and Turks were wiped away)—a usage which while
recognizing differences between the two communities is based on
the idea that certain behavioural ethics are applicable to all.[150] In the
same vein, therefore, when our historians speak of the straightening out
of the Gulabdasis, they invoke shara again: *sharā manā ke chhore* (they
were made to accept shara).[151]

To describe Gulabdasi heterodoxy, The two historians use a range
of other terms. Gian Singh deploys 'khulasa', to point towards the libertinism of the Gulabdasis, a word that carries connotations of openness, frankness, and in this case, free living (loving). Some hint of free
living is also provided by Shamsher Singh Ashok, the late scholar of
Punjabi literatures, who refers to the Gulabdasis as *azād-khyāliye*, or

---

[147] Katherine Ewing, ed., *Shari'at and Ambiguity in South Asian Islam* (New
Delhi: Oxford University Press, 1988).

[148] J.S. Grewal, 'The Shari'at and the Non-Muslims', in his *Miscellaneous
Articles* (Amritsar: GNDU, 1974), pp. 118–22.

[149] Grewal, 'The Shari'at and the Non-Muslims', p. 118.

[150] Gian Singh, *PP*, p. 1294; Ganesha Singh, *BMD*, p. 127.

[151] Gian Singh, *PP*. p. 1295.

independent-minded.[152] And when Gian Singh speaks of the Gulabdasis turning around, he says that their *khulāse* and *fukre* (arrogance, instigation) came to an end. He also uses *rair* (*machyo rair apāre*), perhaps a word pointing to the chaos unloosed by the Gulabdasis at the peak of their popularity. Ganesha Singh uses *maryāda*—another term that points to conventions and conduct rules—to speak of the Gulabdasis flouting the rules of varnashramadharma.[153] *Behayāyī* (shamelessness), *haṅkārī* (egoistical), *abhimānī* (arrogant), *vitandevādi* (argumentative, cussed), and *phisādī* (discordant) are some of the choicest words reserved by him for the Gulabdasis.

Between the apparent contradictions in Gulabdas's praxis and thought and the resounding critique presented by the Sikh historians, how do we understand Gulabdas's behaviour? Is there a way to reconcile the apparent gap between his bhakti-dipped Vedantic theology and his seemingly prideful and singular attitude? There are two ways at looking at the conundrum of Gulabdas: That he was a person who had the strength of character to put the logic of his thought into practice, uncaring for the façade of remaining within shara; and that he was inspired by, or perhaps even in touch with, a radical stream of thought that existed in Punjab, which across the divides of Hindu and Muslim communities agreed on the significance and the location of god/godly within the self. Whether such a way of thinking can be termed a 'school' is moot, but the fact was that this was a very attractive philosophy, and appealed to many in Gulabdas's age across communities, besides his own disciples who fanned out in Punjab and Sindh. In Punjab, especially after the death of Gulabdas, and with his seat inherited by his adopted son Hargobind, many deras were established by his prominent disciples, spread across various parts—Ferozepur, Patiala, Ropar, Ambala, Jullunder, Karnal, Amritsar, Kasur, Pothohar, Sialkot, Sultan, Sindh, and Balochistan.[154] After the Partition of 1947, many centres came to be spread in parts of Haryana and Rajasthan as well.[155] Sindh as an important centre is not only known from Vishan Das' account, but Ganesha Singh also mentions important Sindhi followers of Gulabdas.[156]

---

[152] Ashok, *Shirin Farhad*, p. 5
[153] Ashok, *Shirin Farhad*, p. 5.
[154] Sewak, 'Gulabdasi Sampradaye', p. 115.
[155] See Chapter 8.
[156] Ganesha Singh, *BMD*, p. 130.

Solipsism—the belief that one's own self is the only knowable truth—that can be derived from advaita monism, that sees the universe in organic, non-dualistic terms, was very much a possibility. The centrality of the soham mantra and the insistence of Gulabdas on calling himself Brahm give a strong inkling to his solipsistic thought. It was with the logic of such belief that Gulabdas dissented against caste differences, condemned varnashramadharma, and kept his sect open to all castes. It may have also led him to review gender relations, though in this context we have contrary evidence. On the one hand we know Piro to be his important disciple who lived in his establishment, a literary figure and a religious personage who commanded respect. On the other, there is evidence that he did envisage traditional roles for women—this is also mentioned in his writing—and had a rather conventional notion of good and bad women, as of women's bodies.[157] It was Piro who in her writing and action extended the logic of his philosophy, expanding through her insistence the space that women could occupy in society.

Logic or *tark* through which implications of advaita could be forwarded was also dear to him. He was described by Ashok as a Vedanti who was *tarkvādī, dhārmic Brahm mubīsiañ vich pravīṇ* (skilled at logic and disputing on Brahm, invoking a public platform for debate).[158] Not for nothing were the Gulabdasis seen as disputants and egoistical by Ganesha Singh, and as a group that did not lie. It is worth thinking if the logic of solipsism also made the Gulabdasis individualistic, as they examined and interrogated the self to locate the divine. Individualism and the idea of the self, particularly an inner self is seen as a western development, and a trait of modernity in India.[159] South Asian cultures are generally seen to give preference to collective identity, whether of caste, community, family or kin group over individual growth. A sect that stressed the connection between god and the self, so much so that it pushed them into challenging social norms and living according to their own (non) principles, may be seen to be promoting a home-bred individuation. This individuation was not a consequence of liberalism of the West, but rather of an autochthonous libertinism, as some would have it, itself a product of a non-dualistic philosophy.

---

[157] Sewak quotes verses from a handwritten manuscript of Gulabdas, *Anubhav Khaṇḍā*, where he first speaks of a good woman as a man's *shakti* or power, and as one who is obedient to her husband, and then of a foolish woman. (Sewak, 'Gulabdasi Sampradaye', p. 165.)

[158] Ashok quoted in Sewak, 'Gulabdasi Sampradaye', p. 126.

[159] See the Introduction.

An alternative way of looking at the Gulabdasis is to take seriously the passing references in the writings of the two Singhs that hint at their association with some faqirs of a Sufi order. Gian Singh, in his effort to both own and disown Gulabdas, accuses certain faqirs of introducing khulasa living to him: *rind faqīr khulāsiayoṅ kī un saṅgat karī badherī* (he kept company of debauched faqirs).[160] These faqirs are named as Bullehshahi by Ganesha Singh, apparently referring to a group of Bulleh Shah's followers based in Kasur,[161] and Ashok names the particular faqir with whom Gulabdas kept company as Khaki Shah, also calling Gulabdasis Sufiana in orientation and saying that at a particular time in Punjab the Gulabdasi sect spread as ferociously as a dust storm.[162]

The significance of this Sufi connection is perhaps to be found in the Gulabdasis being in dialogue with Sufi groups that adhered to the heterodox philosophy of Mansur al-Hallaj, the mystic martyr from Baghdad who gave to the world his singular expression *an'āl haq*—I am the Absolute Truth or I am God—considered blasphemous and pantheistic by the orthodox who tortured and hanged him in 922 CE.[163] Mansur, however, inspired enraptured love among many Sufis who considered him to be a model of suffering, including many in Punjab, a land he had supposedly visited in his peregrinations. According to Annemarie Schimmel, at least one way of interpreting Mansur's meaning was that 'God was visible in every trace of creation', and she also points to scholars who compared 'this mystical statement and the *aham brahmāsmi* of the Upanishads'.[164] 'An'āl haq' as it was invoked by the Gulabdasis appeared as a theological equivalent of the soham mantra, and Piro in her poetry at least once made this equivalence explicit: *kaho sabūtī an'āl haq yeh kalmā sācho* (affirm an'al haq the true *kalma*).[165] Kalma, of course, refers to the Quranic formula, the *kalīmā*, a basic belief in tauhid, the Unity or Oneness of god. I have argued elsewhere that groups like the Gulabdasis invoked this equivalence, revelling in cultural conversations and absorbing and incorporating similar elements from different

---

[160] Gian Singh, *PP*, p. 1293.

[161] Ganesha Singh, *BMD*, p. 127.

[162] Ashok, *Shirin Farhad*, p. 5.

[163] Schimmel, *Mystical Dimensions of Islam*, 62–77.

[164] Schimmel, *Mystical Dimensions of Islam*, 62–77.

[165] 160: 30. On theological equivalence, see Tony K. Stewart, 'In Search of Equivalence: Conceiving Muslim–Hindu Encounter Through Translation Theory', *History of Religions* 40, no. 3 (2001): 260–87.

traditions.[166] Certainly, Bulleh Shah's poetry has multiple references to both Mansur and an'āl haq, as did many other Sufis' verses in Punjab, and it is also a known fact about him that he challenged caste—*zāt*—practices.[167] Thus, when groups like the Gulabdasis, the followers of Wazir Singh, or some Sufis challenged what they considered untenable social norms—shara—they must have a sense of solidarity with a tradition with which they aligned themselves; a public which they invoked, a counterpublic on which they relied.

The apparent contradictoriness of Gulabdas's life may have caused consternation among some circles, whether the Nirmala historians put off by his disrespect for any conventions or the colonial ethnographers with their Victorian upbringing, horrified at the sheer diversity of socioreligious life in India, or appalled at the 'loose' morals of its myriad people. However, Gulabdas's theological enunciation and social non-conformism did create cultural interstices which could be exploited by some to carve out small crevices in society, through which they could make a place for themselves, challenging identities into which society slotted them, figuratively writing their own shara. We now turn to Piro, the Muslim prostitute who became Gulabdas's disciple shunning her profession and religion to follow her own path.

---

[166] Malhotra, 'Panths and Piety'.

[167] Malhotra, 'Panths and Piety'. Bulleh's poems are available in *Bulleh Shah ki Kafian*, edited by Namwar Singh (New Delhi: National Institute of Punjab Studies, 2003).

Part II

2 A 'Life Story' in an Autobiographical Fragment

The felt need to tell a person's story is among the most powerful of cultural impulses.

—Stuart Blackburn[1]

Autobiographical truth is not a fixed but an evolving content in an intricate process of self-discovery and self-creation, and, further, that the self that is at the center of all autobiographical narrative is necessarily a fictive structure.

—Paul John Eakin[2]

The title of this chapter suggests that Piro, the low-caste woman (*sūdar nārī*), a Muslim, and a prostitute (sudar vesva), and the protagonist of this section of the book, crafted a story of/for herself, not so much of her life, but of a moment that came to define it, or so she would have us

---

[1] Stuart Blackburn, 'Life Histories as Narrative Strategy: Prophecy, Song, and Truth-Telling in Tamil Tales and Legends', in *Telling Lives in India: Biography, Autobiography and Life History*, edited by David Arnold and Stuart Blackburn (New Delhi: Permanent Black, 2004), p. 203.

[2] Paul John Eakin, *Fictions in Autobiography: Studies in the Art of Self-Invention* (Princeton: Princeton University Press, 1985), p. 3.

FIGURE 2.1   A bejewelled Piro in a contemporary rendition based on an older print. Note the handkerchief shaped like a bird, seen in some Gulabdasi depictions of individuals, though it is difficult to decode the meaning of this representation. (This picture is easily available in the Gulabdasi dera at Hansi.) *Source*: Sant Vijender Das.

believe.[3] This was a moment when she decided to leave her known life and profession, probably in a brothel in Lahore, and also her religion, and enter the dera of Guru Gulabdas as a novitiate. The decision to abandon her known life had severe consequences, Piro suggests, including

---

[3] Piro's autobiographical verses, the *Ik Sau Sath Kafian* or One Hundred and Sixty Kafis (hereinafter *160 Kafis*), are available in a manuscript form, ms. 888, in the Bhai Gurdas Library, at Guru Nanak Dev University (GNDU), Amritsar. The first eight kafis or verses are missing here but I have used this manuscript throughout. The eight missing kafis along with the rest are now easily available in the published collections of Piro's complete works. These are: Sant Vijender Das, ed., *Sant Kavyitri Ma Piro* (Panchkula: Satluj Prakashan, 2011) in Devnagari script, and Veer Vahab, ed., *Piro Kahe Saheliyon* (Jalandhar: R.B. Printing Press, 2012) in Gurmukhi script. Piro refers to herself as a sudar nari, a sudra woman, at many places in the *160 Kafis*. Her Muslim antecedents are an important organizing principle of her *160 Kafis*. She once calls herself a sudar vesva, a low-caste prostitute in kafi 9.

attempts by her former guardians and co-religionists at reconversion to Islam and her abduction; and perhaps even a spectre of homelessness. Piro took recourse to putting down in writing the story of events that happened to her which changed the course of her life—the *Ik Sau Sath Kafian*—in fluid rhyming verses. Piro's rhymed story bears no title.[4] In the manuscript under consultation, the scribe concludes her poetry with a line informing the readers that the *160 Kafis* had ended, which I have used as the unpretentious title for her kafis. Each of her 160 kafis was of six lines, with every two consecutive lines rhyming, Piro giving us her story in a pithy 960 lines.

Before listening to Piro's story it is important to point out that many scholars of the autobiography and the autobiographical prefer to use the terms *life writing* or *life narrative* for a more inclusive study of the heterogeneous practices that constitute self-referential writing, or its presentation in diverse media.[5] These terms are seen to be particularly appropriate for non-Western and premodern societies, though the appropriation of the term 'autobiography' by the modern West has not gone without a challenge.[6] Some scholars of biographies and self-referential writing prefer to use the terms *life history*, or even *life story*, to draw attention to their narration in oral, fragmentary, and allusive forms, and also question that such narration must necessarily have to be true, or that it even matters if related events occurred or not.[7] While these questions will be discussed further later, suffice it to say at this juncture that the use of the term 'life story' here is to adumbrate the fabricated nature of storytelling, the design and rhetorical skill deployed to relate a tale just-so. The tension in the autobiographical narrative between 'truth-telling' and 'truth effect' on the one hand and the 'imaginary' and the 'fictional' on the other is a problematic that is explored both as a theoretical question that

---

[4] In the published versions of her kafis, her narrative begins with a simple 'Ath Kafian Likhayate' (Further Written Kafis) with no title or the traditional *mangalacharan* or an invocatory verse.

[5] Sidonie Smith and Julia Watson, eds, *Reading Autobiography: A Guide for Interpreting Life Narratives*, second edition (Minneapolis: University of Minnesota Press, 2010), p. 4.

[6] Anshu Malhotra and Siobhan Lambert-Hurley, eds, *Speaking of the Self: Gender, Performance and Autobiography in South Asia* (Durham: Duke University Press, forthcoming).

[7] David Arnold and Stuart Blackburn, eds, *Telling Lives in India: Biography, Autobiography and Life History* (New Delhi: Permanent Black, 2004), p. 9.

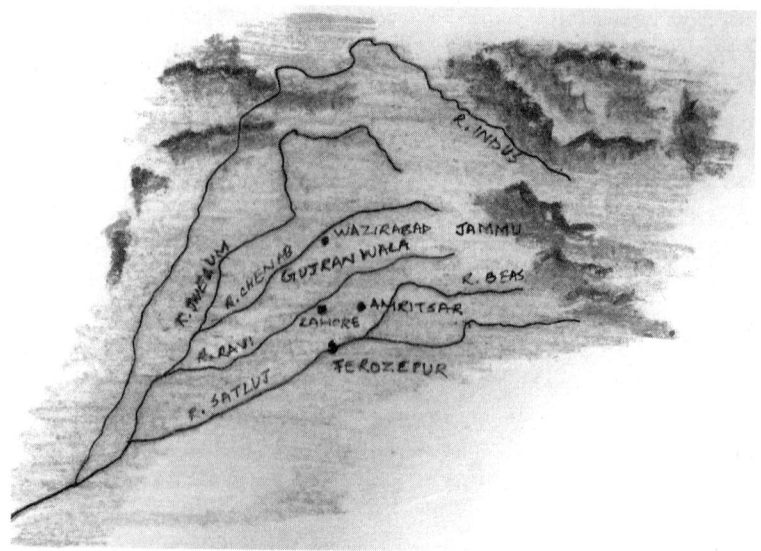

FIGURE 2.2   A map of Punjab showing places mentioned in Piro's *160 Kafis*, and where her story unfolds (map is not to scale).
Source: Courtesy of Aditi Kodesia.

inevitably arises in studying the autobiographical text and in the specific context of Piro's tale.

Thus, Piro's 'life story' is not the story of Piro's life; far from it, for she remains elusive. What we know of her comes mainly from elliptical references in her other works besides her *160 Kafis*, which obsess over a chain of events that are triggered by her momentous decision to become a disciple of Gulabdas. Thus too the *160 Kafis* are fragmentary, not only in the material shape of the manuscript when it was discovered, but also because for all the salience of the related incidents, they cover a miniscule fragment of her life.[8] We grapple with disjointed references to create some template of her life, to fill up the holes in what comes across as a fragmented life, particularly in her early years. The events she describes, however, were a part of her life that compelled her to put them down in writing—the process of its composition, then, an essential

---

[8] Ms. 888 was serendipitously discovered by Santokh Singh (Shahryar), a librarian at GNDU, from *raddi*, or discarded rubbish, and he played an important role in popularizing Piro and doing scholarly work on her.

step in speaking of her subjectivity, in constructing a self-identity. Let us begin by listening to Piro's story.

PIRO TELLS HER TALE

The following paraphrase of her story, the narration of her narration, is by necessity a summation of Piro's tale, one that carries none of the poetic skills she deploys, or the literary ruses and allusions she resorts to, or the rhetorical strategies she uses, though these will be pointed out and discussed later.

Piro begins the *160 Kafis* by addressing her friends (*saheliyo*) invoking the quintessential moment in a girl's life—her marriage—when friends separate and each girl finds herself alone, and despite her wailing, is helplessly bundled off to her marital home. The meaning of this bridal imagery is made clear soon enough—it is a metaphor for the journey of the soul-bride, which must find its way across this ocean/river of worldly existence (*bhei tarinī saritā, bhav sāgar*) and cross over to her groom/god's place.[9] Though this imagery was commonly used by male saints representing themselves as brides eager to meet their master-god, or to evoke *virāha*, the unbearable separation from the groom-god, in Piro's usage the impact of the metaphor changes; for unlike male saints who take on women's role, she does not need to masquerade in a man's voice. Marriage and the cruel departure at a young age from the parents' shelter, in fact, was the fate of most girls in Piro's time.[10] The situation for women is hence plausible, imbricated in a palpable materiality rather than in the realm of imagination. The impact of the bridal topos is then to reject a certain future for an improbable life of spirituality, a choice rarely available to women, and one that put on trial Piro's dedication to that path.

[9] Bridal imagery—the soul-bride meeting the god-groom—is common among both bhakti and Sufi saints. In Punjab, Sheikh Farid (1173–1265), whose verses are enshrined in the Guru Granth, was perhaps the first to use this conjugal metaphor of the soul-bride meeting the death-groom. See Sant Singh Sekhon, *A History of Punjabi Literature*, vol. 1 (Patiala: Publications Bureau Punjabi University, 1993), pp. 20–4.

[10] For the role-playing in women's voices, see Carla Petievich, *When Men Speak as Women: Vocal Masquerade in Indo-Muslim Poetry* (New Delhi: Oxford University Press, 2007).

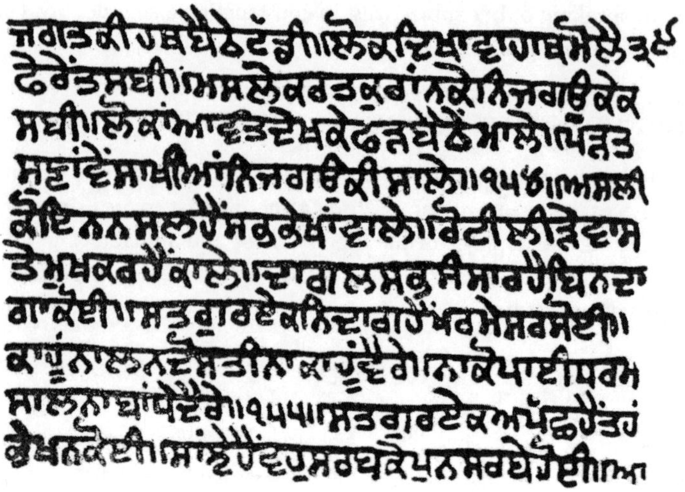

FIGURE 2.3 A page from Piro's *160 Kafis* showing *kafis* 154 and 155. *Source*: Courtesy of the author.

Later, she again addresses her friends, and this time it is clear that the friends hailed are former co-prostitutes. She admonishes them for dressing up without having an actual groom to dress up for or please, that is, they do it for professional reasons rather than as chaste brides dressed for grooms: *binā suhāg singār kar bibchār kahāvo* (dressing without a groom is called being unchaste).[11] Again, the impression created is about a real situation rather than an imaginary one, Piro urging them to find a real 'groom' by looking for a guru-god as she has. Thus, even when old images are deployed by Piro in her uncompromisingly feminine voice, the semantics of released imagery impacts differently from that of men's usage and creates a materiality absent therein.

Piro's story progresses by her averring that a guide/guru, someone who will show the way, is required to assist the soteriological crossing. Piro then explicitly refers to her Islamic faith by naming its potential religious men who could have helped her in this cause, but who all fail, in fact, in doing so. It might be stated here that not only in the *160 Kafis* but also in most of her other poetic expressions the theme of not finding succour in Islam's religious personnel (and subsidiarily in Hindu religious persons), including its qazis and mullahs, is incessantly made, the latter two particularly reviled for shouting

[11] 160: 35. (Kafi numbers from the *160 Kafis* are marked as '160: xx'.)

from roof tops (*ūche bāṅg pukārde*), but utterly lacking real knowledge: *pīr fakīr auliye maiṅ sarab manāye, aisā koī nahiṅ disdā maiṅ bharam vaṅjhāye* (I placated saints, mendicants and the holy, but couldn't see any who'd clear my doubts).[12] Again, foregrounding her obsession with religious identity, and paradoxically its overcoming, Piro makes clear that only the one who has made irrelevant this distinction between Hindus and Turaks,[13] will be the one who would help her cross over: *Turak–Hiṅd kī had te jo āp laghesī, Pīro kahe saheliyo veh pār karesī* (The one who will move beyond the limit of Turakness and Hinduness, friends the one will help in ferrying across).[14]

After making a case for her search for a spiritual guide, Piro immediately introduces Gulabdas into her narrative, relating that in the Moti Bazaar of Lahore came a charismatic man: *Pīro sohne saṅvale mukh sadā haṅsde* ([Says] Piro [he] was a dark complexioned looker with a smiling face).[15] He was dressed regally in weapons, turban and an aigrette, and had called an assembly. He was surrounded by his disciples, one holding an umbrella over him and another fanning him with a fly whisk, and he charmed the people of Lahore. While important men and nobles stood around, Piro relates that he picked her from the crowd and asked her to sit next to him, even as her friends warn her that he is powerful (*zorāvar*), and she but a low-caste prostitute (sudar vesva). On being asked why she has come to the door of an ascetic (sant), she answers him with humility that she has lost interest in material things, and thinking of the certainty of death, wishes to be at his feet. What follows is Piro's eulogy to a guru who provides succour for low-caste men and women—aspects of her writing that will be discussed in subsequent chapters.

Noting her disenchantment from material goods, she introduces herself as one disinclined from the world—*ham bhaī udāse*. She also emphasizes breaking all her previous relations before coming to him—*picchle āī raṅd ke*. However, the Turaks she has left behind are unhappy, *phiran kalānde*, and follow her asking that Piro as their daughter/sister—*dhī bhaiṇ*—be sent back with them, and why she has come taking off her fine clothes and ornaments? Piro, after roundly abusing them, suggests, rather surprisingly, that she herself asks her guru to send her back with them—*bhejo in ko saṅg jī*—saying that

---

[12] 160: 4.

[13] The term 'Turak/Turk', though pointing to an ethnic group at an earlier time, refers to Muslims in nineteenth-century Punjab. Piro uses it quite clearly to indicate a Muslim, though occasionally she also uses the term 'Musalman'.

[14] 160: 5.

[15] 160: 6.

she'd be back if the guru would give her shelter—*balam pannā dīje*. Immediately thereupon, Piro hints at the harsh treatment she would meet at the hands of the Turaks, anticipating in her retrospective writing what she would show as an occurrence later. Among the Turaks she depicts herself as one against many, a lone woman fighting her righteous battle: *Turak sab āye ek se tum dās akalī* (Turaks came all together and your slave was alone).[16]

Piro then portrays that the primary concern of the Turaks was apparently a putative 'conversion' of hers, or rather her apostasy, her giving up/taking off of her (earlier) faith: *is majbar lāhī*.[17] To rectify this apparently anomalous state, the Turaks then call the mullahs, upholders of religious orthodoxy, the authority figures who come with their religious and legal books to question Piro on her transgression and expect her to reconvert to Islam. Piro puts these words in the mullahs' mouth to underscore their anger: *kahe mulāṅre kāfre kyoṅ dīn gavāyo, kāhu ne tujhe bigāṛiyo jin sūr khilāyo?* (Say the mullahs O' infidel, who spoilt you and made you eat pig?).[18] Piro then speaks of the mullahs asking her to read the kalma and other Islamic prayers in order to reassimilate her into Islam. In the ensuing dialogue of Piro with the mullahs and the qazis, in charge of Islamic jurisprudence, she not only presents herself as capable of defending the choice of her guru, but also as repeatedly insulting them, and significantly getting the better of them in tête-à-tête: *hameṅ bosī ek haraf yeh lākh sunāye* (we utter but a word while she makes us hear lakhs).[19] Thus, Piro presents herself as using speech and argument to outdo those who traditionally were used to talking down to people.

The failure of the mullahs to win her back is followed by the clan (*kutumb*) making an appeal to her to reincorporate her into the Islamic faith, using sweet talk and persuasion (*mīṭhe mīṭhe bain*) as the threat of force and punishment has had no effect on her (*sam dam ar ḍanḍ bhed*). Importantly, the clan is composed of friends (*saheliyaṅ*), perhaps hinting at those in her former profession who ask her to return to Islam: *Jo guṇ unke bed meiṅ haī vahi kurāne, rāh chhoṛo tum kāfraṅ nij āo imāne* (The virtues of their Vedas are in the Koran too, leave the path of the infidels and come back to your faith).[20] Piro is not only able to out-argue her friends who acknowledge her superior status, but also to persuade them about the rightness of her chosen path.

16 160: 21.
17 160: 24.
18 160: 26.
19 160: 31.
20 160: 33.

The failure of the friends then gets the 'Muslim men' angry (*Musalmān nar*), whom Piro taunts by ridiculing their religion as one devoted to outward appearance: *indrī mūchh katāī ke* (snipping the penis and the moustaches).[21] The humiliation at the hands of a woman frustrates the men: *dīn hamāra rad ke eh kaisī jāe* (how she is going on humbling our religion).[22] After further cursing these men, calling them 'dogs of religion' (*majbāń ke kūkre*), Piro presents herself as so strong in her determination and will that the Turaks are hard-pressed to find a way out: *bahut takṛī dekh ke sabh hoī lachāre, yeh nahiń muṛesī moṛyań hai baī muhāre* (seeing her strong all feel helpless, she is not going to turn she follows her will).[23] Through these exchanges Piro also shows her interlocutors to be conscious of the power of her guru, both as an accomplished person (*kāmal*) with important men as disciples and as one who commands loyalty in the vicinity of Lahore. Piro then says that seeing her unwavering loyalty to her guru, her opponents then hatch a plan to abduct her at night (*rātoń rāt*) and take her away from Lahore to Wazirabad (near Gujranwala). However, Piro sniffs out the sinister plan in their move and is taken there against her will, suggesting again in anticipation of its later manifestation, that she would be kept captive: *vasdā chhoṛ Lahore ko maiń bande chalī* (leaving a flourishing Lahore I am going to a prison).[24]

The next part of her narrative then moves to Wazirabad where Piro says she's kept imprisoned in a four-storeyed building with locks put in place and sentinels posted outside four doors. In the midst of enemies, due to the liberality, equanimity, and fearlessness of her character (*samtā aur udārtā nirbhaitā nale*),[25] Piro says she befriends two women, Jano and Rehmati, who are ready to help her and suggest that she inform her guru of her situation. With their help she is able to get an amanuensis (*munsī, lakhārī*) to her and makes him write a supplication (*arjī*) to her guru pleading to be taken out of her dire straits. The next few verses are epistolary in nature, where Piro dictates to the munsi her message to the guru. The message, among other things, underlines the power of the guru, and how desperately Piro wishes to be with him and gaze at him: *Āsak jiveń mabūb ko jiuń tu chāsu parse, tiuń man merā satguro tum darsan tarse* (Like a lover looks for his beloved in the four directions, so my heart thirsts for your countenance).[26]

---

[21] 160: 40.
[22] 160: 41.
[23] 160: 47.
[24] 160: 51.
[25] 160: 56.
[26] 160: 72.

Piro then informs—imaginatively painting a picture of events that she is not a witness to—that the letter reaches the guru on the third day, and generates wrath among his disciples on the treatment meted out to her. The guru subsequently dispatches two of his disciples, Gulab Singh and Chatar Singh, on a rescue mission to Wazirabad. On arriving there, the two encamp in an orchard and befriend its gardener (*mālī*), and along with Jano and Rehmati he becomes one of the five conspirators who will help Piro escape. The gardener, in disguise, is able to enter the house where Piro is captive, informing Piro and her friends of the presence of the disciples. Thereupon the two friends of Piro go to meet Gulab and Chatar Singh in the orchard.

The disciples, according to Piro's narrative, are prepared to fight uncaring for their lives. They make quite a splash in Wazirabad: *Sīs talī par rakh ke vich phire nisaṅge, lohu bhariyā akhiyāṅ hath mehṅdī raṅge* (Playing with their lives they roam fearless, with reddened eyes and hands reddened with henna),[27] alerting her captors to their presence. The fallout of such swashbuckling behaviour is that Piro's condition of imprisonment is made harsher.

Piro at this stage introduces a woman called Mehrunissa, who once again, after failing to persuade Piro with sweet words assuring her of all material comforts if she only reassimilates within Islam, resorts to offering Piro a choice of accepting Islam or facing incarceration in chains: *Kaī chhoṛo dharam kāfārāṅ hoī musalmānī, kaī pag pae jaṅjīr mo baho baṅdī khānī* (She said leave the religion of the infidels and become a Muslim woman, she said or wear chains on your feet and sit in jail).[28] Piro is also threatened with being taken to the town of Rajouri (in Kashmir?), where Mehrunissa implies her guru would not be able to help her.

Before these plans could be set into motion, Piro speaks of her escape from her captivity because of the support of the disciples, the gardener, and her friends. However, her actual escape from the prison Piro presents as a miracle unfolded by her guru, the locks falling away at her touch and the guards rendered blind by him. Indeed, the whole town of Wazirabad, including the guards of its gates, are unable to perceive the three disciples make good their escape, as they cannot see them, while the disciples are able to see them all. It is only after they move away from the gates of the city that the enormity of the occurrence is understood—*sehar Wajirāvād mo kūkāṅ paīyāṅ* (in the town of Wazirabad chaos ensued)[29]—and Piro's captors begin the pursuit of the three disciples,

[27] 160: 99.
[28] 160: 102.
[29] 160: 117.

sending horsemen and soldiers. The three, also riding horses, move towards the river, resting only after reaching the banks of the River Ravi. They feel safe after crossing the river (and entering Lahore?): *kusal bhayo man tīn ke jab Rāvī lānge* (the three felt relief after crossing Ravi).[30]

On reaching Chathianwala Piro presents the three as giving proof/being a witness (*sābatī*) to each other's bravery and good conduct, each extolling the role of the other two in accomplishing this task and remaining loyal to the guru. Interestingly, the Muslims at this juncture are referred to as 'mlechha', a term connoting those outside the Indic civilization context,[31] perhaps Piro wishing to overcome the ambiguity of her recently converted status by drawing attention to her not belonging to the 'outcastes'. The steadfast loyalty to the guru on Piro's part is, therefore, highlighted by Gulab Singh who speaks of her resisting their efforts of converting her: *Sarā manāvan vāste bahu hoe akoṇe, kaid malechhāṅ jhaliāṅ tum charan na chhoṛe* (They undertook a lot of trouble to make her adhere to the Shari'ah, she suffered their incarceration but did not leave your feet).[32]

The last part of Piro's narrative then turns to the praise of the guru, emphasizing his glory, the radiance of his personality, and his non-biased attitude towards all, whether high caste or low, man or woman, a Hindu or a Turk. Besides a fulsome critique of the religion of the Hindus and the Muslims, this part of the text also censures other sects and panths, presumably competitors to the Gulabdasis in recruiting novices and in salvific choices, including the Sanyasis, Bairagis, Madaris, Sikhs, Khalsas, Akalis, Nirmalas, the worshippers of graves and cremation grounds, and so on. Piro also explicates on the salience of the consort, the Shakti of the Lord himself, a role that she envisages for herself. While thanking her guru for enlightening her and preparing her for the true path, she then expounds on her understanding of the unique doctrines of her own sect, ending her narrative by reiterating her loyalty and servitude to her guru.

---

[30] 160: 122.

[31] For a discussion on the term 'mlechha' see Romila Thapar, *Somanatha: The Many Voices of a History* (Viking Penguin Books: New Delhi, 2004), p. 141. For multiple terms connoting Muslims with their diverse semantic accent, including the term 'mlechha' see Brajadulal Chattopadhyaya, *Representing the Other? Sanskrit Sources and the Muslims (Eighth to Fourteenth Century)* (New Delhi: Manohar, 1998), pp. 28–60.

[32] 160: 124.

PIRO'S STORY'S 'TRUTH EFFECT'
AND CORROBORATIVE EVIDENCE

This summary of the overt story that Piro relates has a ring of plausibility. Piro emphasizes the suffering she undergoes in order to see the manifestation of her innermost spiritual desires in a sequence of episodes that could well have occurred. Piro creates a throbbing reality, naming some of the persons involved in the events and the places that featured so prominently in the whole escapade, especially Lahore and Wazirabad or the River Ravi, on whose banks Lahore is situated. In other words Piro 'fixes' her story with people, places, and topographical indicators in some sort of reality, creating a 'truth effect'.[33]

In fact, if we follow one of Piro's statements, the advice she gives to Gulab and Chatar Singh when in Wazirabad, asking them to be cautious, warning them of the rule in those parts of the firangi—*aithe rāj firangiāṅ mat rollā pāvo* (here the firangi rules do not be riotous)[34]—it may even help us place the incident she relates in the early 1830s. That Piro was comfortably ensconced at Chathianwala, the abode of her guru, at the time of the sanguinary battles between the Sikhs and the British is apparent from the Sikh historian Gian Singh's reference to the 'Satluj' clash, the Anglo-Sikh wars of 1845–9, and his prior reference to Piro living with the guru in his work *Panth Prakash*. Also the bid to tame and suppress the sect in the 1850s as mentioned by our other Nirmala Sikh historian, Ganesha Singh, in his *Bharat Mat Darpan*, makes the Piro incident into a Sikh period affair.[35] Furthermore, Ganesha Singh in his account made an important observation about the anecdote of a conflict around Piro's arrival in the Gulabdasi dera, his version almost matching that of Piro's, but with some significant details added on. Ganesha Singh gives an account of how Piro *kañjarī* (prostitute) came to stay with the guru after she fell for his charms, an occurrence resented by her guardians

[33] See the discussion in Jeanne Openshaw, *Writing the Self: The Life and Philosophy of a Dissenting Bengali Baul Guru* (New Delhi: Oxford University Press, 2010), p. 108.

[34] 160: 97.

[35] On Gian and Ganesha Singh's accounts see Chapter 1, where the reference to the Anglo-Sikh wars is discussed.

(*wāras*), who then took her away to Gujranwala.[36] He also notes that Gulabdas dispatched Kala Singh and Chatar Singh to bring her back, a train of events and cast of characters that resemble Piro's account, though are not identical with it. Ganesha Singh adds a detail that spells out the incendiary and scandalous nature of the affair when he notes that another 'friend' of Piro's, one Ilahi Khan, promised the help of the army (*fauj*), and urged Piro's 'brothers' to take on Gulabdas. Gulabdas, according to this account, was surrounded near the tomb of the saint Mian Mir in Lahore, where, however, two hundred of his own supporters arrived to help him and a skirmish followed. According to Ganesha Singh, the fight came to an end only after the intervention of 'Maharaj', presumably Ranjit Singh himself, and subsequent to that Gulabdas and Piro settled in Chathianwala.[37] Scholars have identified Ilahi Khan with Ilahi Baksh, an important general of Ranjit Singh who commanded his artillery.[38] If that was the case, we can actually understand the furore Piro's departure to the dera of Gulabdas must have caused, considering she was on the fringes of the Lahore court, apparently coveted by an important army man. In Piro's narration, the guru seemed already settled at Chathianwala when she first joined him, though not according to Ganesha Singh. Certainly Piro first encountered Gulabdas in Lahore, as she narrates. The firangi in Piro's reference can then be identified with Paolo de Avitabile, an Italian general of Ranjit Singh, who controlled Wazirabad in the early 1830s.[39]

Looking at the strong parallels in Piro's and Ganesha Singh's accounts, and giving due consideration to the garnishing of the story the two may have taken recourse to, one to present her subjectivity and unstinting

[36] Wazirabad is located at present in the district of Gujranwala. Both Gujranwala and Wazirabad towns were beautified under Ranjit Singh. Wazirabad is located on the eastern banks of River Chenab, around a hundred kilometres north of Lahore, on the banks of the River Ravi. See Edward Thornton, *A Gazetteer of the Territories under the Government of the East India Company and of the Native States of the Continent of India*, vol. 4 (London: W.H. Allen and Company, 1954).

[37] Mahant Ganesha Singh, *Bharat Mat Darpan* [hereinafter *BMD*] (Amritsar: Vaidak Bhandar, 1926), p. 128.

[38] Sewak, 'Gulabdasi Sampradaye', p. 92; On Ilahi Baksh see Radha Sharma, *The Lahore Darbar* (Amritsar: GNDU, 2001), pp. 92–3.

[39] According to Thornton's *Gazetteer*, Avitabile was responsible for reconstructing Wazirabad in the European style, with 'wide streets, and a handsome and commodious bazaar'. The bazaar is mentioned by Piro as the place where the guru's disciples made a splash. Thornton, *A Gazetteer*. On Avitabile see Sharma, *Lahore Darbar*, pp. 62–6.

loyalty to her new guru and his philosophical ruminations, and the other perhaps a victim of time, rumour, and hearsay we can still conclude that some disturbance had certainly occurred at the time of Piro's arrival at the Gulabdasi dera. If that is true, what made Piro's narrative so exceptional, her embellishments a strain to comprehend and present her story? There are several reasons that suggest the extraordinary effort Piro made to push the envelope of self-representation, her account of events presented within a carefully chosen cultural palimpsest that set the tone for their likely reception, drawing on contexts that gave her story the cultural links she favoured and a moral aura she sought. First, the account of her 'abduction' drew clear linkages to let us say the primary, if not the originative kidnapping, that of Sita, the queen of Lord Ram at the hands of the demon Ravan in the epic Ramayana, a parable that sharply separated out good from evil, her depiction discussed later in the chapter. Second, Piro's version of her confrontation with the mullahs and the qazis drew on region-specific as well as pan-regional traditions of questioning the authority of religious figures, self-appointed or otherwise. It specifically linked her to the episode of Hir's refractory showdown with the qazi who tries to preach good womanly conduct to her while she questions the legitimacy of his pronouncements in the amazingly popular qissa of Hir and Ranjha in Punjab. It simultaneously drew on the Sufi tradition of Punjab, especially the Qadiriya Sufis and their reviling of the mullahs, some even doing so by taking on the persona of Hir;[40] the pan-regional links visible in a similar strain within the bhakti movement and its ridiculing of the religious authority figures—issues that will be discussed in detail in the following chapters. It might be emphasized that for Piro the bhakti inheritance of her sect was significant and she constantly tries to legitimize her own actions by seeking parallels from the bhakti legacy. Third, the appropriation of the bhakti, and to an extent the Sufi, traditions in her repertoire of cultural resources opens up the reasons why Piro chose to submit her personal conflict in the language of a religious face off. The charges of conversion and apostasy made by Musalman/Turak men in Piro's narrative may well resemble the situation as she saw it, but her interpretation also carried the metaphoric weight of a bhakti and Sufi inheritance that opened up for questioning the external religiosity of men of formal faith as against the sants' and fakirs' own interiorized spirituality. This story in turn may provide clues to approach the incipient and often incoherent voices that appear in Piro's text, along with meaningful silences, perhaps

---

[40] Petievich, *When Men Speak as Women*, pp. 38–41.

hinting at life as a prostitute, a woman with sometimes frustratingly little say in the manner in which she may live her life. However, before turning to some of these issues central to Piro's self-fashioning in this and the next three chapters, it is important to understand how an autobiographical narrative works, creates subjectivity, and constructs a self.

THE AUTOBIOGRAPHICAL NARRATIVE

Georges Gusdorf suggested in the 1950s that autobiography was not a universal phenomenon and that it was culturally specific to the West, attributing it particularly to the 'Copernican Revolution', the dissociation of man from cosmic cycles to looking at life as an 'autonomous adventure'.[41] Self-reflexivity, an aspect of the development of interiority and of psychological maturity, was also seen as a Western attribute, variously dated from Augustine's *Confessions* in the fourth century, Montaigne's *Essays* in the sixteenth century, to Rousseau's *Confessions* in the eighteenth century.[42] Many scholars of India have also maintained that the autobiographical narrative is a product of modernity, introspection being a new attitude that was cultivated from the nineteenth century, though reflections on the most personal and the intimate continued to be avoided by men who chose to reflect on their lives and times.[43] The value of women's autobiographical genres, whether diaries, journals, or memoirs, which too began to emerge in nineteenth-century India, particularly Bengal and Maharashtra, was primarily taken to be their sociological interest, their focus seen to be on changing domestic and ritual practices.[44]

As the first epigraph to this chapter suggests, the cultural impulse to relate stories of individual lives is very strong, and in India, as elsewhere,

[41] See the discussion in Eakin, *Fictions in Autobiography*, pp. 199–202. Also Anshu Malhotra and Siobhan Lambert-Hurley, 'Gender, Performance and Autobiography: An Introduction,' in their *Speaking of the Self* (Durham: Duke University Press, 2015).

[42] Malhotra and Lambert-Hurley, *Speaking of the Self*, pp. 2, 18–19.

[43] A.R. Venkatachalapathy, 'Making a Modern Self in Colonial Tamil Nadu', in *Biography as History: Indian Perspectives*, edited by Vijaya Ramaswamy and Yogesh Sharma (Hyderabad: Orient BlackSwan, 2009), pp. 30–52; Udaya Kumar, 'Autobiography as a Way of Writing History: Personal Narratives from Kerala and the Inhabitation of Modernity' in *History in the Vernacular*, edited by Raziuddin Aqil and Partha Chatterjee (New Delhi: Permanent Black, 2008), pp. 418–48.

[44] Partha Chatterjee, 'Women and the Nation', in his *The Nation and Its Fragments: Colonial and Post-Colonial Histories* (Princeton: Princeton University Press, 1993), pp. 135–57.

multiple genres and media have been employed to tell these tales at all times. These include recounting individual lives through collective practices like oral folk stories and other performance traditions.[45] While writing of others' lives has always been a part of a culture's repertoire, presented in cultural-specific ways, the moot question is the status of expressing the self in societies heretofore seen as denigrating the individual as against the communal. Two persistent shibboleths of autobiographical traditions have come to be challenged in recent times. On the one hand, historians have shown through multiple examples that individuals wrote of the self and in varied ways constructed self-identity, particularly in the early modern period, though the focus in India may be on the 'self in society'.[46] On the other hand, scholars of the autobiography in the West are increasingly suggesting that the idea of individual autonomy in the West is a cultural myth, as most individuals, but especially women and other marginalized sections of society, wrote about 'relational' selves.[47]

The idea of the self related to others or constructed in relation to others is not only that of a permeable, less bounded Indian self, 'dividual' as against the individual, as posed by McKim Marriott.[48] It is also the notion that a self is fabricated with an audience in mind and is, therefore, inherently a performative practice.[49] Marilyn Booth, writing about nineteenth-century Egyptian women auto/biographers, posits that the self is a semiotic formation performed between the narrator, the historical subject, and the (feminine) reader.[50] Sidonie Smith and Julia Watson point to something similar when they speak of the autobiographical truth as an 'intersubjective exchange' that takes place between the narrator and the reader. This creates a multifaceted truth, autobiographical writing producing a 'polyphonic site of indeterminacy rather than a single,

---

[45] Blackburn, 'Life Histories', p. 204.

[46] Arnold and Blackburn have introduced this term. See the Introduction in their *Telling Lives in India*, p. 19.

[47] See the discussion in Kathryn Hansen, *Stages of Life: Indian Theatre Autobiographies* (Ranikhet: Permanent Black, 2011), pp. 299–314.

[48] McKim Marriott, 'Hindu Transactions: Diversity without Dualism', in *Transactions and Meanings: Directions in the Anthropology of Exchange and Symbolic Behavior*, edited by B. Kapferer (Philadelphia: Institute for the Study of Human Issues, 1976), pp. 109–42.

[49] Malhotra and Lambert-Hurley, *Speaking of the Self*.

[50] Marilyn Booth, 'Locating Women's Autobiographical Writing in Colonial Egypt', *Journal of Women's History* 25, no. 2 (2013): 36–60.

stable truth'.[51] Jill Ker Conway has shown how given 'cultural scripts', that is, cultural models on which selves are often designed—whether of a heroic figure overcoming obstacles to achieve self-realization, a bildungsroman narrative that envisages social acceptance and reintegration after a struggle with the self and the world, or a romantic heroine of the Victorian period—were dominant ideas that shaped the writing of individual lives.[52] Further, following the work of Louis Althusser, who discussed how ideologies of the dominant classes and the state 'hailed' or 'interpellated' individuals' lives, that is, how institutional discourses moulded their lives, the notion of the autonomous sovereign self has come to be questioned.[53] Piro's autobiographical story, though written in the nineteenth century, resembles a premodern narrative in its form, language, and rhetorical make-up. The interplay between her individual subjectivity and relational self without which the storied fragment of her life cannot be understood must, therefore, be borne in mind.

Two further issues about the autobiographical narrative need to be put into perspective before we analyse Piro's account. Autobiographies are seen to be intrinsically *performative*, as they are regarded to be *fictional*, both aspects to an extent a product of the nature of memory. Autobiography as performance, on the 'page' rather than the 'stage'—though the former may be seen as unfolding the theatrical possibilities of one's life—is essentially about self-presentation.[54] The retrospective nature of the autobiographical text makes for several rhetorical acts to be performed through it. These include, as Smith and Watson note, 'justifying ... own perceptions, upholding ... reputations, disputing the accounts of others, settling scores, conveying cultural information, and inventing desirable futures among others', many of these being important aspects of Piro's text, in particular her desire to secure her future within the Gulabdasi sect.[55]

---

[51] Smith and Watson, *Reading Autobiography*, p. 16.

[52] Jill Ker Conway, *When Memory Speaks: Exploring the Art of Autobiography* (New York: Vintage Books, 1998), p. 8.

[53] Smith and Watson, *Reading Autobiography*, p. 55. Also see Roy Porter, ed., *Rewriting the Self: Histories from the Renaissance to the Present* (London: Routledge, 1997).

[54] The expression 'on stage or page' is from Sherrill Grace, 'Theatre and the Autobiographical Pact: An Introduction', in *Theatre and Autobiography: Writing and Performing Lives in Theory and Practice*, edited by Sherrill Grace and Jerry Wasserman (Vancouver: Talonbooks, 2006), p. 13.

[55] Smith and Watson, *Reading Autobiography*, p. 13.

Thus, specificity of the audience for whom a text may have been composed and its likely reception are all issues that work towards the framing of a performance.

Fictional aspects of the autobiographical act, on the other hand, sit at odds with its apparent intention of 'truth telling', the 'autobiographical pact' of authenticity to which Philippe Lejeune pointed to when he spoke of the distinguishing characteristics of the genre.[56] Lejeune's notion was that the authorial signature that establishes the narrative as autobiographical truth—this happened to me or this is my life—must be read as a contract between the author and the reader. Yet, many autobiographers are aware of the fictional quality of their writing, just as many struggle to establish the truth of their autobiographical account. For the literary critic Paul de Man, autobiography remains an indeterminate creation, not quite a 'genre', as it attempts to give a face, a mask, or a figuration to a specular, mimetic self, while threatened by 'defacement', and 'disfiguration'. Thus, the autobiographical mirror does not reflect as much as it refracts, perhaps even distorting a life according to one's reasons. Speaking of the autobiography's fictional quality, de Man writes: 'We assume that life produces the autobiography as an act produces its consequences, but can we not suggest ... that the autobiographical project may itself produce and determine the life and that whatever the writer does is in fact governed by the technical demands of self-portraiture and thus determined, in all its aspects, by the resources of his medium?'[57] While all may not agree with de Man's bleak assessment of the autobiography, what he suggests is that the demand of writing itself may produce a particular kind of life, to say the least, giving autobiography an undefined status, neither fish nor fowl, so to speak. This indeterminacy creates a degree of doubtfulness regarding the autobiography, as Eakin has noted. While we are comfortable with the autobiographical in fiction, we are discomfited by fiction in autobiography, even though storytelling, and that is what the autobiographical act performs, is as much an 'art of memory', as it is an 'art of imagination'.[58]

Memory, as the growing literature on its unstable nature demonstrates, is always constructed from the present location and consciousness. The telescoping of time, the freezing of a moment, the sequencing of time,

---

[56] Philippe Lejeune as discussed in Eakin, *Fictions in Autobiography*, p. 20; and in Smith and Watson, *Reading Autobiography*, p. 11.

[57] Paul de Man, 'Autobiography as De-facement', *MLN* 94, no.5 (1979): 919–30.

[58] Eakin, *Fictions in Autobiography*, pp. 2–3, 9.

the remembering, the disremembering, the memorializing, the silences, and the erasures, are all a product of a presentist perspective.[59] The past, in a sense, is continually reinvented to meet the changing requirements of the present.[60] The formation of memory, or conflation of events of the past, as Alessandro Portelli has discussed, also entails what an individual or a community might remember as most salient and meaningful, or as an intrinsic aspect of self-identity. In a society, thus, who remembers and what is remembered, who is tasked with remembering, and what is forgotten and on what silence is imposed, are all important issues. How memory may be dammed or how it flows, and what may trigger its torrent, whether sight, smell, touch, event, or an object, are significant vectors in its formation.[61]

If memory is refurbished according to the needs of a constantly changing present, then experience, on whose basis the autobiographical act is dependent, mediated as it is through language and memory, is already an interpretation, as argued by Joan Scott.[62] Storytelling further requires this experience, an interpretation, to be compounded with memory, to be put in a sequence, for better understanding or effect. Thus, a degree of imagination and fictional quality lie embedded in constructing the self. Eakin, therefore, looks at autobiography as an art of self-invention. In his analysis, self-discovery and self-invention are inseparable processes that go together.[63] In Piro's text we will see that the fictional element becomes even more pronounced as she relies on various available 'cultural scripts', well-known tales, whether of a Sita or a Hir, to enhance the effect her own story would produce. Indeed, separating her story from the known stories she relies upon is fruitless, for it is by telling those well-known tales, that she builds her own as she attempts to construct its receptivity. While relying on cultural scripts is likely a trait of modern autobiographies as

[59] Eakin, *Fictions in Autobiography*, p. 21–2; Smith and Watson, *Reading Autobiography*, pp. 22–30; Malhotra and Lambert-Hurley, *Speaking of the Self*; Alessandro Portelli, *The Death of Luigi Trastulli and Other Stories: Form and Meaning in Oral History* (Albany: State University of New York Press, 1991).

[60] Eakin, *Fictions in Autobiography*, p. 36.

[61] A.K. Ramanujan, 'The Ring of Memory: Remembering and Forgetting in Indian Literatures', in Molly Daniels-Ramanujan and Keith Harrison, *A.K. Ramanujan: Uncollected Poems and Prose* (New Delhi: Oxford University Press, 2001), pp. 83–100.

[62] Scott as discussed in Smith and Watson, *Reading Autobiography*, pp. 32–3.

[63] Eakin, *Fictions in Autobiography*, p. 55.

well, is there any specificity of premodern autobiographic narratives, especially of women that we should note?

SELF-REFERENTIAL TEXTS IN PREMODERN INDIA AND WOMEN'S SELF-IDENTITY

As already alluded to, historians in recent years have studied and written about self-referential writing by men of the early modern period in India. Besides the memoirs of Mughal emperors Babur (*Baburnama*) and Jahangir (*Tuzuk-i-Jahangiri*) that present well-known examples, other instances have been brought to the fore and have elicited a growing interest.[64] Mukund Lath drew attention to the Jain merchant Banarasidas' *Ardhkathanaka* or *Half a Tale*, and in recent years other scholars have analysed different aspects of this fascinating account of a contemporary of the great Mughal, Akbar.[65] The tussle between individualist elements in this tale, and the overarching societal norms for the well-bred that worked across religious and to an extent class divides have been discussed. C.M. Naim has translated and introduced Mir Taqi Mir's eighteenth-century autobiography, particularly commenting on its rhetorical purposes and self-fashioning. While the poet was keen to present his father as an accomplished Sufi, it is in the surprising inclusion of scatological humour towards the end of his text that Naim tells us about the author's desire to be regarded as adept at incorporating all norms of a pedigreed noble.[66] David Shulman has discussed the biography of the eighteenth-century successful Tamil politician, Ananda Ranga Pillai, working with the French. Keen to push modernity to an earlier period than is accepted, and for its indigenous origins than is normally conceded, Shulman notes that the interest in this text, among others, is also because it is driven by an 'autobiographical impulse', 'an imagination of the self', as Pillai

---

[64] Stephen Dale, 'The Poetry and Autobiography of the *Babur-nama*', *The Journal of Asian Studies* 55, no. 3 (1996): 635–64.

[65] Banarasidas, *Ardhakathanaka*, edited and translated by Mukund Lath as *Half a Tale* (Jaipur: Rajasthan Prakrit Bharati Sansthan, 1981). Also see Farhat Hasan, 'Presenting the Self: Norms and Emotions in *Ardhakathanaka*', in Ramaswamy and Sharma, *Biography as History*, pp. 105–22.

[66] C.M. Naim, translated, annotated, and introduced, *Zikr-i-Mir: The Autobiography of the Eighteenth Century Mughal Poet: Mir Muhammad Taqi 'Mir'* (New Delhi: Oxford University Press, 1999).

also kept a diary of his everyday activities.[67] Jeanne Openshaw has analysed the autobiography of a Baul/Bartaman Panthi guru, Raj Krishna
or Raj Khyapa, who—though he lived into the first half of the twentieth
century—derived his interiority and sense of self (for example, in the
joint signature in his songs with his partner) from various indigenous
Bengali traditions.[68]

Many scholars of life narratives of the early modern period in India
have commented on the absence of penetrating self-introspection,
though there are exceptions, as for instance seen in the delightful exposition of Banarasidas' good and bad qualities by Rupert Snell.[69] This,
of course, did not mean a lack of interiority, as Openshaw shows, but
only that its sources were rooted in local traditions. Similarly, the historian Barbara Metcalf notes that Muslim autobiographers, even in the
modern period, wrote not to discover or introspect on a self as much as
to fulfil the achievement of intrinsic qualities present in them, making
auto/biographies perform didactic pedagogical tasks of exemplarity.[70]
Metcalf presents these as qualities inherited from an Islamicate tradition, which may be as she suggests, but are also visible in other ways in
Indic traditions, for example, the genealogical prediction of success as
Shulman shows, or as a fulfilment of a destiny whose signs are visible
from childhood.

In comparison to the growing volume of men's auto/biographical
voices in the early modern period, it is difficult to come across women's
self-referential narratives in India in the same period. This has to do
often with the lack of access to literacy and education for women even
from the elite sections of society, as it is a product of notions of decency
that required self-effacement and self-deprecation from them.[71] Though

---

[67] David Shulman, 'Cowherd or King? The Sanskrit Biography of Ananda Ranga
Pillai', in Arnold and Blackburn, *Telling Lives*, pp.175–202.

[68] Openshaw, *Writing the Self*.

[69] Rupert Snell, 'Confessions of a 17th-Century Jain Merchant: The
Ardhakathanak of Banarasidas', *South Asia Research* 25, no. 1 (2005): 79–104.

[70] Barbara D. Metcalf, 'The Past in the Present: Instruction, Pleasure, and
Blessings in Maulana Muhammad Zakariyya's *Aap Bitii*', in Arnold and Blackburn,
Telling Lives, pp. 116–43.

[71] Malhotra and Lambert-Hurley, Introduction, in *Speaking of the Self*. Also see
Sylvia Vatuk, '*Hamara Daur-i-Hayat*: An Indian Muslim Woman Writes Her Life',
and Francesca Orsini, 'The Reticent Autobiographer: Mahadevi Varma's Writings',
both in Arnold and Blackburn, *Telling Lives*, pp. 144–74 and 54–82 respectively.

conventions of humbleness were seen in men as well, it did not stop some of them from expressing their sense of self as we have seen, the restraint being far more effective for women who were often in seclusion, literally and metaphorically. In recent years, however, some scholars have attempted to read genres other than the autobiographical by women—like the Mughal princess Jahanara Begum's Sufi treatise or the compendium of ghazals of the famous eighteenth-century courtesan from Hyderabad, Maha Laqa Bai Chanda—as well as their architectural endowments, as instances of self-fashioning and self-referentiality.[72]

It is only the seventeenth-century Marathi saint Bahinabai's verses, *Atmanivedana* (Self-Presentation/Self-Dedication), that present us with an autobiographical text, where she speaks especially about her early years and struggle to both fulfil her marital duties and become a Brahmin disciple of the sudra saint Tukaram against the wishes of her husband.[73] Though the poems of other women bhakti saints (and male saints) can have autobiographical references, Bahina's autobiographical narrative remains sui generis. It is in this sense that Piro's *160 Kafis*, composed almost two hundred years later, while smaller and focused on an episode, presents an exciting find indicating a continuity of expressing subjectivity by women within the bhakti tradition.[74] In this context, Tanika Sarkar's reading of Rassundari's *Amar Jiban*, the first woman's autobiography in Bengal published in 1868, at least partially within the bhakti frame is significant. At many points Sarkar draws our attention to the peculiarly nineteenth-century aspects of this remarkable work, including its material production, prose, readership, and self-absorption. And despite Rassundari's divergence from the erotic–devotional demeanour of medieval Vaishnav bhakti of Bengal, her autobiographical act cannot be wholly understood outside Vaishnav referents as Sarkar emphasizes when she says that 'many histories ... interanimate and transact with one another' in its composition, rather than any 'derived' cultural act from

---

[72] Afshan Bokhari, 'Masculine Modes of Female Subjectivity: The Case of Jahanara Begum', and Shweta Sachdeva Jha, 'Tawa'if as Poet and Patron: Rethinking Women's Self-Representation', both in Malhotra and Lambert-Hurley, *Speaking of the Self*.

[73] Bahinabai has been discussed in detail in a subsequent chapter. Her verses and their translation are available in Justin E. Abbott, *Bahina Bai: A Translation of Her Autobiography and Verses* (New Delhi: Cosmo Publications, 2005).

[74] Piro's engagement with bhakti devotion has been explored in Chapter 4.

the West.[75] So strong does the bhakti trope remain, lending a vocabulary to self-representation, that even in the twentieth century a Bohra Muslim and a Gandhian, Raihana Tyabji, imagines her erotic–devotional relationship with Krishna as his gopi or cowherd woman Sharmila, as analysed by Siobhan Lambert-Hurley.[76]

While Piro's engagement with bhakti devotion to give herself a voice is discussed in Chapter 4, it is important to emphasize the continuing relevance of the bhakti tradition that was used creatively by women well into the nineteenth century and beyond to construct their subjectivities by using its relative openness to the marginalized to achieve a degree of autonomy. We now turn to what made Piro's mid-nineteenth century text 'premodern', in form and composition; its imaginative and fictional elements, as well as its truth effects; and in her deft use of myriad cultural resources at her disposal to weave a story she wished to relate.

160 KAFIS: RHETORIC AND FORM

The narrative Piro organizes in the 160 Kafis is well crafted. Though not following the more conventional pattern of beginning a poetic composition with a dedication to a guru, mentor, or any other personage (mangalacharan), she nevertheless follows convention enough to be respectful towards her guru throughout the text, declaring her subservience to him by repeatedly calling herself his slave (dasi). This was as much a conventional stance of a pupil towards the teacher as a rhetorical strategy of a cornered and vulnerable person against forces that seemed to her were determined to thwart her bid for autonomy.

Piro wished to relate a specific story of her discipleship and the sincerity of her spiritual quest; of her abandoning her former religion and profession and so of her honest and heartfelt attachment to her novitiate status as to her new found faith; and of the cruelty, belligerence, and sheer illegitimacy of the demands of those opposed to her and ergo the fairness of her own endeavour. Piro's wilful abandonment of her known life, likely in a brothel in Lahore, and her 'crossing over'—here a literal

[75] Tanika Sarkar, 'A Book of Her Own. A Life of Her Own: Autobiography of a Nineteenth Century Woman', in *From Myths to Markets: Essays on Gender*, edited by Kumkum Sangari and Uma Chakravarti (New Delhi: Manohar, 2001), pp. 85–124.

[76] Siobhan Lambert-Hurley, 'The Heart of a Gopi: Bhakti Devotionalism as Self-Representation?' in Malhotra and Lambert-Hurley, *Speaking of the Self.*

move involving a change of place and religion and not only a figurative makeover in a spiritual sense—must surely be seen as a scandal. For a woman who, as her own writing suggests, was a low-caste Muslim prostitute, to come to the dera of a higher-caste Sikh, albeit an advaita advocate with his own singularities, was a step that violated several instances of social decorum at once. The challenge to social propriety that her move involved were multiply played: of religion (a Muslim in a Sikh establishment), of caste (a low-caste in a dera of the dominant caste of Jat), of gender (a woman in a monastic establishment), and of sexual behaviour (the allegations of intimacy with the guru as later Sikh historians hinted, and so of norms of sexual restraint and celibacy).[77] All this meant that Piro had to construct a narrative that would, despite all her violations, portray her in a sympathetic light. Piro required a tale that could erase her wrongdoings, perhaps towards those who had rights over her, her guardians and friends, and endear her to those among whom she wished to build a new life—her guru and his disciples. Hence, Piro had to create a story that would banish her blemishes from sight/site, and beguile her perhaps reluctant guru and the dera inmates with praise and blandishments, as well as sincerity and seriousness she spouted. Piro aimed for redemption, both spiritual and social, one that would help her integrate with and be incorporated into the society she chose. Piro had to fabricate a saga that would convince others of her intent, as it would show her in a subservient light, mitigating through the sheer wizardry of her words the sharp edge of her exceptionally subversive act.

For what else did Piro have besides speech as a weapon she could deploy to achieve her ends, to 'talk back' to a society that gave little space to the variously marginalized, and to her, who carried the triple burden of a low caste, her gender and her disreputable profession?[78] Acquisition of language is often associated with the emergence of self-awareness.[79] Therefore, self-discovery and self-identity are processes associated with self-invention in the unfolding of the autobiographical act, what

[77] See Giani Gian Singh, *Sri Guru Panth Prakash* (Patiala: Bhasha Vibhag, 1970, first published 1880) and Ganesha Singh's *BMD*.

[78] The expression 'talk back' has been taken from bell hooks' work *Talking Back: Thinking Feminist, Thinking Black*, as cited in the introduction to 'Writing the Self', in *Women Writing Women: The Frontiers Reader*, edited by Patricia Hart and Karen Weatherman with Susan H. Armitage (Lincoln: University of Nebraska Press, 2006), p. 3.

[79] Eakin, *Fictions in Autobiography*, p. 8.

Eakin calls the *'verisimilitude* of the re-creation of self in the language of autobiographical discourse'.[80] And Piro is certainly self-aware of the power of her speech, namely her triumph as she depicted in her confrontation with Islamic religious authorities, or her humility as expressed in relation to her guru. Further, it is only by putting in writing her experiences, by using language and words, and by 'naming' herself incessantly in her poetry, that she escaped becoming another nameless victim of history.[81] Therefore, language and speech were central to self-identity, to the restoration of the self, to becoming who she wanted to be.

Piro told a tale whose intent was *justificatory*, of her actions that dismantled the societal discourse of a given place of a woman, who was, moreover, a low caste and a prostitute. It was also a story meant to be *reconciliatory*, convincing the doubters of her sincerity towards her new life, a dialogue with the audience, as discussed earlier, that she had in mind. The *interlocutory* nature of her narrative, a story built, as earlier suggested, between the autobiographer and the reader, especially those with whom she now wished to share her life. Piro's narration was *performative*, she performed her role, delicately balancing the effects of her steely resolve with a portrayal of feminine vulnerability and pliability. And her story was *fictional*, not in the sense that the events she recounted did not happen and were solely a product of her fertile imagination—though on their veracity one can hardly be sure despite the countervailing evidence that supports the broad contours of her story. Rather, it was fictional in the sense that she uses myths, legends, and tales—of Sita of Ramayana, of Hir of the qissa of Hir–Ranjha, and of major bhakti saints and minor characters of bhakti mythology—to craft her own story, her imagination at play in organizing and structuring her story, in designing its rhetoric, in producing its affects and effects. Speaking of Rassundari's autobiographical act, Sarkar writes that 'it was through writing a book that the life she wanted to express could live'.[82] For Piro one could say that

---

[80] Eakin, *Fictions in Autobiography*, p. 213.

[81] Eakin discusses the Chinese–American author Maxine Hong Kingston's feeling of oppression in her mother's story of the 'no name woman', the woman who cannot be named, because she defied and brought shame to her society. Paradoxically, she must be simultaneously forgotten and remembered: forgotten, to show how society punishes the deviant, and remembered, so all women will remember the fate of defiance. It is by writing and through speech that Kingston invents herself. Eakin, *Fictions in Autobiography*, pp. 255–75.

[82] Sarkar, 'A Book of Her Own', p. 117.

it was by writing a life others (albeit fictional characters) lived as her own that she could live a life she wished to live.

But how does one write a story of one's life—even if it was just of a fragmentary but a life-changing moment—when cultural inheritance does not permit such a telling by failing to provide noteworthy examples that could be emulated? The most significant narrative form in Punjab was the qissa; Punjabis were enamoured by their myriad tales of love, loss, transgression, and occasional reintegration, whether these were the stories of Hir–Ranjha, Sohni–Mahiwal, Shirin–Farhad, Sassi–Punnun, or Puran Bhagat. Related as the qissa was to the *masnavī* form used for longer narratives, both consisted of rhyming couplets that told a story. Stories and anecdotes from Guru Nanak's life were told in hagiographical literature of the *Janam-sākhīs*, and quite likely hagiographies of signifi-cant bhakti saints circulated in Punjab as elsewhere in northern India.[83] However, little existed by way of speaking about oneself; and the little that did, like Bahina's account of her dilemmas and travails, was outside Piro's access.[84] Innovation in creating a form that would be adequate to the task she wished to accomplish was the need of the hour.

Piro turned to the poetic form of the kafi, particularly used by the Sufis, and popular among the populace. Many common people of Punjab, even at present, memorize and recite kafis of known Sufi saints. The poetic expression referred to as kafis is virtually a form that incor-porates any rhyming lines. This simple form suited Piro who probably did not have sufficient training in poetics, unlike her guru who used complex metres to compose his verses. Though she also wrote siharfis, and some *shabad*s (short rhyming poems), these were again simpler forms to which she could adapt her poetry. The Punjabi verses of Piro,

---

[83] On Janam-sakhis see W.H. McLeod, *Early Sikh Tradition: A Study of the Janam-sakhis* (Oxford: Clarendon Press, 1980).

[84] One has no way of knowing if Piro was familiar with the part of Guru Gobind Singh's *Dasam Granth* that is called *Bachittar Nāṭak*. This has a section called *Apnī Kathā* (My Story), seen to be autobiographical, where the tenth guru traces his lineage going back to creation, including the family of Ram and Sita, and his Sodhi lineage through the Bedi clan of Nanak. It included the guru recalling his previous births, a trope also present in Bahinabai's *Atmanivedana*. However, Piro's is not a genealogical narration, it is a storied narrative. Robin Rinehart, 'The Guru, The Goddess: The *Dasam Granth* and Its Implications for Construction of Gender in Sikhism', in *Sikhism and Women: History, Texts and Experience*, edited by Doris R. Jakobsh (New Delhi: Oxford University Press, 2010), pp. 40–59.

interspersed and influenced by Braj, with Urdu words often incorporated as well, were written in the Gurmukhi script in a six-line format, following a simple metrical pattern where the last words of every two lines rhymed. The use of a mix of Punjabi and Braj written in Gurmukhi was part of the Sikh sacred and secular literary tradition from at least the eighteenth century and perhaps earlier.[85] Despite Piro's Muslim background to which she referred often in her *160 Kafis* and other poetry, her use of language suggests whatever formal training she had in poetics was within the Gulabdasi establishment. It is quite possible that she used an amanuensis for writing, as was the custom, and as she took recourse to in her tale as well, but her language use cannot be explained by that.

What is more exceptional about Piro's kafis is that she picked up the genre of kafis, traditionally non-narrative, to tell tales. Annemarie Schimmel described kafis as 'little songs composed by the Sufis for their followers'.[86] Explicating the Sufis' use of this poetic form, Carla Petievich has emphasized the use of the feminine voice in these compositions, giving examples from the kafis of Shah Hussain in the sixteenth century, and Bulleh Shah in the eighteenth century in Punjab.[87] Noting that kafis were to be sung to music, till at least the advent of print culture, their most notable feature being the refrain (*rahāo*), repeated after every stanza, she also points out that their distinctive feature, much like the ghazal, was that they did not follow a narrative sequence.[88] Piro made the kafi pliant to her need to narrate her life, using its simpler metrical structure to build a narrative about events she wished to recount. In that sense, her narrative can be seen to be a hybrid innovation of the non-narrative kafi of the Sufis and the qissa that narrated a tale. In her rhyming couplets that follow the AA BB CC pattern in each of the six lines, she allowed its fluid simplicity to tell her story.

Further, it is possible that the kafi that allowed men to write as women, the masquerade in the feminine voice to which Petievich refers, allowed a woman to voice her thoughts, and perform her act. Sufis like Shah

---

[85] See Chapter 1.

[86] Annemarie Schimmel as quoted in Carla Petievich, *When Men Speak as Women*, p. 9.

[87] On the popularity of Bulleh Shah's kafis and compositions today, see Anshu Malhotra and Farina Mir, 'Punjab in History and Historiography: An Introduction', in *Punjab Reconsidered: History, Culture and Practice*, edited by Anshu Malhotra and Farina Mir (New Delhi: Oxford University Press, 2012), pp. li–lii.

[88] Petievich, *When Men Speak as Women*, p. 16.

Hussain or Bulleh Shah could take on the voice and persona of Hir
to speak of their desire for the mystical union with their Ranjha-god,
or lament their separation from Him. Piro, with her unconventional
autobiographic impulse, perhaps found the kafi most amenable to her
purpose. For Piro spoke in an uncompromising female voice, not for
her any masquerade; she wished to relate her story alone: the story of a
complaining woman indicting those who wronged her, a woman humble
before her guru, resilient in her faith, a woman, moreover, determined
to create a niche in her new environment in the dera. Piro's narrative,
as it followed the episodes of her momentous metamorphosis from a
prostitute to a religious neophyte, was completely self-absorbed, without
any distractions from her story.

While Piro determinedly uses her voice, her 'I', the reference to the
self is both in the first- and third-person voices, a trait not that uncommon in the Indian context.[89] Piro often refers to herself in the *160 Kafis*
in the third person, especially in the signature line, which was normally,
and against the grain, the first one in a number of kafis, but could also
occur in the last line (the more traditional placement), and sometimes
anywhere in the middle as well. Thus, Piro could indicate her point of
view with the use of the third person as *Pīro pāk palīt te mil sāhab sache*
(Piro the impure became pure on meeting the true master)[90] or report
her action as *Pīro ṭurī nisaṅg ho gur nām dhyāye* (Piro walked fearlessly
meditating on the name of the guru).[91] However, Piro often switched to
the first person almost as soon as she inserted her presence in the third,
for instance, *Pīro kehsī satguru houṅ tumrā parnā* (Piro says satguru [I] am
your extension)[92] or *Pīro kehsī satguru houṅ dās tumārī* (Piro says satguru
[I] am your slave),[93] the verb 'houn' (am) giving an immediacy to her
person, and a palpable reality to her narrative. One may note that Piro,
whether in the third or the first person, was carrying forward the deep-
seated Indic tradition of placing one's identity (*chhāp* or *bhaṇīta*) in one's

---

[89] Openshaw refers to a similar tendency in the writing of her Bartaman
Panthi guru, Raj. See her *Writing the Self*. Also see Snell, 'Confessions of a
17th-Century Jain Merchant'.

[90] 160: 27.

[91] 160: 112.

[92] 160: 69. *Parna* is a length of cloth which ties the bride and the groom during
the marriage ceremony, and the word can, therefore, mean marriage as well. This
enhances the effect of the metaphorical tying to her guru that Piro refers to.

[93] 160: 24.

verse, claiming it as one's own. Scholars have questioned if the 'chhap' meant an authorial or an autobiographical 'I', as later poets within the tradition used names of popular saints, often the initiator of a tradition, to expand their corpus, as for example within the Sikh Guru Granth. However, it is quite clear in our case that Piro is using her own name and voice.[94]

The elliptical reference to the self in the third person allowed certain possibilities in composing the text not available in the first person. Snell's critique of Lath's prose translation into English of Banarasidas' verse in Braj is instructive in this regard. By translating Banarasidas in the first person voice throughout, Snell suggests Lath is insensitive to the subtleties and ambiguities latent in the poem.[95] Among the openings a third-person voice made, which in effect permitted the distancing of the self from one's person without necessarily detracting from one's saga (in fact, we will see that it added to the dramatic effect Piro hoped for), was the movement back and forth in time, sometimes predicting or foreseeing events that will occur as action later. This is what Shulman calls a 'prospective idiom' in a retrospective narrative.[96] At many times in her text then, Piro anticipates what will happen later, for example, she speaks of her bad treatment at the hands of her guardians even as she is leaving her guru's abode the first time. Similarly, she anticipates the miracle her guru would perform to permit her escape: *Yeh mār janjīr jandre takṛaī karseṅ, ṭursāṅ satgur nām laī, sarbe jhaṛ parseṅ* (They will strengthen [imprisonment] by chains and locks, [I'll] walk saying the name of the guru and they will fall off).[97] It also facilitated the reporting of events, for instance, Piro could report what occurred in the guru's establishment when her letter written from Wazirabad reaches there, a reportage which must necessarily fall in the realm of the imaginary, as she was meant to be

---

[94] See a discussion on these issues in J.S. Hawley, 'Author and Authority', in his *Three Bhakti Voices: Mirabai, Surdas, and Kabir in Their Times and Ours* (New Delhi: Oxford University Press, 2012 [2005]), pp. 21–47.

[95] J.S. Hawley, 'Author and Authority'. According to Snell, the first-person voice in *Ardhkathanaka* is restricted to a very short authorial preface. Those who rely on Lath's translation tend to give finality to Banarasidas' observations. He is shown to move from a darker past to a reformed self, missing the subtleties he conjures, for he is writing only from the point of view of 'half a life', even though he died soon after its completion.

[96] Shulman, 'Cowherd or King?', p. 182.

[97] 160: 96.

incarcerated in Wazirabad. The reportage mould also facilitated the
rehearsing of conversations among other dramatis personae in her story,
dialogues between them related in first- and second-person speech:
*Pūchhat Jāno Rehmatī kī nām tumhāre, Singh Gulāb Chatar Singh yeh
nām hamāre* (Jano and Rehmati asked what are your names, Singh Gulab
and Chatar Singh these are our names).[98] All this fluidity of depicting
location, action, and dialogue enhanced the theatrical unfolding of her
narrative, the prosopopoeia, the trope of the autobiographical narrative to
which de Man drew attention, Piro's simultaneous presence and absence
in the text.[99] It finally also made possible for Piro to make statements
praising her guru, giving them the status of indisputable facts: *Dās Gulāb
majūd haī satgur abnāsī, Pīro naiṇ nihār ke taṅh hoī dasī* (Das Gulab
is the indestructible true guru, admiring his visage Piro has become
his slave).[100]

To underscore her rhetorical strategy, let us now turn to the character she most specially sought to portray, her taking on the persona and
demeanour of Sita, the epic heroine of the Ramayana. Her emulating and
staging of Sita's story is a central episode in her saga, a lynchpin to her
self-portraiture. Additionally, while this depiction seemed to downplay
a supposed licentious past, it also hid a deep and unsettling hurt at the way
perhaps daughters were treated by her clan. The references to daughters
seem almost incidental, often incoherent. It was as if Piro was attempting
to prise open a seal of silence in which the question of how girls may have
been exploited in the business of prostitution lay. The subtext of the treatment of daughters was, however, tackled far more tentatively than the
issue of apparent religious animosity, Piro concentrating her angst on the
question of a religious face off (discussed in the next chapter), deflecting
towards that issue all her accumulated anxieties.

PIRO AS SITA

Quite audaciously for a Muslim low-caste prostitute, Piro took on the
role of the prima donna of 'Hindu' wifely devotion and chastity, Sita, the
wife of Lord Ram, the prince-king of Ayodhya in the epic Ramayana.
The juncture at which she introduces herself as Sita in her narrative is, of

[98] 160: 93.
[99] de Man, 'Autobiography as De-facement'.
[100] 160: 151.

course, after her 'kidnapping', comparing her own ill judgment at persuading her guru to let her go with her clan to Sita's ill-considered lust for the golden deer:

Pīro kehsī satguro ab houṅ bhar pāyo
Kītā man kī mat kā huṇ āge āyo
Muskal kiyo satguro man mat hamārī
Hamro pāchhe āpko bhī bhaī lachārī
Mrig pīchhe jiuṅ Rām ko Sītā bhaṭkāyo
Āp dukhī man mat karo mat vakhte pāyo.

Piro says true guru now I met my just deserts
I followed my heart and it landed me in regrets
My bad sense has created the straits
You too are feeling helpless because of my fate
Like Sita made Ram wander in search of the deer
Please do not trouble yourself or lose your cheer.[101]

Though the last line of the verse purportedly requests the guru to refrain from bothering himself over her, the intention of the lines was in fact to galvanize him into action, and she manipulated her words to simultaneously create the effect of emphasizing that his reputation was at stake, as it was for Ram, and, therefore, the divine analogy was used to underscore the significance of undertaking her own rescue. If one is mindful of the retrospective nature of her narrative, it is important to note that Piro attributes to her words, sent in a missive, the power of influencing the course of action her guru follows, even as she remains subservient in her humble submission to his power:

Pīro kahsī satguro ham nahī chārā
Hamrī lajjā āpko yeh birad tumhārā
Arjī āī charan mo kar meher dakhīje
Jaisā bhaṇā āp kā man āve kīje
Sīya kaidoṅ Rām jiyuṅ bal laī chhaḍaī
Pīro upar satguro tiuṅ ho hushāī.

Piro says satguru I have no recourse
My honour is in your hands and your reputation is at stake
As the supplication reaches your feet show benevolence
Fulfil your will and do as your heart pleases
As Sita's release was secured by Ram with force
Piro asks satguru to bestow on her his magnanimity.[102]

---

101 160: 67.
102 160: 79.

The ambience of the epic was further created by direct and indi-
rect allusions to persons and events from the text. Thus, if Piro was
Sita, and the guru Ram, then the disciples, Gulab Singh and Chatar
Singh, who came to Wazirabad for her rescue, were Hanuman and
Angad, loyal supporters of the lord, who breached the defences of Lanka/
Wazirabad to carry back Sita: *Bolyo Aṅgad Hanumān tum āgyā pāveṅ,
Laṅkā ākho phūk kar ghar Siyā le āveṅ* (Said Angad and Hanuman we
seek your command, if you permit we'll burn Lanka and bring Sita to
our land).[103] In Piro's writing, the orchard where the disciples sought
refuge in Wazirabad resembled the Ashok Vatika, the site of Sita's captivity; and the gardener who helped the disciples was rewarded among
other things with a golden ring, which again had a distinct recall of the
one Hanuman presented to Sita.

Through these narrative strategies Piro becomes the self-fashioned
Sita, endowing her own character and her version of events with ethical righteousness while simultaneously being able to depict herself as
the wronged person in the saga she relates. The irony of her portrayal
of Sita was not just that of a prostitute taking on the mantle of a chaste
wife, but also unlike the conventional Sita, silent and suffering, Piro was
neither, putting down in writing her complaints against her supposed
tormentors, and in the long run living out a fairly comfortable life in
the dera at Chathianwala. Furthermore, though conventionally shown
as the loyal shadow of her husband-god, there existed other traditions that
sought to critique patriarchal institutions by taking a sympathetic view of
Sita's suffering. For instance, women have chosen to lament their own
ill treatment at the hands of their husbands by mourning the fate of Sita,
thereby undermining the moral claims of patriarchy;[104] the fascinating
Chandravati Ramayana, or 'Sitayana' of Bengal of the sixteenth century
even indicting Ram for cruel treatment by pushing out a pregnant wife.[105]

Yet, we find a highly traditional portrayal in Piro's rendition of her
Sita's story. For she chose to draw attention away from a promiscuous past

---

[103] 160: 74.

[104] Velcheru N. Rao, 'A Ramayan of Their Own: Women's Oral Tradition in
Telugu', in *Many Ramayanas: The Diversity of a Tradition in South Asia*, edited by Paula
Richman (New Delhi: Oxford University Press, 1994), pp. 67–88.

[105] An absolutely fascinating account of Chandravati's text has been discussed
by Nabaneeta Dev Sen, 'Chandravati Ramayana: Feminizing the Rama Tale', in *Faces
of the Feminine in Ancient, Medieval, and Modern India*, edited by Mandakranta Bose
(New Delhi: Oxford University Press, 2000), pp. 183–91.

towards the more acceptable and orthodox Sita-like fibre of chaste loyalty, free of sensuous temptations, and so, worthy of not only the shelter of the guru, but in the long run as a practitioner of the ascetic lifestyle and as the guru's partner, and indeed as a 'mother' to his disciples in the dera. But the more immediate reason to cast herself as Sita was to accuse her former community, clan, and their religious heads of cruel and abhorrent behaviour towards her. The epic Ramayana, as some scholars have drawn our attention to, was especially suited to drawing out implacable lines between the morally upright and the ethically repugnant, and could be used historically to mark out the 'divine' and the righteous world from that of the licentious and illicit 'demons'.[106] And Piro chose to demonize her former community and associates. It might be worth recalling her use of the term 'mlechha' at this point in her text to denote the 'Muslim' men who abduct her, underlining their alien non-belonging as against the community of dharma represented by her guru and his disciples. The cultural flavour that the epic carried, the clash between good and evil, was sought to be attached by Piro to her own story, painting an image in black and white for the consumption of her chosen audience, the Gulabdasi disciples and other ascetic orders, perhaps the politically powerful who mattered and may have chosen to arbitrate in the matter.

However, the calumnious charge that Piro made against those with whom she lived as a community till fairly recently does sound like a pro-test too loud, ridden with anxiety to prove her case. While on the surface Piro gave a particular story of her ill treatment and abduction, and made specific allusions to illustrate her tale, her account was nevertheless rid-dled with half-said reproaches and brief utterances that betrayed another tone, one not overtly spoken by Piro, but posed questions that punctuated her text with another set of possibilities not always easy to understand or create a coherent tale from. Fairly early on in her story, for example, it becomes quite clear that Piro *chose* to go back with her 'clan' (kutumb) when they came pleading to her guru, promising to return, one would assume, after 'persuading' her people of the seriousness of her intent towards an ascetic life. That somewhere she felt herself betrayed, misled, even tricked into leaving comes through repeatedly in the *160 Kafis*; but

[106] On how the strategies of 'divinization' and 'demonization' were deployed in the medieval period by politically imaginative kingship, see Sheldon Pollock, 'Ramayana and Political Imagination in India', in *Religious Movements in South Asia 600–1800*, edited by David N. Lorenzen (New Delhi: Oxford University Press, 2004), pp. 153–208.

what also emerges is that she herself did not have the discernment to see what was right. A fair question that can then be posed is that did she leave in the first place because of an attractive offer of some sort placed before her? Or, was it because life in the dera did not seem appealing and she chose to go back only to be let down, and so became desperate to re-enter the dwelling of the guru, a task made all the more difficult by her initial departure, and in the new situation, her complete lack of choice? At least some of these varied nuances in her account are caught in the tone of these lines:

Pīro kehsī satgur houṅ sūdar nārī
Bhāṇā na pachhāṇiyo ab bhaī lachārī
kadar na paī āpkī houṅ gāfal hoī
aūguṇ more dekh ke gur dhāk dayoī
pichhle āuguṇ bakhsiye houṅ bhaī lachāra
thouṅ na koī satguro tum vāñjh hamāra.

Piro says satguru [I] am a sudra woman
[I] did not understand [your] will and am now helpless
I did not recognize your worth having become negligent
Seeing my faults the guru pushed me
Forgive my previous sins for I am helpless
[I] have no place to go satguru except yours.[107]

Though the previous sins Piro refers to could be allusion to her earlier life, the first line does suggest a more recent misjudgement on her part; what also emerges is her desperate fear of homelessness, or alternatively to a life she wished to discard.

On the other hand, Piro kept up a barrage of insinuations against those whom she depicted as her captors, hinting at a betrayal of good faith from those who brought her. Here is a sample of that corrosive accusation brought to the fore every now and then by Piro: *Pīro kahe saheliyo maiṅ bhulī bharme, visvī turkāṅ sukhan par jo nāhiṅ sarme ... dhokhā de gur saran te ham ko le āye* (Piro says friends I fell for a shadow, I believed the Turaks' talk who have no shame ... they misled me and brought me from the guru's shelter).[108]

It is undoubtedly difficult to put a finger on the nature of this betrayal whose refrain stays with Piro. Yet another manner in which it emerges is the subtle reference to the unacceptable way in which 'daughters' are treated by Piro's relatives and associates, which meant Piro's own

[107] 160: 66.
[108] 160: 60.

treatment. In fact, right at the beginning of her narration when her clan comes to the dera looking to take her with them, they assert their rights over her by calling her their daughter/sister: *Pīro hamri dhī bhain so dān mange hain* (Piro is our daughter sister so we ask for her gift).[109] The six-line kafi in which this line is inserted is the address of the Turaks to the guru, presented as a supplication to return their daughter, questioning her reasons to leave, having taken off her jewels (*bhukhan*) and good clothes (*līre*), when all material things (*padārathān*) were available to her. Daughters in high-caste Hindu society are 'gifted' in marriage, a meritorious act that all fathers hope to perform.[110] The semantic transfer of the right to gift a daughter from the clan to the 'Hindu' guru here creates two possibilities. On the one hand, the guru is pressured on a dharmic scale to treat 'his' daughter well, 'gifting' her to her rightful claimants; on the other, it is clear that the clan's daughter must go back to her jewels and clothes, the accoutrements a part of her profession, to further their traditional trade.

At two other instances Piro mentions daughters and their ill treatment. At the moment of her conversation with the mullahs, she indicts them with what seems like an expletive, *dhī ke laure*[111], perhaps pointing to their exploitation of daughters, asking them not to look for them/her, for they would not find them/her.[112] What this statement achieves is probably to toss up two different expectations of daughters into conflict with each other. Piro, it seems, sought to appropriate for herself the high-caste model of treating a daughter with care and earning merit through following prescribed behaviour towards her. One assumes that in Piro's world view this was set against the condemnable act of making a living or earning any other advantage through a daughter. The second reference reinforces this interpretation when Piro makes a more direct statement accusing the same religious figures of using daughters to further the cause of their religion: *majab vadhāvan vāste sath dhiān dese* (they give

[109] 160: 15.

[110] See Anshu Malhotra, 'Killing, Gifting or Selling Daughters: The Pressures on a High Caste Identity', in her *Gender, Caste and Religious Identities: Restructuring Class in Colonial Punjab* (New Delhi: Oxford University Press, 2002), pp. 47–81.

[111] 160: 42.

[112] Piro may have used the word *laure* to mean search, for the hemistich before this asks the addressed *miān* of this kafi to not search. However, Piro's tone is abusive, and the use of *miān* here is offensive, and she may well be calling the mian a daughter-fucker; laura with a longer vowel sound refers to penis.

sixty daughters to strengthen their religion).[113] Sixty was a figurative way of underscoring the willingness to 'trade' in several daughters in order to serve the faith/community. However, what remains somewhat unclear is how religion/religious community is served in this sordid bargain as against the benefit accruing to her professional clan.[114]

While Piro's foregrounding of her personal conflict in religious terms will be discussed subsequently, we may speculate where her background in prostitution placed her in terms of expectations from a daughter. Louise Brown in her study of the contemporary life in Hira Mandi in Lahore has shown the dominance of Shia Islam in these prostitutes' quarters, noting the many 'temporary' marriages that a prostitute is expected to enter, and the way a good-looking and healthy daughter is treated as an asset and a security for the rest of her family.[115] Though it would be difficult to project onto Piro's time the realities of contemporary Hira Mandi, Piro's own narrative, once again, fuels speculation on similar lines. When she speaks of her being forced to leave Lahore for Wazirabad, she accuses her captors of taking her not only against her will—*jor dhagānā* (forcibly)[116]—but also perhaps being tricked into a potential relationship (of temporary wifehood/concubine?): *khachru tumara janīyo ham chhaliyā lore* (I know your wickedness/wiliness of finding a man/lover for me),[117] and then asserting that she would never interact with him as long as she was alive, *mukh is ke kabhī na lagsāṅ houṅ jab lag jīvī*.[118] Was Piro, then, kept captive in order to make her succumb to a demand she refused to bow to? Was the turning to the guru a way of escaping a situation she did not relish? Did she fall for the charms of the guru as disingenuously suggested by the Sikh historian Ganesha Singh?[119] Or was the spiritual urge on her part a genuine one? We do not know the answers though the truth might have been a combination of all of the above. However, it is evident that by assuming the role of Sita, she put herself in a moral order that had echoes in the society she wished to persuade towards her own

---

[113] 160: 45.

[114] The likely meanings of this statement have been discussed in the next chapter.

[115] Louise Brown, *The Dancing Girls of Lahore: Selling Love and Saving Dreams in Pakistan's Pleasure District* (New York: Harper Collins, 2006).

[116] 160: 53.

[117] 160: 50.

[118] 160: 50.

[119] See Chapter 1.

attitude of restraint and rectitude, and pushed her clan and its demands, hopes, and expectations in the realm of the illegitimate and the unethical. Piro's masquerade as Sita, in other words, was primarily aimed at her new community, persuading them to the purity of her intent, the consort-like devotion to the guru, but significantly also of her irreconcilable differences with her former associates. Piro's careful self-fashioning on the one hand and her recusant self on the other, not only in her presentation of her conflict with authority figures of her former community but also from the point of view of her clan to whose authority too she refused to bend, show a person of exceptional will and self-worth. It was surely this remarkable sense of selfhood that allowed her to live and manoeuvre her extraordinary circumstances to her advantage.

In this chapter, we traced Piro's 'life story', a tale she assembles, crafts, and designs to narrate an episode in her life that became life-defining for her. Though the events she recounts were based on some 'truth', an occurrence that happened, Piro's own rendition of it was artful and self-fashioning, for her saga, like most autobiographical accounts as discussed in this chapter, was meant to fulfil several rhetorical ends. These included convincing people in her past and future of the serious intent in her spiritual journey and of finding a place in the dera. Piro's autobiographic impulse, as narrated in a premodern form and language, and expressed through much loved and familiar fictional characters like that of Sita, was an 'imaginative' rendering of a life that grabbed at subjectivity and sought autonomy. Piro's self-identity was not based on a unique life journey that only she undertook, though in retrospect we can see what made her and her story singular: whether her move from a brothel to a monastic establishment, her religious 'crossover', or her poetic expression. She built her tale on allusions and allegories, crafting a story on her resemblance to Sita as we have seen, or Hir, Kubjan, and Bhilni, even a Kabir and a Mansur as we will see, though never letting go of her gendered identity. Her story, as summarized in this chapter, also centrally developed around questions of religious identity, conversion, and conflict. In the next chapter we turn to this aspect of her tale.

3 Agonistic Religiosity, Gendered Self, and a Conversion Narrative

Tāe tapāiā kājiāṅ ne, chāhe sarā de vāste pāe mainuṅ
Kahe kāfar hoī mil kāfarāṅ nuṅ, chorī dhoe kurān pilāī mainuṅ
Maiṅ tā dāsī Gulābdāsjī dī, kahe sāḍe imān meiṅ āye mainuṅ.

The qazis heated up in anger, and invoked the love of shari'ah with me
They said I've become a kafir [unbeliever] after meeting kafirs, and stealthily
asked me to drink [the juice] of the Quran,
[I said] I am the servant of Gulabdas, they said come into our creed to me.[1]

Jāvṇā asī pardes saiyoṅ, Turak Hiṅduaṅ pare kahāvṇa ī,
Asī tiyāg jāṇā mat Hiṅduaṅ dā, nahiṅ Turakāṅ dā kuj dharāvṇa ī
Jithe pahuch na Turak te Hiṅduaṅ dī, Pīro aise makān meiṅ jāvaṇā ī
Pīro Rām jharokṛe baiṭh ke nī, mujrā kul jahān dā pāvṇa ī.

We will go to a foreign land friends, far away from Turaks and Hindus
We will sacrifice the doctrine of the Hindus, nor keep anything of the Turaks
Where neither Turak nor Hindus can reach, we will reach such a place
Piro says sitting at Ram's window, we will dance away the norms of the clan
and the world.[2]

Safal hoyā huṇ janam merā, gurāṅ bhulṛī rāh batāiyo ne,
Kuṅj vāṅg maiṅ paī kurlāṅvdī saṅ, taṅh nām hayāt pilāyo ne.

[1] S2: 3.
[2] S1: 10.

My life is now fulfilled, the guru stopped me from the wrong path
I was wailing like the *kunj* bird, he made me drink the life of Name.[3]

Besides the *160 Kafis*, Piro wrote at least three siharfis, a painti, *Sanjhi Siharfi* with her guru, and a set of short songs/poems set to musical *ragas* called the *Rag Sagar*.[4] The subjects of these writings were diverse, but it is possible to pick many autobiographical verses from them, like the first quotation in the epigraph above where she makes a reference to the recurring theme in her works, of being asked to 'reconvert' to Islam.[5] While no single word Piro deploys can be seen as an equivalent of the English language usage of 'conversion'—the act and process of changing religious (or other) beliefs—her language does indicate unequivocally that she is speaking of a change of religious belief, and the notion of belonging to a community. The cluster of words encountered, for example, in the first quotation above, *sarā*, *kajī*, *kāfir*, *qurān*, *imān*, point unambiguously to a reported dissonance over religious belongingness or its disavowal, the coming into or leaving a religion-based community. Having introduced the idea of religious dissonance, Piro follows it up by her rejection of Hinduism and Islam as in the second quotation. In the third quotation, Piro gushes with fulsome praise of her guru, the one above and beyond the limits of 'Hinduness' and 'Muslimness' as she affirms at different places, who shows her the right path. Piro's life story, as discussed in the previous chapter, obsesses over the consequences of her decision to become a neophyte in the dera of Gulabdas, which included her abduction and incarceration on account of her apostasy from Islam and the pressure put on her

---

[3] *SS*: 4.

[4] These are available in *Sant Kavyitri Ma Piro* compiled by Sant Vijender Das and in *Piro Kahe Saheliyon* compiled by Veer Vahab. One of her siharfis, hereafter referred to as *Siharfi3* (*S3*) is also available in ms 888 at GNDU.

[5] The *Sanjhi Siharfi* with her guru, for example, was about the guru teaching Piro the principals of advaita; the *Rag Sagar* consisted of celebratory songs sung in praise of the guru when the Gulabdasis observed the Holi festival. The siharfis touched upon Piro's spiritual experience as well as the recurring themes in her bhakti- (and sometimes Sufi-) inspired writing. These included the certainty of death, *Kāl* (Time) making the most of this birth, her non-biased guru, and many favourite metaphors through which advaita was traditionally explicated.

to reverse it and to re-enter the fold of Islam. Piro's foregrounding of the motif of conversion—or rather the failed reconversion initiated by her co-religionists—in her writing compels us to explore the reasons why she incessantly brings up this question and what it means to her. The manner in which she expresses her angst over the question also pushes us to investigate how the motif of conversion was understood in Punjab of the nineteenth century, before the polemics of the modern associational movements and census-driven politics created the pathology of numerically competing communities. Piro accuses those out to harm her and thwart her from her chosen path of religious bigotry, and speaks against a piety consisting of externalities of religious symbols. Against this she counterpoises the interiority of the bhakti path, of the benefit accrued through the repetition of the Name, of a single Truth as shown by monist advaita. She speaks of one's solipsistic presence in the universe; and above all, that it is only through the medium of the guru that one can follow the soteriological path.

While she eloquently expounds on the philosophy of the Gulabdasi panth, she also posits a question that only she singularly interrogates— her gendered existence, and what it meant in a world of religious dissension and of soteriological opportunity. This question of her gendered being, so central to Piro's spiritual questioning and growth, will be introduced in this chapter and then further explored in the next two. Women, in the period Piro inhabited, were perhaps seen as incapable of making individual choices, and were expected to adhere to the given religious practice of their kin and community. They rarely took it upon themselves to define their subject-position in relation to any given creed, a situation that clearly irks Piro. In the larger Indic world of ideas and practice, where collective interest is supposedly always placed above stances of individuality, it is in spiritual seeking that a degree of individualism is conceded, at least to men.[6] The manner in which Piro rejects given religious practices and insists upon her individual spiritual choice and subjectivity was radical for her time, a trait of questioning the normative practices she develops in her varied writings. It was

---

[6] Renunciation as a practice has historically been seen to develop with urbanization and individualism. See Gavin Flood, *An Introduction to Hinduism* (New Delhi: Cambridge University Press, 2009), pp. 80–1. For the 'complementariness' of the dialogue and tension between the renouncer and the householder, see T.N. Madan, *Non-Renunciation: Themes and Interpretations of Hindu Culture* (New Delhi: Oxford University Press, 2001 [1987]), p. 17.

by building the trope of conversion, and by rejecting those who might force upon her a given creedal allegiance, that she could assert her subjectivity and choice. In this chapter, I will discuss the layered meanings of conversion, and the emphasis on its outward and public display will be examined in the specific context of Punjab. How Piro's social background in prostitution may have curbed and limited her life choices will be discussed, giving us a clue to understand her adamant will to follow her chosen path. The reasons for Piro's specific 'conversion narrative' will also be introduced, and how her gendered subjectivity shines forth in her poetry will be shown.

THE TOPOS OF CONVERSION

In her writing Piro often mentions her previous Islamic identity, and her shedding it on meeting her guru and subsequently deciding to live in his establishment. In the *160 Kafis* this comes through quite early when she mentions her 'previous' Muslim relations—*pichhle Turak manaut ke jo rehan dukhānde* (the wheedling previous Turak [relations] who stay unhappy),[7] the word *pichhle* or former connoting those relations she has forsaken. Elsewhere, too, Piro makes references to abandoning Islamic rituals when taking to chanting the Name, as for instance: *nivājāṅ roze chhuṭ gaye mastānī hoī* (I became intoxicated and gave up praying and fasting during *rozās*);[8] or again, referring to her abduction and subsequent escape, interpreting it as a release from Islamic practices: *Meher dillī guru ajāta ṭe, turkāṅ kaid te laī chhadāī saiyoṅ, avar kalme, namāz te roze dī, sirākār vigāṛ uthāe saiyoṅ* (Friends the casteless guru showed mercy and freed me from the Turaks' incarceration, and raised me from the harm of *kalma, namaz,* and *roza*).[9] That in this quotation Piro refers to the three basic practices of Islamic faith—the kalima formula which all Muslims affirm, the daily *namaz* prayers, and the ritual fasting in the month of Ramzan—make explicit both her previous belonging to, and her subsequent breaking away from, Islam.

This 'turning away' from Islam and 'turning to' her guru and the Gulabdasi path, to which Piro refers, is what the anthropological literature on conversion analyses as a 'passage', a bid 'to reidentify, to learn,

---

[7] 160: 14. (Kafi numbers from the *160 Kafis* are marked as '160: xx'.)

[8] *S3*: 8.

[9] *S2*: 26.

reorder, and reorient'.[10] Seeing this move as more than 'syncretism', that is, the inhabiting of a cultural pastiche composed of former and the newer identities, or a 'breach' signifying a complete break from the past (though these aspects remain important), conversion is seen in terms of 'a quest for human belonging' that 'expresses new forms of relatedness'.[11] This understanding of conversion points to not only how one may opt for a new identity, but also importantly, how this attempt at belonging to a new community is perceived by the host community with whom relatedness is sought, by the one that has been exited, and also by society at large. One may assume that Piro was formally initiated into her Gulabdasi sect, as is wont in most renunciative orders, which probably also involved formally shedding an earlier religious identity, though Piro does not speak of it. What, however, remains ambiguous in Piro's account is whether such an initiation into the Gulabdasi panth also meant a broad commonsensical affiliation with being a Hindu, or even a Sikh, particularly in the eyes of the common people or her former co-religionists. The latter accuse her of having become a *kāfir*, an unbeliever, as Piro informs us, giving us a clue to how her former community perceived her, albeit this is Piro's depiction. We need to investigate why Piro plays up the Hindu/Muslim imbroglio while telling her story. We also need to make an attempt to understand her often vituperative outbursts in the light of her own cultural placement not only in relation with the people she has forsaken but also regarding those she has adopted, who bestow on her a new identity. Furthermore, the complex of her emotions, outbursts, and sagacious thoughts together can be apprehended only if we also take cognizance of the history of the idea of conversion in Punjab, and keep a pulse on Piro's historical time.

Piro, of course, repeatedly rejects formalist Hindu/Muslim religious identity, clearly stating that her guru is above the limits set by such identities, whereas the ordinary are caught up in them. She refers to him as *bihadī* or outside these mundane limits and so, limitless. Indeed, she explicitly states for herself that she too rejects any formal religious affiliation: *na maiṅ Musalmānī na Hiṅdu hosāṅ; na maiṅ baranāsram mo, na bhekhal rosāṅ* (I am neither a Muslim woman nor a Hindu, I neither

---

[10] Diane Austin-Broos, 'The Anthropology of Conversion: An Introduction', in *The Anthropology of Religious Conversion*, edited by Andrew Buckser and Stephen D. Glazier (Lanham: Rowman and Littlefield Publishers Inc., 2003), p. 1.

[11] Austin-Broos, 'The Anthropology of Conversion', p. 2.

accept varnashramadharma, nor any [order's] costume).[12] This stance is in consonance with the tendency of the late bhakti sects turning to a personal guru for spiritual teaching and emancipation, rejecting both Hinduism and Islam as unquestionably true, as observed by Daniel Gold.[13] However, this did not stop Piro from also asserting that her guru had both Hindus and Muslims as his disciples: *Turak Hind sabh āpke ham chere heve* (We Turaks and Hindus are all your disciples),[14] counting herself among them; she also states that the qualities of Hindus and Muslims were conjointly present in the unplumbed depths of the guru—*sāñjhe Turakāṅ Hinduāṅ guṇ tāṅh athohe*.[15] Rejection of an outward Hindu or Muslim identity, therefore, did not mean that in the ordinary transaction of everyday life such identities did not possess the quality of adhesiveness that stuck to a person, nor even did it mean that the guru, who was above the identities that dogged ordinary mortals, was so because he had in the first instance absorbed their essence. What this means is that a formal desertion of an ascriptive identity may still mean negotiating with given perceptions about the self in the course of life.

Significantly, in all her writings Piro sets up the opposition only between Hindu and Muslim identities, whether to reject such formal identities or incorporate them in the boundless persona of her guru. This trope of invoking Hindu–Muslim oppositional identities can be partly seen as a long legacy of both Sikh and bhakti inheritance of the Gulabdasis. Nanak, the first Sikh guru, is said to have uttered *na ko Hindu haī na Musalmān* (there is neither Hindu nor Muslim) while announcing his enlightenment;[16] and as David Lorenzen has argued, sants and poets like Kabir, Eknath, and Vidyapati in the early modern period in India spoke of distinct Hindu and Muslim identities (if only to reject them), and that these developed in a self-conscious way.[17] Though historians studying political elites have shown that attitudes towards the Muslims varied and

---

[12] 160: 150.

[13] Daniel Gold, *The Lord as Guru: Hindi Sants in North Indian Tradition* (New York: Oxford University Press, 1989), p. 2.

[14] 160: 19.

[15] 160: 151.

[16] W.H. McLeod, *Exploring Sikhism: Aspects of Sikh Identity, Culture and Thought* (New Delhi: Oxford University Press, 2000), p. 27.

[17] D.N. Lorenzen, *Who Invented Hinduism: Essays on Religion in History* (New Delhi: Yoda Press, 2006), pp. 2–3. Lorenzen has argued that setting up a dialogue between two antagonistic figures to define and then reject the common-sense

were a product of the political process, and these could range from their demonization to conceptually incorporating Muslim polities in the early modern period, the bhakti literature more consistently set up Hindu–Muslim opposition, perhaps in order to reject formalist religiosity.[18] More recently, however, scholars studying sant literatures have also argued that the Hindu–Muslim binary must not be overemphasized in their poems, and that angst was also visible for groups similar and intimate to the self, the Shaktas, for example, in Kabir's works. Thus, though the trope of Hindu–Turak opposition may be present, one needs to be cautious and give careful consideration to the contexts in which these works were composed and the specific meanings one may attribute to them.[19] As will be discussed below, and to bring the Sikhs into the equation when discussing Punjab, the ostensible intimacy between Hindu–Sikh identities on the one hand, and the tension between Hindu (Sikh)–Muslim identities on the other, developed and came to be understood in particular ways in Punjab of the eighteenth and nineteenth centuries.

In the setting up of the Hindu–Muslim opposition in Punjab of the mid-nineteenth century, Piro, bhakti's legatee, seemingly ignores the turbulent eighteenth century in Punjab, as she does not delve or expound on the Sikh or Khalsa identity at any length, even as she is aware of them and mentions them, and even though the Gulabdasis can be said to belong to a broader Sikh cultural heritage. The eighteenth century in Punjab was a period of sanguinary struggles between various power brokers, the Mughal governors, the Afghans, the Marathas, and the Sikhs, from among whom the Sikhs ultimately emerged triumphant.[20] Furthermore,

---

understanding of a Hindu and a Muslim was a common trope in bhakti literature. He has discussed Eknath's 'Hindu–Turka Samvad', in *Who Invented Hinduism*, p. 27.

[18] On the political elites, see Cynthia Talbot, 'Inscribing the Other, Inscribing the Self: Hindu–Muslim Identities in Pre-Colonial India', *Comparative Studies in Society and History* 37, no. 4 (1995): 692–721; and Ramya Sreenivasan, 'The Marriage of "Hindu" and "Turak": Medieval Rajput Histories of Jalor', *The Medieval History Journal* 7, no. 1 (2004): 87–108.

[19] See the 'Introduction', in *Religious Interactions in Mughal India*, edited by Vasudha Dalmia and Munis D. Faruqui (New Delhi: Oxford University Press, 2014), pp. ix–xxiv. Also, in the same volume see Heidi Pauwels, 'Diatribes against Saktas in Banarasi Bazaars and Rural Rajasthan: Kabir and His Ramanandi Hagiographer', pp. 290–318.

[20] Purnima Dhavan, *When Sparrows Became Hawks: The Making of the Sikh Warrior Tradition 1699–1799* (New York: Oxford University Press, 2011).

at the fag end of the seventeenth century, the tenth guru of the Sikhs, Gobind Singh, set up the Khalsa, and the literary genres under the aegis of the Sikhs that developed in the eighteenth and the first half of the nineteenth centuries, dealt with fashioning Khalsa identity (the *rahitnāmās*), and celebrated the 'play of the guru' (*gurbilas*), the latter revelling in Pauranic myth and associations with the 'court' of the tenth guru.[21] It is important to keep this history in mind because the Gulabdasis, though closer to sects like the Nirmalas and the Udasis, who in themselves were associated in various ways with the tenth guru, were not outside the processes that shaped relations between different communities and groups in Punjab. In some ways, Piro's ostentatious presentation of the question of her 'conversion' can be explicated only if we keep this background in perspective.

One moment that came to be centrally discussed in the gurbilas literature, starting from the beginning of the genre itself with the *Bachittar Nāṭak* (*The Wonderful Drama*)—believed to have been composed by the tenth guru Gobind Singh—was that of the execution of his father, the ninth guru Tegh Bahadur by the Mughal state under Aurangzeb in 1675, after infliction of extreme torture on him and his associates.[22] What is significant about this moment from our perspective are some of the motifs which stand out in the various gurbilas narrations of the incident well into the nineteenth century.[23] Among these is that the ninth guru offered himself for sacrifice (inasmuch as he asked to be converted before others) in order to ostensibly protect the rights of the Kashmiri pandits to practise their religion and not be coerced into conversion to Islam as the Mughal governor of Kashmir had apparently initiated. The pandits went to the guru for succour and advice, and to protect their

[21] Scholarly writing on these literary genres is extensive. A good place to begin at is Surjit Hans, *A Reconstruction of Sikh History from Sikh Literature* (Jalandhar: ABS Publications, 1988). On the rahitnamas, among others, W.H. McLeod has written extensively. See his *Sikhs of the Khalsa: A History of the Khalsa Rahit* (New Delhi: Oxford University Press, 2003). On the court of the gurus, particularly that of the tenth, see Louis E. Fenech, *The Darbar of the Sikh Gurus: The Court of God in the World of Men* (New Delhi: Oxford University Press, 2008).

[22] On Guru Gobind Singh, see J.S. Grewal and S.S. Bal, *Guru Gobind Singh (A Biographical Study)* (Chandigarh: Punjab University, 1967).

[23] Hari Ram Gupta, 'Guru Tegh Bahadur: A Biographical Study', in *Guru Tegh Bahadur: Background and the Supreme Sacrifice: A Collection of Research Articles*, edited by Gurbachan Singh Talib (Patiala: Punjabi University, 1976), pp. 3–24.

right to bear the 'marks' of their religion, which included the wearing of the forehead mark (*tilak*) and the sacred thread (*janeu*).[24] When incarcerated, the guru, as projected in these narratives, was given the choice of accepting Islam, and along with that the hand of the emperor's daughter, the provinces of Kangra, Atak, Peshawar, and Lahore. Alternatively, being a man of god, he was asked to perform a miracle.[25] The guru explicitly rejected both options and chose to embrace death over conversion or the staging of a miracle. The latter option he reprobated on the grounds, as Anne Murphy has argued, that it represented an intentional demonstration of power, whereas miracles are meant to be the workings of the Lord.[26] Tegh Bahadur's 'supreme sacrifice' for the 'purpose of righteousness', and its interpretation in the *Bachittar Natak* and the later gurbilas inaugurated a new motif in Sikh literature, as Louis Fenech has shown—that of martyrdom, which came to be elaborated by the Singh Sabha polemicists in the late nineteenth century.[27] Later, Guru Gobind's two younger sons, captured by the Mughal officials when the guru was forced to evacuate Anandpur in the Punjab foothills in December 1704, were also executed when they chose not to convert to Islam, adding to the Sikhs' martyr myth.[28]

The condensed account of the topos of conversion as of martyrdom presented above is not to gloss over the complexities of the issues as these came to be subsequently debated in the late nineteenth century by the Singh Sabha activists, or the manner in which scholars of Sikhism

[24] The *Bachittar Natak* reports this as 'The Lord protected the paste mark and the sacred thread; And in Kaliyuga performed a mighty heroic deed; This deed he performed for the protection of Dharma; Gave up his head and not his passion.' (Gupta, 'Guru Tegh Bahadur: A Biographical Study', p. 22.)

[25] Anne Murphy's discussion on the episode of the execution of the ninth guru as represented in various gurbilas has been particularly helpful. See her 'An Idea of Religion: Identity, Difference, and Comparison in the Gurbilas', in *Punjab Reconsidered: History, Culture and Practice*, edited by Anshu Malhotra and Farina Mir (New Delhi: Oxford University Press, 2012), pp. 93–115. Also see J.S. Grewal, *Guru Tegh Bahadur and the Persian Chroniclers* (Amritsar: GNDU, 1976), pp. 78–9.

[26] Murphy, 'An Idea of Religion'. Sikh literature is otherwise replete with miracles performed by the gurus and other holy personages, for example, the Janam-sakhis, the hagiographies on Guru Nanak's life. For a further discussion on the question of miracles, see Chapter 5.

[27] Louis E. Fenech, *Martyrdom in the Sikh Tradition: Playing the 'Game of Love'* (New Delhi: Oxford University Press, 2000), pp. 123–9.

[28] Grewal and Bal, *Guru Gobind Singh*, p. 141.

have discussed the question of the time when sharp distinctions came to mark out Hindu and Sikh/Khalsa identities. For historians like Oberoi, McLeod, and Fenech, there was historically a remarkable fluidity between Hindu/Sikh identities.[29] This is what Oberoi refers to as the sanatan Sikh paradigm, emphasizing diversity within Sikhism, and a broad acceptance of many 'Hindu' social practices, including caste among them. Other scholars have maintained that the rahit and the gurbilas literatures already began to work out distinguishable and sharper Hindu/Sikh identities from the second half of the eighteenth century.[30] Piro in the *160 Kafis* is, in fact, critical of the emerging Khalsa identity, sympathetic to a broader and looser Sikh personhood, but at the same time incorporative of Sikh identity within a capacious Hindu one. In this sense, Fenech is right when he argues that the Singh Sabha understanding of conversion was specifically developed within the colonial/Orientalist perspective.[31] This was a viewpoint which was discomfited with the fuzziness of boundaries, as with hybrid identities, and in Punjab encouraged a Khalsa identity for the Sikhs.[32] What is important to bear in mind here is the growing 'othering' of the Muslims in Sikh literature of the eighteenth century. The 'intractable foe' of the Sikhs was always described as Muslim, whether Mughal or Afghan, as Fenech has observed,[33] even though in the later part of the eighteenth century various Sikh chiefs would both fight or ally with different 'Muslim' chiefs of distinct ethnicity in order to wrest power and territory.[34] This attitude of distancing from the Muslims encompassed Muslim women, so that some rahitnamas specifically ask Khalsa men to refrain from sexual intercourse with Muslim women or interacting with

[29] Thus the question, did Tegh Bahadur make a sacrifice for 'Hindu' religion, which was other than his own?

[30] Harjot Oberoi, *The Construction of Religious Boundaries: Culture, Identity and Diversity in the Sikh Tradition* (New Delhi: Oxford University Press, 1994). Fenech, *Martyrdom in the Sikh Tradition*. On emerging Sikh identity, see Murphy, 'An Idea of Religion'. Also see the 'Introduction' in this book.

[31] Louis E. Fenech, 'Conversion and Sikh Tradition', in *Religious Conversion in India: Modes, Motivations and Meanings*, edited by Rowena Robinson and Sathianathan Clarke (New Delhi: Oxford University Press, 2003), pp. 149–80.

[32] On the role of the colonial state in developing a Khalsa Sikh identity, see Richard Fox, *Lions of the Punjab: Culture in the Making* (Berkeley: University of California Press, 1985), p. 141.

[33] Fenech, *Martyrdom in the Sikh Tradition*, p. 126.

[34] Dhavan, *When Sparrows Became Hawks*.

them.[35] In this context Piro, with her recent abandonment of Islam, and as our sources suggest her intimate relations with her guru Gulabdas, who was broadly associated with Sikh identity, must have found herself in an anomalous situation. Her loud protestations against her Muslim relations and their conniving ways can be seen as overcompensation for the instability of her vulnerable position, as also the enthusiasm of a recent convert. Thus, when she speaks of Hindu–Muslim opposition, she indeed uses an older trope as deployed by various sants in their poetry to which Lorenzen has drawn our attention; but we need to be cognizant of the possibility that in the mid-nineteenth century Punjab, the topos of oppositional religions compressed within it a history of the emerging Sikh/Khalsa identity as well, with its antipathy towards a normative Muslim identity.

The tale of the ninth guru Tegh Bahadur's execution and resistance to conversion to Islam is semiologically rich, especially in its depiction of the righteousness of the demand to display one's religious markers on one's person, in this case the Kashmiri Brahmins' right to sport the tilak and the janeu. The manipulation and use of the body to create identity insignia is as old as civilization itself. The rahitnama literature that developed through the eighteenth and into the nineteenth centuries, worked on bodily symbols effectively to shape a Khalsa identity, particularly the insistence on keeping kes, the uncut hair.[36] More to our point though, the externalities of religious formalism, of which Piro speaks evocatively, were emblems of a faith, and in terms of the discourse on conversion, ready and obvious insignia of a changed identity, to be displayed publicly. The public theatre of conversion or resistance to it was often significant in the premodern worlds, making a spectacle of changed affiliation, or resistance to it, at fractious moments. Ronit Ricci has argued when speaking of the 'Arabic cosmopolis' and the spread of Islam in South and Southeast

---

[35] McLeod, *Sikhs of the Khalsa*, p. 55. In the nineteenth century Giani Gian Singh in his *Tawarikh Guru Khalsa* repeated this injunction to the Khalsa, forbidding them interaction with Muslim women (*musalī*) (McLeod, *Sikhs of the Khalsa*, p. 47). Also see Oberoi, *The Construction of Religious Boundaries*, p. 67.

[36] W.H. McLeod has argued that the normative five Ks of Khalsa identity: *kachh* (long drawers), *karā* (steel bangle), *kirpān* (dagger), *kes* (uncut hair), and *kaṅghā* (comb) in totality did not develop till the time of the Singh Sabha reformers, though a few are mentioned in different rahit literature. See 'The Five Ks', in his *Essays in Sikh History, Tradition, and Society* (New Delhi: Oxford University Press, 2007), pp. 115–23.

Asia through the growth of 'literary networks' and the work of translation therein, that while inner beliefs and convictions remain hidden and elusive, the mere utterance of the *shahādā*, Islamic formula—kalima—was enough to turn one into a Muslim. She speaks of this motif appearing time and again in conversion scenes, 'even when untranslated and potentially unintelligible to the reciter'.[37] Though not an outward symbol as such, the reciting of the shahada was an outward acceptance of a faith and the public portrayal of a changed status. Similarly, Natalie Davis in her study of the remarkable Leo Africanus or al-Hasan al-Wazzan or Yuhanna al-Asad, a sixteenth-century convert from Islam to Christianity, speculates on his memory of witnessing conversion to Islam (submission or surrender to Allah). The moment of conversion, she notes, was a public one of reading the shahada thrice, before witnesses, with the right index finger raised.[38]

In a significant confrontation with the mullahs as reported by Piro in her *160 Kafis*, when they hoped to bring her back into the fold of Islam, Piro depicts being asked by the mullahs to say the kalma, its very utterance sufficient to declare her Islamic status: *awal kalmā yād kar paṛh sifat amāne, hosī pāk palīt te saitān harāme* (first remember the kalma and read the recuperating *sifat aman*, so be purified you illegitimate devilish woman).[39] The same mullahs also accuse her of having 'lost' her faith (*dīn*) on being persuaded to consume pig—*kāhu ne tujhe bigāṛayā jin sūr khilāyo* (who spoilt you by making you eat pig)[40]—by presumably the Gulabdasis. Thus, the insignia of religious affiliation, particularly at the time of 'conversion' (or the threat of its possibility), at the liminal moment of changing identity (or holding on to one when under threat) was publicly displayed, declared, or shown. It was an important marker of who one was, how one wished to be seen, and how one was perceived. This was the public aspect of a new identity, 'a newly inscribed communal self defined through the gaze of the others'.[41] Anthropologists have emphasized that

---

[37] Ronit Ricci, *Islam Translated: Literature, Conversion, and the Arabic Cosmopolis of South and Southeast Asia* (Ranikhet: Permanent Black, 2011), p. 215.

[38] Natalie Z. Davis, *Trickster Travels: The Search for Leo Africanus* (New York: Faber and Faber, 2008), pp. 63, 78.

[39] 160: 26. 'Sifat amane' probably refers to a recuperating (*shifa, shafa*, to restore to health) verse, meant to purify or recover from the stigma of being a kafir. I thank Seema Alavi for suggesting this interpretation.

[40] 160: 26.

[41] Austin-Broos, 'The Anthropology of Conversion', p. 2.

though conversion might occur as a single act, the convert is, however, an 'encultured being', carrying aspects of an older identity, though anxious to relate to the new community. Therefore, the quest of the convert in her changed status is not for a *utopia* but a *habitus*, that is, a 'continual embedding in forms of social practice and belief ... ritual dispositions and somatic experience'.[42] This argument is persuasive as it sensitizes us to the embodied cultural being transitioning into a new self and status, reorienting the self to changed social and bodily structures and habits. However, the point that needs to be underscored for the argument being presented here is that because conversion, in terms of filling into and in the long term living a new identity, cannot be achieved at the moment of change of affiliation, the public declarations of its achievement through signs and symbols become all the more significant. To put it another way, because the process of conversion into a new religious filiation might be gradual or one of constant negotiation, it is important to deploy a symbolic repertoire to display more immediate results. Changed insignia may even play a role in facilitating the reorientation towards the new identity. Alternatively, to display one's religious marks becomes important when one is explicitly rejecting conversion, as with the Kashmiri Brahmins, emphasizing a continuing adherence to marks under threat.[43] Thus, in many ways, whether through new Khalsa practices or through a complex understanding and chronicling of conversion, the idiom of religious symbols was a known and a much used one in Punjab. And so when Piro insistently brings it up in her *160 Kafis* and elsewhere, she was reverting to a semiotic language that had traction there.

However, when Piro brings up somatic semiotics tied to religious affiliation, she does so to reject their power, showing them as bogus externals. I will argue that by ridiculing embodied religious symbols she achieves two ends. On the one hand, by recounting the fracas around her own religious identity—the much ado about her having become a kafir thwarting the symbols of Islamic faith—and by underscoring where she

---

[42] Austin-Broos, 'The Anthropology of Conversion', p. 2.

[43] Of course, one may hide one's identity to escape persecution. Importantly, according to Sikh tradition, Gobind Singh created the Khalsa with their distinct bodily markers because there were Sikhs in the audience that witnessed the ninth guru's execution but were too afraid to openly show their Sikh affiliation. On the other hand, some cultures recognized the political compulsion of 'precautionary dissimulation' to escape persecution. See the discussion on the practice of *taqiyya* among Muslims in Davis, *Trickster Travels*, pp. 188–9.

belongs in her new-found Gulabdasi identity, she attempts to overcome the ambivalence that her recently changed status may have caused. On the other hand, by rejecting formalist identity she anchors herself in bhakti, and in Punjab Sufi, traditions that mercilessly ribbed those tied to religious formalism. Thus, Piro manages to simultaneously speak of religious insignia, even while rejecting their significance.

At many places in Piro's *160 Kafis*, therefore, we encounter her associating men of Hindu or Muslim denominations with their somatic religious marks:

> *Kūṛe majab banaut ke kar kūṛe dāve*
> *Liṅg mūchh ko kāt ke phir Turak kahāve*
> *Hiṅdu baṇe baṇaut ke dhar janyu chotī*
> *Baṇe baṇaut na nāriaṅ gal dono khoṭī.*

They make false creeds by making false claims
Snipping the penis and the moustache they call themselves Turak
Hindus are made by the wearing of the sacred thread and the top knot
Women cannot be made, thus, both are counterfeit.[44]

Drawing attention to the externalities of faith, Piro seemingly draws equivalences between the Muslims with their specific somatic symbols and the Hindus with theirs. At other places, too, this strategy of equivalences is deployed in order to reject both identities, which in essence are declared to be similar. Thus, *Hiṅdu paṭh haiṅ bed ko yeh Turak Kurāne* (Hindus read the Vedas and the Turak the Koran);[45] or later, she speaks of the Muslims and Hindus both as showmen out to fool the innocent, but really as men with grasping hands, the former differentiated as cow slayers (*gau ke kasbī*) discussing the Koran, and the latter as sitting in cow shelters (*gau kī sāle'*);[46] or even equivalent in their ignorance: *Hiṅdu anne sāhab te yeh Musle kāṇe* (Hindus are blind sir and these Muslims one-eyed).[47] The purpose of these statements was to underscore the falsehood of the ways of the Hindus and the Muslims, both, in fact, similar in their cussed insistence on religious form as seen in its symbols, as against the enlightened path of her guru, tuned to interiorized growth.

Further, two things stand out in Piro's statements that reject Hindu–Muslim identity. Firstly, the whole tenor of her writings point out that

---

[44] 160: 44.
[45] 160: 18.
[46] 160: 154.
[47] 160: 19.

she underlines her antagonism towards the Muslims far more sharply than towards the Hindus, whether in her confrontation with the mullahs, Muslim men, or Mehrunissa, the woman she encounters in her captivity, as outlined in the previous chapter. This was so because they were the ones who assaulted her independent choice or worked towards impos- ing their wishes on her. Moreover, her repudiation of Muslims must be seen in the light of her anxiety to underscore her successful conversion to Gulabdasi tenets. The precariousness of her situation then shaped her narrative that desperately attempted convincing her various interlocutors of the sagacity of her choice. Of course, the attempted denial of choice to her was a matter also of her gender, her womanly status instrumental in the community of men denying her choice—the angry Muslim men she refers to in her *160 Kafis*. Thus, also, her gendered identity surfaces almost every time she ridicules the externals of Hindu or Islamic faiths. It is to examine some aspects of her gendered self that we now turn.

PIRO'S GENDERED SUBJECTIVITY

Every time Piro brings up the outward signs of religious identity, she avers that these symbols define only men and are redundant for women, as in the above quoted verse. Here she ridicules what she calls spurious and empty bodily symbolism, whether of a style of facial hair or circumcision, a top knot or sacred thread, both somatic pairs a requirement for Muslim or Hindu men and inapplicable to women. Indeed, every time she brings up prescriptive somatic signs, she follows it up by stating the impossi- bility of their defining women's religious selves. It is important to note that the difficulty of the same signs marking women's religiosity as that of men was not only a function of physical or biological difference, but was centrally a cultural one. While women may not have facial hair or a penis, the fact that the Muslim faithful were identified with these meant that only men's public religiosity was salient, women in Muslim societ- ies were theoretically confined to the *zaif*—the non-discursive domestic realm.[48] Similarly, the signs of highborn socio-religious standing for the

---

[48] Faisal F. Devji, 'Gender and the Politics of Space: The Movement for Women's Reform 1857–1900', in *Women and Social Reform in India*, vol. 2, edited by Sumit Sarkar and Tanika Sarkar (Ranikhet: Permanent Black, 2011 [2007]), p. 103. It is another matter that today the fully veiled female body is itself a religious marker of Islam.

Hindus reflected that women were traditionally denied knowledge that would allow them a twice-born status to sport the sacred thread or the top knot, and came to be associated with sudras, the lowest category in the varna hierarchy, the difference being that with the Hindus a class of men was also denied the same. The Khalsa, too, worked out somatic symbols only for men, with the incorporation of women into the symbolic system being attempted only under the aegis of a very small group within the Singh Sabha reformers late into the nineteenth century.[49] Piro's contention, therefore, was that the mainstream religions were incapable of defining women's piety and must be rejected on those grounds.

Choṭī janyu Hindpaṇā yeh bāt na koī
Nārī kā kīj haī tis dono nāhī.

Top knot, sacred thread, Hinduness, what is this?
What will you do with a woman, she has neither?[50]

Liṅg mūch ko kāt ke yeh Turak banāhī
Nārī kya banāvso tāṅh dono nāhī.

Snipping the penis and the moustache they make Turaks
What will you make of a woman, she has neither?[51]

Baṇyo Sikh baṇaut ke lak kachhā pāyo...
Nārī Kachh na pāī le tis kae kareṅse.

You make Sikhs by putting drawers on their loins
A woman will not wear drawers, what will you do?[52]

---

[49] This was the Bhasaur group. See Doris R. Jakobsh and Eleanor Nesbitt, 'Introduction–Sikhism and Women: Contextualizing the Issues', in *Sikhism and Women: History, Texts and Experience*, edited by Doris R. Jakobsh (New Delhi: Oxford University Press, 2010), p. 12.

[50] 160:132.

[51] 160: 133.

[52] 160: 136. Here, Piro is clearly speaking of the Khalsa identity, but still calls it 'Sikh', though the semantic weight of both terms is not identical. This is evident from the next two lines of the verse: *Sikhyā Sikhī chhoṛ ke tāṅh baṇat banāyo; Pāhul chhoṛ akhaṇḍ ko khaṇḍe kī deseṅ* (Setting aside the teaching of Sikhness they have manufactured new things; Leaving the initiation in the name of the indivisible one, they now give by the double-edged sword). The play on the word 'khand', literally to fragment, is ironical, with 'akhand' signifying the Supreme Indivisible Being, and 'khanda', to splinter, as the Khalsa among the Sikhs, signifying a double-edged sword.

Matters of formal religiosity that so occupied men, Piro suggests, were
not only meaningless triviality, but what got her gall was the power that
men asserted over women, bandying about as leaders of communities
with rights over them. Piro portrays the saga of her abduction and incarceration in these terms, the wholly illegitimate and bogus positing of
rights over her person by her clan. Piro makes this amply clear in her
kafi quoted above where she speaks of Muslim men and their somatic
religiosity. Therein she continues: *Musalmān nah nar ko kyoṅ tāṅ har
lāveṅ ... thoṛī jaisī bāt mo korāhme mache* (Then why do the Muslim men
kidnap a woman ... and make a riot of a small thing?).[53] The 'small thing'
she refers to was the exercise of her autonomous will in choosing her
own salvific path, and so an assertion of control over her life and personhood, which was sought to be denied to her by her forcible kidnapping
and confinement. At another place, and in almost identical language,
Piro again brings up the outward and somatic religiosity of men (*nar*),
implying its vacuity, on the strength of which, however, they exercise very
real power over women (*nārī*): *liṅg mūchh nar kātke tum dīn banāyo, nārī
na tumre dīn mo kyuṅ tāṅ har lāyo* (snipping the penis and moustaches
of men you make your religion, women are not in your religion then
why abduct her?).[54] The emptiness of Muslim men's religiosity, for Piro,
then, unravelled the power they possessed over women, for the externals
of their religion disallowed membership to women. Hence, in the logic
proffered by Piro, women could not be Muslim (or Hindu) and, therefore,
were outside the control of men of these religions, and so autonomous.
One may suggest that the disability that the religious elite men placed on
women (and low castes in Hinduism) was upended by Piro in denounc-
ing men's rights over women (and low castes). Elsewhere, too, Piro
questions these apparently assumed rights of men over women of their
communities, fuming against the sordid bargains men apparently made,
exchanging women, for instance, in the name of their religions. Here is
Piro's lament:

> *Pīro kahe pukār ke sabh majbī rāteṅ*
> *Majbāṅ ke sab kūkre kyā bole bāteṅ*
> *Apne-apne majab ko dono parveseṅ*
> *Majab vadhāvaṇ vāste saṭh dhiāṅ deseṅ*
> *Na sukh vāṛe Turak ke na Hindu chauṇe*
> *Sukh dar dās Gulāb ke jāṅh parmat bhauṇe.*

[53] 160: 133.
[54] 160: 39.

Piro says aloud that all are in the darkness of religion
Dogs of religion what can they say?
They both make [others] enter their religions
To inflate [numbers] they are willing to give sixty daughters
There is no happiness in the house of the Turaks, nor should one choose
the Hindus
Happiness is at the door of Das Gulab where the Supreme One roams.[55]

In the previous chapter, it has been suggested that Piro, as a 'daughter'
in a brothel, perhaps, felt constrained by the institution of concubinage,
temporary marriages, or other short-term sexual relationships that were
imposed upon women by her profession and clan. Here I will attempt to
conjecture any further meanings we can attribute to this statement, but
before that let us briefly visit the speculative writing on Piro's background.

Piro's writing gives us very tentative glimpses of her past life, as of
her present one, except for one specific incident in her life, a shaping
anecdote of her becoming a Gulabdasi novitiate, which we have discussed
at length in the previous chapter. While there are fairly obvious autobiographical references in her various writings other than the *160 Kafis*, it
is very difficult to place them in any sequential way in her life, though
a number of writers have done just that.[56] However, from her different
verses her Muslim past does emerge clearly, as I have shown, as too the
fact that she had foregone her Islamic identity. Indeed, one may push
the point to suggest that Piro underscores at many places her sense of
disaffection with Islam and the knowledge given by the Islamic religious
persons, and that she turned to Gulabdas to discover her self.

Lāī akal pehle kājīyāṅ dī kalmā sarā dā tāṅh paṛhāiyo ne
Rakh rojiyāṅ paṛhā nivāj sarā, tinhoṅ nām rasūl janāyo ne
Dekho kehar kiyā inhā kājiyāṅ ne, haī sī hor te hor batāiyo ne
Karam bakhsī karī Pīro Ārafāṅ ne, har apna āp janāyo ne.

I learnt from the qazis first, they taught me the kalma and the Shari'ah
I kept rozas, and bowed to the Shari'ah, they taught me of the Prophet
See the wrong the qazis have done, it was something else and they said
something else
The Gnostics saved me, they showed me to know myself.[57]

---

[55] 160: 45.

[56] The first scholarly article that does that is Devendra Singh Vidyarthi, 'Punjabi
di Pehli Istri Kavi', *Khoj Darpan*, vol. 1, no. 2 (1974): 89–95. Others have been
discussed in Chapter 7.

[57] *SS: 24.* Knowing the self was a part of monist doctrine.

Piro foregrounds her professional identity, calling herself a sudar vesva, a low-caste prostitute. Our late nineteenth-century source of Gian Singh's *Panth Prakash* refers to her as 'kasbi' and 'musali', underlining her low-caste religious identity along with her professional identity as a prostitute/whore through these terms.[58] He calls those who also became Gulabdas's disciples because of her *besiyā* and kanjari, implying prostitutes, even using the term *kanchanī*, prostitute/dancing girl, once. Our other Nirmala historian Ganesha Singh calls her a kanjari, all, therefore, underlining her past in prostitution.[59]

There are two prevailing opinions on how Piro landed in prostitution. Devendra Vidyarthi, the first scholar to work on her poetry, reports that he started working on Punjabi women poets in 1943 in Lahore and received valuable information from the well-known Punjabi literary figure Kushtaji on the background of these poets.[60] Though he lost all he had collected in the melee of the Partition, his interest in this project, particularly Piro, was revived when the erudite Punjabi scholar Shamsher Singh Ashok tasked him to work on Punjabi handwritten manuscripts in Patiala. According to Vidyarthi, Piro came from a family of small-time landowners in Gujranwala. She lost her mother when she was very young. Her father kept the company of Sufis and holy men, and she subsequently ran away with one such older man who took her to Lahore. He died after a few years and Piro was left to fend for herself taking recourse to prostitution.

The other story has been popularized by Vijender Das, the present guru of a branch of the Gulabdasis in Hansi, Haryana, in his compilation of Piro's writings to which he has given an elaborate introduction.[61]

---

[58] The term 'musali' was used by Gian Singh to mean a low-caste Muslim woman. He uses the term in the same way in his *Tawarikh Guru Khalsa* as quoted by McLeod, *Sikhs of the Khalsa*, p. 47. According to Ibbetson, a musali referred to a low-caste Muslim Chuhra (scavenger/sweeper). See D.C.J. Ibbetson, *Punjab Castes* (Patiala: Bhasha Vibhag, 2000 [1883]), pp. 294–5.

[59] See Chapter 1.

[60] Munshi Maula Bakhsh 'Kushta', was a poet, scribe, and a compiler of the biographical accounts of Punjabi poets. Among other writings, Kushta compiled *Punjabi Shairan da Tazkra*. (R.P. Malhotra and Kuldeep Arora, eds, *Encyclopaedic Dictionary of Punjabi Literature* [Delhi: Global Vision Publishing House, 2003], pp. 306–7.)

[61] Sant Vijender Das, *Sant Kavyitri Ma Piro* (Panchkula: Satluj Prakashan, 2011). See Chapter 8 for a further discussion on Vijender Das, his writing, and his guruship.

Vijender Das assumes sectarian Gulabdasi authority for his voice derived from what he has heard from an older sant, Milkhi Shah, of his sect. Broadly keeping with Vidyarthi's recounting of Piro's early loss of her parents, he differs from him by stating that Piro came from a family of the low-caste musicians and genealogists, the Mirāsīs, and that her own uncle (*chāchā*) pushed her into their 'traditional' trade of singing and dancing (performing *mujrā*) after she lost both her parents.[62] Vijender Das builds his narrative of pathos around the idea that Piro was always spiritually inclined, and she felt trapped as a caged bird in the brothel, a house of sin, using neologisms—*pāpāgar, vaishyālaya*—to describe the brothel. He also quoted her appropriate verses to buttress his argument, as for instance:

> *Daso saheliyo meriyon nī, main te sach dī rāh puchhāvniyān*
> *Jis rāh main pīr faqīr gaye main tan ose nun nit dhiyāvniyān.*

> Tell me my friends, I ask for the path of truth
> The road taken by holy men, I daily think of that.[63]

In Das's rendition of Piro's story, a client of Piro once chanced upon her singing of her spiritual yearning and suggested she go to Gulabdas in Chathianwala to seek spiritual solace. He helped her reach there one early morning when Gulabdas was out on horseback for his daily ride, and who out of compassion gave her shelter.[64] The only problem with this 'cultural script' of the rescue of a helpless woman (*vivash, ablā*) is that Piro herself reports meeting the guru in Lahore's Moti Bazaar as he gave a discourse to those assembled there, as discussed in the previous chapter.[65] Thus, it is difficult to ascertain how Piro came to be a prostitute, or even if she

---

[62] The term 'mujra', a singing and dancing performance particularly by prostitutes, is used by Piro herself as in one of the verses quoted in the epigraph. Piro never shied away from her past in prostitution; indeed, in this verse she defiantly uses it to mock pious niceties of Hindus and Turaks. The term 'mujra' is also used by Gian Singh, who says disapprovingly that after Piro many other prostitutes became Gulabdas's disciples and in his establishment, instead of communal singing and storytelling of the religious kind, mujras started taking place (*kirtan kathā thor nit mujrā hui kanchanī kero* [Giani Gian Singh, *Sri Guru Panth Prakash* (Patiala: Bhasha Vibhag, 1970, first published 1880), p. 1294]). Following him Ganesha Singh too uses this term. See the next chapter for further discussion.

[63] *S1*: 9.

[64] Das, *Sant Kavyitri Ma Piro*, pp. 7–10, 20–6.

[65] On cultural scripts see Chapter 7.

was born into a family that pursued this profession. After all, her Islamic background, about which we know for sure, does not give any clue to how she came to be in Lahore or in this profession.

It is also difficult to say if Piro always had a spiritual yearning; but what is relevant for our discussion here is that her abandonment of her profession and religion had consequences, which she reports in the *160 Kafis*. Significantly, neither Gian Singh in the late nineteenth century, nor Vidyarthi perusing handwritten manuscripts in the 1950s and the 1960s mentions any conflict over Piro's person, the latter having come across her siharfis, but not her *160 Kafis*. However, Piro's narrative and the reportage of Ganesha Singh, as mentioned in Chapter 1, speak of a discordant situation developing out of her bold step.[66] While Piro speaks about it in terms of her abduction and forcible imprisonment in Wazirabad, Singh informs that Gulabdas's men clashed with a general of Ranjit Singh, the gunner Ilahi Khan Jarnail (Ilahi Bakhsh), who instigated Piro's brothers, and the two sides had a run-in near the tomb of Mian Mir in Lahore.[67] In this skirmish apparently many were wounded, and the situation was brought under control when Maharaja Ranjit Singh himself intervened, subsequent to which Gulabdas and Piro settled at Chathianwala. The development of this fractious situation explains the recurring references in Gulabdas's writing, and also in that of his disciples including Piro, that he had to face humiliation and he frequently displayed his angst against Ranjit Singh.

The facts that Piro was on the fringes of the court of Ranjit Singh and that the Maharaja may have himself intervened to settle the matters between the rival claims over Piro—her guardians and brothers on the one side and Gulabdas on the other, with whom Piro threw in her lot—propel us to probe Piro's status further. What did it mean to be a prostitute, a possible concubine, and a vulnerable woman who had little control over her life, whose sexual favours and access to her person could be bought? We must also turn our attention to the social situation of many women in the precolonial period—women from the highest to the lowest sections of society—who were either honourably married as daughters of feudatories and subordinates, or captured after defeat, and

---

[66] Mahant Ganesha Singh, *Bharat Mat Darpan* [hereinafter *BMD*] (Amritsar: Vaidak Bhandar, 1926), p. 128.

[67] Ganesha Singh reports that Gulabdas was surrounded, but then two hundred of his Sikh followers arrived and had a brush with Ilahi Khan's men. Ganesha Singh, *BMD*, p. 128.

kept in varying states of unfreedom. A look at the time and court of Ranjit Singh will give a glimpse of the material realities of women's lives in the period that Piro inhabited.

The most powerful man of Punjab in the first four decades of the nineteenth century, Ranjit Singh, was not gifted with good looks. He was said to be dark and his face was pitted with marks, the result of small pox, which also took one of his eyes. According to Emily Eden, the sister of Governor General Auckland, who accompanied him in his tour of north India in 1838, he looked 'exactly like an old mouse with grey whiskers and one eye'.[68] Be that as it may, Ranjit Singh had regal tastes and was said to be rather fond of horses and women. Legendary tales regarding both circulated; for example, the stories of the horse Laili, which he was said to have acquired with cunning and deceit, or his courtesan wife Moran, towards whom he was said to be particularly solicitous.[69] These 'objects' of his desire sometimes came to him when aggrandizing his empire, whether in war, or while strategizing alliances in order to avoid one, when enjoying the fruits of victory, or when asserting authority over enemies and subordinates.

He is said to have had forty-six women in his harem, of which there were 'four categories': (*a*) nine wives 'duly married according to the Sikh custom', (*b*) nine widows (some of defeated chiefs?) whom he married by the informal ceremony of *chādar andāzī*, or putting a sheet over a woman, (*c*) seven courtesans, and (*d*) his many concubines; the first three categories having the status of queens.[70] Some of these liaisons were clearly made to further political alliances, for example, his first and second wives, Mehtab Kaur, the daughter of the powerful Kanhaiya

---

[68] Emily Eden as quoted in Khushwant Singh, *Ranjit Singh: Maharajah of the Punjab* (London: George Allen and Unwin Ltd, 1962), p. 7.

[69] For details, see Fakir Syed Waheeduddin, *The Real Ranjit Singh* (Patiala: Publications Bureau Punjabi University, 1981). Kartar Singh Duggal, *Maharaja Ranjit Singh: The Last to Lay Arms* (New Delhi: Abhinav Publications, 2001). Duggal has devoted a short chapter to Ranjit Singh's acquisition of the magnificent horse, Laili, from the defeated Afghans (from whom he also managed to usurp the Koh-i-Noor diamond), and another on the 'Affairs of the Heart', whereas Waheeduddin's chapter on wives is called 'Unequal Sweethearts, Equal Wives'. The presentation of Ranjit Singh's various sexual relationships in both books is presented as the legitimate dalliance of a very popular king.

[70] Duggal, *Maharaja Ranjit Singh*, pp. 63–7. Waheeduddin, *The Real Ranjit Singh*, p. 165.

misal[71] chief Gurbaksh Singh and his equally powerful widow Sada Kaur's daughter; and Raj Kaur of the Nakai misal.[72] Both these wives had sons, two of whom eventually succeeded Ranjit Singh, though for very short periods of time.[73] On the other hand, the two daughters of Sansar Chand, the ruler of Kangra (now in Himachal Pradesh), Guddan and Raj Banso, whom Ranjit Singh married in 1829, can be seen to be 'tributes' seized from a feudatory chief. In the biographies of Ranjit Singh, these two wives are presented as blue-blooded Rajput princesses, though Ranjit Singh is said to have married them after an expedition conducted especially for their sake. However, other sources inform us that after the death of Sansar Chand, and in the time of his son and successor Anirudh Chand, Ranjit Singh hoped to marry his courtier Dhian Singh's son, Hira Singh, whom he treated like a son, to one of Anirudh's sisters. Unhappy with this demand Anirudh had the sisters, daughters of Sansar Chand's wife Prasanna Devi, married in secrecy and haste to Raja Sudarshan Shah of Tehri Garhwal. However, Sansar Chand also had two daughters by his concubine Gulab Dasi, who wed Ranjit Singh in 1829. Anirudh had probably abdicated his throne by this time.[74] While the anecdote of Anirudh Chand's sisters from his father's wife and those from his concubine tells us about the different statuses of children from varied states of matrimony and sexual liaisons, the story of which children from which kind of a wife/sexual partner may inherit a kingdom, or would be in line for succession, indexes stark hierarchies within the harem and the domestic realm.

We also hear of at least two Muslim courtesan wives of Ranjit Singh, Moran Sarkar and Gul Bahar Begum. This is significant, because as a Khalsa man, and despite the parallel emergence of rahit literature that sought to define the norms for Khalsa men including a distancing from

---

[71] *Misal/misl* refers to eighteenth-century Sikh band of soldiers organized under a commander or leader, a *misaldār*. Among the powerful misaldars were Ranjit Singh's grandfather Charhat Singh Sukerchakia.

[72] Sada Kaur played a very important role in guiding the young Ranjit Singh to power in Punjab.

[73] Waheeduddin, *The Real Ranjit Singh*, p. 165. These were Raj Kaur's son Kharak Singh, and Mehtab Kaur's son Sher Singh.

[74] This has been pieced together through trawling the internet: https://en.wikipedia.org/wiki/Sansar_Chand; and the official Kangra district website: hpkangra.nic.in/abtus_history.html. Both sites were accessed on 20 December 2014.

Muslim women, as discussed earlier, he openly married Muslim women. According to some accounts, he was summoned to the Akal Takht in Amritsar, recognized as a seat of Sikh religious authority, after marrying Moran. He was handed a punishment of flogging, and a fine of over one lakh rupees was imposed upon him. These he accepted, though ultimately the counsel revoked the flogging.[75] Of course, as a king Ranjit could do what others could not, but his marriages to Muslim women do tell us about the famed 'secularity' of his times, quite in contrast to the religious dissension, albeit regarding her own person, that Piro suggests. His various biographers present him as a devout Sikh, but one who was non-discriminatory in his attitude, and who employed men of all religions in his court and army.[76]

Ranjit Singh was said to have been smitten by Moran, a courtesan of Amritsar, at the age of twenty-two, and married her in 1802. She is the only queen in whose name Ranjit struck a coin which bore the figure of a peacock (*mor*) 'in keeping with the queen's name ... and which she acquired because of her style of dancing'.[77] There are many tales about Ranjit's love and respect for Moran, including that she did not observe purdah and appeared with the Maharaja publicly, and that in 1831 at Ropar, Ranjit Singh was reminded of his own relationship with Moran when he saw the British governor general Lord William Bentinck's fondness for his wife— a story that even found its way in the work of the official diarist of the

---

[75] Duggal, *Maharaja Ranjit Singh*, p. 63. Other accounts present the Nihang chief Phula Singh as having imposed this punishment on Ranjit Singh. See Aruti Nayar, 'Moran, the Mystery Woman', *The Tribune*, 24 August 2008. Available at: http://www.tribuneindia.com/2008/20080824/spectrum/main3.htm, retrieved on 28 November 2014.

[76] Khushwant Singh begins his biography of the Maharaja with the anecdote of Ranjit Singh's purchase of a very expensive Quran from a calligraphist which he then presented to his senior minister Fakir Azizuddin, saying that 'God intended me to look at all religions with one eye'. K. Singh, *Ranjit Singh*, p. 7. Duggal has devoted a whole chapter to his 'secularism', also informing us that there were more than forty Muslim officers in his forces including two generals, one of whom was Ilahi Bakhsh. *Maharaja Ranjit Singh*, pp. 125–30. One assumes this is the same Ilahi Bakhsh of the Piro affair.

[77] Waheeduddin, *The Real Ranjit Singh*, p. 168. Khushwant Singh refers to her name as Mohran, which invokes *mohar*, stamp/coin in her name, referred to as *Moranshahi* currency. See his *The Real Ranjit Singh*, p. 7, and Duggal, *Maharaja Ranjit Singh*, p. 64.

king, Sohan Lal Suri's *Umdat-ut-Tawarikh*.[78] There is a bridge named after Moran near Amritsar called in common parlance *Pul Kanjarī* (Prostitute's Bridge), and she is said to have had a mosque built in Lahore.[79] Whether Ranjit was reminded of Moran or not, we also learn that it was at Ropar that he saw another courtesan of Amritsar, Gul Begum, dance before his English guests, and captivated by her decided to marry her, and this wedding was also recorded by Suri.[80] This queen, too, did not observe purdah, and accompanied him on an elephant in royal processions.[81]

The hierarchies that existed in the domestic arrangements of Ranjit Singh—between queens who were in seclusion and those who had relatively more freedom, and could be seen in public as former courtesans; those who were designated queens and duly married and those who were mere concubines; yet others who were 'slave girls'—manifested themselves in other ways as well. The death of Sansar Chand's daughter, Raj Banso, is of particular interest in this regard. Apparently Ranjit Singh, who occasionally held durbars or courts for his queens, once asked a dancing girl, Allah Jowai, which of his queens she thought to be the most beautiful. Hesitating to offend all but one queen, Allah Jowai had to point out one, because of the insistence of the Maharaja. She indicated Raj Banso, upon which Ranjit Singh asked her if she did not find Moran Sarkar of comparable beauty. Raj Banso, it is reported, was so offended by this comparison with a former courtesan that she took an overdose of opium and died in her bed chamber, much to the grief and remorse of the king.[82] The tale, whether true or apocryphal, points to the extraordinary effort the queen had to make to prove her Rajput ancestry and its uncompromising ways as far as the purity of its women was concerned, particularly as she was born to a concubine. The other sister, Guddan, was one of the four wives of Ranjit Singh who committed sati on his funeral pyre, along with seven slave girls.[83]

[78] Duggal, *Maharaja Ranjit Singh*, pp. 63–4; Waheeduddin, *The Real Ranjit Singh*, p. 170.

[79] A play on Moran has been written by Manveen Sandhu called *Moran Sarkar*, which was staged at Amritsar. Nayar, 'Moran, the Mystery Woman'. By all accounts his Muslim wives practised their religion.

[80] Duggal, *Maharaja Ranjit Singh*, p. 66.

[81] Duggal, *Maharaja Ranjit Singh*, p. 66.

[82] Waheeduddin, *The Real Ranjit Singh*, p. 168.

[83] J.M. Honigberger wrote his eyewitness account of the satis committed by the queens and slave girls of Ranjit Singh. See the note of Edward Thompson in

The high-caste ceremonies at Ranjit Singh's death, different marriage patterns he adopted in life, including the relatively informal *chādar
andāzī* liaisons, and the manifold categories of wives and concubines he
kept in his harem, points to a fluid situation on the ground as far as
acceptance and prevalence of different kinds of sexual relationships in
society are concerned. Along with that it demonstrates the availability
of several categories of women often serving as slaves, whether readily
bought in the market, or procured as captives through wars, exchanged
through strategic alliances, or those forced to sell selves or children due
to indigent situations, as has been well documented for long periods
of Indian history.[84] Such commodification of women was a part of the
history of Punjab as well where selling of women—*bardāfaroshī*—was a
practice that went on at least until the end of the nineteenth century.[85]
The litterateur Krishna Sobti, known for some of her novellas on Punjabi
women exploring, among others, issues of their sexuality, captured the
precarious life of one such woman, Pasho, who for various reasons
entered this market at the time of flux during the Anglo-Sikh wars in
Punjab. The remarkable changing of hands and ownership that Pasho
experienced, moving from one household into another of different castes,
religions, and social positions, speaks of the inherent instability of some
of their lives.[86] The use of labour and reproductive labour of these women
and their progeny has been commented upon by historians. The unequal
status of the children of different categories of women as compared to the
children of wives married according to high-caste rituals has also received
attention, particularly when the desire for purity of descent and inheritance increased in society.[87] Significantly, the labour that went into honing

---

Emily Eden, *Up the Country: Letters Written to Her Sister from the Upper Provinces of
India* (London: Curzon Press, 1978 [1930]), pp. 407–8.

[84] See the Introduction and the various essays in *Slavery and South Asian History*,
edited by Indrani Chatterjee and Richard M. Eaton (Bloomington: Indiana University
Press, 2006).

[85] On the persistence of selling or trafficking of women—*bardafaroshi* (slave
trading)—into the colonial period see Anshu Malhotra, *Gender, Caste and Religious
Identities: Restructuring Class in Colonial Punjab* (New Delhi: Oxford University Press,
2002), pp. 65–7.

[86] Krishna Sobti, *Dar se Bichhuri* (New Delhi: Rajkamal, 1984 [1958]). I thank
Francesca Orsini for drawing my attention to this novella.

[87] Ramya Sreenivasan, 'Drudges, Dancing Girls, Concubines: Female Slaves in
Rajput Polity, 1500–1850', in Chatterjee and Eaton, *Slavery and South Asian History*
(Bloomington: Indiana University Press, 2006), pp. 136–61.

the arts of a dancing girl was also appreciated. Ramya Sreenivasan, for example, speaks of the high value placed in Rajput polity on the skills of well-trained and coveted *pātars* (dancing girl).[88] Lahore and Amritsar in Punjab were well known for the arts of the dancing girls, which produced the likes of Moran, Gul Bahar, or Piro, where their training, it is said, began by the age of five and continued for up to nine years. They were, it seems, renowned for their physical charms, the whiteness of their teeth, and their beautiful hands and feet![89]

In this Punjab of the middle decades of the nineteenth century then— where dancing girls and courtesans flourished as did the trade in women who could be purchased as slaves, concubines, and wives, where sharp hierarchies existed between the various categories of women, their kin and their progeny—what chances did Piro have of asserting her individual choice? What chances did she have of establishing her will when a some-what important general of the kingdom, Ilahi Baksh, as Ganesha Singh has informed us, coveted her? In the face of the fact that a woman like her represented potential sexual liaisons, reproductive capacity, and skill in music and dance to those who had authority over her person, could Piro hope to act autonomously? The enormity of Piro's transgression in her refusal to become a concubine or a sexual partner to a nameless charmer (*chhaliyā*), or a vile person adamant in acquiring her (*paṅbar*), as Piro reports, must be gauged keeping this background in mind.

> *Pīro kehsī kachiyoṅ kyuṅ chhitar joṛe*
> *Khachru tumrā jaṇiyo ham chhaliyā loṛe*
> *Paula karat salām mam is paṅbar bīvī*
> *Mukh iske kadī na lagsāṅ hauṅ jab lag jīvī.*

> Piro says unripe ones why shouldn't you be beaten by shoes?
> I know your wiliness in finding me a lover
> I was asked to first greet this vile person as a wife(?)
> But I will not interact with him as long as I have life.[90]

It is with this background in mind then that we must interpret her statement of trading in daughters, the metaphorical sixty daughters she refers to—*majab vadhāvaṇ vāste saṭh dhiāṅ dese*[91]—her accusation of her

[88] Sreenivasan, 'Drudges, Dancing Girls, Concubines', pp. 136–61.

[89] G.S. Chhabra, *Social and Economic History of the Panjab (1849–1901)* (New Delhi: Sterling Publishers, 1962), pp. 87–8.

[90] 160: 50.

[91] 160: 44.

abductors as exploiters of daughters/girls. Was Piro then hoping to escape her fate as an exploitable woman whose sexual or reproductive labour could be readily marketed or be made available to different bargainers by dressing her grievance in the language of religious acrimony? Let us understand her 'conversion narrative' to draw some conclusions.

PIRO'S CONVERSION NARRATIVE

Scholars working on life writing discuss conversion narratives as structured around the idea of a radical transformation of the self, 'from a faulty "before" self to an enlightened "after" self'.[92] Even if, as we have seen, the process of conversion was slow, filled with negotiations and tensions, it may be presented as a dramatic public event, as, for instance, Piro's abduction and escape. Though the notion of a conversion narrative is steeped in evangelical Christian ethos—a moment of epiphany or new beginnings—the idea of sharp and significant change in life has been applied to various situations, particularly to religious transformations. Thus such moments of revelation, of 're-routing' life on a different track or new spiritual directions has been especially noticed in tales of bhakti saints.[93] For women bhakti saints like Mirabai, the sixteenth-century Rajput princess, or Mahadeviyakka, the eleventh-century Kannada poet, the time of marriage and its unambiguous rejection are presented as radically transformative in stories about them.[94] In his study of renegade women who consciously chose conversion in order to escape variously difficult domestic situations, Eric Dursteler particularly emphasizes the desire to escape unwanted marriages.[95] In this sense, Piro's rejection of concubinage or wifeliness, as the case may have been, and her turning to Gulabdas and his sect can be seen in a similar light: a definitive disengagement with any form of domestic arrangement in preference of a spiritual path. The aural reception of the guru's discourse in Moti Bazaar of Lahore that Piro tells us about can be taken to be that momentous

[92] Sidonie Smith and Julia Watson, *Reading Autobiography: A Guide for Interpreting Life Narratives* (Minneapolis: Minnesota University Press, 2000), p. 266.

[93] David Arnold and Stuart Blackburn, eds, *Telling Lives in India: Biography, Autobiography and Life History* (New Delhi: Permanent Black, 2004), p. 14.

[94] Arnold and Blackburn, *Telling Lives in India*, p. 27n18. See Chapters 4 and 5 for more on women saints.

[95] Eric Dursteler, *Renegade Women: Gender, Identity, and Boundaries in Early Modern Mediterranean* (Baltimore: The Johns Hopkins University Press, 2011), p. 115.

time of transmutation, the 'before' and 'after' of which were essentially two different lives of the same person. Was this something that Piro could do only by repudiating Islam rather than staying within its fold? Did the cleaving from the past and the obligations of her life in prostitution also require an identity makeover so that it became acceptable to the world and, indeed, to her? Of course, her forsaking of her profession and religion were public events, as Ganesha Singh informs us. However, here I seek to draw a relation between those events and her vocal and vociferous repudiation of her earlier religious identity. It is as if by asserting her soteriological choice that the other choices she made in life—of abandoning her professional life and its guardians—could also be avouched and validated.

The question that also arises is why did she, in the writing of her story, make religious acrimony over her person so central, built on assumedly fractious and agonistic religious relationship between the Hindus and the Muslims? At one level, this was because there was in fact a confrontation over her person. However, some of her statements are baffling and we need to understand what they could possibly indicate. For when she writes of 'giving sixty daughters to expand religion/s', she seems to almost anticipate the game of harnessing numbers to shape community identities and politics that began to surface from the late nineteenth century. More plausibly, her statement seems to point ostensibly to the instance of the offer made to the ninth Sikh guru Tegh Bahadur by Aurangzeb, of the hand of a daughter for the gain of adherents for Islam. Her statement can be seen as an evocation of that deeply wounding affray, for in no way does its literal interpretation makes any sense for the situation that Piro may have actually confronted. Certainly, there was not meant to be any growth in community numbers in a bargain to which she may have been subjected, except that she would stay a Muslim. By harping on a divisive moment then, and by underlining the religious cleft between Hindus and Muslims, did she hope to rid herself of the patriarchal control of her wardens? By stepping outside their religion, was she not also effectively stepping out of their hold on her life and person, which she may not have been able to do had she stayed within Islam? For was the question also not about the temerity of a woman in asserting her choice, her autonomy, of how she may lead her life? Piro's description of the many offended by her act—the brothers, religious figures of the mullahs, Muslim men—all suggest a thwarting of patriarchal rights by an upstart woman, and its unacceptability to the extent of her forcible kidnapping. However, was Piro exchanging one patriarchal control for another within her Gulabdasi establishment? Though undoubtedly the authority of the guru, often conflated with god in Piro's writings, was supreme, there is no doubt that Piro bargained for relative autonomy and an alternative life path for herself where she could be more of her own mistress. One may suggest that she used the theatrical power of a conversion and its narrative to shape her life and assert her autonomy.

Finally, conversion narratives are directed towards the community one is seeking to become a part of. As discussed earlier, a conversion might involve an individual's change of world view, a spiritual awakening of a single person, but 'it occurs in a context of institutional procedures and social relationships'.[96] For Piro the severing of one set of social relationships was sharply made, where she underscored her 'hyper-distinctiveness' from the community she abandoned, but conversion was more than a 'transcendental promise', and involved a cautious approach to tackling 'prosaic structures of everyday situations' in the community that she wished to be included.[97] It would have been naïve on her part to assume a smooth transition to a completely novel environment. I have suggested elsewhere that her transgressions, in terms of her gender, religion, caste, and profession, were too enormous to find easy acceptability in a monastic establishment.[98] It is possible that she may have faced hostility from at least some of the members of the Gulabdasi establishment. The implacable denunciation of her former co-religionists in her writing may point to her inordinate effort to be absorbed within her new environment, and also her total devotion towards her guru. The absolute severing of her former ties and the drama that she builds around it on the one hand, and a complete acceptance of the authority of the guru on the other, may be understood partly as strategies for easing her way into the sect.

Whatever conjecture we may draw of Piro's intentions, the constraints of her circumstances, or of the pathos of her conversion narrative, what does emerge keenly is her trenchant need to portray her gendered subjectivity. It would also be a deep cynicism on our part if we dismiss her turn towards the Gulabdasi sect, and her own orientation towards bhakti

---

[96] Buckser and Glazier, *The Anthropology of Religious Conversion*, p. xi.

[97] I take these phrases from Deepak Mehta, '"Naming" Conversion: Being Muslim in Old Delhi', in *My Favourite Levi Strauss*, edited by Dipankar Gupta (New Delhi: Yoda Press, 2011), pp. 118–44.

[98] Anshu Malhotra, 'Telling Her Tale? Unravelling a Life in Conflict in Peero's *Ik Sau Saṭh Kāfiāṅ*', *The Economic and Social History Review* 46, no. 4 (2009): 541–78. Also see Chapters 1, 2, and 7 of this book.

devotion, as merely a way out of a life she no longer wished to lead. How Piro understood and developed her gendered being within a devotional bhakti ethos, with her cognizance of her anomalous and sexually charged past will be outlined in the next chapter. The counterfoil of religious dissension discussed here will also be examined, not as religious harmony but in Piro's bhakti-steeped world view as the uselessness of formal and externally oriented religiosity. How the advaita monism so central to her Gulabdasi community was developed in relation to like-minded theologies available in Punjab and how Piro understood these will be shown. From Piro's statements as seen in this chapter where she critiques outwardly inclined male public religiosity as inapplicable to women, we see her having arrived at a view that an interiorized piety was worth aspiring to, and, in fact, amenably suitable for women.

4   A Low-Caste Muslim Prostitute and Bhakti Religiosity

Cultural Imaginary and the Ability to Imagine Otherwise

Rākho sarnī asaran ko houṅ sūdar nārī
Jāt ajāt na dekhiyā tum Kubjāṅ tārī
Chākhat beraṅ Bhīlṇī chuṇ miṭhe li āī
Tumī piyāre prem ke tahuṅ jūṭhe khāī
Tārī Gankā Ajāmal na pāp vichāre
Pīro kehsī satguro tum nīch udhāre.

Keep this shelterless woman at your feet for she is a sudra woman
You did not look at caste or castelessness when you ferried Kubjan
Bhilni picked the sweet berries after tasting them
You who crave for love had the soiled remains
You ferried across Ganka and Ajamal unmindful of their sins
Piro says satguru you liberate the lowly.[1]

I contend that our ability to imagine ourselves otherwise—that is, our
ability to imaginatively distance ourselves from our habitual modes of
self-understanding and to envisage, in imaginative representations, alternate
possibilities for ourselves—plays an important role in practical reflection and
deliberation about the self, and hence in self-definition....

---

[1] 160: 11. (Piro, *Ik Sau Sath Kafian* [*160 Kafis*]) ms. 888 [Amritsar: Bhai Gurdas
Library, GNDU]. Kafi numbers from this text are marked as '160: xx'.)

Innovative cultural imaginary plays a ... liberating role. In representing
what might be possible it abstracts us from our habitual understandings of
ourselves and others and so begins to loosen the grip of dominant imagery.

—Catriona Mackenzie[2]

I open this chapter with a quotation from Piro where she portrays herself
as being a low-caste sudra, and enumerates various low-caste women
who were 'ferried across',[3] that is, those who reached their soteriological
destinations, despite being women and of low caste. They, moreover, had
sexually charged personas insofar as they nurtured inappropriate desires,
provided sexual services, or led debauched lives.[4] In Vaishnav legends,
we come across Kubjan, a hunchback (as her name suggests) maid of
the evil uncle-king Kansa of Lord Krishna. She desired Krishna, and her
wish was not only fulfilled but her beauty too was restored. Shabari, the
Bhilni, in the well-known parable is said to have selected sweet berries
for Lord Ram by tasting them first, offering him the soiled remains,

---

[2] Catriona Mackenzie, 'Imagining Oneself Otherwise', in *Self and Subjectivity*,
edited and with a commentary by Kim Atkins (Malden: Blackwell Publishing,
2005), pp. 284–99.

[3] She refers to one high-caste man, Ajamil, who, however, leads a degraded life.

[4] The journey from this world to the next is often metaphorically presented
as the crossing of a waterway—a river, a stream, or an ocean. In Bhakti and Sufi
imaginaries, the guru/*murshid*, is the facilitator who enables this journey, figuratively a boatman who helps the disciple to cross. In Bhakti metaphysics the repetition of the name of the Lord, expressed as the Word or the Name, is also a path to
spiritual emancipation. Here is an example of Piro's rendition of this journey and
the relationship with the guru:

Āo milo saheliyo ral maslat kariye
Bhaye samund athāh haī kaho kis bidh tariye
Pīro Nām jahāj hai gur khevaṭ merā
Pauṇ prem chalāvsī pār hosī ḍerā

Come friends let us consult together,
The ocean is of unplumbed depth say which way shall we swim?
Piro says Name is my boat and Guru my boatman,
He'll blow the breeze of love, and we will encamp on the other side. (*S1*:1).

allowing a gastronomical mixing of fluids, which has sexual overtones.[5] Gan(i)ka refers to Jivanti, the courtesan who buys a parrot and teaches it to recite 'Ram Ram' every morning. The day the two die Vishnu's messenger takes them to heaven because they have the name of god on their lips—the simple devotional formula of repeating the Name as a route to liberation in bhakti ethics,[6] referred to as 'accidental' liberation by Wendy Doniger.[7] In the same category is Ajamil, a pre-Kaliyuga (before the present degenerate iron age) evil Brahmin seduced by a prostitute. Frightened by Death's messengers in his last moments, he begins to call out to his son Narayan, a name of Vishnu, who is pleased and saves him from hell.[8] Piro, as a low-caste woman and a prostitute, can be said to underscore the point about her own emancipatory future, made possible by the alternate cultural imaginary inherent in bhakti devotion that eased the path of liberation for those seen as degraded.

The feminist philosopher Catriona Mackenzie discusses the manner in which a self may acquire personal autonomy. She gives attention to the development of what are called 'autonomy competencies', 'skills in deliberation, decision making, and action, all of which depend upon a unified and valued self-conception'.[9] Developing an integrated sense of self-worth, Mackenzie posits, is a dynamic aspect of one's reflexive ability that facilitates one to either externalize or appropriate aspects of ourselves that our 'internal observing self' can distinguish as worth rejecting or embracing.[10]

---

[5] On the relationship between gastronomy and sexuality, see Ann G. Gold, 'Sexuality, Fertility and Erotic Imagination in Rajasthani Women's Songs', in *Listen to the Heron's Words: Reimagining Gender and Kinship in North India*, edited by Gloria G. Raheja and Anne G. Gold (California: University of California Press, 1994), pp. 30–72. Also see Anshu Malhotra, *Gender, Caste and Religious Identities: Restructuring Class in Colonial Punjab* (New Delhi: Oxford University Press, 2002), pp. 164–5. Wendy Doniger writes, 'Food and eating function in South Asia to define the person more than anything else, even sex.' See her *On Hinduism* (New Delhi: Aleph, 2013), p. 70.

[6] D.N. Lorenzen, *Praises to a Formless God: Nirguni Texts from North India* (Albany: SUNY Press, 1996), p. 268.

[7] Doniger, *On Hinduism*, p. 239.

[8] Lorenzen, *Praises to a Formless God*, p. 263.

[9] This is discussed in Kim Atkins' commentary on Mackenzie. Atkins, *Self and Subjectivity*, p. 280.

[10] The internal observing self is shown to be discerning, helping guide one's self-conception through reflecting on 'one's values, ideals, commitments and cares'. This is distinguished from one's 'internal audience', which is 'caught up

In other words, when we observe ourselves we may accept or reject aspects of ourselves. Mackenzie also emphasizes that our self-conception is mediated through social relationships and the cultural imaginary at our disposal. Thus, our self-worth is also dependent upon social recognition, a self-knowledge we acquire in social relationships that value our self-conception, commitments, and ideals. Oppressive social conditions and relationships, therefore, can hamper or truncate our self-knowledge and worth. Mackenzie importantly speaks of the cultural imaginary, the repertoire of culturally available images and representations on which the imagination draws, as part of the process through which we achieve integration, self-transformation, and a unified autonomy. This activity of imagining can, in Mackenzie's thought, abstract us from our habitual modes of understanding, opening up a 'space within which to envisage new possibilities of self-definition and self-understanding'. Imagining is liberating because we do not restrict ourselves to what is, but what might be possible, 'loosening the grip of dominant imagery', though 'representations can act like compulsions to constrain the imagination, enforce habitual patterns of thought, and stymie self-understanding and self-definition'.[11] Thus, an enabling social environment and an integrated sense of self-conception facilitate alternative imaginations, helping us become agents with autonomy, shaking loose the hold of the dominant imagery.

In this chapter I wish to draw from Mackenzie's valuable analysis of how an agent becomes autonomous while interacting in society, with an enabling sense of self-worth. I use this insight to speak of Piro's self-conception, her ability to imagine otherwise, drawing from the cultural imaginary provided to her by bhakti's devotional (and in certain contexts Punjabi Sufi) repertoire of tales, fables, and legends. I argue that Piro could have felt hobbled and constrained in ordinary social circumstances and in her quest for a meaningful spiritual life, as she was a low-caste woman. She was, moreover, a prostitute, seen to embody not just loose sexual morals but epitomizing sexual surplus, and was a Muslim in a 'Sikh' monastic order. Thus, the quadruple burden she bore—female sex, a sexualized past, low caste, and her religion—could have stymied anyone, casting a shadow over her sense of self-worth, or the ability to

---

within the imaginative project and emotionally identifies with it'. Atkins, *Self and Subjectivity*, p. 285.

[11] Atkins, *Self and Subjectivity*, p. 294.

imagine alternatively. However, once ensconced in the Gulabdasi dera and its intellectually enriching and relatively socially liberal environment, she could further hone her autonomy competencies already present in her person. She could then envisage for herself a socially valuable role, and her soteriological ambition could be fulfilled. Further, she could do this by not only not denying her past with its incumbent stigmas, but also by exploiting bhakti's proclivity for finding a home in, and solace for, the marginal and the downtrodden, including opening spaces for the lower castes and women.

That the way of bhakti had a special affinity for the low castes and women has been well demonstrated by scholars.[12] As according to A.K. Ramanujan's discussion, if the *dharmashastras* with their 'context-sensitive' nature, their axiomatic organization on differentiation which creates different rules for separate castes, can be taken to be normative, then bhakti must be seen to be anti-structural, its spirit egalitarian and anti-hierarchic.[13] Offering an alternative vision that challenged the 'inexorable contextuality'[14] of the dharmashastras, bhakti, in Ramanujan's formulation, 'satirizes the caste system, the male–female divisions, the rich, the priests, sacred time and sacred space, and so on'.[15] Further, bhakti revels in reversal, so that the low castes and women were seen as natural devotees or bhaktas. While the high-caste twice-born males, as Ramanujan shows, had to shed their status, the security that birth and wealth bestowed on them, and become open to 'downward mobility', or 'equalizing downwards', the low castes and women, being unprivileged, had neither status nor egos to lose, and so were always already open for bhakti.[16] Even saints' wives sometimes were better placed to recognize the Lord than the twice-born saints, as, for example, Purandharadasa's wife recognized Lord Vitthala before he did when god came to them in the disguise of a mendicant Brahmin.[17] And the low-born males, as

---

[12] See the two essays of A.K. Ramanujan, 'On Women Saints' and 'Men, Women and Saints', in *The Collected Essays of A.K. Ramanujan*, edited by Vinay Dharwadker (New Delhi: Oxford University Press, 2013 [1999]), pp. 261–94.

[13] See another two essays of Ramanujan, 'Where Mirrors are Windows: Towards an Anthology of Reflections' and 'Is There an Indian Way of Thinking? An Informal Essay', in Ramanujan, *The Collected Essays of A.K. Ramanujan*, pp. 6–51.

[14] Ramanujan, *The Collected Essays of A.K. Ramanujan*, p. 48.

[15] Ramanujan, *The Collected Essays of A.K. Ramanujan*, p. 28.

[16] Ramanujan, *The Collected Essays of A.K. Ramanujan*, p. 285.

[17] Ramanujan, *The Collected Essays of A.K. Ramanujan*, p. 276.

Ramanujan discusses, did not have to struggle with their own traits to attain the Lord, as much as they had to fight the Brahmins who hindered their access to the temple image to see their Lord.[18]

Bhakti devotionalism and its ways, then, can be demonstrated to provide the cultural imaginary that Mackenzie speaks of, the enabling representational repertoire that someone like Piro required, and exploited, to assert her autonomy and demand a space in her Gulabdasi environment. However, matters were not so simple, for though bhakti emphasized the potential to challenge the rules of the dharmashastras, it could also occasionally accommodate them. To stay with Ramanujan a little longer, he shows not only context-sensitivity as an important organizing principle of the Indic cultures, but also speaks of 'reflexivity' as their significant trait. Using the specular metaphor, Ramanujan speaks of a dialectic relationship between the self and its other, of the dharmashastra culture and its alternatives, whether bhakti, folklore, or tantra. This reflexivity opens 'windows' for mirroring and distorted mirroring, of parodying and having family resemblances with the other, where inversion, subversion, and conversion were all a possibility.[19] Speaking of the relationship between bhakti and the Vedas specifically, with the Vedas as the fount of dharmashastra rules, Ramanujan notes that 'some bhakti poems reject the Vedas fiercely, others pay lip-service to them, and still others respect them and go their way'.[20] Though never submitting to the dharmashastra and its rules and ideology, bhakti could have varied readings, dealings, and relationship with it. In this scenario, how easy or difficult was it for Piro to 'imagine otherwise', that is, other than what the dominant tradition showed her to be her particular place in society and societal expectations from her fulfilling that assigned role?

In an important article J.S. Hawley discusses the moral order of bhakti, examining it in conjunction with that of the dharmashastras.[21] According to Hawley, bhakti ethics do not altogether negate those of traditional morality so much as challenge and supplement them. Qualities that have a significant place in the dharmashastras, but are associated with specific castes, in bhakti imaginary come to be placed in

---

[18] Ramanujan, *The Collected Essays of A.K. Ramanujan*, p. 287.

[19] Ramanujan, *The Collected Essays of A.K. Ramanujan*, p. 8.

[20] Ramanujan, *The Collected Essays of A.K. Ramanujan*, p. 26.

[21] J.S. Hawley, 'Morality Beyond Morality', in *Three Bhakti Voices: Mirabai, Surdas and Kabir in Their Times and Ours* (New Delhi: Oxford University Press, 2012 [2005]), pp. 48–69.

new and surprising contexts so that they reconfigure ethics and accept-able morality. Thus fearlessness, normally a male kshatriya trait, comes to be associated with a woman (Mira); generosity, normally seen as a whim of the rich, with a penniless bhakta (Narsi Mehta); and service, the lot of the sudra and the outcaste, with erstwhile rulers (Pipa and his wife Sita). As Hawley puts it, ordinary virtue is 'reshaped by being set in a new context'.[22] Most of all, conventional morality that works by dividing social types (context-sensitivity for Ramanujan) is overturned because bhakti sets about constructing a community that brings people together in satsang, that is, bringing together socially disparate sections to praise the Lord. This bhakti tendency to push for a subtle, and at times subversive, shift of meaning and message, I wish to add, creates the possibility of a radical challenge to conventional morality. However, it can also sometimes coexist and reconcile with, if not outright endorse, traditional ethical codes.

The aspect of bhakti that allowed it to reconcile with traditional values of society has been particularly highlighted by feminist scholars. Kumkum Sangari, for instance, argues that prescriptions of Brahminical texts were available as an ideology that was absorbed and reflected in the verses of the bhaktas.[23] Others have suggested that though making space for women, the bhakti way was difficult for married women, and there were only a few married women bhaktas who could pursue the bhakti way and remain married.[24] Unlike married male saints, women could not reconcile marriage and the devotional path.[25] Ramanujan plotted this pattern for women saints in his landmark essay, additionally noting that though women were bhaktas, they were rarely seen as gurus.[26]

In an inversion of the ashrama system that saw *sanyas* or asceticism as suitable for the fourth and last stage of life, and which expected those seeking spiritual emancipation to live a life of wandering, deprived of the comforts of home and hearth, bhakti endorsed householder life. It is

[22] Hawley, 'Morality Beyond Morality', p. 64.

[23] Kumkum Sangari, 'Mirabai and the Spiritual Economy of Bhakti', *Economic and Political Weekly* 25, no. 27 and 28 (1990): 1464–75 and 1537–52.

[24] There were very few women who continued in their marriages once they took to the bhakti path. Among them was Bahinabai, discussed in the next chapter.

[25] Uma Chakravarti, 'The World of Bhaktin in South Indian Traditions: The Body and Beyond' in her *Everyday Lives, Everyday Histories: Beyond the Kings and Brahmanas of "Ancient" India* (New Delhi: Tulika Books, 2006), pp. 275–92.

[26] Ramanujan, 'On Women Saints'.

commonly accepted that a number of male bhaktas were householders, Kabir and Nanak among them.[27] Though there do not seem to be extensive legends that actually explore the relationship between a male bhakta and his spouse, the marital status of the bhakta is nevertheless important to position the bhakti way as distinct.[28] For women devotees, however, there emerges an axiomatic incompatibility between marriage and bhakti. Uma Chakravarti points to a fundamental tension between unstinting loyalty and service to be rendered to the earthly god, the husband, in accordance with prescriptive wifely duties as outlined by the dharmashastras, and unhindered devotion also to be offered to the chosen (male) god.[29] The question of the sexuality of the female devotee also takes centre stage in Chakravarti's analysis and she highlights the dissonance between marriage and bhakti for women devotees. The four women under her lens either refuse marriage (Avvaiyar) or walk out of it (Karaikkal Ammaiyar, Mahadevi Akka) or marry their god (Andal). Thus, unlike male bhaktas, who have little problem reconciling their devotion to their gods, and being the recipients of their wives' devoted services (Chakravarti discusses Tiruvalluvar, the famous Sangam poet and brother of Avvaiyar to make the point), pursuing bhakti becomes a complicated problem for women bhaktas that tests their loyalty towards their dual gods.[30]

In this chapter I will show that the inherent subversive tendencies of bhakti were sought to be exploited by Piro, who pushed for more radical possibilities opened by it, seeking to widen its ambit to include a low-caste woman, a prostitute, and a Muslim. Deploying Mackenzie's ideas that a sense of self-worth allows an empowering recourse to cultural representations, I will show the manner in which bhakti's cultural imaginary provided Piro with a legacy that she deftly employed,

---

[27] Lorenzen mentions that the Kabirpanthis dispute Kabir's marriage, calling him a lifelong celibate. However, other legends and hagiographies of Kabir see him as a married householder with a wife, mother, and children. D.N. Lorenzen, *Kabir Legends and Ananta-Das's Kabir Parchai* (Albany: SUNY Press, 1991), pp. 18–19.

[28] The ascetic's behavioural codes may not have been discarded entirely, and may have in fact been incorporated and infused with householdership. See the 'Introduction'.

[29] Chakravarti, 'The World of Bhaktin'.

[30] This is also true for the fourteenth-century Kashmiri mystic Lal Ded, who too walked out of marriage. See Lynn Teskey Denton, *Female Ascetics in Hinduism* (Albany: State University of New York Press, 2004), pp. 156–9.

establishing her autonomous agency. Taking a cue from Ramanujan, I will speak of how a 'feminized' bhakti, that is, wherein the attributes of the humble and the marginalized were eulogized, was sought to be underscored by Piro. While the ambience of the Gulabdasi dera and its self-conscious monism that styled itself against the dogma of varnashramadharma made it more amenable to challenging the rules of caste, Piro had a harder time stretching bhakti ethics to accommodate a prostitute. Arguing along with Hawley, I will show that when sexual ethics was approached from the side of bhakti, ordinary morality could be transmuted to yield one in which there was place for a prostitute. Piro carefully picked and appropriated apt bhakti legends and fables, dipping into bhakti's representational repertoire to scan those that could reconcile with the idea that a sexualized past did not hinder a salvational future. By the mid-nineteenth century, and as the sant tradition developed around the person of the guru through the eighteenth century, the guru came to be seen as both human and transcendent simultaneously, and was the focus of disciples' devotion.[31] Piro, though unabashed about her past, hoped to be seen as a consort of the guru. Thus when feminist scholars point to the structural differences between the spiritual paths of men and women bhaktas, it does indicate what was in the realm of possibility for women devotees. Piro, the courtesan, living in the interstices of the narrow opening made by bhakti representations of sexualized women, but unable to fully overturn the dharmashastra morality in relation to them, hoped to be seen as a consort of the guru, though not his wife. Although Piro's sexuality was not contained in wifehood, consort-hood may be seen as imposing a degree of restraint on a prostitute's sexuality, though Piro never repudiated her past, but rather openly owned it. However, it left the question of sexuality somewhat ambivalent, as I will show. Thus, bhakti enabled dharmashastra ethics to be tweaked if not overturned, widening the inhabitable crevices for a woman like Piro.

Finally, as a Muslim woman, Piro had to go beyond the imaginary provided by bhakti's cultural store to dip into Punjabi Sufi attitudes and emotions. As discussed in Chapter 1, the Gulabdasis were open to sharing devotional attitudes with the Sufis. There were theological equivalences that they highlighted between advaita-inspired monism

---

[31] Daniel Gold, *The Lord as Guru: Hindi Sants in North Indian Tradition* (New York: Oxford University Press, 1987), p. 6.

and the Sufi concept of the unity of godhood. Piro, on her part, obsessively delved not only on the meaninglessness of externalized religiosity as shown in the last chapter, but also on the monist/Sufi path that sought one truth (haq) in the universe. By using the cultural inheritance of her Punjabi milieu, Piro was able to underline that all divine seekers were on the same path.

CASTE IN BHAKTI AND GULABDASI IMAGINARY

Scholars have commented on the historical persistence of marginal, subaltern groups that have existed on the fringes of society, characterized by opposition to the norms of the dominant order, including to caste and varnashramadharma—the normative order of castes and stages of life as expounded in the dharmashastras.[32] However, these are often viewed as remaining on the fringes, unable to change or challenge the dominant social order, opting out of the ordinary and the normal.[33] To what extent the dialectics between affirmation of caste and its negation by certain groups could potentially alter the order of castes is worth a debate, especially as many sects were able to reach out to householders, gathering at least some following from among them. It is at the same time important to record the manner in which opposition to caste was built up by orders. This gives an insight into how and to what extent society could be imagined without this pervasive institution, and how it may have empowered individuals and groups.[34] The Gulabdasis and some other sects in Punjab, for example, the followers of Wazir Singh, were strongly opposed to the strictures of the varnashramadharma, declaring their selves as outside its organizing reach, indeed building their identity through this oppositional stance.

The voluminous and growing scholarship on caste has criticized the Dumontian model that deemed South Asia under the thrall of religion and dharma. This model delineated the four-varna linear hierarchy with

---

[32] These were what Doniger calls 'the caste-oriented texts such as The Laws of Manu'. See *On Hinduism*, p. 39.

[33] See the discussion on marginal sects in Partha Chatterjee, 'The Nation and Its Outcastes', in his *The Nation and Its Fragments: Colonial and Post-Colonial Histories* (Princeton: Princeton University Press, 1993), pp. 173–99.

[34] Chatterjee, having discussed the marginality of minor sects, also argues for an implicit impulse for change in the manner in which labouring people dealt with caste. Chatterjee, 'The Nation and its Outcastes', p. 199.

the Brahmin on top and sudra at the bottom, organized around degrees of purity and pollution, showing it as false and misleading.[35] The multiple axioms through which caste operates—from the workings of discrete jatis, endogamy, occupation, *jajmānī* (service provided to a patron), dominance and the power of the king or the dominant group—makes the discussion on caste around any single principle partial at best and obfuscating at worst.[36] The historical change in the operation of caste, particularly of its understanding by the colonial state and its instruments of government and in the fluid politics of the postcolonial state, makes discussion on the issue a highly contentious one.[37] Taking cognizance of the complexity of the issue, here I wish to briefly touch upon the range of Piro's semantic play with the question of caste, why she opposes varnashramadharma, or how she seeks to equate herself with low-caste male saints.

As argued in Chapter 1, monism among the Gulabdasis was geared to bestow theoretical and theological equality to all, for its pantheistic understanding meant that god was omnipresent. Of course, not all achieved their inherent potential, and, in that sense, only the guru reached the state of perfection—he was *kāmil* and arif, a perfect mystic, a Gnostic. This immediately reintroduces an implicit hierarchy within the ascetic order, but this must not be overplayed. The implication of monist theology was that caste was seen as an attribute of the body that did not adhere to the soul, and so the spiritual seeker, having abandoned worldly existence, becomes casteless. It is the body that is birthed and dies, participates in endogamous unions, procreates, perpetuates hierarchy, or otherwise indulges in a variety of polluting tasks, and so can be graded.[38] The soul, an element of the universal Truth, haq, was part of god, soham. Though embodiment was a reality for all, and so much more for a woman who had to consider her gendered body when justifying her ascetic inclinations, the soul's castelessness provided an argument that could be exploited.

---

[35] For a critique of linear hierarchy as developed by Dumont, see Declan Quigley, *The Interpretation of Caste* (Oxford: Clarendon Press, 1995), pp. 142–69. For an excellent summary of sociological and historical debates around caste, see Ishita Banerjee-Dube, *Caste in History* (New Delhi: Oxford University Press, 2008), pp. xv–lxiv.

[36] Quigley, *The Interpretation of Caste*; Banerjee-Dube, *Caste in History*. Also see the essays in Satish Deshpande, ed., *The Problem of Caste: Essays from Economic and Political Weekly* (Hyderabad: Orient BlackSwan, 2014).

[37] See the discussion in Chapter 6.

[38] Chatterjee, 'The Nation and Its Outcastes', p. 194.

This understanding of Gulabdasi theology is significantly present in Piro's writing. She declares herself to be outside religion, the bonds of varnashramadharma, and those accruing as a result of being entangled in worldly relations, described as the varied ways to experience shame/honour (*lāj*). Additionally, and implying a critique of other sects which took pride in their particular rules, including those of specific attires, she calls her sect, rather disingenuously, a non-sect—one that did not initiate a panth (though, of course, they were seen as such).

> *Na maiṅ Musalmānī na Hiṅdu hosaṅ*
> *Na maiṅ baranāsram mo na bhekhal rosaṅ*
> *Hamre lāj na kul kachhu lok na lāje,*
> *Lāj na bed kateb kī ko paṅth na sāje.*

> I am neither a Muslim woman nor a Hindu
> Neither within varnashrama, nor keep any raiment
> We have no shame of the clan or of the world
> No shame of the Vedas, nor of the book [Quran], and have not organized a panth.[39]

Interestingly, the castelessness she explicitly states, *ajāt*, was expressed in the language of caste, *jāt*, a species, in this instance without any defining characteristics. Here Piro, for example, describes her guru when she depicts herself in conversation with the mullahs, the upholders of Islamic faith: *sāiṅ jāt ajāt haī tum jātī rāte* (the master's caste is casteless, while you are caught within caste).[40] Similarly, Piro makes her 'friends', her former colleagues, refer to her as outside normative relations, of having achieved a 'divine' caste after meeting her guru: *yeh to jāt khudaī kī mil sāhab sache* (she is of the divine cast[e] after meeting the true master).[41] What was thus implied was that those on the path of spiritual seeking were outside the reach of caste taxonomy—even if castelessness itself was expressed as a caste—befitting a holy personage. The utilizing of the very concept that was sought to be demolished can be seen as the limits imposed upon her expression, both by language and imagination. It may also indicate the inescapability from the pervasiveness of the institution of caste that one necessarily adhered to even as one was outside it. However, one must not undermine the significance of these statements which, in fact, condemned caste. An attribute of the body, caste could be

[39] 160: 150.
[40] 160: 28.
[41] 160: 37.

expressed by Piro as a stain (dāg), whose tyranny people bore, even as they had a choice to reject it:

Āye jahān te dekhyā e, āpo apne man parchāī baiṭhe
Jis vāste manukh deh dhārī, soī āye ke yahāṅ bhulāī baiṭhe
Sabhī pache haiṅ baran āsrame saīyoṅ, āpo apne dāg lagāī baiṭhe
Sufal hovsī aye jahān Pīro, joī ārafaṅ dā mat pāye baiṭhe.

In this world one sees, people amuse themselves variously
The reason for which they assumed the human body, they have forgotten that totally
Friends all are stuck within varnashrama, making their own stains
Piro says their coming to this world will be successful, if they follow the teaching of the mystic saints.[42]

In this understanding, everyone had a choice to abandon caste and come out of its tentacles by following the mystical path. However, it was also perhaps clear that it required a rejection of worldly relations, the domain where caste had its pincer hold, and to seek a life outside the normative by following a chosen guru, as Piro supplicated to her guru: Tusī jāt te āp ajāt hoe sānu jāt te pār laṅghāvṇa haī (You have become casteless abandoning caste, you have to make us cross over from casteness).[43] To be within caste, then, was the lot of the ordinary, and even the spiritually inclined had to seek a way out of its reach. In this verse Piro also calls herself a low caste (maiṅ nīch jāt), who required guidance from the guru to break the shackles of caste, to cross over to a state of castelessness.

At this juncture I wish to draw attention to another persisting refrain in Piro's writing: where she equates herself with the low-caste saints, those closer to god because of their low status, and those not ruled out for liberation because of their caste. The monist intellectualism of the Gulabdasis pushed Piro to declare the emptiness of caste among the enlightened or those on the path to spiritual knowledge: a desire to transcend caste. However, the emotional states that could give voice to her situation of a low-caste woman seeking acceptance in the guru's establishment, and one asserting the rightness of seeking emancipation, inclined her towards bhakti's devotional repertoire. Here she wished to identify with the low caste. It is my contention that though bhakti devotion had an easy acceptance among the Gulabdasis, Piro invested heavily in its idiom. She owned it as her specific imaginary because it provided her with an emotional current with which she could

[42] S2: 1.
[43] S1: 27.

identify and explicate her case. I will underscore Piro's borrowing from and identification with Kabir, the foremost of the bhakti saints of north India, perhaps because his low caste and the ambiguous status in relation to his Muslim background aroused in Piro an affinity with him.[44] As a recalcitrant personality, nominally Muslim but more critical of its theology than accepting of its tenets, Kabir, the hagiographical person depicted as constantly at loggerheads with religious authorities, both Muslim and Hindu, seemed to Piro a person after her own heart.[45] At the same time, Kabir had little to offer in terms of the soteriological path a woman may tread, and that too a prostitute embodying sexual excess.[46] How Piro's gender and profession further skewered her position besides her caste background, which also meant a further exploration and innovation in her cultural imaginary and its deployment, is a question that I will discuss in the next section.

Keeping company of the holy and the good—the sadhu *sangat*—and identifying the self with sants was an important aspect of affiliating with the bhakti tradition, creating a chain of ties. Piro carefully enumerates those low-caste saints in the company of whom she wished herself to be included, emphasizing that lowness in caste hierarchy did not result in the closing of the opportunity for emancipation. Rather it opened the door wider, as Ramanujan has shown.

> *Nāmā chhīpā tāriyo ar Saiṇā nāī*
> *Kabīr julāhā udhāriyo tum bhaye sahāī*
> *Chor ya rajuwāriyoṅ par kirpā kīnī*
> *Bālmik nis tāriyo tum jāt na chīnī*
> *Pīpa jāt chamār thā ar Sadhnā kasāī*
> *Pīro kehsī satguro tum nīch tarāī.*

You ferried across Nama the cloth printer, and Saina the barber
You helped in the liberation of Kabir the weaver

---

[44] On Kabir's foremost status among bhakti saints, see D.N. Lorenzen, ed., *Bhakti Religion in North India: Community, Identity and Political Action* (New Delhi: Manohar, 1996), pp. 1–32.

[45] On Kabir's Muslim name and his birth as a Muslim, see Charlotte Vaudeville, *A Weaver Named Kabir* (New Delhi: Oxford University Press, 2005), pp. 46–7.

[46] For Kabir, illusion or *maya*, that metaphor for the momentary and delusional snares of the world, was personified as a woman, even a harlot, trapping the unaware. See the poems on maya, including one where he calls her a harlot, in Vaudeville, *A Weaver Named Kabir*, pp. 207–8. Greed was also feminized by him. Vaudeville, *A Weaver Named Kabir*, p. 158.

You bestowed grace equally on thieves and kings
You helped Balmiki cross over, uncaring of his caste
Pipa was a leatherworker, and Sadhna a butcher
Piro says satguru you ferry the downtrodden.[47]

Kabir's sharp and acerbic poetry—a hallmark of his verses that many
scholars have commented on—was especially attractive to Piro. She often
adopted his demeanour, some of the themes that are associated with
him, and even occasionally the tradition of the *ultībamsī* or the 'upside-
down' mystical language—the paradoxical, allusive, and esoteric use of
language that he sometimes favoured.[48] As noted, her attraction to his
oeuvre may have been because he matched her own ambiguous relation
with the Muslim community, or because his irreverent tone towards
religious authority matched the moods that Piro evoked. Piro's refractory
statement of being neither a Hindu nor a Muslim can be taken to be a
reiteration of the same sentiment in Kabir, *Na ham Hindu na Musalmān,*
allah rām ke piṇḍ parān (I am neither Hindu nor Muslim, Allah–Ram is
the breath of my body), which are also similar to Nanak's words upon
enlightenment, *Na ko Hindu hai na ko Musalmān* (there is neither Hindu
nor Muslim).[49] These mordant moods were also present in the poetic
outpourings of many Sufis of Punjab, particularly the Qadiriyas, and Piro
clearly imbibed from both these sources, as I will show later.

---

[47] 160: 12. The reference is to the popular tale about Valmiki, a low-caste
dacoit, before he took to Ram bhakti. For the transformation of Valmiki from
a grammarian, ascetic, and the author of Ramayana into a 'brutish' character
under the 'pressure of bhakti', see Julia Leslie, 'The Implications of Bhakti for the
Story of Valmiki', in *The Intimate Other: Love Divine in Indic Religions*, edited by
A.S. King and J. Brockington (New Delhi: Orient Longman, 2005), pp. 54–77.
Did Piro confuse Ravidas with Pipa? Pipa is a royal in bhakti hagiographies, and
Ravidas, a Chamar involved in leatherwork.

[48] On the personality of Kabir that comes through the hagiography, see John
S. Hawley and Mark Juergensmeyer, *Songs of the Saints of India* (New Delhi:
Oxford University Press, 2008), pp. 35–45. On the harsh tone and the intellectual
content of Kabir's Bijak collection, see Linda Hess, 'Kabir's Rough Rhetoric', in
The Sants: Studies in a Devotional Tradition of India, edited by Karine Schomer and
W.H. McLeod (New Delhi: Manohar, 1987), pp. 143–65. For an authoritative study
of Kabir, including comments on his mystical language with its roots in the Nath
tradition, see Vaudeville, *A Weaver Named Kabir*, pp. 102–3.

[49] W.H. McLeod, *Exploring Sikhism: Aspects of Sikh Identity, Culture and
Thought* (New Delhi: Oxford University Press, 2000), pp. 24, 27.

Other themes like the march of Death/Time in its relentless inevitability, the certainty of death and so making the most of this life, as seen in the poems of Kabir, were also present in Gulabdas's writing, as was the importance of repeating the Name. However, the simplicity of Piro's style and the undercurrent of pathos in some of her verses make her poetry poignant, and her connect with Kabir an emotional affair. Kal/Time that 'eats' up all in its path is expressed in Piro's lines thus:

Kāl khaṅvdā chaṅgyā maṅdyāṅ nuṅ, kāl age na kise ne pher kīte
Koī bachde kāl te saṅt Pīro aur mar ke kāl ne zer kīte.

Time eats the good and the bad, No one can hide from Time
Piro only some sants are saved from Time, Time smashes the rest to smithereens.[50]

The immanence of death and, therefore, the plea to make the most of this birth was an important notion within the bhakti devotional world, particularly seen in Kabir's poems. Here Piro shakes herself awake:[51]

Pīro baṅdiye jāg le huṅ jāgaṇ velā
aise janam malāvṛa phir hoe na melā.

Piro woman, awaken, it is time to rise
You will get but one birth.[52]

Piro's baiting of mullahs and pandits is also akin to Kabir's shaming them on the outward orientation of their religiosity. For Piro, her own confrontation with the mullahs, whose authority she challenged and whose consequences she suffered, as discussed in the previous chapter, was similar to the tortures that Kabir's hagiography suggests he bore. These included being tied and thrown into the River Ganges on the orders of Sultan Sikander Lodi at the behest of qazis,[53] the upholders of the Shari'at or Muslim law. One of Piro's verses made a reference to the torture of Kabir, as also of the tenth-century west Asian Sufi mystic-martyr, Mansur al-Hallaj, at the hands of authorities, and it may not be farfetched to assume that Piro imagined her own ordeal along similar

[50] *S1*: 14.

[51] Vaudeville, *A Weaver Named Kabir*, pp. 190–4.

[52] *S3*: 3.

[53] Priyadas, the eighteenth-century hagiographer of bhakti saints, relates this incident. Vaudeville, *A Weaver Named* Kabir, p. 45.

lines, the trial that all truly evolved figures go through and emerge triumphant.

Pīro kehsī satguru in sarā piyārī,
gote diyo Kabīr ko in binā vichārī.
sūli diyo Mansūr ko khal samas lāhī,
aur dukhāye keṭre ham ket sunāhī.

Piro says satguru they love the Shari'a,
Without giving it a thought they tried to drown Kabir,
They hanged Mansur flaying him,
What more suffering shall I relate?[54]

Moreover, her critique of circumcision as practised by Muslims—*use sampūraṇ bhejiyo tum dāg lagāiyo* (you were sent complete but have put a stain)[55]—resembles Kabir's taunting of this Islamic ritual, where he notes that if god wanted him to be a Turak, He would have circumcised him himself.[56]

It is in Piro's use of the paradoxical language that one especially senses Kabir's presence in her mystical writing. Piro imitates the manner in which Kabir alludes to the inexpressible experience of the mystical *sahaj* state—the sugar of the mute—the adage according to Charlotte Vaudeville that was borrowed from Nath and Tantric traditions. Focusing on the soham mantra, Piro shows the significance of its repetition (like the repetition on Nam/Name) by unravelling its mystical dimensions, and exposing its inexpressible joys.

Soham nām pukārda kyoṅ maiṅ te nasāṅ
Gūṅgā guṛ ko khaī jo maiṅ man vich hasāṅ.

Soham the word is calling out, why do I run?
Like jaggery to the mute, I smile to myself.[57]

Similarly, Piro mimics the 'eastern' (*pūrbi*) language of Kabir, associated with mystical depths and terse esotericism borrowed from the Naths, to demonstrate her ineffable experience. The following are her words:

Pīro bolī pūrbī samjhe nahiṅ koī,
jo pūrab kā hovsī samjhegā soī.

---

[54] 160: 22.
[55] 160: 40.
[56] Vaudeville, *A Weaver Named* Kabir, p. 47. See the poem in question, p. 227. Also Hawley and Juergensmeyer, *Songs of the Saints*, pp. 35–6.
[57] S3: 7.

> Piro speaks the Eastern language, no one understands,
> The one from the East, only he will understand.[58]

They are almost verbatim of Kabir's:

> My language is of the East—none understands me: He alone understands
> me who is from the farthest East.[59]

This mimesis of Kabir and a reflexive identification with him was a space from which Piro could contest the false hold of caste as a shibboleth while also claiming a place in the company of the low-caste saints to challenge the power of the high and the mighty. There was an emotional investment in this parallel that she drew between her situation and that of Kabir and others. Nor was this simultaneous inhabiting of low casteness and no casteness necessarily contradictory. For it was important to dwell with the low to show solidarity and then thwart the institution in which the high castes invested so fundamentally.

What made Piro a low caste, sudar vesva as she referred to herself, was, of course, her profession of prostitution—traditionally related to the kanjar community in Punjab—which was seen as degraded. Whether born into this community or joining it at a later stage in life, prostitution was held to be a base profession. If born outside this profession, we do not know what Piro's caste may have been, though as a Muslim—mlechha— she may be seen as outside caste, but in the sense of a debased other, like the untouchable, whose degradation within the Brahminical system can be understood only in relation to the high caste. Further, as a woman, Piro in the dharmashastra tradition was of course a sudra, all women were designated as such, and when Piro called herself a sudar nari this was also the sense she evoked. Let us then turn to how Piro worked with the ambiguous motif of prostitution in bhakti imaginary.

A COURTESAN OR A CONSORT? BHAKTI AND THE AMBIGUITY OF BEING A PROSTITUTE

As the opening quotation in this chapter shows, Piro was aware of the various Vaishnava, Pauranic, and bhakti legends, those that spoke of the salvific possibilities in the lives of people seen as depraved. These included the prostitute, the redemption of a fallen woman being a particularly poignant motif in many world religions.[60] Though spiritual

---

[58] *S3*: 15.

[59] Vaudeville, *A Weaver Named Kabir*, p. 118.

[60] A Mary Magdalene in Christianity or an Ambapali in Buddhism comes to mind.

liberation in some of these legends was accidental, as with Ganika Jivanti or Ajamil—the latter's debauched nature stemming from his relationships with prostitutes—Piro self-consciously willed her move towards liberation, speaking of these parables to legitimize her spiritual future.

Though seen as 'feminized', inasmuch as bhakti made space for women, bhakti was not an easy path for all women. While men often took on the persona of women, speaking to their gods often in the mien of women, emasculating their selves and debasing their manly egos, bhakti, as discussed, was not easy for wives and women to undertake. Most women stepped out of material marriage, abandoning husbands or marrying their celestial, incorporeal gods. Except for the eighteenth-century high-caste Maharashtrian saint Bahinabai, who stayed within an abusive marriage, there are very few examples of women bhaktas who could sustain marriage and devotion to their gods. Bahinabai, too, had an unhappy life, and cannot be seen to have straddled her two roles harmoniously.[61]

Among the north Indian women bhaktas, Piro alludes in a definitive way to only one woman saint, the most popular among them, Mirabai. Allusions to Mira's poetry are fairly obvious in some instances in her writing, though oblique in others. In an unmistakable imitation of Mira, Piro writes, *Pīro pī pyālṛā matvārī hoī* (on drinking from the cup Piro became intoxicated),[62] recalling the famous incident of Mira being rejuvenated rather than felled by the poisoned cup sent by the prince (*raṇa*) to kill her, intoxicated as she was on her Lord.[63] At a few other places, Piro evokes the *vairāgya* mood of Mira—of suffering in separation—a dominant emotion in much bhakti and Sufi poetry of India, and a very important motif in the songs of Mira. An example of mimicking Mira in a state where she refers to herself as a *jogan* or a *yoginī* (female ascetic) is the following:[64]

Pīro kahe saheliyo maiṅ soham te chalī
Bhukh naṅg Kabūl kar darvesī kallī

[61] Anne Feldhaus, 'Bahina Bai: Wife and Saint', *The Journal of American Academy of Religion* 50, no. 4 (1982): 591–604. Also see Denton, *Female Ascetics*, pp. 142–5. See the discussion on Bahinabai in the next chapter.

[62] *S3*: 18.

[63] On Mirabai and how her poetry reflected her biography, see Hawley and Juergensmeyer, *Songs of the Saints*, pp. 119–40.

[64] Mira's poetry as a jogan or a yogini, where the haunting emotion is of abandonment, even death, has been discussed by J.S. Hawley in 'Mirabai as Wife and Yogi', in his *Three Bhakti Voices*, pp. 117–38.

Darsan karan vāste main jogaṇ hoī
Jisde saīyon vichhṛī var pāyā soī.

Piro says friends I am going to meet soham
Having accepted hunger and nakedness, like a lone mendicant
To get a glimpse (of Him) I have become a jogan
Friends from whom I had separated, I have found that mate.[65]

Even while imitating Mira, the symbolic substance of Piro's verses remains different from that which Mira expounds. While separation, abandonment, and isolation were the leitmotif in some of Mira's most moving poetry, Piro's verses here affirm her monist and solipsistic orientation of finding her mate–guru, a happy achievement, lending a different mood from the desperate loneliness of Mira.[66]

That Piro evoked Mira at all was interesting for several reasons. In Punjab, Mira's songs were excised from the version of the *Adi Granth*, the Sikh sacred text, prepared in the early seventeenth century because of the erotic nature of her poetry. Mira was thus considered a contumacious figure who defied family and clan norms in abandoning marriage and familial life.[67] Such obstreperousness associated with Mira has had high castes of most north Indian regions squirm in discomfort,

---

[65] *S3*: 11. Another example of such a mood would be: *Rang te bhaī ke rang saīyon, sohṇe piyā de viyog te roīyān main; main tān hāl te bhaī behāl saīyon, jaṭṭan khol virāgan hoīyan main* (I am coloured in his colour, friends, I wail in separation from my beautiful beloved; my condition has become pathetic, I have become an ascetic having opened my hair) (*S2*: 10).

Piro uses the feminine form *darvesi*, as she does when she calls herself *jogan*. Her gendered identity is always affirmed in her poetry.

Var can mean both a boon and a prospective bridegroom. Here the latter sense is evoked. Bridal and marriage imagery was also a staple of bhakti poetry.

[66] For an analysis of Mira's searing sorrow on feeling abandoned by her Lord as expressed in Mira's poetry, see Hawley, 'Mirabai as Wife'. On Mira's isolation within the bhakti community of her time and the embracing of Mira by the low castes in Gujarat and Rajasthan, see Parita Mukta, *Upholding the Common Life: The Community of Mirabai* (New Delhi: Oxford University Press, 1997), pp. 23–5.

[67] Pashaura Singh, *The Bhagats of the Guru Granth Sahib: Sikh Self-Definition and the Bhagat Bani* (New Delhi: Oxford University Press, 2003), pp. 145–6. A late seventeenth-century text of Punjab, the *Prem Ambodh*, discusses Mira but tames her defiance as a form of *pativrata* religion. See J.S. Hawley and G.S. Mann, 'Mirabai in the Pothi Prem Ambodh', *Journal of Punjab Studies* 15, nos 1–2 (2009): 199–223.

including her native Rajasthan as shown by Parita Mukta.[68] Perhaps for that very reason, Mira's refractoriness held an appeal for Piro, for she too, like Mira, abandoned her clan, however disreputable, to pursue her own spiritual path. However, ultimately Piro hoped to be accepted as a consort of her guru, though not a wife, and so she could not overplay her affiliation with Mira who, after all, did not wish for a human partner. Also, howsoever recalcitrant Mira may have been, her legends stop her from crossing into sexual impropriety, as I will index presently, even though she is depicted as coming to the very brink. In this sense, the rather minor figures of a Jivanti, Kubjan, or a Bhilni had greater appeal for Piro, for their very sketchiness in bhakti lore could be used by her to make the statement that low-caste and sexually impious women were emancipated by god. The ambiguity of Mira's biographical details elicited ambivalence from Piro; she was attracted to her, yet unable or unwilling to make her a role model.

How did bhakti traditions regard the figure of the prostitute, besides those that accidently reached liberation like a Jivanti or an Ajamil? If the bhakti way provided an alternative to the conceits of the dharmashastras where womanly sexuality, her *strīsvabhava*, was meant to be contained within wifehood, her *strīdharma*, and which condemned the sexual excess associated with the prostitute, how did bhakti view the matter?[69] J.S. Hawley in his discussion on bhakti morality through its hagiography, cited earlier, brings up the case of sant Pipa's wife, Sita, which can be described as a theme of 'almost falling into prostitution', though this is not the purpose of Hawley's discussion.[70] In this story, the threatened honour of a respectable woman is ultimately preserved. The movement towards a temporary occupation of liminal space defined by the fear of

[68] Mukta says that Rajputs refer to Mira as a *kulnāsi*, a destroyer of family and clan values. (Mukta, *Upholding the Common Life*, pp. 49–66.) In Sangari's analysis that questions Mira's rebellious stance, Mira imbibed the dominant feudal and patriarchal values of her society, and her verses often display a Mira observing herself through the harsh gaze of society. (Sangari, 'Mirabai and the Spiritual'.) However, Mira's contumacious biography and poetry exceeds the normative boundaries sought to be imposed on her.

[69] On the view of the *shastras* on women's nature and duties as interpreted in an eighteenth-century text, see Julia Leslie, *The Perfect Wife: The Orthodox Hindu Woman According to the Stridharmupuddhati of Tryambakayajvan* (New Delhi: Oxford University Press, 1989).

[70] Hawley, 'Morality beyond Morality'.

loss of honour reintroduces the importance of the familiar argument of maintaining sexual rectitude. The fact that the protagonist is willing to contemplate the overstepping of the line that divides honourable behaviour from dishonourable one, is not meant to elevate the status of those who follow 'degraded' professions like prostitution. Instead, the idea is to underline that if the bhakta is truly sincere towards the duties entrusted to her, she will be saved from a terrible fate. The import of the saga of Pipa, a king, and his queen, Sita, is precisely this. Developed around the idea of the royal couple normally used to receiving the humble service of others, its order is inverted within the bhakti paradigm. The couple is shown eager to serve the community of the bhaktas, and willing to go to any lengths to achieve that aim. Living in poverty, the appropriately named Sita, the devoted wife, follows her husband in his impecunious life of a bhakta. She is shown willing to prostitute herself by standing in the bazaar in the hope of earning money to feed the bhakti community. On another occasion, she bargains her body to a lascivious merchant for the same reason. On a rainy night when the streets are impassable, her husband, Pipa, carries her for her tryst to the merchant's house so that she can keep her side of the sordid bargain. On both occasions Sita's honour is saved because the depth of hers and her husband's devotion shames and changes the outlook of those earlier willing to exploit her. As discussed by Hawley, there is a reversal of ordinary values in this bhakti parable insofar as who is the rightful recipient of service or what constitutes an ideal household. Vasudha Dalmia in her discussion on the same story in the context of the Vallabha sect also importantly comments that marital fidelity does not emerge as an absolute value.[71] Yet from the viewpoint of prostitution, there is an affirmation of it being a degenerate institution in relation to the moral and sexual economy of the household. The portrayal of a wife eager to become a prostitute so she can fulfil her higher call of community service does not condemn prostitution as such. However, holding back the wife from a possible crossing over to a 'depraved' life does reassert the salience of wifely dharma, even if not in the absoluteness of the dharmashatric model.

Similar stories also circulated around Mirabai, where the motif of sexual transgression became complex. Mira emerges in most accounts

---

[71] The story appears in the corpus of tales called the *Chaurasi Vaishnavan ki Varta*. See Vasudha Dalmia, 'Women, Duty and Sanctified Space in a Vaishnav Hagiography of the Seventeenth Century', in her *Hindu Pasts: Women, Religion, Histories* (Ranikhet: Permanent Black, 2015), pp. 173–88.

determinedly defiant of ordinary morality, but also without having com-
promised herself in any way. According to Hawley, in the condensed life
story of Mira available in the *Bhaktamāl*, her single-most important trait
is her fearlessness.[72] This Rajput princess is shameless in her passion-
ate devotion to Krishna and thinks nothing of thwarting her *pativrata*
(the ideal of a devoted wife) religion or the demands of propriety in her
marital household. She neither consummates her marriage to the rana,
insisting on her fidelity to Krishna, nor seeks to please her husband's
family, choosing to spend time in the company of sadhus. Yet two episodes associated with her, as elaborated in Priyadas' eighteenth-century
Bhaktirasabodhinī, stop short of her crossing into sexual misdemeanour.
In one episode Mira is heard whispering with someone in her room and
rumours of a liaison are spread. When the rana demands to see who is
with her in her chamber, he can only find the idol of Giridhar, her favourite image of Krishna, the mountain-lifter. In the second episode, Mira
comes across a dissolute sadhu out to take advantage of her by insisting
that Krishna himself wishes her to submit to his advances. Mira's predicament is overcome appositely by her very quality of shamelessness.
She lays out the pleasure bed in the presence of the satsang, urging the
sadhu to do Krishna's bidding in front of all and thereby shaming him
into abandoning his carnal desire.[73]

The bhakti imaginary in the saintly episodes discussed above plays
with the idea of prostitution, even envisaging the celebrated bhakta
Pipa facilitating his wife's contemplated impropriety, not to speak of
the ever popular Mira's consent to a tryst with the dissolute holy man.
The message that a bhakta can do anything to achieve the welfare of the
bhakti community emerges powerfully, and to that end episodes with
sexual innuendos are developed. However, as mentioned earlier, the
crossing over does not happen and womanly virtue remains safe. It is
only in one story of the Vallabha sect that a prostitute is accepted as a
devotee, even though she has been with many 'worldly masters'. The story
remains important though couched in a language of purity/pollution (her
emaciating the body through hunger purifies her), and other Vaishnavas
are asked to desist from following her way.[74]

---

[72] Hawley, 'Morality beyond Morality', pp. 50–5.

[73] Hawley, 'Morality Beyond Morality', pp. 50–5.

[74] Vasudha Dalmia, 'Forging Community: The Guru in a Seventeenth-Century
Hagiography', in her *Hindu Pasts*, pp. 141–72.

I will now turn to another bhakti anecdote to which Piro makes a direct reference in her verses, one where Kabir keeps the company of a prostitute. The episode is discussed by D.N. Lorenzen as part of Ananta-Das's *Parchāī* of Kabir of the early seventeenth century, a story also available in Priyadas' anthology of the early eighteenth century. As Kabir's fame grows and people begin to flock to his place, Kabir decides to rid himself of them and his fame by going early one morning to the house of a prostitute, putting his hands around her neck, and grabbing a vessel filled with holy water. Pretending the water to be liquor, and in the company of the prostitute he goes to the market, where people, as he expects, begin reviling him. While the next part of the story depicts Kabir establishing his superiority over the Brahmins' ritualistic punctiliousness in the heart of orthodox Jagannath Puri, the role of the prostitute for Kabir is simply to rid him of milling crowds and worldly fame.[75] The fact that Kabir does not make love to the prostitute or drink liquor can be said to establish his purity and moral reticence. Even though the prostitute is not the focus of the story, it needs to be emphasized that there is no second-hand redemption for her by association with Kabir, his antics the sole concern of the author.

In Piro's very brief recalling of this episode, this association of Kabir with a prostitute becomes an enabling one, underscoring the significance of such an association. In her interpretive frame it is the special obligation of the guru to protect the interests of the vulnerable in society, as Vishnu did.

> *Bipar bantā chher ke ghar Kubjān āṇī*
> *Charnī lāī Ranghri chhorat Khatrānī*
> *Gankā nāl Kabīr ne mil yagat dekhāye*
> *Gaurī god Mahādev bhāṇā vartāyo.*
> *Kau lā charnī lāī kar yag niṅd karāī*
> *Raṅgī Rām chamārī ā nij pās biṭhāī ...*
> *Charchā arath ajog bahu saṅtan kar diyā*
> *Yāroṅ Dās Gulāb hī achraj na kiā.*

Unmindful of dangers you brought Kubjan home
You kept Ranghri at your feet leaving Khatrani
Along with a prostitute Kabir saw the world
Gauri in the lap of Mahadev followed the will of the god.
You suffered the humiliation of the world but kept them at your feet

---

[75] D.N. Lorenzen, *Kabir Legends*, pp. 29–32.

Ram coloured the Chamar woman making her sit next to him ...
Unseemly rumours were spread about many sants
Friends, Das Gulab did not (alone) do something amazing.[76]

Piro's reference to her guru Gulabdas facing the humiliation of the world
on her account, and encouraging him to keep his association with her
and also rescue her (the juncture at which this verse appears is when
she sends him her supplication for undertaking her rescue) is important.
She gives him various mythical examples of God's association with low-
caste women, women who were not necessarily pure, the reference to Kabir
with Ganka being a giveaway, but that their past did not inhibit their liberation by the Lord. Indeed, this was a statement to encourage her guru to
not be embarrassed about being associated with her, and in the manner
of Kabir to be unafraid in keeping the company of a prostitute. Thus,
even a story that on the surface does not appear particularly empowering
becomes so in the manner in which it is presented by Piro.

Piro makes the point about the uplifting of the low caste and women
repeatedly. Here is another example:

> Pīro kehsī satguru tum parupkārī
> Dekh prem udhār ho ki purkhā nārī
> Ūnch nīch na dekh ho tum prem piyāre
> Pāpī āye charan mo tum sahaj udhāre
> Auguṇ hārī satguro huṅ sūdar nārī
> Rehne dīje saran mo tum jore jhārī.

Piro says satguru you are kind
Seeing love you deliver, whether men or women
You don't distinguish between the high and low
You liberate the sinners who come at your feet

---

[76] 160: 76–7. Piro's poetry is full of such references. For example, *Radhe
rākhī saran mo tum kisan balāsī; aur Arain Kasainī tum rākhī dāsi* (160: 142) (You
merry Krishna kept Radha at your feet; and kept the Arain and the Kasain as
your slaves); Arain refers to a woman from the horticultural caste, and Kasain
to a butcher woman. Again, *Ae dās Gulāb piyāre jin harnākas rāvaṇ māre, tārī
Kubjāṅ Karmābaī* (The beloved Gulabdas who killed the demons Harnakashyap
and Ravan, and saved Kubjan and Karmabai) (*RS*, 'Hori Kumach Dī'); this refers
to the myth of demons Harnakashyap and Ravan killed by Vishnu, the first in the
form of man-lion, Narasimha, and the second as Ram. 'Khatrani' must refer to a
local legend as the Khatri caste is mostly found in Punjab. The point again was
the preference for a lower-caste woman from among the dyers to the high-caste
Khatrani.

> Beaten by bad qualities satguru I am a sudra woman
> Let me stay at your feet cleaning your shoes.[77]

Perhaps Piro felt insecure, or she felt the need to remind her guru that he was doing the right thing in keeping his faith in her. While these are plausible explanations, a third one is also important, which is Piro's validation of the bhakti imaginary that created a space for the likes of her. Through the repetition of the notion of benevolence towards the low and the outcast, Piro could also be seen to celebrate the liberal potential within bhakti's alterity. Furthermore, Piro felt pious enough to aspire for a place next to the guru, to be seen as his consort. And she hoped to occupy this space as a low-caste former prostitute rather than through obfuscating or obliterating her past. Of course, her repetitive references to her low caste meant a constant recalling of her background. Moreover, the Gulabdasis attracted other prostitute followers after Piro joined their ranks as discussed in Chapter 1. I will explicate these two aspects of Piro's ambition and life before I close this section.

To elaborate on the first point about her eventually successful desire to be acknowledged as the consort of the guru, one must first turn to how the guru was imagined in her writing. It is this relationship of drawing succour from him that helps in understanding Piro as demure, docile, and subdued in manner. The enormous emphasis in her poetry on salvation through the mystical persona of the guru carries forward the bhakti legacy of the reliance on the guru to reveal esoteric knowledge and personally lead the disciple on the path of deliverance. The tradition of guruship is old in India, and scholars have traced its origins to the obscure and arcane sects of Buddhist Siddhas and Tantric yogis, including the Nath yogis, seen as precursors to nirguni (formless) bhakti.[78] Equally important in north India is the Sufi concept of *pīr–murīd*, laying stress on the complete dependence of the murid (disciple) on the pir or the *murshid* to help reach the stage of annihilation of the self in the divine (*fanā*). Both these traditions are well established in Punjab, and there is no doubt that both influenced Piro.

The salience of the guru as the focus of piety is seen in the multiple names with which Piro addresses him. The guru could at once be the human guru, an avatar of Vishnu, or god himself. The term most employed by Piro is satguru (true teacher), in keeping with the bhakti

---

[77] 160: 138.
[78] See the 'Introduction'.

FIGURE 4.1   A picture of Piro and Gulabdas as depicted by the Gulabdasis at Hansi. The picture of Gulabdas is superimposed in the background.
Source: Sant Vijender Das.

tradition. Terms such as *sāhu*, *sāhab*, *saīṁ*, and *mālak* are also used, underscoring the status of the guru as the master. Soham, the mystical mantra of the Gulabdasis, is also used to refer to the guru in Piro's writing. She also addresses her guru with words that have an Islamicate heritage such as murshid (preceptor), arif (Gnostic), *hajoor* (honoured one) or *beparvāhe* (nonchalant). Modes of address that could cross into an erotic usage are also deployed like *saīyaṅ*, *piyā*, and *balam* that carry the connotation of a lover, more in line with the erotic chord in some *saguṇa* (god with attributes) bhaktas' songs, or those in the mood of viraha. Piro at other times uses terms seen otherwise in the context of nirguna bhakti, *akhaṇḍ* (complete/indivisible), *jaṇī-jāṇo* (all knowing), *antaryāmī* (all knowing), *nirankāre* (formless), *abnāsī* (indestructible) and *bihad* (without limit), but also avatar (incarnation of a god), as in saguna bhakti. Here is a poetic, erotic evocation of the guru.[79]

> *Pīro kehsī satguru houṅ daras piyāsī*
> *Kaṅval khire rav dekh ke jiuṅ jal mīn tarāsī*
> *Kāmī chāhe rūp jyuṅ jyuṅ chor hanerā*
> *Kavi khire sās dekh jyuṅ jyuṅ lobhī dhan kerā*
> *Āsak jiveṅ mabub jyuṅ tu chāsu parse*
> *Tyuṅ man mera satguro tum darsan tarse.*

> Piro says satguru I thirst for your visage
> Like the lotus blooms on seeing the sun and the fish thirsts for water
> Like the amorous looks for beauty and the thief for darkness
> Like the poet blossoms on seeing the moon and the greedy on seeing wealth
> Like the lover sees his beloved in all four directions
> So my heart thirsts satguru for your sight.[80]

In her quest to be regarded as the guru's consort, Piro once again resorts to mythological examples, in this instance recalling consort goddesses who could be considered as spouses of the most popular gods of the Hindu pantheon. Her endeavour to be a Sita to Ram-guru has already been discussed in Chapter 2. Sita was the most devoted of wives, and as elaborated earlier, Piro sought to imitate her stance of devotion, as well as underline the worthiness of her person. What is striking is her attitude—as seen also in some earlier examples of her cited verses in this chapter—a demeanour of servility, an emphasis on being regarded as a humble, non-threatening person. The note of subservience to the superior and divine spouse, to whom respect and service (*sevā*) is due emerges strongly in the following verse:

> *Aradh sarirī sakat jī tum āp upāī*
> *Bohru sevā vāste tum charnī lāī*
> *Brahmaṇī Brahmā hoe ke tum sev lagoī*
> *Tumte hoe kar Lachhmī tum charan maloī*
> *Pārbatī Siv hoe kar tum sev lagāī*
> *Siya saktī Rām hoe tum charanī lāī.*

> You created the half-bodied Shakti
> You kept her at your feet to serve

---

[79] This is part of the address to the guru to rescue her from captivity.
[80] 160: 72.

Brahmani was meant to serve Brahma
You created Lachhmi to stay at your feet
Shiv's Parvati you put at his service
Siya, the shakti of Ram, you kept at your feet.[81]

The demeanour of the sudra-like (and sudra) woman towards the guru
can here be replicated in the respectful attitude of the Hindu wife to her
spouse-god. The evocation of domestic hierarchy in this instance resembles the injunctions of the dharmashastra, though Piro's place could never
be that, neither in the monastic Gulabdasi establishment nor as a former
prostitute who did not give up her association with others of her ilk.

Yet her effort to be seen as a consort of the guru was successful.
The literary trope popular in bhakti poetry, of speaking in the voice of a
woman, often assumes the stance of a bride pining for her husband. The
bridal imagery is fairly ubiquitous in bhakti poetry, the ideology of 'service and suhāg' that Sangari speaks of in the poetry of Mira that diluted
for her Mira's social rebellion.[82] Piro, too, uses this image to indicate the
degree of her spiritual attainment: Piyā Pīro pāye ke suhāgan hoī (On finding piya Piro has become an auspicious bride).[83] This line, as the rest of
this verse, blurs the distinction between god, guru, and spouse-god, as it
does the variance between physical and spiritual union. In many verses
of this siharfi, Piro exults in her complete physical and mystical union
with her god/guru/spouse-god—Pīro piyā āp haī maiṅ bhin na piyā (Piro
is piya, I am not separate from piya)[84]—not only stressing the need to
find god and guru within oneself, but also baring the bliss of attaining
that state. The ultimate reality is imagined in terms of both a physical
and mystical union with the divine, akin to that of a bride with her
groom, an endorsement of the conceptual reach of the idea of a suhāgan.
Furthermore, available iconography of the sect shows her sitting next to
Gulabdas on a raised platform, while some key disciples surround them,
including the heir-apparent to Gulabdas's gaddi (seat) shown fanning
them (see Figure 4.2).[85]

---

[81] 160: 141. 'Half-bodied Shakti' refers to the androgynous Ardhnareshwar.

[82] Sangari, 'Mirabai and the Spiritual Economy of Bhakti'.

[83] S3: 10.

[84] S3: 14.

[85] This picture is available in Sevāk's thesis, 'Gulab Dasi Sampradaya'. It shows
a bejewelled Piro sitting with Guru Gulabdas on an elevated seat while the heir
apparent to the gaddi, Hargobind, fans them with a flywhisk. Notice the turban
with an aigrette, halo, and umbrella, the insignia of royalty, on the guru's person.

FIGURE 4.2 A bejewelled Piro sitting alongside Guru Gulabdas on an elevated seat. The heir-apparent to the gaddi, Hargobind is shown holding the flywhisk. Gulabdas holds a rose (*gulab*), wears a turban and aigrette, and his head is framed by a halo, while he sits under an umbrella, all insignia of his magnificence.
The names of Guru Gulabdasji, Piroji and Hargobindji are inscribed in Gurmukhi. They watch a musical performance. The name of the female performer Kalavant is inscribed, though not of the musicians who surround her.
Source: Gian Inder Sewak, 'Gulabdasi Sampradaya: Rachna Ate Vichar', unpublished PhD diss., Guru Nanak Dev University, 1984. Sewak seems to have taken the image from a Gulabdasi manuscript but does not give the source in his thesis.

Also, Gulabdas and Piro were buried in a single tomb whose ruins still stand in the Kasur district of the Pakistani Punjab (see Figure 4.3). Gian Singh describes how the site of their mausoleum is considered sacred by their followers, who visit it with votive offerings during Holi.

A woman (prostitute?) Kalavant (literally, endowed with art, and one may question if this is her name or a generic name?) and men perform around them.

FIGURE 4.3   The extant tomb where Piro and Gulabdas lie buried side by side in Chathianwala, District Kasur, Pakistan. The tomb lies in utter neglect though is listed as an archaeological site by the Pakistan state. It is used as a cattle shed by the villagers.

Source: Courtesy of the author.

Unīs sau uṇtae Pīro mahi jahāṅ dabvāī
Dās Gulāb mās aṭh pīchhe marayo dabyo tithānhīe
Banyo makbarā ek duhoṅ kā mannat chele tāṅke
Phūl patāse ādi charāvat sīs nivāvat jāṅke.

In 1929 Piro was buried where she died
Das Gulab died eight months later and was buried in the same place

A single tomb was made for the two where their disciples ask for boons
They make offerings of flowers and sweetmeats and bow their heads.[86]

This degree of respect for a woman who calls herself the disciple of the
guru shows that Piro had reached the stature of the guru's consort. Piro,
who in the *160 Kafis* makes other disciples address her as 'mai sahib'
(respected mother) and 'mata Piro' (mother Piro), probably depicted the
reality of the situation in her time. At the same time, Gulabdas and Piro
never married, our sources not alluding to such an event. They remained
practising ascetics, keeping themselves above the quotidian requirements
of ordinary lives.

While Piro may have become acceptable in the Gulabdasi dera as the
consort of the guru and as a mother-like figure for other disciples, she
continued her association with other prostitutes, which must, in the least,
be seen as a constant reminder of her having come from their ranks.
Figure 4.2, which shows a soiree in progress, with music and dance, gives
a glimpse of what did occur in the dera, whose textual reference we get
from Gian Singh. It was perhaps an aspect of the antinomian elements
in her sect, or even a common practice in many Sufi hospices, that during annual fairs (*melā* or *urs*) prostitutes came to perform there, both to
celebrate the event or as disciples. My interview with an elder (*buzurg*)
of Chathianwala gave me an indication of the longevity of the practice.[87]
That Holi, the carnivalesque festival associated with overturning of
normal social restraints, was particularly favoured by the Gulabdasis is
apposite, for they prided themselves in flouting norms of caste, class,
and religion. A number of the songs—ragas—which Piro composed and
which were collected in the *Rag Sagar* (Ocean of Songs), celebrate her
guru, who was splendidly adorned with clothes, jewels, and weapons, and
who showed his visage (*darshan*) to his followers who came to play Holi
with him. Piro is often present in these songs in the signature line of the
verses, and as the principal disciple of the guru.

What is noteworthy is that a number of songs acknowledge the presence of prostitutes in the festival, with some hinting at competition to

---

[86] Giani Gian Singh, *Sri Guru Panth Prakash* (Patiala: Bhasha Vibhag, 1970,
first published in 1880), p. 1295. 1929 is the Bikrami Samvat date that corresponds
to 1872 CE.

[87] On 25 May 2008 I visited Chathianwala where the elderly Mohammad Shafi
Ansari recalled a Gulabdasi fair before the Partition of India lasting for eight to
nine days.

attract their numbers to the dera. Of the ninety-nine ragas recorded, eleven mention dancing girls. That prostitutes often participated in festivals held in the honour of various Sufi pirs in Punjab is apparent from the *Rag Sagar*, and also other accounts.[88] One may speculate that the reference to rising commercialism in their relations with the faqirs, as some songs suggest, may point to a changing perception of prostitution and courtesan culture with the establishment of the Raj.[89] But it also tells us about Piro's regular association with women from this profession. The references to prostitutes singing and dancing are numerous, their presence considered auspicious on this occasion of breaking down of social barriers.[90]

[88] On 26 May 2008 Dr Tabassum Kashmiri, a scholar in Pakistan, recalled his youth in the 1950s in Punjab. He spoke of the Nurpur mela at the Shah Char Charag Dargah near Rawalpindi, where, according to him, prostitutes (*tawa'ifs*) came from all over Pakistan and even India to participate in the proceedings. These included their dances (*mujrās*). In her book on the prostitutes of Hira Mandi in Lahore in contemporary Pakistan, Louise Brown writes in detail of a prostitute's visit with her family to the urs of Shahbaz Qalandar to Sehwan, Sind. Louise Brown, *The Dancing Girls of Lahore: Selling Love and Saving Dreams in Pakistan's Pleasure District* (New York: Harper Collins, 2006), pp. 95–107. Shahbaz Qalandar was also said to have converted prostitutes to Islam. See William Dalrymple, 'The Red Fairy', in his *Nine Lives: In Search of the Sacred in Modern India* (London: Bloomsbury, 2009), pp. 112–45.

[89] Historians have argued that the colonial state's Victorian values changed the perception and cultural understanding of the courtesan. See Veena Oldenburg, 'Afternoons in the Kothas of Lucknow', in *Shaam-e-Awadh: Writings on Lucknow*, edited by Veena Oldenburg (New Delhi: Penguin, 2007), pp. 111–31. In one song composed by Gulabdas, he reprimands gankas or dancing girls for performing mujra for monetary gain: *karke mujrā gur darbāre paisā leve hath pasāre* (after performing mujra at the guru's court they ask for money with extended hands). He then chastises them, *kahe Gulāb suno rī gankā, lobh tajo tum kuṛe dhan kā* (says Gulab, listen O ganka, let go of the greed for falsely claimed money). ('Rag Dhanasri Shabad' in 'Ath Rag Sagar Granth Mata Guru Piroji' in Sant Vijender Das, *Sant Kavyitri Ma Piro* [Panchkula: Satluj Prakashan, 2011], pp. 212–39, 238).

[90] Prostitutes are regarded as auspicious precisely because they always remain suhagan or married (to their various lovers), never becoming inauspicious widows. For the same reason widows, howsoever sexually disciplined, are never considered auspicious. On the concept of auspiciousness, see Frederique Apffel Marglin, 'Female Sexuality in the Hindu World', in *Immaculate and Powerful: The Female in Sacred Image and Social Reality*, edited by C.W. Atkinson, C.H. Buchanan, and

Gankā āve nāche gāve kar leṅ murādaṅ ān bharī
satgur pīr faqīr jhukāe hath lachhmī āge jor kharī.

Ganka sings and dances fulfilling her desires
The satguru makes pirs and faqirs bow [to him], and Lachhmi stands with
folded hands.[91]

If prostitutes became lay disciples of Gulabdas because of the presence
of Piro, then here was an ongoing association of Piro with her past
that she does not repudiate, indeed, actively participates in keeping
it afloat.

The values encountered in bhakti devotion, as I have argued, could
go along with the dharmashastras, challenge them, or overturn them.
The varied possibilities of conversion to those values, their subversion and aversion to them, or even the perversion of their intent could
be available within the bhakti imaginary. Piro emulated Mira's social
challenge to an extent, but wished for association with a human guru-
god. She used bhakti parables and legends to amplify ever more the
expansive potentiality embedded in bhakti devotion. The unique
openness of the bhakti way for all sorts of deviants of society allowed
not only an entry into the haloed portals of salvation to Piro, but also
enabled her to do so without shedding her sexualized past. This was in
many ways a sui generis contribution of Piro, enlarging its subverting
tendencies further. However, the question of Piro's Islamic past
remains. How did she tackle being a Muslim in a Sikh establishment?
Was she able to demonstrate that whatever attributes from a past one
carried, it was a spiritual future that mattered, that divinity was always
one, indivisible, everywhere, and permeating everything? Let us now
view how certain popular Punjabi Sufi ideas, images, and inheritances
suffused her writing, giving her confidence that all divine seekers
were on the same path.

M.R. Miles (Boston: Beacon Press, 1985), pp. 39–60. Also see the discussion in
Denton, *Female Ascetics*, pp. 34–40. Interestingly, in one verse addressed to her
'friends', Piro calls their marital status false, as they have not turned to the true
master—the guru/god: *Pīro kahe saheliyo kyuṅ kūṛ kamāvo, binā suhāg singār kar*
bibchār kahāvo (Piro says friends why earn falsehood? You are called unchaste
for you dress up without a husband) (160: 35). Though here the meaning of the
prostitute's auspiciousness has been turned around, it plays on the same semantic
field where they are considered auspicious.

[91] *RS*, 'Hori Sorab di'.

SEEKING THEOLOGICAL EQUIVALENCES

Besides Piro, at least one more Muslim, Mohammad Shah, mentioned in multiple sources, was a member of the Gulabdasi sect. However, unlike Piro, who sought a relationship as a consort of the guru, Mohammad Shah went on to set up an independent establishment in a nearby village, a privilege perhaps unavailable to women.[92] Piro's use of the term 'mlechha' for her kidnappers and erstwhile community after her ordeal of abduction and incarceration, an epithet that denoted them as outsiders and low barbarians, gives us a sense of the discomfort she may have felt because of her Muslim background even in a liberal and antinomian sect. On the other hand, we do know of the 'Bullehshahi' influence on Gulabdas, as mentioned by our Sikh sources, which traced the libertine ways of the Gulabdasis to the apparently corrupting influence of the popular Sufi Bulleh Shah (1680–1758) and his followers, who were also based like Gulabdas in the Kasur district of Punjab.[93] In this section I will focus on demonstrating how the Gulabdasis often deployed certain Sufi terms and concepts making them pliable and adaptive to their own theological premises. More specifically, I will show Piro's investment in amplifying this innate, inchoate tendency of the Gulabdasis, delineating her effort to enhance inclusive predilections of her sect. By using a vocabulary that borrowed and sought equivalences with Sufi concepts, and by knitting in the familiar emotional thread in her poetry that sought to challenge authority figures that weighed against the weak and the vulnerable, Piro underscored the unifying vision of true religious seekers, and challenged the need for formalist religion. I will contend that it was Piro's singular contribution through her poetic outpourings and cultural imaginaries that fructified into and enlarged the syncretistic vision of her sect.

The term 'syncretism', used cautiously and advisedly above, has, in recent times, lost some of the traction it held earlier. It has been critiqued by historians with expertise in textual sources[94] and anthropologists looking at religions in practice, especially in active and contested sites.[95]

---

[92] See Chapter 8.

[93] See Chapter 1.

[94] Carl W. Ernst, 'Situating Sufism and Yoga', *Journal of the Royal Asiatic Society* 15, no. 1 (2005): 15–43.

[95] Peter van der Veer, 'Syncretism, Multiculturalism and the Discourse of Tolerance', in *Syncretism/Anti-Syncretism: The Politics of Religious Synthesis*, edited by Charles Stewart and Rosalind Shaw (London: Routledge, 1994), pp. 196–211;

They see syncretism as an inadequate concept because it assumes an amalgamation of separate religious traditions, allowing the viewing of religions as self-contained entities that can be mixed and harmonized into a synthesis. That is to say, the processual and open-ended character of religions is overlaid with the idea of their inherent completeness.

In South Asia the term has carried a positive connotation as historians used examples of syncretism to show religions in practice. The term 'syncretism' was invested with the load of demonstrating composite cultures, shared religious sites, and religiously mixed following of tombs and saints that acted as an antidote to the pathology of communalism that scarred colonial and postcolonial histories. Negating the burden of colonialist accusations that saw the colonized as intrinsically divided, the concept of syncretism was deployed to show the nascent nation's 'composite' culture. As Shahid Amin puts it, syncretism in this understanding comes fully formed, bleaching histories of conquest and conflict.[96] Peter van der Veer shows that the mixed following of a saint may not exclude hierarchies of access in these sites, nor how the saint may be perceived in different terms by the Hindus and Muslims who come to worship.[97] However, scholars aware of such critiques have nevertheless insisted that many shrines continue to be spaces of Hindu–Muslim amity.[98] Still, wary of such usage today, historians are carefully examining their own conscious or unconscious implication in the agendas of writing 'secular' histories.[99]

While syncretism as an analytic is no longer used uncritically, scholars have begun a more nuanced reading of what ostensibly appear to be shared cultural practices. Pointing to the rigidity of religious categories post the historical processes associated with colonialism, some suggest that sharp religious divisions may not have been the norm earlier, nor may have

---

Robert M. Hayden, 'Antagonistic Tolerance: Competitive Sharing of Religious Sites in South Asia and the Balkans', *Current Anthropology* 43, no. 1 (2002): 205–19.

[96] Shahid Amin, 'Un Saint Guerrier: Sur la Conquete del' Inde du Nord par les Tures au xi Siecle', *Annales–Histoire, Sciences Sociales* 6, no. 2 (March–April 2005): 262–92. I thank the author for sharing the English version of the paper with me.

[97] Van der Veer, 'Syncretism, Multiculturalism and the Discourse of Tolerance'.

[98] See the discussion on syncretism in Pnina Werbner and Helene Basu 'The Embodiment of Charisma', in *Embodying Charisma: Modernity, Locality and the Performance of Emotion in Sufi Cults*, edited by Pnina Werbner and Helene Basu (London: Routledge, 1998), pp. 3–27.

[99] Neeladri Bhattacharya, 'Predicaments of Secular Histories', *Public Culture* 20, no. 1 (2008): 57–73.

instances when elements from both traditions appear been considered as aberrations.[100] Another historian shows that in Punjab saint veneration was a form of piety shared by all people.[101] An important argument based on interaction and relatedness of cultures has been put forward by Tony Stewart in the context of the seemingly syncretic language used to establish Islamic theological ideas in medieval Bengal. Stewart does not see the language that deployed Hindu equivalents to convey the ideas of Islam as a case of syncretic amalgamation. Rather, he prefers to see in this borrowing a desire to locate 'theological equivalences' on the part of religious figures disseminating Islamic ideals in this peripheral region of India.[102] The theology of the interlocutors was rooted in Islamic traditions, but the project of its diffusion required a language that was easily comprehensible to the people. In an argument that also underlines the need for greater care in assuming syncretism from outward appearances of convergence, Carl Ernst studies the extensive texts that showed a relationship between the Sufis and Yogis of India. Acknowledging the many points of equivalence and cultural conversation between them, Ernst stresses that exchange often took place from being grounded in one's tradition, and included an inclination towards contestation and appropriation.[103] Ernst's argument that emphasizes location within inherited cultural traditions is echoed among a number of scholars today, and may be seen as a reaction to an older, blither, scholarly inclination that viewed Sufi development in India as a product of non-dualist advaita monism within Indic sources.[104] I believe this argument that underscores gaining

[100] Robin Rinehart, 'Interpretations of the Poetry of Bulhe Shah', *International Journal of Punjab Studies* 3, no. 1 (1996): 45–63.

[101] Farina Mir, 'Genre and Devotion in Punjabi Popular Narratives: Rethinking Cultural and Religious Syncretism', in *Punjab Reconsidered: History, Culture and Practice*, edited by Anshu Malhotra and Farina Mir (New Delhi: Oxford University Press, 2012), pp. 221–60.

[102] Tony K. Stewart, 'In Search of Equivalence: Conceiving Muslim–Hindu Encounter through Translation Theory', *History of Religions* 40, no. 3 (2001): 260–87.

[103] Ernst, 'Situating Sufism and Yoga'.

[104] Lajwanti Rama Krishna, *Panjabi Sufi Poets A.D. 1460–1900* (New Delhi: Ashajanak Publications, 1973). Robin Rinehart discusses a number of Hindu and Sikh scholars who are inclined to see Sufism as a product of Vaishnav and advaita influences. See her 'Interpretations of the Poetry'. On a critique of Rama Krishna along these lines, see Christopher Shackle, 'Punjabi Sufi Poetry from Farid to Farid', in Malhotra and Mir, *Punjab Reconsidered*, pp. 3–34.

insights from within one's cultural location and seeking interaction from being ensconced there is a significant one, though I wish to demonstrate that religious exchange was eagerly sought by some. Certain individuals and groups had enormous stakes in pushing forward such proclivities, and it is they who attempted to sustain interaction and open-endedness between cultures. They were the agents of transmission, the ones more receptive to newer ideas or familiar ones in different garbs. Does such cultural fluidity, curiosity, and exchange result in some kind of hybridity, bricolage, or even syncretism, terms that highlight interaction leading to a new cultural product, a mosaic of different elements, or even a synthesis emerging over a time? Or can one stay embedded in an inherited culture, but revel in commonalities and familiarities that encourage a universal humanistic outlook? Dominique-Sila Khan underlines the salience of traditions that thrive on exchange and their import in impacting society: 'Syncretic and liminal traditions or communities can be perceived as cohesive forces in the social fabric, powerful links in the uninterrupted chain of religious traditions.'[105] It is towards such cultural expression that I wish to indicate, an ease with theological concepts that emerge from within the legacy of one's tradition, but where there is also an appreciation of sameness elsewhere, a carousing in equivalences that one finds in parallel traditions. I demonstrate how individuals like Piro invested in developing such syncretistic predilections based on variegated borrowings, for these manifold cultural possibilities not only rendered their own lives more meaningful but also opened doors for others.

The mystical tradition within Islam developed in the crucible of Islam in West Asia; its evolution has been discussed by scholars like Annemarie Schimmel in some detail.[106] Grounding Sufi practices in Islam, and also Sufi asceticism, scholars have argued for the Quran as the basis for its terminology, though the influence of Christian mysticism on Sufism has been acknowledged.[107] However, even scholars like Aziz Ahmad, known for their 'Muslim separatist position',[108] concede that 'from the

---

[105] Dominique-Sila Khan, *Crossing the Threshold: Understanding Religious Identities in South Asia* (London: I.B. Tauris Publishers, 2004), pp. 6–7.

[106] Annemarie Schimmel, *Mystical Dimensions of Islam* (New Delhi: Yoda Press, 2007 [1975]).

[107] Aziz Ahmad, 'Sufism and Hindu Mysticism', in *Sufism and Society in Medieval India*, edited by Raziuddin Aquil (New Delhi: Oxford University Press, 2011), pp. 31–51.

[108] Raziuddin Aquil, 'Introduction', in his *Sufism and Society in Medieval India*, p. xii.

fifteenth century onwards Sufis in India seem to have begun noticing a resemblance between Ibn al 'Arabi's formulation of the doctrine of ontological monism and their second-hand information about the prevalence of similar doctrines in the Vedanta'.[109] Thus, the commonalities between the advaita monist doctrine of the pantheistic permeation of the Brahman in the universe and the Sufi belief in *wahdat-ul-wujūd*, or the Unity of Existence, were noticed, and, I will argue, were developed by interested sections from within both the Islamicate and Indic traditions who invested in such cultural conversations.

Ahmad points to such predilections among the Qadiri and Shattari Sufi orders, particularly popular and widespread in Punjab, Bulleh Shah often referred to as a Qadiri–Shattari Sufi.[110] Here I will show how Bulleh Shah, the most popular Sufi mystic of Punjab, was an influence and inspiration to the Gulabdasis and Piro.[111] Known for his openness to 'Hindu' imagery, scholars have traced a strong presence of Krishnaite and Nath elements in his verses.[112] Ranjha, the flute-playing cowherd in the most famous of Punjabi ballads of *Hir–Ranjha*, with whom Hir falls in love, was a Krishna-like figure.[113] Others though have rightly maintained that Islamicate and Quranic references are very significant in his work, and the recourse to the union of Hir and Ranjha could mean an embracing of

---

[109] Ahmad, 'Sufism and Hindu Mysticism', p. 46.

[110] Bulleh Shah's sheikh murshid Shah Inayat is referred to as a Qadiri–Shattari. See Jit Singh Sital, *Bulleh Shah: Jivan te Rachna* (Patiala: Punjabi University, 2002), p. 14. Rinehart calls Shah Inayat a Shattari Sufi and notes that they were particularly influenced by the pantheism of Ibn-i-Arabi (1160–1240). Rinehart, 'Interpretations of Poetry'.

[111] Shackle, otherwise in disagreement with Rama Krishna's thesis, agrees with her on the popularity of Bulleh Shah in Punjab. See his 'Punjabi Sufi Poetry', p. 22.

[112] Denis Matringe, 'Krsnaite and Nath Elements in the Poetry of the Eighteenth Century Panjabi Sufi Bullhe Shah', in *Devotional Literature in South Asia: Current Research 1985–1988*, edited by R.S. McGregor (Cambridge: Cambridge University Press, 1992), pp. 190–206. Carla Petievich cites U.F. Usborne's 1905 translation of Varis Shah's qissa where Usborne refers to Bulleh's friendship with Darshani Nath as a possible source for his knowledge of Indic philosophy. See her *When Men Speak as Women: Vocal Masquerades in Indo-Muslim Poetry* (New Delhi: Oxford University Press, 2007), p. 36.

[113] Petievich also links Ranjha with the Biblical and Quranic figure of Joseph, the favourite son of a prosperous father, dispossessed of his birthright by jealous elder brothers. (Petievich, *When Men Speak as* Women, p. 38.)

immediate and personal mystical experience that being in the confines of traditional Hinduism or Islam could not express.[114]

The impersonation of the feminine voice in Bulleh's kafis has been extensively commented on by scholars.[115] He often presented himself as Hir to the divine or preceptor figure addressed as Ranjha. The other popular sixteenth-century Qadiri Sufi who too spoke as Hir, Shah Hussain, is sometimes referred to as a *malāmī*, or a blameworthy deviant, for a number of reasons, but primarily because he did as he pleased, ignoring the dictates of the shari'at, including singing and dancing with abandon.[116] Bulleh was also known to have masqueraded as a dancing girl for a while to please his spiritual preceptor, after he turned Bulleh out of his circle of disciples for neglecting to follow the dictates of Islamic law.[117] As Carla Petievich has noted about the two Qadiri Sufis, this image of a dancing dervish both enhanced the femininity cultivated in their poetry and linked them to the devotional poetry of north India (Mirabai was known to wear bells and dance) as also to the Mevlevi Sufi order associated with Jalal al-din Rumi (d. 1273).[118] Bulleh's poetry also evoked images of work and leisure associated with a woman's life. Scholars like Richard Eaton have spoken of how the songs of the Sufis in the Deccan deployed images that were reminiscent of women's work and gathered followers from among women.[119] Bulleh's poetry, too, was suffused with

[114] Rinehart, 'The Interpretations of the Poetry' However, it is difficult to accept the view of scholars who insist that Bulleh accepted formal Islam and his antinomian utterances were nothing more than an attempt to 'shock' people into reality. See Mustansir Mir, 'Teachings of Two Punjabi Sufi Poets', in *Religions of India in Practice*, edited by Donald S. Lopez, Jr (Princeton: Princeton University Press, 1995), pp. 518–29.

[115] Petievich, *When Men Speak as Women.*

[116] In Hussain's case also for relations with his companion, a Hindu boy Madho Lal. See Scott Kugle (commentary and translation), 'Haqiqat al-Fuqara: Poetic Biography of 'Madho Lal' Hussayn', in *Same-Sex Love in India: Readings from Literature and History*, edited by Ruth Vanita and Saleem Kidwai (New Delhi: Macmillan, 2000), pp. 145–56.

[117] Sital reports that Bulleh stayed with a dancing girl for a while learning her craft. Sital, *Bulleh Shah*, pp. 21–2. Also see Petievich, *When Men Speak as Women*, p. 42fn14.

[118] Petievich, *When Men Speak as Women*, p. 37.

[119] For the discussion around *chakkī-nāma* and *charkhā-nāma* poetry, see Richard M. Eaton, 'Sufi Folk Literature and the Expansion of Indian Islam', in Aquil, *Sufism and Society*, pp. 70–81.

images of women's work: the spinning circle (*trinjan*), women fetching water from the well, spinning to make their dowry, and bridal imagery including that of a bride pining for the absent husband. As a former prostitute and dancing girl, and as a woman self-consciously writing as one, there was much in Bulleh's verses that attracted Piro to him.[120] But before exploring the metaphysical aspects of Gulabdasi and Sufi monist orientations in Piro's poetry, I look at how Sufi terms were used and understood by the Gulabdasis.[121]

I wish to begin by reiterating that the Gulabdasis spoke from being placed in the advaita tradition, nurtured within certain Sikh sects.[122] Also, Piro's and Gulabdasi writing is in a language that is part of Sikh inheritance, that is, Punjabi, with its links to Sadhu Bhasha, and Braj, rather than that of the Sufis who used Punjabi dialects like Majhi and Multani.[123] One may suggest that while the syntactical base was Punjabi for both the Gulabdasis and the Sufis, the vocabulary could veer one way or another. However, it needs to be underscored that there were many points of interaction and connection between these traditions, including a familiarity with concepts and themes, and in invoking certain emotional states. What is significant about Gulabdasi poetry is that its practitioners could switch codes to words and terms that were Islamicate in origin, seamlessly appropriating and incorporating Sufi terminology within their poetry. Piro's deployment of the term 'fana' (annihilation of the self in divine) exemplifies this comfort with Sufi concepts. Here is an example of her verse in praise of the guru: *Har dīd kahat fanāhu haī kahāṅ kare yakīnā; khole chasmā jikar kā har darsan chīnā* (every glimpse says annihilate and believe; you open the eye of the heart to discern divine vision).[124] In some verses in her poetry there are references to the Sufi

---

[120] I have earlier discussed how Piro emulated Hir in her confrontation with the mullahs.

[121] Bruce B. Lawrence has noted the thematic equivalences between Sant and Sufi traditions as well as mildly critiqued the scholarly tendency to deny this influence on Sants. See his 'The Sant Movement and North Indian Sufis', in Schomer and McLeod, *The Sants*, pp. 359–73.

[122] See Chapter 1.

[123] See the discussion in Malhotra and Mir, *Punjab Reconsidered*, pp. xxviii–xxix. Also see Denis Matringe, 'Hir Varis Shah, A Story Retold', in *Narrative Strategies: Essays on South Asian Literature and Film*, edited by Vasudha Dalmia and Theo Damsteegt (New Delhi: Oxford University Press, 1998), p. 19.

[124] 160: 147. *Jikar* or *jigar* is literally liver, and carries the connotation of the heart.

way and stages associated with the Sufi's spiritual progress towards the divine (*shariat, tarīqat, haqīqat, mārfat*), for example, *sabati rakhsāṅ satguru te, jinhā mritak lī jivāī mainūṅ; pare sarā tarīq haqīqtī de, mārfatī mo āp janāī mainūṅ* (I'll keep faith in the satguru who brought me alive from the dead; away from shari'at, tariqat and haqiqat, he put me on the path of marfat).[125]

In a similar vein, occasionally in Piro's poetry one catches glimpses of words and the affect of Bulleh, the mimesis being unmistakable, though her verse may develop along the non-dualist advaita path. Thus, when Piro says *Pīro piyā āp hai maiṅ bhin na piyā'* (Piro is herself the beloved, I am not separate from the beloved)[126] or *Piyā Pīro pāe ke suhāgaṇ hoī* (On meeting the beloved Piro has become an auspicious bride),[127] one is reminded of Bulleh's *Piyā piyā karte hamī piyā hoe* (On calling the beloved repeatedly I have become Him)[128] or his popular *Rānjhā Rānjhā kardī maiṅ āpe Rānjhā hoī* (On calling to Rānjhā I have become Rānjhā).[129] Or when Piro says *Pīro nāl kuchajiāṅ maiṅ chaj na lītā, velā pichhe bītiyā maiṅ kuj na kītā* (Piro kept the company of the clumsy and did not learn skill, time went by and I did not do a thing),[130] it is reminiscent of Bulleh's *Maiṅ kamīnī kuchajī kojhī, beguṇ kauṇ vichārī* (I am mean, clumsy, and ugly, who'll think of the one without qualities).[131] While often Piro's poems celebrated and revelled in finding her guru, the preceptor who awakened and slaked her spiritual thirst, and Bulleh's poems evoked the mood of separation from his preceptor/divine figure but owed his spiritual wealth to him, the figure of the preceptor loomed large in their poetry. Thus, Piro can be said to employ a vocabulary and evoke an emotional chord that had

---

[125] *S2*: 4. Piro refers to being transported on to the mystical path (marfat) from the more ritualistic, legal one of shari'at, and perhaps even skipping the early stages on the Sufi path.

[126] *S3*: 14.

[127] *S3*: 10.

[128] 'Piya Piya Karte Hamin Piya Hoe', in *Bulleh Shah ki Kafian*, edited by Namvar Singh (New Delhi: National Institute of Punjab Studies, 2003), p. 146.

[129] 'Ape Ranjha Hoï', in N. Singh, *Bulleh Shah ki Kafian*, p. 184.

[130] *S3*: 19.

[131] 'Main Kusmbhara Chun Chun Harï', in N. Singh, *Bulleh Shah ki Kafian*, pp. 171–2. There are other verses where Piro uses a broad idea present in Bulleh's poems. For example, her use of the pair of words *adal* and *fazal* (justice and grace) in *S1*: 6 is similar to the use of the pair by Bulleh in 'Sahavareyan Ghar Jana' in N. Singh, *Bulleh Shah ki Kafian*, p. 50.

great familiarity in Punjab, even if the emotional state she described was not identical to Bulleh's. By establishing these connections she placed herself in the tradition of the seekers of divine grace, even if one speaks of union and the other of separation.

It was most significantly in the rejection of the externalities of ritualistic and legalistic religion, and in the assertion of a greater and universal truth that all could embrace, that Piro most emulated Bulleh. She mocked the keepers of religious formalism much like Bulleh, and pointed towards the larger pantheistic, solipsistic truth. That they thought that those in authority were self-aggrandizing comes through repeatedly in following verses of Bulleh and Piro.

Bulleh mocked the Quran scholars:

> Becoming a Quran scholar [*hāfiz*] you memorize it
> Constant reading makes you glib
> Then your attention is drawn towards favours
> Your heart goes wandering like a messenger.[132]

Thus when Piro iterates similarly of Islamic scholars she is expressing a shared sentiment.

> *Gāfal sāiṅ nām bin tum kāfar kājī*
> *Sarghī ghar ghar khāvso kar jagat muthājī.*
>
> Oblivious of the name of the master, infidel qazis
> You go begging from door to door for meals like the indigent.[133]

Similarly, Bulleh, and following him Piro, accuses religious authorities of deviously trapping the innocent in their snares, whether by spouting knowledge purportedly found in the holy books or by recommending pilgrimages.[134]

Bulleh says:

> We are tired of reading the Vedas and the Quran
> We've damaged our foreheads prostrating
> God is neither at pilgrimage, nor Mecca.[135]

---

[132] 'Ik Alaf Parho Chhutkara Hai', In N. Singh, *Bulleh Shah ki Kafian*, p. 43.

[133] 160: 28.

[134] This is a theme present in the poetry of a number of Qadiri Sufis of Punjab, including the seventeenth-century mystic Sultan Bahu. Malhotra, 'Panths and Piety'.

[135] This verse appears in Bulleh's famous 'Ishq di Navioṅ Naviṅ Bahār', in N. Singh, *Bulleh Shah ki Kafian*, p. 37.

And Piro's statement had the familiar ring:

Kāzī īn kurān kī sab Turak fasāye
Hindu ghere paṇḍtāṅ, paṛh bed sunāye.

Qazis trap the Turaks in the honour of the Quran
Hindus are tricked by the pundits who read the Vedas to them.[136]

While examples of deriding corrupt religious authority can be multiplied as both Bulleh and Piro reviled such self-important personages
with impunity, I wish to now turn to Piro's and Gulabdasis' pantheistic,
monist theology and see how they appropriated aspects of Sufi thought,
which was particularly popular in Punjab. Piro's sophisticated engagement with the theology of her sect was built on the cornerstone of the
Vedanta belief in the identity between the Self/Atman and Brahman
(Supreme Being), the notion that the deepest part of our being is one
with the essence of the world.[137] This idea found expression in the mystical mantra of Soham (I am S/He)[138] of the Gulabdasis, as with Gulabdas
calling himself Brahm. The continuum between the body, the empirical
reality, the undifferentiated consciousness, and the universe is seen in
Piro's words: *ek sarīr anātmā, ātam brhamāṇḍe,*[139] and again *baṭak tukham
kā rūp jyoṅ houṅ sarab akhaṇḍe* (like a tree is a form of seed so I am one
with the universe).[140] God as the essence of the world pervades it: *sarab
rūp moṅ jaṇīyoṅ jyoṅ nīr tarānge* (and is found in every form, like waves in
water).[141] The same thought can be seen in Gulabdas's words: *ek bīj jiveṅ
bat phail rahā har tara hai yagat bilās terā* (like a seed spreads as a tree
you play expansively in the universe).[142] The Supreme Reality was both
immanent and transcendent for the Gulabdasis, and their path involved
the solipsistic belief of locating within the self the essence of creation.

[136] 160: 152.

[137] On advaita see S. Radhakrishnan and Charles A. Moore, eds, *A Source Book
in Indian Philosophy* (Princeton: University of Princeton Press, 1957), pp. 506–7.

[138] On the self-understanding of female spiritual leaders and their theological
identification with a feminine deity see Rita DasGupta Sherma, '"Sa Ham–I am
She": Woman as Goddess', in *Is the Goddess a Feminist: The Politics of South Asian
Goddesses*, edited by Alf Hiltebeitel and Kathleen M. Erndl (Sheffield: Academic
Press, 2000), pp. 24–51.

[139] 160: 148

[140] 160: 144.

[141] S3: 16.

[142] This line is from an incomplete siharfi (20) of Gulabdas in Ms. 888.

This philosophy of the Gulabdasis came overlaid with the ideas of bhakti, as I have discussed throughout this study. In Piro's writings, the ultimate Reality is imagined in nirguna terms, though she takes recourse to Vaishnav imagery when required. However, the ability to follow the path to seek Reality rested on the guru, illuminating the significance of the preceptor both in the ascetic tradition and within the bhakti imaginary, as within Sufi praxis. Piro captures these esoteric ideas in her verse that refers to this formless Supreme Being, arrived at through working out different negations, but underlines the positive role of the guru:

Sāiṅ hameṅ ajāt haī na hiṅdu turkā
janam maraṇ to bāhra na nārī purkhā
hadāṅ pare behad haī na hadāṅ māhī
Pīro guru dikhāvsī aiuṅ dekhe nāhī.

The master is without attributes neither Hindu nor Turk.
Outside birth and death, neither woman nor man.
Beyond bounds, is limitless, not confined within limits.
Piro says guru will reveal, unfathomable otherwise.[143]

While expounding the ideals of non-duality between the Self and the Supreme, Soham, an expression of Piro's immediately opens up the universe of Islamicate Sufi heritage—an'al haq (I am the Absolute Truth). This expression is attributed to the mystic martyr of Baghdad, Mansur al-Hallaj, who inspired in the Islamic world deep enraptured love among some Sufis who looked at him as a model of suffering, but also venomous hatred from the orthodox, who tortured and hanged him in 922 CE.[144] Schimmel, writing the history of Sufism through its classical period, notes that scholars have compared this mystical expression to the Upanishad's *aham brahmāsmi* (I am Brahman). She also shows the strong controversies, interpretations, and reactions an'al haq garnered in the Muslim world, particularly on whether it should be seen in pantheistic or strictly monotheistic terms.

Here the important point is the manner in which the expression an'al haq was used in Punjab to elucidate the idea of the Unity of Being, and how theological equivalence was made with advaita philosophy. In Punjab, the resonance of an'al haq was twofold—its association with Mansur, the Sufi who ostensibly visited Punjab in his peregrinations, and the theological

---

[143] *S3*: 4.
[144] Schimmel, *Mystical Dimensions*, pp. 62–77.

interpretative possibilities opened up by the expression itself. The popularity of Mansur in Punjab can be seen in the multiple references to him in the poetry of a number of Punjabi Sufis, including Bulleh, and also in that of Piro and Gulabdas.[145] The references to him link up with the idea of dogmatic and bookish knowledge, and wrongly applied power by those in authority to perpetuate it, and invariably speak of his bearing tortures to proclaim his truth. The self-image of the Sufi in this context is of his being the impecunious man of god—a faqir—tortured for his truth, and willingly accepting suffering. Thus, any allusion to Mansur is almost always in reference to his torture and unjust hanging.[146] To quote Bulleh as an example:

> Beloved, be careful when you fall in love, or you'll regret it later.
> There, one had his skin flayed,
> One was cut open with axes,
> One was hanged at the gallows,
> There, you too will be beheaded.[147]

The Gulabdasis equally speak of the tortures of Mansur and others in the same emotional frame as the Sufis of Punjab. Gulabdas writes: *has has ke khal lahaiyāṅ ne chāṛe sūliyāṅ haq pukārde nī* (smiling while being flayed, they have climbed gallows calling out haq [truth]).[148] And Piro echoes:

> *Pīro kehsī satguru in sarā piyārī*
> *gote diye Kabīr ko in binā vichārī*
> *sūlī diyo Mansūr ko khal samas lāhī*
> *aur dukhāye keṭre ham ket sunāhī.*

> Piro says satguru they love the shara
> Without giving it a thought they tried to drown Kabir
> They hanged Mansur flaying him
> What more tortures shall I relate?[149]

---

[145] These references are also found in the Punjabi verses of the seventeenth-century Qadiri Sufi Sultan Bahu. See Jamal J. Elias, translated and introduced, *Death Before Dying: The Sufi Poems of Sultan Bahu* (Berkeley: University of California Press, 1998), p. 86.

[146] Mansur was often mentioned in conjunction with other tortured souls like Shams Tabriz, said to be the preceptor of the great Jalaluddin Rumi. In Punjabi folk parlance he was skinned alive.

[147] 'Pyarian Sambhal ke Nehu Laga', in N. Singh, *Bulleh Shah ki Kafian*, p. 142.

[148] Ms. 888.

[149] 160: 22.

The image of the tortures that al-Hallaj suffered with stoicism in Baghdad became the stuff of myth, appropriated and made their own by varied groups like the Punjabi Sufis and the Gulabdasis. This was the image of the righteous suffering for their unbending adherence to justice and Truth, the haq that Mansur called out to. Piro's indignation at her face-off with the mullahs, discussed earlier, exhibits this sense of injustice, the ill treatment that was inevitably meted out to the righteous by those seemingly upholding the tenets of Islamic law.

How was an'al haq, the signature words of Mansur that opened a long history of scholarly discourses, interpreted by the Gulabdasis? In Piro's writing, an'al haq at one level extends the usage of 'Mansur' to highlight the continuous history of persecution.

Jeko ne sat kehat haiṅ taṅh khal lahese
jeko kehsī an'āl haq bardār kareṅse.

Those who speak the Truth, they strip their flesh
Those who say an'al haq, they disinherit them.[150]

Bulleh Shah too uses the term in this sense and tongue-in-cheek he cautions:

Bullyā gair sharā na ho ...
Muṅho na an'āl haq bago
Chaṛ sūlī ḍhale gāveṅgā.

Bullya don't step out of shariah ...
Don't say an'al haq
Or you will be singing (swinging) on the gallows.[151]

Piro, however, also employs the term as a mantra, a chant specifically of her sect. In her interlocution with the mullahs when they wish to bring her back into the fold of Islam and urge her to recite the Quranic formula, kalima, Piro proffers an'al haq as the right chant: *kaho sabūtī an'āl haq yeh kalmā sācho* (affirm an'al haq the true kalma).[152]

However, the term is most often deployed to highlight the permeation of the one Truth in the universe. It is in this sense that it is used as a theological equivalent of the pantheistic, non-dualist ideas of the Gulabdasis.

[150] 160: 140.
[151] 'Pyarian' in N. Singh, *Bulleh Shah ki Kafian*, p. 143.
[152] 160: 30.

It refers to the one Reality that infuses the universe, the Truth that the guru opens one's heart to:

> *Khol kuvāṛe jikar ke tum dayo hamāre*
> *haq majūd dikhlāyo kul ālam yāre.*

> You have opened the doors of my heart
> Showing the Truth that pervades the universe.[153]

Thus, as a mantra, similar in its import to soham, as a universal Reality, and as the Truth that penetrates the world as the self, an'al haq resonates with multiple valences with the Gulabdasis as it does with the Sufis.

Finally, the solipsistic pantheism that seeks to locate the divine in the self, the only knowable reality, can also be seen in the more esoteric and opaque verses of both Bulleh and Piro. Though, once again, the larger philosophical contexts in which they were located may be different, the referencing of Mansur's cry is significant, drawing attention to the permeation of a universal Truth or haq. Piro's translucent verse reads:

> *Haīni saīyoṅ merīyoṅ maiṅ kehar kītā*
> *Maiṅ vich saīṅ vasda maiṅ bhaye na lītā*
> *Pīro darsan rab dā maiṅ jis val jovāṅ*
> *Neṛe kehte sahargoṅ mat maiṅ hī hovāṅ?*

> O friends of mine I have caused a calamity
> The master resided in me but I did not recognize this
> Piro says there is divine visage wherever I turn
> He is close say the wise, perhaps it is me?[154]

This verse, reminiscent of the ulti bamsi of Kabir, and which speaks of the divine within the self, and the self as divine, also resembles in spirit the elliptical stanza of Bulleh's famous kafi *Bullah kī jāṇā maiṅ kauṇ* (What does Bullah know who I am?) where Bulleh, too, seems to speak of the self as the only knowable truth.

> *Awal ākhar āp nuṅ jāṇā*
> *Na koī dūjā hor pachhāṇā*
> *Maithoṅ hor na koī sayāṇā*
> *Bullah Shah khaṛā hai kauṇ?*

> I recognize myself as the first and the last
> I don't recognize anyone else

---

153 160: 144.
154 S3: 26.

There is no one wiser than I
Bullah says who is (left?) standing?[155]

Though hesitant to trace all Sufi pantheism in India to roots in Western Asia, the eminent scholar of Punjabi literatures, Christopher Shackle, does speak about this particular kafi of Bulleh's as a 'direct transcreation' from the Persian ghazal of the great Jalal al-din Rumi, insofar as both in the course of their poetry negate belonging to any established religious identity.[156] This, I suggest, is only part of the story this poem tells us, though undoubtedly a significant part. In my understanding, the poem is also in conversation with various groups in Punjab and India that were open to mystical ideas that showed similarity—echoing, reflecting, or enlarging their own beliefs.

Bulleh's poem can be seen to be an aspect of Punjabi popular culture that celebrated absorption, appropriation, and imbibing of similar ideas that flourished within ostensibly separate traditions in society. While such assimilations and incorporations did not make these traditions the same, they did open syncretistic plausibility, in other words, working with cultural porosities that encouraged connecting the dots that were theological equivalences. Syncretism in this understanding must be seen as an attitude that revelled in variegated borrowings, celebrated mimesis, and found the self in the myriad splintered specular images. Further, individuals like Piro, whose very existence thwarted the comforts that came with fixed identities and given nomenclatures, pushed the boundaries that enhanced cultural pluralism, inflating the more incipient tendencies that were present in her sect.

Piro's fertile cultural imaginary worked with bhakti religiosity as imbricated in its legends and fables, and the emotions and attitudes released by Sufi poetry, particularly of Bulleh, to enhance the potential towards spiritual attainment that her own life represented. Piro drank deeply of the Punjabi cultures she imbibed in her life and in the intellectual ambience of her dera. However, it was she who strove to widen its ambit, making it more inclusive of the socially marginalized and the deviant, even as she established her autonomy and agential self within the social world she lived in. Let us turn to the next chapter to further understand the expression of her agential self.

---

[155] 'Bullah ki Jana Main Kaun', in N. Singh, *Bulleh Shah ki Kafian*, pp. 148–9.

[156] Shackle, 'Punjabi Sufi Poetry', in Malhotra and Mir, *Punjab Reconsidered*, p. 27.

5 Miracles and Women Bhaktas
Understanding Piro's Agency

Pīro satguru meher te guṇ tino palle
Samtā aur udārtā nirbhaitā nalle.

Piro with the generosity of the satguru has three qualities
Equanimity and liberality, and along with these, fearlessness.[1]

Pīro turī nisaṅg ho gur nām dhiyāye
Vāhī jaṅdre gir pare jaiṅ hāth lagāye
Pehro pās kharotiaṅ sab buhe khole
Satguru kīyo āndhle much koī na bole
Niksī veh veliyoṅ rav bhayo parkāse
Bohro turī nisaṅg ho satgur parvāse.

Piro walked fearlessly on the name of the guru meditating
All the locks fell away with her hands a touching
All the doors were opened by the nearby standing guards
Satguru blinded them and they couldn't utter any words
She departed as the sun shone in the horizon
Under the power of the guru [she] fearlessly left her prison.[2]

---

[1] 160: 56. (Piro, *Ik Sau Sath Kafian* [*160 Kafis*], ms. 888 [Amritsar: Bhai Gurdas Library, GNDU]. Kafi numbers from this text are marked as '160: xx'.)
[2] 160: 112.

These lines from Piro's *160 Kafis* show her in two different attitudes. In the first, Piro speaks of her own inimitable qualities although she attributes her acquisition of these to the grace of the guru. These allow her to organize and direct, to a large extent, her own rescue from captivity, the event of her abduction around which, as we have seen, her narrative is woven. In the second, though Piro is ostensibly the actor, she appears more of a puppet performing to the script written and set into motion by her guru. She is literally relating the miracle that made her escape from the clutches of her guardians and co-religionists possible—the bolts giving way at her touch and the sentinels turning (momentarily) blind. What are we to make of her agency between this self-conscious awareness of her own talent, the display of bold initiative that initially led her to the guru's establishment and then inaugurated her ultimate release from incarceration on the one hand, and the attribution of her success to the miraculous, mystical, even mysterious powers of the guru on the other? I take up the question of Piro's agency in this chapter, and explore the modes of its operation. I begin with a discussion on the centrality of the concept of agency in women's autobiographical writing in the Western tradition, and then ask how we may comprehend and locate this concept in South Asia, especially in early modern women's autobiographical writings.

Although this chapter is based on Piro and her autobiographical narrative immersed in bhakti religiosity as discussed in the previous chapter, I will also at various points draw from the autobiographical writing of Bahinabai (1628–1700), *Atmanivedana* (Self Revelation/ Dedication). Bahinabai was a woman saint from the Marathi bhakti tradition.[3] Besides their shared gender and the fact that they both developed their spiritual yearning within the bhakti tradition, it is to the existence of their autobiographical writing that I wish to draw attention. While various women saints who found, as this work shows, a more hospitable environment within the folds of bhakti left behind

[3] For the translation of her autobiography and other poems, see Justin E. Abbott, *Bahina Bai: A Translation of Her Autobiography and Verses* (New Delhi: Cosmo, 2005 [1929]). On the Maharashtrian bhakti tradition, see Charlotte Vaudeville, 'Pandharpur, City of Saints', in her *Myths, Saints and Legends in Medieval India* (New Delhi: Oxford University Press, 1996), pp. 199–219.

corpuses of devotional songs and hymns, autobiographical writing is rare. It is striking that both Bahini's, as she called herself, and Piro's autobiographical writings are episodic. They concentrate on certain events: Piro on her encounter with her guru, her incarceration, and her escape; and Bahini on her association with a cow, calf, Jayaram Gosavi, and her guru, Tukaram—who appeared in a dream—all connected in a sequence of happenings in the eleventh year of her life. However, unlike Piro, whose story is more fragmentary, Bahini also provides us with details about her life, parents, husband, the state of her mind at a particularly desperate juncture in her life, her previous births, and the approach of her death. When writing one's own life story, or aspects of it, what can or cannot be preserved for posterity becomes an important issue for the author. This in turn has implications for the question of agency, the power of self-representation operating within the norms of a tradition that Piro and Bahini nurtured and identified with.

Miracles or marvellous and inexplicable occurrences, albeit of the more unpretentious kind, occur in the two cases analysed, giving a glimpse of a world permeated with enchantment. These happen, in my understanding, to underline the salience of these women, even as the women handed formal agency that brought about transformational change in their lives to divine or guru-initiated occurrences. The specificity of the miracles associated with these women is enunciated later in this chapter. It may be briefly noted here that miracles and their performance had a special place in both bhakti and Sufi religiosity.

Within feminist scholarship the concept of agency has been pivotal in addressing the issue of women's subjectivity, and of women as subjects of history. The liberal, progressive template that has informed much feminist writing and politics has valourized the individual to act against structural constraints, often in spite of oppressive conditions, if possible through collective and confrontational politics towards transformational trajectories. Thus 'assertion' and 'resistance', as Padma Anagol suggests, are 'twin aspects of women's agency' that work with women's volition to overturn structures of power that fetter their lives.[4] However, in understanding women's agency in history in early modern contexts, confrontational, collective, and resistance-oriented politics may not be possible, and degrees of consent and compliance may occur along with

---

[4] Padma Anagol, 'Agency, Periodization, and Change in the Gender and Women's History of Colonial India', *Gender and History* 20, no. 3 (2008): 603–27.

resistance and subversion, often as modes of self-empowerment. Janaki Nair speaks of the question of female agency in history, cognizant as she is that the further back we go in history the more 'dispersed, episodic or discontinuous' women's struggles become. Discussing whether women's agency takes the form of consent, transgression, or subversion, she explicates that the question 'can neither be wholly contained within a delineation of structures of oppression nor exhausted by accounts of female presence in history, but must be posed within specific contexts and placed along a continuum where various forms of agency may coexist'.[5] A similar argument emphasizing contingent contexts is put forward by the anthropologist Saba Mahmood in her study of the veiling practices among some women in contemporary Egypt.[6] I propose here that agency must be seen as operative within specific cultural and temporal contexts in a continuum of varied actions that could range from resistance to consent. Thus, agency must be understood, grasped, and its meaning sought in its particular milieu. A liberal explanatory paradigm may not always be useful in understanding why women may take on subordinate roles and a submissive mien, and yet be conscious of their roles as agents. Notions of agency tied only to resistance or subversion of dominant patriarchal structures that animate many feminist projects in the West may be inadequate to understand agentive action in different cultures, and in different periods of time.

UNDERSTANDING THE SELF AND AGENCY

As a retrospective narrative, the autobiographical text is apparently steeped in agentive awareness. Agency here is seen to connote self-reflexivity, one that sees the individual as autonomous, active, and in charge, though imbricated in multiple impinging and power-informed cultural formations. In the Western tradition of the autobiography, a sense of agency is seen as axiomatic, for it underscores the psyche, the inner self and character, reflecting and taking charge of its actions—the creation of a subject. In post-structuralist critique of the certainties that shaped Enlightenment

[5] Janaki Nair, 'On the Question of Agency in Indian Feminist Historiography', *Gender and History* 6, no. 1 (1994): 82–100.

[6] Saba Mahmood, *The Politics of Piety: The Islamic Revival and the Feminist Subject* (Princeton: Princeton University Press, 2005).

discourse, the making of subjectivity has come to be seen as far more complex than a question of individual free will or autonomy.[7] Jill Ker Conway, for example, writes of the 'cultural scripts' that often unconsciously dictated the framing of life writing in the West, whether it be the archetypal 'secular hero' overcoming odds to emerge triumphant, or the 'romantic heroine' of the nineteenth century, passive and acted upon by people and circumstances.[8] However, so central is the notion of agency, tied to the idea of unique, unified, and autonomous selves, that Conway urges the taking charge of our lives and assuming agency for our actions. The use of tropes that deny or distort such agentive power, including the grammatical use of passive voice, is critiqued by her, condemned for its lack of moral responsibility for the actions reported.[9] However, the overwhelming reach of a culture's demands for appropriate roles have a way to intrude into apparently self-representational writing through editorial and marketing interventions, even when not imbibed by the autobiographers, as shown by Linda Peterson. The nineteenth-century Victorian publishers fitted normative gendered roles—for instance, the romantic heroine discussed by Conway—to the works of an earlier generation of Quaker women authors even when such roles did not exist and were irrelevant.[10] The pervasiveness of cultural norms—whether in governing lived perspectives or (re)shaping memoirs—complicates further the notion of ostensibly unfettered individual agency. This suggests that both the represented self and its reception are historically contingent, shaped by cultural norms that govern societies.

In recent years the autonomy of the individual self has been destabilized by a timely reminder that even as the individual came to occupy centre stage in the intellectual and cultural development of the West, the bureaucratic and disciplinary machinery of the modern state was reducing the individuated persona to an anonymous blip in the mechanics of state

---

[7] Sidonie Smith and Julia Watson, *Reading Autobiography: A Guide for Interpreting Life Narratives* (Minneapolis: University of Minnesota Press, 2010), p. 54.

[8] Jill Ker Conway, *When Memory Speaks: Exploring the Art of Autobiography* (New York: Vintage Books, 1998).

[9] Conway, *When Memory Speaks*, pp. 178–9.

[10] Linda H. Peterson, 'Institutionalizing Women's Autobiography: Nineteenth Century Editors and the Shaping of an Autobiographical Tradition', in *The Culture of Autobiography: Constructions of Self-Representation*, edited by Robert Folkenflik (Stanford: Stanford University Press, 1993), pp. 80–103.

power and its discursive terrain.[11] Scholars like Althusser discussed the interpellation of subjects by the many socio-political structures that shaped people even as they seemingly assumed their own subjectivity. Foucault brought home the unobtrusive but ubiquitous power of discursive regimes that impinged on people, constituent of their selves.[12] Yet, significant scholarship has emerged that emphasizes the assertion of agency through creating spaces from within the working of plural systems, for example, Michel de Certeau's 'transverse tactics', the reuse or reordering of constraining systems, or through flexible networks of language that are difficult to monitor.[13] Similarly, Judith Butler's location of agency in the ruptures between multiplicities of norms governing an individual that do not align illuminates the spaces for reconfiguration and redeployment.[14] In other words, when conflicting norms are laid out, one can work around them to assert personal choice. What this scholarship on the mechanics of agency shows are the diverse ways in which systems and structures, including relational cultural formations that impact a person, can be manoeuvred by the marginalized, such as women, to assume agential initiative. As Mahmood notes, agency 'in this form of analysis is understood as the capacity to realize one's own interest against the weight of custom, tradition, transcendental will, or other obstacles'.[15] Undoubtedly, this manner of tactical manoeuvring will be visible in the way Piro, or for that matter Bahinabai, worked to create spaces for themselves, manipulating plural and sometimes contradictory cultural norms to gain power over their circumstances and selves. However, what this elaboration of agency and the constraints upon it still do not explain is the occasional giving up of agential initiative, or being informed by agency even when living within given social norms.

According to Mahmood, the concept of agency needs to be delinked from progressive politics that views resistance as agency. Many scholars

---

[11] Roy Porter, ed., *Rewriting the Self: Histories from the Renaissance to the Present* (London: Routledge, 1997).

[12] Smith and Watson, *Reading Autobiography*, pp. 55–6.

[13] Smith and Watson, *Reading Autobiography*, pp. 56–7.

[14] Smith and Watson, *Reading Autobiography*, p. 58. Also, Sidonie Smith, 'Performativity, Autobiographical Practice, Resistance', in *Women, Autobiography, Theory: A Reader*, edited by Sidonie Smith and Julia Watson (Madison: University of Wisconsin Press, 1998), p. 110.

[15] Mahmood, *Politics of Piety*, p. 8. Mahmood makes these comments in the context of women's mosque movement in contemporary Egypt.

of South Asia, looking at the multifarious and insidious ways in which patriarchies obtrude on women's lives, have also often enough modelled their writings on the hegemonic Western liberal feminist discourse. It is generally felt in this perspective that it is through resistance— whether enacted in everyday life and its minutiae,[16] as lifestyle itself,[17] or as intentionally undertaken to alter gendered power relations[18]—that agency is exercised.

However, liberal feminism's universalist claims as well as its definitions of normative subjectivity have recently come under intense critical scrutiny.[19] Women's agency in different contexts has come to be seen across various academic and activist contexts as disrupting the 'normative definition of a unified, autonomous subject exerting her will freely toward clearly defined and transparent ends', as Mahua Sarkar posits while exploring the multiple ways in which Muslim women were produced as invisible in colonial India.[20] Though resistance and subversion are viewed as constitutive of agency, that the process of negotiation with structures of power may also involve capitulation or negotiation is increasingly being understood.[21] Walter Johnson similarly critiques the notion of agency as saturated with categories of nineteenth-century liberalism that smuggle in 'the jargon of self-determination and choice', making it difficult to consider the extent of choicelessness or constraints faced by those outside modern, liberal conventions of structures of power.[22] Thus, if we are not to eschew the use of agency altogether, for it still shows

---

[16] Anindita Ghosh, 'Introduction', in *Behind the Veil: Resistance, Women and the Everyday in Colonial South Asia*, edited by Anindita Ghosh (Ranikhet: Permanent Black, 2007), pp. 1–20.

[17] Veena Talwar Oldenburg, 'Lifestyle as Resistance: The Case of the Courtesans of Lucknow', in *Contesting Power: Resistance and Everyday Social Relations in South Asia*, edited by Douglas Haynes and Gyan Prakash (Berkeley: University of California Press, 1991), pp. 23–61.

[18] Padma Anagol, 'From the Symbolic to the Open: Women's Resistance in Colonial Maharashtra', in Ghosh, *Behind the Veil*, pp. 21–57.

[19] Mahua Sarkar, 'Introduction: Writing Difference', in her *Visible Histories, Disappearing Women: Producing Muslim Womanhood in Late Colonial Bengal* (New Delhi: Zubaan, 2008), pp. 1–26.

[20] Sarkar, 'Introduction: Writing Difference', p. 21.

[21] Sarkar, 'Introduction: Writing Difference'.

[22] Walter Johnson as quoted in Cornelia H. Dayton, 'Rethinking Agency, Recovering Voices', *The American Historical Review* 109, no. 3 (2004): 827–43.

how the self may inform action and work on the course of one's life, we have to be able to apply the concept to societies that are historically and temporally situated in their own circumstances.

Along with this insight emerges the awareness that subjecthood is not a linear march towards what has been defined for it by liberal feminism. Indeed, Butler speaks of the opacity of the 'I' to itself, embedded as the self is in varied social conditions that encroach upon it prior to the I's reflexive self-knowledge, though she speaks of the ethicality of opening the I to others.[23] In contexts outside the realm of modernist discourse, where subjectivity is determined within complex and layered traditions with their embedded norms, including that of bhakti, agency has to be framed in its own location. Caroline Bynum also makes a similar point though she does not explicitly speak of agency. Studying the symbolism of food in medieval European women saints' religiosity, Bynum asserts that these women have been hitherto viewed through the lens of modern feminism, or through the vantage point of the male religious. Hence, among other distortions, a presentist perspective has not allowed these women to be understood on their own terms.[24] As Mahmood would have it, the historically contingent and culturally specific notions of the architecture and expression of the self and its potentialities need to be taken into account.[25] Thus within late bhakti religiosity, the idea of the self and its trajectory toward divine realization play a determining role in individuals' adherence to certain social and cultural roles—a warning that predetermined understandings of agency may be far too narrow.

Does such a reading of agency that looks beyond resistance—whether frontal or surreptitious—to historical structures wherein subjectivities unfold mean that feminists who advocate such a reading are in effect endorsing patriarchies that oppress women? Or are they by their reading displaying how women dealt with their situations, sometimes changing them and others reinforcing existing social conditions, and at still others being agentive even as they conform to or transform certain social and cultural practices? For the outcomes of transgression or subversion could mean a solidifying of patriarchal bulwarks against further attack and change, or could work towards assimilation or accommodation with

[23] Smith and Watson, *Reading Autobiography*, pp. 58–9.
[24] Caroline Walker Bynum, *Holy Feast and Holy Fast: The Religious Significance of Food to Medieval Women* (Berkeley: University of California Press, 1987), pp. 29–30.
[25] Mahmood, *Politics of Piety*, pp. 34–9.

change. In either case it is important to focus on the cultural openings available to women, and the logics of their action. These issues are particularly important in the spiritual domain where across different cultures women have been markedly present.[26] As noted in the previous chapter, bhakti religiosity allowed some women to carve out spaces for themselves and emerge as active participants within its ranks. Speaking of the multitudinous religious traditions of South Asia where women are visible, Sondra Hausner and Meena Khandelwal point to the respect these women accumulate by displaying persistence to stay the course against odds that are stacked more heavily against them than they are against men. In the face of overwhelming pressure to adhere to marriage and procreativity, the chosen path of women saints can ultimately garner them power, spiritual space, and respect.[27] Visibility, respect, and the wielding of power can undoubtedly lead to destabilizing structures that sustain patriarchies without necessarily overturning them, particularly because patriarchies—linked to other power structures—constantly reconstitute themselves. The same can, of course, be said for all manner of subversive action. In brief, it is far more rewarding to look at women's lives and actions—their agency—in historical circumstances that produced them rather than debate their lives or their life histories in anachronistic terms.

It will be pertinent at this juncture to briefly recollect how the self is seen in South Asia, and more specifically within the devotional tradition under study, in order to explicate the complex ways in which agency can be understood. Recent scholarship focused on India, as discussed in Chapter 2, has underscored the significance of the individual as against the tendency to see Indians as collectivities of caste or kinship networks. At the same time, the emphasis is on the self in society rather than the autonomous, isolated self.[28] Speaking of the Baul (*Bartamān-Panthī*) religious tradition in Bengal, Jeanne Openshaw notes the fluid notion of the self in Indic cultures as against the reification of the individual in the West, with its stress on a single, continuous self: the notion that though a person may change and develop, she or he is fundamentally the

[26] Bynum, *Holy Feast and Holy Fast*.

[27] Sondra L. Hausner and Meena Khandelwal, 'Introduction: Women on Their Own', in *Nuns, Yoginis, Saints and Singers: Women's Renunciation in South Asia*, edited by Meena Khandelwal, Sondra L. Hausner, and Ann Grodzins Gold (New Delhi: Zubaan, 2007), pp. 1–47.

[28] David Arnold and Stuart Blackburn, eds, *Telling Lives in India: Biography, Autobiography and Life History* (New Delhi: Permanent Black, 2004), pp. 3, 19.

same being between birth and death. Referring to the blurring of lines in India between biographies, autobiographies, and even hagiographies, Openshaw notes the constant switching between first and third person voices in the writing of these genres. This is partly because the self in Indic traditions is fluid, 'dividual', linked through birth, death/renunciation (social death), and rebirth, which may involve forgetting the past life (renunciation) but also often involves remembering past births.[29] A.K. Ramanujan remarked on how evolved souls of holy men like the Buddha were said to have a complete recollection of their past lives. This was a remembering in order to master the past and get rid of it, to ultimately escape the cycle of transmigration, of birth, death, and rebirth.[30] Linked through births with the logic of karma, for example in Bahinabai's text, is the belief that actions in this birth will be carried onto the quality of life in the next, that the self can be said to have a different meaning, field of play, and purpose in the Indic religious and devotional thought. Similarly, Openshaw stresses that the interiority that her Bartaman Panthi guru, Raj, displays in his autobiographical writing may seem 'Western' insofar as he reflects on events rather than merely describing them, and otherwise writes of an 'inner life', qualities viewed as distinctive of Western autobiographies.[31] This interiority that she observes, however, is best understood as evolving from a Vaishnav bhakti tradition.[32] She quotes Tanika Sarkar's understanding of the autobiography of Rassundari Debi in emphasizing a 'devotion centred selfhood' that developed through her Vaishnav religiosity.[33] Bahinabai's musings, too, on the state of her mind can be understood in the context of her Varkari Vaishnav bhakti.

Looking at Bahinabai's autobiographical writing and her poems—which Anne Feldhaus refers to as autobiographical in an extended sense—Feldhaus shows how Bahini recalled her twelve previous lives,

---

[29] Jeanne Openshaw, *Writing the Self: The Life and Philosophy of a Dissenting Bengali Baul Guru* (New Delhi: Oxford University Press, 2010), pp. 103–7.

[30] A.K. Ramanujan, 'The Ring of Memory: Remembering and Forgetting in Indian Literatures', in *A.K. Ramanujan: Uncollected Poems and Prose*, edited by Molly Daniels-Ramanujan and Keith Harrison (New Delhi: Oxford University Press, 2001), pp. 83–100.

[31] Focusing on externalities rather than the interior is also seen as a trait of the labouring people's first-person accounts in the early modern period in the West. Dayton, 'Rethinking Agency', p. 840.

[32] Openshaw, *Writing the Self*, p. 114.

[33] Openshaw, *Writing the Self*, p. 139. Also see Chapter 2.

before this final thirteenth one, indicating a seamless self through different births and possible identities.[34] Significantly, in her successive births
Bahini remained a woman, but her caste and marital status 'improved'.
Bahini achieved Brahminhood and marital status in her last four lives. It
may be mentioned that the crisis in Bahini's life stemmed partly from her
choice of bhakti devotion by going against the Vedic religion and rituals
her much older Vedic Brahmin husband—described as a materialist by
Bahini—believed in. The problems also arose because she chose Tukoba
or Tukaram, a low-caste sudra as a guru, though she herself was from a
Brahmin family, and according to the Brahminical code of conduct, to
which she too paid obeisance, she should have looked at her husband
as her god, serving him for her redemption. While I will comment on
aspects of Bahini's life later, what is noteworthy here is the hierarchical
nature of her self-evolution through different births, if we can call it that,
from a lower caste to the highest, and from the single status to that of a
married woman, in effect aligning with Brahminical precepts, which in
many ways she never abandoned. The paradox of accepting and overturning (by choosing a sudra guru and bhakti piety) Brahminical codes of
conduct created immense tensions in her life that Feldhaus and others
have written about.[35] The apprehending of agency in Bahinabai's conflicted life, and also Piro's, therefore, becomes a matter of understanding
the wider notions of the self and religiosity in the particular social milieu
in which they lived and chose to find fulfilment, along with seeing the
way in which they surveyed and used their circumstances.

AGENCY AND THE PLACE OF MIRACLES IN PIRO'S STORY

In the *160 Kafis*, to briefly recall its content, Piro details a single anecdote
with its chain of events, which is clearly shown as a life-defining one, not
only literally a 'conversion narrative' because it shows her crossing religious

[34] Anne Feldhaus, 'Bahina Bai: Wife and Saint', in *The Journal of American
Academy of Religion* 50, no. 4 (1982): 591–604. Also Abbott, *Bahina Bai*, pp. 50–61.

[35] For an introductory note and selected passages of Bahina's verses, see Susie
Tharu and K. Lalita, eds, *Women Writing in India Volume I: 600 BC to the Early
Twentieth Century* (New Delhi: Oxford University Press, 2007 [1991]), pp. 107–15.
Eleanor Zelliot, 'Women Saints in Medieval Maharashtra', in *Faces of the Feminine
in Ancient, Medieval and Modern India*, ed. Mandakranta Bose (New Delhi: Oxford
University Press, 2000), pp. 192–200.

boundaries, but also metaphorically, as it explains and justifies the changed course of her life.[36] Its autobiographical nature is noteworthy as it is surprising, for the rest of her repertoire of writings is of a different genre—poetry that probed metaphysical and spiritual questions, though autobiographical references are available therein.

Piro in the *160 Kafis* presents herself as a low Muslim prostitute disenchanted with material things and seeking a life of spiritual fulfilment by taking asylum in the dera of Guru Gulabdas in the middle years of the nineteenth century in Punjab.[37] In Piro's telling, coming to his dera was not, however, a simple affair of putting to practise one's desire. For in her train followed her guardians, clan, and Muslim men, all claiming her back to her profession and religion, for there was an assumption that having joined a Sikh sect she had turned into an apostate and an unbeliever. Having somehow tricked her, as Piro alleged, or otherwise persuaded her into going back to them in Lahore, rather than the nearby village of Chathianwala where the dera according to Piro was located, her Muslim relations and associates began persuading her to reconvert to Islam. It is in this context that Piro introduces a note of habitual conflict between Hindu and Muslim men as delineated in Chapter 3, though her vehemence comes across more strongly in relation to Muslim men and priests whom she depicts as pushing her into stances and situations adverse to her interests. Her adamant refusal to succumb to their pressure of re-entering into their fold, according to Piro, goads them into abducting her, taking her away from Lahore to Wazirabad, an old town near Gujranwala. This was a ruse to try and use incarceration and distance from her guru to reincorporate her into her former religion, and Piro notes that she at this juncture is offered a choice between prison if she stays recalcitrant, and a life of luxury if she chooses Islam. Piro writes about her being able to communicate with her guru about her captivity through a missive sent to him, written with the help of an amanuensis, summoned by Rehmati and Jano, the new friends she makes in her adversity. The guru sends two of his disciples, Gulab Singh and Chatar Singh, to rescue her. Her escape from her prison comes about in Piro's narrative because of a number of reasons. These are looked at in some

---

[36] A life-transforming event especially related to religious experience can be referred to as a 'conversion narrative'. See Arnold and Blackburn, *Telling Lives in India*, p. 14.

[37] For details of her autobiographic narrative, see Chapter 2.

detail below. In the rest of her story, Piro speaks of being pursued by her captors, but in the company of her rescuers is able to reach her guru in Chathianwala, where the three disciples, including Piro, speak of each other's valour and steadfast loyalty to the guru.

In the narration of her tale, Piro at various points of time refers to her exceptional qualities, as the epigraph to this chapter shows, of a perspicacity of character that makes for clear thinking and action in time of crisis. Her many attributes included her ability to stand her ground in the face of overwhelming pressure to follow the dictates of others; she was called wilful (*haī baī muhāre*, she follows her will);[38] she had the ability to think for herself; she was able to rouse intense loyalty in her friends, Jano and Rehmati, who were willing to help her despite the danger they faced if exposed, and who cried bitterly and asked to accompany her when she escaped; and her ability of portraiture of the respect that the two disciples sent to rescue her gave her, addressing her as *maī sāhib* (respected mother) or *mahārāj* (a kingly prefix normally reserved for the honoured male).

Her very first step of deciding to leave or flee the brothel in Lahore must itself be taken to display her will in commandeering her life. At other times, she highlights her determination to stay on the course she chooses, an unusual choice of living a monastic life. She speaks of her refusing to bend to the persuasions or threats of different groups of people who she shows as enjoining her to recommit to her older life and religion: her former guardians who demand their rights over their daughter/sister, her clan and friends who try to cajole her through sweet talk, and the angry Muslim men. She also describes her tête-à-tête with Islamic religious authorities who pressurize her into coming back into the fold of Islam, where she bests them in arguments—Piro portraying herself as a woman with a mind of her own and with the ability to argue out her case. As she put it, Piro created problems for the Turaks (*Pīro Turkāṅ sāmne kar masle tāṛe*) in her stubborn refusal to give in, and in her determination to keep to her chosen course.[39] And so she was an exceptional woman using words in speech and writing to defend her decision. She also mentions the courage of the disciples who come to rescue her—they are compared to the characters of the epic Ramayana, Angad and Hanuman, known for their bravery. More significantly, there

[38] 160: 47.
[39] 160: 43.

is the reference to the planning and strategizing of the escape between Piro, her friends, the disciples, and the gardener of the orchard where the latter find refuge. Piro presents herself as giving command in the unfolding of her escape:

Pīro kahe saheliyo tum bāg bhadhāro
Singh Gulāb Chatar Singh yeh bāt chitāro
Ghoṛe kaṭhī pāe ke baho nisaṅge
Hoṅ tursāṅ satgur sev ko hath mehṅdī raṅge.

Piro says friends go to the orchard
Relate this to Gulab Singh and Chatar Singh
With horses and carts let them sit fearless
Having coloured hands with henna [I] will go to serve the guru.[40]

While taking cognizance of her qualities and exceptional characteristics, Piro simultaneously highlights the omniscient guru who miraculously brings about her release. She describes her incarceration as a difficult one, and escapes from a prison that was well-guarded and difficult to access—she is imprisoned in a room, in her account, on the top floor of a four-storeyed house, with its four doors bolted, and sentinels placed outside them. At another juncture she mentions at least five people guarding her room.[41]

As discussed in Chapter 2, Piro's storytelling moves forward and backward in time; it is simultaneously retrospective in narration and prospective in foretelling, a temporality trick that creates space for different actions and performance situations to occur at the same time. Piro, who evidently committed her story on paper after the incident she relates had occurred, could also in the same text write, at various points, in the manner of predicting events. For instance, from the very start of her travails we are told about the power of the guru to set things right. The two disciples—whose conversation with the guru too is reported by Piro—are encouraged by the guru to undertake their mission with the words:

Jinke man meiṅ sābatī mil dono jāo
Kāraj karsī satguru tum sobhā pāo.

With the two together and your hearts firm
The guru will accomplish the deed but the accolades will be yours.[42]

[40] 160: 107.
[41] 160: 110.
[42] 160: 83.

This was the guru as an omnipotent figure in the late bhakti tradition, divine and human at the same time.[43] Mere mortals like Piro craved the grace of such a guru:

> *Pīro kahe piyāriyoṅ vo beparvāhe*
> *Unko loṛ na hamrī ham un kī chāhe.*

> Piro says friends he is nonchalant
> He does not need us but we desire him.[44]

In a string of hyperbolic similes, Piro compares the desire of her heart for her guru with that of a lotus awaiting sunlight to blossom, of fish for water, of the sensualist for beauty, of a thief for darkness, of a poet for the sight of the moon, and of a greedy man for treasure.[45] And like the great god Vishnu and his earthly incarnations, Ram and Krishna, the world and its activities were the guru's 'play'—an indulgence on account of ordinary humans:

> *Pīro kahe satguru tum ketī berā*
> *Khel rachāye jagat maiṅ kar dūr andherā.*

> Piro says satguru you are our support
> You created play [khel] in the world and banished darkness.[46]

Thus, the miracles organized by the guru must be envisioned as a part of the great design of the god-guru—first, of the unlocking of the doors, then of the guards' stupor, and finally of the inability of the guards and people of Wazirabad town to see them as they passed through its streets and gates:

> *Jāvat turī bājār mo kaṅh dīse nāhī*
> *Pehru āgaye sahar ke darvāje māṅhī*
> *Satguru ke partāp te vo āndhe hoī*
> *Laṅg tinā ke vīch moṅ un khabar na koī.*

> She walked through the bazaar but could not be seen
> [Even though] the guards came to the town's gates
> With the blessing of the satguru they became blind
> [She] passed between them but they had no clue.[47]

---

[43] Daniel Gold, *The Lord as Guru: Hindi Sants in North Indian Tradition* (New York: Oxford University Press, 1989).

[44] 160: 64.

[45] 160: 72.

[46] 160: 76.

[47] 160: 113.

The concept of karma is based on this life and the actions and deeds accomplished therein that have repercussions in subsequent births and, therefore, militate against non-action. Thus, Piro's own strategizing and planning, her own qualities, remained important. We, therefore, have within the same text the juxtaposition of Piro underscoring her own agency even while denying it—Piro acting and being acted upon. Piro in her story emerges as the woman to whom ordinary folk began to pay respects, including the guru's disciples sent to rescue her, while she remained the woman who considered herself innocuous, a nobody, in front of the majesty of the guru.

While the portraiture of the guru as a divine being elevated above human mortals behoved the attitude of a desperate woman seeking refuge and a novitiate status, one may also speculate on other possible readings of the miraculous in her text. This is a good place to be reminded of the fracas and a skirmish described by the Nirmala historian Ganesha Singh in his brief on the Gulabdasis, between Piro's purported suitor (Singh calls him her friend, *dost*) Ilahi Khan and Gulabdas's men near the tomb of Mian Mir in Lahore, which resulted in the wounding of many of Gulabdas's followers.[48] Is this in fact what occurred after Piro was brought back from Wazirabad/Gujranwala?[49] While Piro mentions her rescue in all its details and intrigues, apparently effected by Kala Singh and Chatar Singh in Ganesha's Singh's writing, she makes no reference to this violence, whether as part of the rescue or as having occurred subsequently. Why? The sordid details of her sexual availability and vulnerability as a prostitute—or that of inordinate desire that refused denial on the part of the powerful Ilahi Khan—that his pursuit of Piro represented on the one hand and the bloodlust that the violent clash between the guru, his followers, and the men of Ilahi Khan and her guardians represented on the other were elided by Piro. Instead, she delineates the guru's miracle in meticulous detail.

Piro's 'convoluted agency' and 'incitement', as discussed in Chapter 2, that is, her skilful use of words and language to transform her ordinary life into one of epic proportions by emulating Sita, as she did, and goading her Ram-guru to rescue and protect her, lent her life the meaning she sought to give it. Similarly, her words now alchemized violent action

---

[48] Mahant Ganesha Singh, *Bharat Mat Darpan* (Amritsar: Vaidak Bhandar, 1926), p. 128. For a discussion on Ganesha Singh's account see Chapters 1 and 3.

[49] Ganesha Singh mentions her being taken to Gujranwala by her guardians. Wazirabad is a town in the district of Gujranwala.

spurred by base human emotions of desire and possession into those infused with divine purpose, working as god's miracle enacted by her god-like guru. Perhaps Piro's autobiographical life story, which set out to legitimize her actions and elevate her status, refused the unremarkable ordinariness of the routine—the lust and violence that may have marred her life. It was the extraordinary and the marvellous that she wished to narrate, the story that made her life meaningful, and gave her the status she hoped for.

As Piro and her story travelled between places and performances, so it moved between an active and a passive voice.[50] Piro had a first-person presence, but also a third-person narration in the *160 Kafis*, a proclivity that Openshaw also notes for the Bengali Baul guru's autobiographical writings, especially his songs. She could register her presence in the first person, even as she addressed her guru in the second, as '[I] have come to your feet you who are honored and true' (*houṅ charnī lagī āye ke tum sāhib sache*).[51] She also referred to herself in the third-person passive voice as in 'Piro says friends go quickly' (*Pīro kahe saheliyo tum sīghar jāvo*).[52] Note that the 'I' in the first example is implied in Punjabi, and in both the examples the person/s addressed are referred to in the second person *tum* (you). In Indic literature down the ages, the convention of the author placing their names in the 'signature' line of the verse was well established, referred to as bhanita or chhap. This was true of the poetic collections of various bhakti saints, even when their songs were available in more than one tradition/recension. Due to the lack of any one 'authentic' source for their poems, scholars have speculated on the possible growth of corpuses of these saints by their followers and disciples who wrote in the names of their gurus. Thus the implied authorial 'I' in these songs is often more than an autobiographical 'I'—sometimes a collective 'I' that imbibed the spirit of a saint's oeuvre.[53] As Openshaw has remarked about her study on Bartman Panthis, a disciple can write an autobiography, and a biography may be dictated by the subject.[54] In the case of Piro's writing from the mid-nineteenth century, however, it is undoubtedly Piro clearly referring to herself when she intones 'Piro

[50] See Chapter 2.

[51] 160: 11.

[52] 160: 91.

[53] J.S. Hawley, 'Author and Authority', in his *Three Bhakti Voices: Mirabai, Surdas and Kabir* (New Delhi: Oxford University Press, 2005), pp. 21–47.

[54] Openshaw, *Writing the Self*, p. 103.

says', the normative form of chhap. However, unlike the poems of bhakti saints, since Piro narrated an episode and her own story, she deploys her chhap unconventionally, her signature appearing anywhere in her verse, often in the first line itself, sometimes in the middle lines, not necessarily the normative last line. As a legatee of complex and plural traditions, and as an innovator within these, Piro's autobiographical fragment opens multiple ways of reading it.

So what does Piro's tale, the reportage of the specific miracle of her escape, and the singular way of her narration—as a person present in the action of her story and as one relating the impinging of people and circumstances on her—mean for her agency? Indubitably, social and cultural conventions, both behavioural—as the exaggerated respect for the guru and self-effacement in relation to him, more particularly of a woman, and especially one of a low caste and a degraded occupation— and textual, the blurring of first and third person voices, were at play here. The question of her agency is, therefore, more complicated than the manner in which Conway raises that of taking moral responsibility for one's actions. However, if we pose the question in another way, that is, what did the attribution of ultimate agency to the guru do for Piro, we may arrive at a different perspective. The idiom of miracles in premodern literatures, and life, was a common one, though it spoke of the uncommon. In the context of bhakti hagiographies, the particular tradition that Piro turned to model, live, and explain her life, the play of miracles was ubiquitous and used for various ends. What did Piro's, or for that matter Bahina's, miracles do for them in the corpus of such divine and wonderful events?

THE POWER OF MIRACLES

In any premodern society, miracles formed an important medium to grasp the world—to understand it, explain it, relate to it, and organize it. Miracles were not mere magic, which was perhaps more commonplace, even for the ordinary to perform, manipulate, and transform their lives, though there could be more spectacular magic associated with the holy or the learned. Miracles invariably spoke of the extraordinary; those blessed with divine favour and had direct access to godly grace. Miracles were a means through which the evolved often communicated their special status to the hoi polloi and to those blinded by power, or even used them to establish a superior status in relation to others like them.

The world of the bhakti (and Sufi) saints was steeped in myths that used the miraculous to underline the greatness of the saint, for example,

Sheikh Farid, the Chishti Sufi whose verses are also found in the *Adi Granth*.[55] In bhakti legends, the innate godly quality of the bhakta, the devotee, was sometimes hidden from view. This was particularly true if the saint was a humble person, following a lowly profession, like a number of bhakti saints were, including the foremost among them, Kabir, a weaver *(julāha)*, or Raidas, a leatherworker *(chamār)*—who are both referred to in Piro's *160 Kafis*, though Kabir particularly left a mark on her. In some of these stories, the saint had to 'prove' his saintliness, precisely because it was difficult to believe in it, or the purport of the story was to establish it and make others acknowledge the guru's power. The performance of the miracle, as of other dramatic acts associated with a saint's life, and the theatrical mode of getting across one's message— in other words the performativity associated with the miracle—made for a spectacle of exemplarity.[56] The drama of a saint put through the test was often employed in narrating the saints' life, its purpose being to garner awe and appropriate humility from those who up until then did not believe in the saint's special status. Kabir's poetry portrays him as unrelenting in his mocking of religious authority, and it is perhaps this grain from his verses that spurred the fabricating of legends around him.[57] The story associated with Kabir, for example, of his torture by Sultan Sikander Lodi at the behest of the qazi, mullahs, and the pandits, that is, the various religious and judicial authorities of Benaras, because his beliefs were considered seditious, is one such account. In this tale, Kabir is awarded the death sentence, and is sought to be killed by first being tied and thrown into the river Ganges, then by being pushed into a blazing fire, and finally by being trampled by an elephant. All attempts to kill him fail, and the sultan has to acknowledge Kabir's miracles as the handiwork of an evolved soul.[58]

[55] On the miracles, *karāmat*, of the Sufi Shaikh Baba Farid of Pak Pattan, Punjab, see Raziuddin Aquil, 'Episodes from the Life of Shaikh Farid-ud-Din Ganj-i-Shakar', *International Journal of Punjab Studies* 10, no. 2 (2003): 25–46.

[56] Hester Goodenough Gelber, 'A Theater of Virtue: The Exemplary World of Saint Francis of Assisi', in *Saints and Virtues*, edited by J.S. Hawley (Berkeley: University of California Press, 1987), pp. 15–35.

[57] Linda Hess, 'Kabir's Rough Rhetoric', in *The Sants: Studies in a Devotional Tradition of India*, edited by Karine Schomer and W.H. McLeod (New Delhi: Motilal Banarasidass, 2004), pp. 143–65.

[58] This legend is found in Priyadas' *Bhaktirasabodhini*, an early eighteenth-century commentary on Nabhadas' *Bhaktamal*, a sixteenth-century bhakti hagiography. For

A story of similar import is related about Mirabai, the most famous woman bhakta of north India who is said to have lived in the fifteenth century, and who is also obliquely referred to in Piro's poetry, though not the *160 Kafis*. The most prominent quality of Mira as seen in her hagiographic literature was her fearlessness. Mira, a Rajput princess, was married as per custom at a young age. However, she refused to consummate her marriage or follow the norms of modesty expected of a high-status bride. She considered her idol of Krishna her husband, and insisted on breaking Rajput traditions guiding royal princesses by keeping the company of holy mendicants devoted to Krishna. To teach Mira a lesson, she is sent a cup of poison by the rana, the prince-ruler, as the offering from the feet of the god, the *charanāmrit*, that she was bound to have. This attempt at eliminating Mira in fact transmutes into her moment of glory. The poison miraculously transforms into ambrosia at her touch and she glows with greater health.[59]

Remarkably, demonstrating the intertextuality and the dialogic process among the various traditions within South Asia, the same story of the enacting of a miracle could circulate in different contexts and with different protagonists. The Janam-sakhis, hagiographies on the life of the first Sikh guru Nanak report his visit to Mecca. At night Nanak slept with his feet pointing towards the Ka'aba. On the qazi's questioning him on the disrespect shown to the holy site, Nanak asks the qazi to turn his feet in any direction where there was no god. Wherever the qazi turned his feet the Ka'aba came to stand there.[60] In this miracle-tale, not only is Nanak able to show that he is a man of god much more than the qazi of Mecca, but the story also has competitive connotations to it. The relative merit of religious traditions was put to the test, establishing the superiority of the one over the other. Simon Digby, also studying various

---

a discussion on this miracle, see Charlotte Vaudeville, *A Weaver Named Kabir: Selected Verses with a Detailed Biographical and Historical Introduction* (New Delhi: Oxford University Press, 2005 [1993]), p. 45. For a short biographical sketch of Kabir and Ravidas, see J.S. Hawley and Mark Juergensmeyer, *Songs of the Saints of India* (New Delhi: Oxford University Press, 2008), pp. 8–61.

[59] See Hawley and Juergensmeyer, *Songs of the Saints*, pp. 118–40. Also see J.S. Hawley, 'Mirabai as Wife and Yogi', in his *Three Bhakti Voices*, pp. 117–38; and Parita Mukta, *Upholding the Common Life: The Community of Mirabai* (New Delhi: Oxford University Press, 1997).

[60] Navtej Sarna, *The Book of Nanak* (New Delhi: Penguin/Viking, 2003), pp. 101–2.

hagiographical materials, relates a similar story about Gorakhnath, the famous Nathpanthi Jogi, member of an esoteric medieval sect, said to have left an imprint on Kabir. On his visit to Mecca, Gorakhnath lay down with his feet pointing towards the temple, and again the temple turns wherever his feet are dragged.[61] Interestingly, an identical story is also related about the south Indian woman saint, Avvaiyar, though in her case the location shifts from Mecca to a temple in south India.[62] Digby also narrates accounts of miracles performed in the spirit of contestation, mostly involving religious personages from different traditions, as in the flying contest between a Sufi and a Jogi. In these, the accomplishments of one holy man and the superiority of his religious tradition over the other were demonstrated in a test of personal prowess.[63]

In the miracles discussed above, the active agency of the saint in question, including some women saints, is established. It is they who perform the miracle, or are the medium through which god is revealed, thereby showing to all who witness it their special relationship with the divine order and their elevated stature. In another category of miracles, it is not the saint who performs but rather miracles happen around the person of the saint, the circumstances of their occurrence enhancing the celestial aura of the saint. Auspicious auguries connected with the birth, the growing up, or the death of a holy person are examples of these, as when on Kabir's death Hindus and Muslims fighting to claim his body only found a pile of flowers.[64] In the world of multitudinous miracles then, how did Piro's or Bahinabai's miracles fit in? How shall we read them?

Bahinabai, as mentioned earlier, was born in a Brahmin household, and was married at the age of three to a man several years her senior. Her marriage was a difficult and violent one, her husband often beating her, more so when Bahini began to have visions of the famous low-caste saint Tukaram, associated with Pandharpur Varkari bhakti.[65] Bahini in *Atmanivedana* describes in detail her special relationship to a cow and

[61] Simon Digby, trans., *Wonder-Tales of South Asia* (Jersey: Orient Monographs 2000), pp. 219–20.

[62] Uma Chakravarti, 'The World of the Bhaktin in South Indian Traditions: The Body and Beyond', in her *Everyday Lives, Everyday Histories: Beyond the Kings and Brahmanas of 'Ancient' India* (New Delhi: Tulika Books, 2006), pp. 275–92.

[63] Digby, *Wonder-Tales of South Asia*, pp. 229–33; also Aquil, 'Episodes from the Life of Shaikh Farid'.

[64] Hawley and Juergensmeyer, *Songs of the Saints*, p. 39.

[65] Vaudeville, 'Pandharpur: City of Saints'.

its calf, gifted to her husband, particularly the latter when she was eleven years old.[66] The manner in which the calf became attached to Bahini, following her everywhere, sleeping in her bed, and being fed by her became something of a wonder.[67] According to her account, the calf would even follow her to hear the recitation of pauranic *kathās*, parables from the Puranas, and listen in keenly, behaving in an appropriate and attentive way. Though Bahinabai does not use the word miracle to describe her experience, she does dwell at length on this episode in her life. She also gives an account of a famous katha performer, Jayaram Gosvami (Gosavi), who gave the two—Bahini and the calf—his blessings, after the calf was left outside the hall one day during his katha performance due to the room being filled with devotees, causing distress to both Bahini and the calf. The Gosvami even explains to her miffed husband the bond between Bahini and the calf, describing the latter as an evolved soul from previous birth (*yogbhrashṭā*) that would help Bahinabai reach salvation.

What I wish to emphasize in this marvellous story that Bahinabai left for posterity of a calf's and a little girl's mutual attachment is the proxy 'miracle' that happens to her. Bahinabai, unlike the saints noted earlier, is neither the agent of this near miracle nor the initiator of her remarkable relationship with the calf. It is the calf that chooses her, seeks her out, and accompanies her. But what did Bahinabai's recording, indeed delving on this specific incident, do? In my reading it was meant to highlight her own esteemed status, perhaps manoeuvre within a highly restrictive and difficult marriage of a slip of a girl to a much older man. It is possible that the autobiographical tone, unlike the later-inscribed hagiographies of saints, did not allow attributing to oneself miraculous powers, and so she looked for an alternate way to underscore her chosen status. It is also probable that being a woman in an ordinary domestic situation, Bahinabai dared not see herself as capable of performing amazing deeds. Yet the extraordinary could happen to her, without her apparent will, as it were, and this circuitous route could still allow her to be seen as someone special, chosen for a spiritual path.

[66] Abbott, *Bahina Bai*, pp. 8–24.

[67] Ruth Vanita also analyses the importance of the cow and calf in the life of Bahinabai, seeing them as empowering her, fulfilling her life beyond domesticity, and endowing her with autonomy and joy. See 'I'm an Excellent Animal: Cows at Play in the Writings of Bahinabai, Rukun Advani, Suniti Namjoshi and Others' in her *Gandhi's Tiger and Sita's Smile: Essays on Gender, Sexuality and Culture* (New Delhi: Yoda Press, 2005), pp. 290–310.

The relationship Bahini shared with the calf allowed for several status and role reversals in her life. Jayaram Gosavi, the respected spiritual leader, to whom the little girl along with her calf went to listen, came now to her twice. Once after she was beaten and tied by her husband, who found inappropriate the Gosavi's blessing his wife, and the whole kerfuffle caused by the calf's devotion to Bahini; and a second time after the death of the calf when Bahini herself fell into a long state of unconsciousness in which Tukaram became her guru and gave her a mantra to chant.[68] The special status that ostensibly the calf's devotion to her gave her, in fact, exacerbated the crisis in her marriage, her husband giving her a sound beating and tying her up. This eventually led to the death of the calf, which refused food despite her husband relenting and releasing Bahini. As the calf died Bahini fell in a faint, in which state she had a vision of Tukaram, who later, in another vision, gave her a mantra, becoming her guru. It is the guru, then, who comes to the disciple, even if in a dream, a dream whose contents became common knowledge so that she started to be an object of devotion herself. Bahini's husband seeing her collecting devotees around her decided to leave her for a life of mendicancy, pushing Bahini into giving up her devotion and accepting her wifely duties over those of a bhakta. Even as this happened, her husband fell ill, was nursed by Bahina, and realized that his illness was a result of his insulting his wife's guru. From then on, he too converted to her bhakti religiosity, and though the troubles of Bahini's life continued, her husband was from this moment her ally rather than her adversary.[69] In one of the most spectacular role reversals that take place, Bahini speaks of her husband performing a low bow (*sashtāṅg namskār*) before the sudra guru, though he required an elderly Brahmin to show him the falsity of his stand.[70]

What did this unsolicited miracle in Bahini's life mean? Bahini's miracle was one in which the cow, the calf, and Tukaram are entangled together, the cow sometimes referred to as a mother, as is Tukaram, and the calf alternately presented as a spiritual partner, her own self, and as her daughter.[71] One may argue that the miracle creates the supernatural as the active agent, and the self as being led in a drama that is bigger than

[68] Abbott, *Bahina Bai*, pp. 15–23.

[69] Feldhaus, 'Bahina Bai: Wife and Saint'.

[70] Abbott, *Bahini Bai*, p. 29.

[71] Abbott, *Bahini Bai*, p. 36.

one's limited and, in her case a very constricted, universe. Bahini, unlike most women saints, was one of the few who reconciled marriage, with its attendant notion of husband as god for a devoted wife (pativrata), to devotion to a guru and through him god. As has been argued by many feminist scholars, and as discussed in the previous chapter, women saints found it impossible to reconcile marriage to bhakti—a situation conducive to worshipping dual gods, earthly husbands being unable to handle either shared service (seva) or divided loyalty.[72] Though Bahini's reconciliation of marriage and devotion may have been a fraught one, it was nevertheless singular. How did a mere girl manage that? One may argue she did so with help of her surrogate miracle, which created a spectacle of her special status, announcing to the world god's favour. Further, one can argue from a liberal feminist perspective that Bahini, even if unconsciously, manoeuvred in her favour the situation as it developed, manipulating her circumscribed circumstances to resist the oppression of her violent husband. By underlining her chosen status—through highlighting the devotion of the calf to her—Bahini though initially risked her bhakti religiosity, ultimately managed to follow her heart. In this clash between hegemonic Brahminism and a subaltern religiosity, not only did she reverse her husband's penchant for Vedic rituals, caste concerns, and Brahminical asceticism, but also turned him towards her faith, guru, and bhakti. This was, then, a subversion that battled difficult circumstances and emerged triumphant. Bahina, the passive and voiceless sufferer, found a vocation and a voice—a nondescript Brahmin girl left behind a corpus of songs (abhaṅgs) and her story for posterity.

But what about Piro? Unlike Bahinabai, Piro was a consciously self-determined person, her subjectivity shaped and contoured by none other than herself. The confident tenor of her voice—whether in taking the initial decision of becoming a novice in guru Gulabdas's dera, or in later plotting and carrying out her escape—leaves one in no doubt about her being in charge of herself in her depiction despite her adverse circumstances. Yet, she too chose to shrug off the ultimate responsibility for her actions, making her 'powerful' (zoravar) guru the final saviour. Though Piro was in her narration the medium of the miracle that enabled her situation, the miracle was performed by her adept and perfect (kāmal) guru. Such a stance on the part of Piro can be understood from a variety of perspectives. It was the correct demeanour of a disciple towards her

[72] Chakravarti, 'The World of Bhaktin'.

guru, especially of a female novice, in a culture that seldom allowed independent action to women. Piro, as I have noted earlier, transgressed multiple cultural codes in seeking refuge in the dera. She moved from a brothel to a monastic establishment, from a Muslim background to a Sikh sect, and, moreover, defied guardians and community censors in both her former abode and her new refuge in pursuing her chosen path. In such a predicament, by attributing her escape to the mysterious and divine work of the guru, Piro could garner the respect of her new community by showing her guru and god's grace on her. For who could question her credentials for choosing this rather uncommon path if her guru picked her as the select? Thus, right in the beginning when she visits Lahore's Moti Bazaar to see the guru, she makes clear his choosing her as a special favourite:

> *Dekh anāth garīb ko sad pās bathāhiṅ*
> *Bhūp khaṛe darbār mo na puchhe koī.*
>
> Seeing [this] poor orphan he called her and made her sit close ...
> No one asked after the kings who stood in his court.[73]

In fashioning her autobiographical fragment—which single-mindedly dwelled on this one incident of her kidnapping and rescue—Piro could be seen to be tactically ensuring a secure future where she would find acceptability and respect. Again, in a liberal feminist reading, one can argue that Piro was strategizing and asserting her agency in bettering her place in society, as in resisting forces that acted against her desires and will.

UNDERSTANDING AGENCY

However, the moot question is if there is another way of reading Bahini's and Piro's agency. Since almost all societies are patriarchal, there is an enormous satisfaction in knowing the manner in which women coped with cultures and traditions that apparently did not give them their due. When women used their wit and intelligence to subvert existing subaltern conditions of their existence, it gives us not merely vicarious pleasure in tracing their actions, but throws light on the way subalterns make do in ideologically and materially oppressive situations. At the same time, the anachronism of expecting a universal humanist concern

---

[73] 160: 8.

animating all societies, the genesis of the idea of rights for all individuals, is unreal. Feminists from the liberal tradition, as indeed all feminists to a greater or lesser extent, too are cognizant of this anomaly. For
example, the feminist historians' efforts in the West to look at the private
sphere not only as a site of politics and women's oppression but also as
a space where women shared enriching experiences can be said to be a
product of a sensitive historicity that hopes to study societies, including
their own, on their own terms.[74]

Saba Mahmood, in her study of the mosque movement among
women in contemporary Egyptian society has sought to comprehend
what prompts women to take on aspects of their culture that seem patriarchal, exploitative, and sometimes imbibed against the wishes of the
male members of their families. She explores the meaning of veiling for
women deeply immersed in inculcating piety in their lives.[75] In the light
of Western societies' increasing intolerance towards the veil, it has come
to symbolize a doubly irreconcilable essence of Islamism: it is seen as
either a sign of women's oppression in Islamic societies, or an aggressive
cultural marker of ethnic and cultural identity that refuses assimilation.
That women in the piety movement deploy a different logic—one that
seeks a relationship between embodied modesty as engendering an
interiorized expression of it—hardly ever impresses the liberal feminist
critics of the practice as shown by Mahmood. For a movement that springs
from trying to live the word of god—howsoever patriarchal that may be
to those outside its realm—one assumption that animates it is that of
the overwhelming notion of the will of god. Comparing two broadly conceived imaginaries—Islamic and Western—at work in understanding of
agency, Mahmood notes that one religious imaginary is the one 'in which
humans are considered only partially responsible for their actions, versus
an imaginary in which humans are regarded as the sole authors of their
actions'.[76] This insight, which probes the relationship forged by communities between humanity and god, can be applied to women in the bhakti
imaginary as well. In this context one may quote Mahmood further on the
significance of understanding the working of agency. Mahmood insists
on the need to 'analyse agency in terms of the different modalities it takes

[74] Sue Morgan, ed., *The Feminist History Reader* (London: Routledge, 2006),
pp. 7–8.
[75] Mahmood, 'Agency, Gender and Embodiment', in her *Politics of Piety*,
pp. 153–88.
[76] Mahmood, 'Agency, Gender and Embodiment', p. 168.

and the grammar of concepts in which its particular affect, meaning, and form resides'.[77] In other words, the cultural and temporal specificities have to be kept in mind while employing the notion of agency.

The bhakti imaginary was based on personal devotion to a chosen god, and later bhakti especially encouraged the mediation of the guru to reach this goal.[78] The disciple, in this imagination, held the preceptor as all-powerful, for without the guru's guidance it was impossible to reach divine fulfilment. The guru, in turn, often displayed his own exemplarity by performing miracles, exhibiting god's favour that blessed him as well as made him a receptacle of knowledge incomprehensible to others. In this ethos Piro's or Bahini's agency lay in actively choosing a path, and then following its precepts to reach the given goals. Although the bhakti imaginary was seen to be especially favourable to women and other sub-alterns, gender still created certain barriers, as discussed in this work, in relation to Bahinabai as a wife, and perhaps Piro as a Muslim, low-caste prostitute. The training of the self towards complete submission was a requisite in the particular path chosen by these women. In Bahini's case, her agency appears more diffused as she continued to struggle between an ostensibly ordained fate of marriage and domesticity and one of bhakti and discipleship. For Piro her choice and agency were more apparent as she self-consciously and boldly followed her heart. Her audacity as her volition, however, should not detract from Piro's determination to respect and imbibe the culture of her bhakti. She considered herself putty in the hands of her guru, giving the guru his due, in a cosmos imagined as his sport. Indeed, her agency lay in activating this relationship with her guru, and allowing him to shape her, moulding her for the religious path. At no point does she seem unaware of her will. At no point, too, does she question or thwart his power.

---

[77] Mahmood, 'Agency, Gender and Embodiment', p. 188.
[78] Gold, *The Lord as Guru*.

Part III

6 Caste in the Colonial Public Sphere

The Conundrum of Sant Ditta Ram/ Giani Ditt Singh

Bulleh Shāh kahī eh kāfī
Jo merī hālat par kāfī
Jo bolāṅ tāṅ man ḍar khāve
Chup rihā bhī mūl na jāve.

Bulleh Shah uttered this kafi
That appositely speaks of my situation
If I speak out my heart trembles with fear
But it is also impossible to remain quiet.[1]

What followed the above brief panegyric and mimetic poem were the famous lines of one of the most popular Sufi saints of Punjab.[2] I quote these

---

[1] Giani Ditt Singh, *Nakalī Sikh Prabōdh*, in *Panth Ratan Bhai Ditt Singh Giani, Rachnavali – Bhag Athvan* edited by Pritam Singh (Mohali: Published by the editor, 2007), p. 103.

[2] *Jhooṭh ākhaṅ je bachdā haī, sach ākhe bhāmbhaṛ machdā haī, dil duhāṅ galāṅ te jachdā haī, jach jach ke jībhā kehṅdī hai, muṅh āī bāt na rehṅdī haī.* The lines speak of saving oneself embarrassment and avoiding hullabaloo by speaking falsehood, but they also underline the impossibility of withholding truth that inadvertently trips out from a slippery tongue.

lines not because Ditt Singh reiterated the truth of Bulleh Shah's words nor
to show his facility with writing verse (though he clearly had that—note the
pun on the word 'kafi', meaning both a verse form and enough/adequate).
I do so to highlight the irony of borrowing from a Sufi close to the heart
of the Gulabdasis—and located within Punjabi popular culture—that Ditt
Singh now wished to turn his back on and banish from a reformed Sikh
personhood in the very pamphlet in which he began with this quotation.
This demonstrates his concurrent inhabiting of two increasingly opposed
worlds as envisaged by the Punjabi reformers of the Singh Sabha towards
the last decade of the nineteenth century, the two worlds still not discretely
disparate, as he may have preferred. Ditta Ram, who started his public life
as a Gulabdasi preacher and ended it as a Singh Sabha provocateur, worked
towards creating these dichotomous worlds, though the borders between
them were sometimes blurry even to him. This chapter gives a glimpse
of the changing dynamics of the Punjabi publics by the last decade of the
nineteenth century, from the radical Gulabdasi counterpublics as discussed
in Chapter 1, to the conservative identity politics of the Punjabi public
sphere at the fin de siècle, as a former Gulabdasi struggled to disavow a
more pluralist inheritance in the changed atmosphere of the colonial world.

In this chapter I will track these changes by concentrating on how the
idea of caste came to be formulated by the Sikh reformers of the Lahore
Singh Sabha in late nineteenth-century Punjab by reading the life and
select writings of a stalwart among them, Giani Ditt Singh. In the writings
of Gulabdas and Piro we have witnessed how advaita theology and bhakti
religiosity placed the Gulabdasis in opposition to the dictates of varnashramadharma. Ditt Singh may well have preached the evils of caste or the
castelessness of the universal Brahman in his life as a Gulabdasi preacher.
As a Singh Sabha ideologue too he had to show why caste differentiation
was to be shed, as the Sikh gurus excoriated the institution. Yet, he tied
himself in tangles while doing so. Let us see why.

Ditt Singh is a particularly apposite figure to study the protean stands
of the Singh Sabha on caste as he was a 'Rahtia' or a 'Ravidasia', polite
terms that nevertheless carried the stigma of a Sikh 'untouchable' Chamar.
An unambiguous stance on the meaning(s) of caste (or its irrelevance)
would surely have better served him and the Tat (pure) Khalsa community, which the Sabha and Singh were invested in constituting. However,
as the chapter will demonstrate, Singh's marked ambivalence on caste,
sometimes repudiating it and at others insisting on its centrality to social
life, reflected deeper anxieties on the issue: whether in constituting community, denigrating popular culture, or in imagining the opportunities
and energies its absence may release.

As the Punjabi reformers of different hues initiated and participated in the project of creating modern subjectivities unmarked by the
taints of caste,[3] the question of caste came to be incessantly debated,
among others, by the Arya Samaj and the Singh Sabha. For the Sikh
reformers culling a Khalsa identity, freeing the Sikhs from what came
to be perceived as the debilitating influences of the 'boa constrictor'
of Hinduism, became a project in itself.[4] Caste in its myriad manifestations came to be associated with Hinduism's deleterious effects,
even as they imagined and discursively sought to produce a casteless
Sikh past of the time of the gurus. As the project of forging Sikhs into
a Khalsa identity gained momentum, and every custom and ritual
came to be examined for its appropriateness towards this endeavour,
practice came to be slotted as Hindu, Muslim, or Sikh. Yet, variable
stands on caste persisted, exemplified here in Ditt Singh, and doing
away with the institution became more difficult than has been hitherto
recognized. Harjot Oberoi, W.H. McLeod, and Tony Ballantyne have
all suggested the successful efforts of the Singh Sabha in achieving
the Tat Khalsa identity, which included the need to free Sikhism from
the stranglehold of caste.[5] Perhaps we need to pause and re-examine

[3] As modern middle-class identities were shaped, there came to be an embar-
rassment with the idea of caste. See Anshu Malhotra, *Gender, Caste and Religious
Identities: Restructuring Class in Colonial Punjab* (New Delhi: Oxford University
Press, 2002), p. 2. On delegitimizing of caste for middle-class identity, see Sanjay
Joshi, 'Introduction', in his *The Middle Class in Colonial India* (New Delhi: Oxford
University Press, 2010), pp. xxxix–xl.

[4] Tony Ballantyne, 'Resisting the "Boa Constrictor" of Hinduism: The Khalsa
and the Raj', *International Journal of Punjab Studies* 6, no. 2 (1999): 195–216.

[5] Harjot Oberoi comments on the success of the Tat Khalsa in defining
Sikh identity and separation from what he calls the sanatan paradigm. See his
*The Construction of Religious Boundaries: Culture, Identity and Diversity in the Sikh
Religion* (New Delhi: Oxford University Press, 1994). W.H. McLeod has consistently
noted the issue of caste in the making of Sikh identity, but has discussed caste as a
persistent social problem rather than one stemming from the ambiguity of stand.
See his *Who Is a Sikh: The Problem of Sikh Identity* (Oxford: Clarendon Press, 1989),
pp. 62–81. Ballantyne emphasizes the continuing diversity of the Sikhs and has
brought in the perspective of the Sikh diaspora. However, he does not note the
ambiguity on the issue of caste, and, in fact, quotes Ditt Singh to iterate the Lahore
Sabha's apparently unambiguous stance on caste. See his *Between Colonialism and
Diaspora: Sikh Cultural Formations in an Imperial World* (New Delhi: Permanent
Black, 2007), pp. 57–8.

the certitudes of this historiography by looking at a figure germane to Sikh reformism.

Sociologists have debated for a long time the polysemic significations of the term caste—its association with occupation, ritual purity, bodily substance, social privilege, and the like.[6] The term will be used in all these senses here. Historians have been particularly concerned with questions of the persistence of the institution from earlier times[7] or its specific transmutations in the colonial period.[8] Thus, the moral valence that the term 'dharma' may have—say when Singh as a Gulabdasi faqir in the earliest phase of his career rejected varnashramadharma—may be different from what caste came to mean in a public sphere formed by Orientalist knowledge projects, colonial governmentality, and reformist reformulations. But how did these varied understandings impinge on quotidian life? How did individuals like Ditt Singh, who straddled precolonial and colonial times, understand and express the changing connotations of the institution? The variability of Singh's position on caste, as of others like him caught in the vortex of destabilizing change, is a product of their times, implicated in and constitutive of their efforts at self-fashioning and disciplining society in debates that swirled in the public sphere. Such vacillation persisted despite the trajectory of Singh's life that indicates his personal quest and attraction for public forums that would downplay, if not obliterate, the reach of caste. While it was difficult for the upper castes to forgo the privileges granted by that status—after all, the universal modernity of the middle class in India was often shaped by upper-caste men[9]—there was no given clarity in the positions espoused by the Dalits either. The peculiarly colonial ideas of the immutability of caste, the attractions of upward mobility and its deployment for community identities as undertaken by Singh or alternative potentialities of the institution are delineated here, discussed through the case of Ditt Singh.

[6] For a succinct discussion on various perspectives, see Ishita Banerjee-Dube, 'Introduction: Questions of Caste' in *Caste in History*, edited by Ishita Banerjee-Dube (New Delhi: Oxford University Press, 2010), pp. xv–lxiv.

[7] Susan Bayly, 'Introduction', in her *Caste, Society and Politics in India: From the Eighteenth Century to the Modern Age* (Cambridge: Cambridge University Press, 2005 [1999]), pp. 1–24.

[8] Nicholas B. Dirks, *Castes of Mind: Colonialism and the Making of Modern India* (Princeton: Princeton University Press, 2001).

[9] Joshi, *The Middle Class*, pp. xxxvi–xliv.

In the wake of the resurgence of the debate on caste within Sikhism in the context of assertion of Dalit identity in Punjab today, Ditt Singh's variable stand on the issue will illuminate the historical period when this legacy was redefined. This may lend a perspective on the persistence of the institution of caste within Sikhism, despite a salient desire to fight it. The indeterminacy and lack of fixity on caste and community identity, from the writings of one primarily associated with the development of identity politics, shows the complexity of the issue at hand. This chapter will begin with a survey of the historiographical understanding of the historical role of caste within Sikhism. This will be followed by a glimpse of Ditt Singh's life, stressing the significance of his Gulabdasi background, his move into the Arya Samaj, and finally his association with the Lahore Singh Sabha. The last section will take up some of his writing to examine his varying stands on caste and the contexts in which his arguments were constituted and expressed.

THE QUESTION OF CASTE IN SIKHISM

W.H. McLeod was a historian constantly engaged with the question of caste in the course of his enormous contribution to Sikh Studies. This is visible in his important effort at analysing Sikh sacred scriptures and the anecdotal accounts of the first guru's life (Janam-sakhis) to study the life and teachings of Guru Nanak, placing him within the larger north Indian sant movement.[10] McLeod underlines the theoretical rejection of vertical caste hierarchies in Nanak's teachings, drawing attention to his egalitarian vision of emancipation available to all castes without any disability attached to being born of a low caste. This was in consonance with other sants, men of god often low born, who preached against the rules of varnashramadharma, the broad category of the varna divisions and stages of life that placed the Brahmin on top of the social heap, the sudra at the bottom, and the untouchable outside its ambit. The sants also ridiculed the idiom of purity and pollution in caste practice that rates as superior one who is least soiled with bodily waste and its management. At the same time McLeod draws attention to the continued horizontal operation of caste, in the sense in which rules of caste endogamy were adhered to

---

[10] W.H. McLeod, *Guru Nanak and the Sikh Religion* (New Delhi: Oxford University Press, 1996 [1968]). Karine Schomer and W.H. McLeod, eds, *The Sants: Studies in a Devotional Tradition of India* (New Delhi: Motilal Banarsidass, 1987).

even in the lives of the gurus, as they all married within their ascribed sub-castes. McLeod observes the persistence of this aspect of caste rules particularly among the Khatris of Punjab, the category to which all the gurus belonged.[11]

Significant from the point of view of the fashioning of the Tat Khalsa—the pure Khalsa identity—is McLeod's work on the prescriptive literature of the Sikhs. The rahitnamas, produced in the eighteenth and the early nineteenth centuries, is the corpus of literature that pronounces the code of conduct of the Khalsa.[12] The importance of rahit literature for the purpose of understanding its deployment by the vociferous advocates of the Lahore Singh Sabha is twofold. Firstly, the rahit, its study, and what was attributed to it became the basis for laying the rules for 'correct' Sikh/Khalsa conduct—appearance and personal grooming, costume, rituals, and other social and behavioural indicators—that would mark the Sikhs as a separate community. As McLeod shows, the Sabha intellectuals deliberated on and sieved through this literature, picking up elements that *they* attributed to the tenth guru's period, in consonance with his vision as *they* saw it, while rejecting anything that smacked of being Hindu. They tended to overlook the specific circumstances of the rahit's evolution over time. Second, the eighteenth century, the time of the composition of some of this literature, became the 'heroic' age of the Khalsa for the pamphleteers and public men of the Singh Sabha, adept at investing the writing of history—a community's existence and survival in its difficult past—to mould community identity.[13] The struggle of the Sikhs against the Mughals and Afghans was seen to potentially possess emotive power that could be exploited to forge a separate identity. Bhai Vir Singh, the famous Sikh literary figure, successfully welds together history with new literary forms like the novel to develop a sense of community. Often using the eighteenth century as a backdrop to create moral fables featuring Hindus, Muslims, and Sikhs as distinct types,

---

[11] W.H. McLeod, 'Caste in the Sikh Panth', in his *The Evolution of the Sikh Community: Five Essays* (New Delhi: Oxford University Press, 1996 [1976]), pp. 83–104. More recently, his 'Sikhs and Caste', in *Textures of the Sikh Past: New Historical Perspectives*, edited by Tony Ballantyne (New Delhi: Oxford University Press, 2007), pp. 104–31.

[12] Among McLeod's contribution on the subject is his *Sikhs of the Khalsa: A History of the Khalsa Rahit* (New Delhi: Oxford University Press, 2003).

[13] See Louis Fenech, *Martyrdom in the Sikh Tradition: Playing the Game of Love* (New Delhi: Oxford University Press, 2005 [2000]).

Vir Singh uses the didactic novel to spell out the characteristics of the Khalsa Sikhs.[14]

Studying the six rahitnamas of the eighteenth century, McLeod comments on the cultural background of the 'Hindu' world against which the rahit was formulated.[15] The attitude towards the institution of caste could vary in this prescriptive literature from its virtually complete acceptance in daily social conduct in say the Chhibber Brahmin Chaupa Singh's *Rahitnama* to the more circumspect *Rahitnama* of Daya Singh that discountenances caste.[16] Recently, Purnima Dhavan has shown the simultaneous growth of rahit literature along with that of the *gurbilas* in the eighteenth century. While the former attempted to draw boundaries around Khalsa social conduct, the latter used the devotional idiom and Pauranic myths to figuratively partake in the court of the tenth guru and its warrior tradition. Thus diversity, Dhavan notes, was intrinsically a part of the Sikh world of the eighteenth century.[17]

From this bricolage world, where one could be a Sikh and/or a Khalsa, a *kesdhārī*[18] or a *sahajdhārī*,[19] or, indeed, an Udasi, Nirmala, Akali, Nihang, Nirankari, Namdhari, Sarwariya, or even a Hindu–Sikh, the Lahore Sabha from the late nineteenth century embarked on the project of homogenizing the Sikhs and defining Sikhism.[20] While Oberoi stresses on the distinction between the uniformity promoted by the Tat Khalsa (Lahore group) and the pluralist sanatan positions among other reformist groups

[14] Bhai Vir Singh, *Sundri* (New Delhi: Bhai Vir Singh Seva Sadan, 1983 [1898]).

[15] McLeod, *Sikhs of the Khalsa*, p. 52.

[16] McLeod, *Sikhs of the Khalsa*, p. 130.

[17] Purnima Dhavan, *When Sparrows Became Hawks: The Making of the Sikh Warrior Tradition, 1699–1799* (New York: Oxford University Press, 2012).

[18] One of the five ks, kes or unshorn hair, mandatory for Khalsa Sikhs. The others being in parlance of the Sabhaites, kachh (long drawers), *kaṛā* (steel bangle), *kirpān* (small sword), and *kaṅghā* (comb). The tenth Guru, Gobind Singh, is said to have initiated the Khalsa sect, exhorting the Sikhs to turn Khalsa by taking the *khaṇḍe ki pāhul* (double-edged sword) initiation ceremony, and to maintain certain bodily and behavioural practices, the start of the rahit. However, exactly what these practices were is not clear, the early rahit not even mentioning all five or the same five ks. The Singh Sabha sought to create uniformity on such somatic symbolism. McLeod, *Sikhs of the Khalsa*.

[19] The Sabhaites interpreted sahajdhari as those gradually turning Khalsa. However, the term could refer to the Sikhs who believed in ineffable bliss (sahaj) as the highest spiritual goal.

[20] Oberoi, *Construction of Religious Boundaries*.

(for example, the Amritsar Sabha), McLeod shows the contemporary historian's tendency to overplay the differences between the two.[21] I suggest that Ditt Singh, an early member of the Lahore group, represented an equivocating figure sometimes working for an exclusive Sikh identity and at others pushing for Hindus and Sikhs to jointly abjure 'Muslim' practices. He was keen to establish the Sikhs as a third community of Punjab, distinct from the Hindus, yet found it difficult to theoretically and socially work out this separation, producing literature ambivalent on both caste and community identity. By turning to the voice of the low-caste reformer, we can show the heterogeneous positions on the question of caste as it came to be discussed in the 1890s.

The apparent success of the Tat Khalsa advocates in homogenizing Sikh identity has been challenged by the unstable and complex relationship of the Dalit Sikhs (the scavenger Chuhra/Mazhabi, and the leather-working Chamar—Ravidasi/Rahtia) to it. In a state where Dalits constitute up to 28.3 per cent of the population[22] (the highest in a state in India), their assertion has led to tensions in Punjab and in the diaspora. This erupted, for example, in the attack on two visiting Ravidasi leaders in Vienna, Austria, by a group of Sikhs in May 2009.[23] The tensions also spilled onto Punjab's streets in the summer of 2007, when the Dera Sacha Sauda's Guru Gurmit Ram Rahim Singh attempted an imitation of the tenth Guru's initiation ceremony for his own followers.[24] This unspooling of caste-based identity politics, albeit a product of social churning in modern Punjab, also has to be understood in a historical light. Though the Singh Sabha in the last quarter of the nineteenth century was dominated by the 'upper castes' of Khatris and Aroras—who were traders, merchants, shopkeepers, and professionals—their legatees in homogenizing Sikh identity and controlling its religious and political organs of power were the Akalis, who represented the rural and landowning Jats. The assertion of identity on the part of the Dalit Sikhs, those who earlier worked the lands of Jat zamindars and provided other menial services, has been at the heart of this conflict.

[21] McLeod, *The Sikhs of the Khalsa*, p. 164.

[22] K.S. Singh, ed., *People of India – Punjab*, vol. 37 (New Delhi: Manohar, 2003), pp. xxvi, xliv.

[23] 'It was Waiting to Happen', *Hindustan Times*, New Delhi, 28 May 2009.

[24] Lionel Baixas, 'The Dera Sacha Sauda Controversy and Beyond', *Economic and Political Weekly* 42, no. 40 (2007): 4059–74.

Historically, on the one hand, the low castes freewheeled between the different religious conglomerations of Punjab, which were themselves fairly fluid and adhered to their own heroic and saintly figures like Lalbeg, Balashah, or Balmiki.[25] The colonial state, with its Orientalist notions of religion, which refused to recognize the piety displayed by the Balashahis or the Lalbegis as constitutive of religion, tended to club them with the dominant communities.[26] The attraction of conversion to Christianity under the aegis of the missionaries in Punjab led to a reaction among indigenous reformers who initiated programmes of low-caste 'uplift'. This move received fillip once the reformers became conscious of displaying enhanced community numbers and imbibed the logic of majorities/minorities, leading to concerted efforts to 'purify' (*shuddhī*) and entice the low castes to join mainstream Hindu/Arya and Sikh ranks.[27]

Caste mobility and change of occupation through conversion to Islam or Sikhism was already available in Punjabi society. Conversion to Sikhism could lead to change in status and nomenclature—Chuhra to Mazhabi (who then gave up scavenging) or Chamar to Ravidasi (who sometimes gave up working leather and took up weaving)[28]—as will be demonstrated for Ditt Singh. Additionally, there were sects on the margins of society which admitted low castes and untouchables into their ranks, such as the Udasis and the Gulabdasis of Punjab, and offered avenues of gaining respect through donning the garb of the sadhu/faqir along with access to literacy and education. Later the Ad-Dharm Movement, under

[25] John C.B. Webster, *Religion and Dalit Liberation: An Examination of Perspectives* (New Delhi: Manohar, 2002), pp. 16–17.

[26] Instructions to census officers in 1931 in Punjab asked them to enumerate as Hindu all Chuhras who were not Muslims or Christians and did not return any other religion. See Mark Juergensmeyer, *Religious Rebels in the Punjab: The Social Vision of the Untouchables* (New Delhi: Ajanta Publications, 1988), p. 73.

[27] On the complex politics of conversion of Dalits, see C.S. Adcock, 'Brave Converts in the Arya Samaj: The Case of Dharam Pal', in *Punjab Reconsidered: History, Culture and Practice*, edited by Anshu Malhotra and Farina Mir (New Delhi: Oxford University Press, 2012), pp. 261–86.

[28] Denzil Ibbetson notes in his 1881 Census Report: 'The scavenger on becoming a Musalman will refuse to remove night soil, and on becoming a Sikh will take to tanning or leather-working. The tanner and leather-worker on becoming a Musalman will give up tanning, and on taking the Sikh *pahul* will turn his hand to the loom, and so forth'. *Panjab Castes* (Patiala: Languages Department, Punjab, 1970 [reprint]), p. 268.

its inspirational leader Mangoo Ram, that started in Punjab in the 1920s offered yet another alternative to the low castes.[29] Ditt Singh, a Rahtia, struggled to free himself personally of constraints that shadowed him because of his caste, and intellectually in working out agendas that would reflect the egalitarian principles that the gurus stood for.

IN PUBLIC LIFE: DITT SINGH'S QUEST FOR RESPECTABILITY

We know little about Ditt Singh's personal life, though in recent years there has been a spurt of interest in him fuelled partly by an eagerness to reclaim him as a Dalit hero.[30] His biographers repeatedly speak of his lowly birth, giving an impression that the question ought to have bothered him, as it does them,[31] for how could someone from a Chamar background not have been affected by its debilitations? In the argument presented here, I also index the part his caste played in determining his career, whether initially with the Gulabdasis or later in the Arya Samaj and the Singh Sabha. The issue of caste became prominent from the late nineteenth century onwards as the reformist Aryas and the Sabhaites attempted a theoretical reformulation of the institution. In the charged atmosphere of the time, when the proselytizing missionaries initiated conversions to Christianity of the Punjabi people (for instance, the stories of the genesis of the Amritsar Singh Sabha and the Kanya Mahavidyalaya, Jalandhar, are about the anxieties putative conversions produced),[32] the

---

[29] On Ad-Dharmis, see Juergensmeyer, *Religious Rebels*.

[30] The preface of Pritam Singh's eight-volume collection of Ditt Singh's writings makes this interest in Dalit literature clear. He speaks of Singh's rise from a downtrodden society (*dabbe-kuchle dalit samāj*), and introduces himself as the author of *Dalit Rattnan di Mala* (*A Necklace of Dalit Gems*). See *Panth Ratan Bhai Ditt Singh Giani – Rachnavali-Part I* (Mohali: author published, 2005), pp. 1–3. Gurditt Singh, a biographer of Ditt Singh, also mentions Singh's humble origins, noting prejudice against him because of his 'poor caste' (*garīb jātī*). See *Giani Ditt Singh: Jiwan Ate Rachna* (Chandigarh: Dharam Prachar Committee, 1998), p. 4.

[31] See, for instance, Giani Amar Singh, *Jiwan Chariter Singh Sabha Lehar de Ughe Sanchalak Giani Ditt Singh Ji* (Amritsar: Gulab Singh Malak Firm, 1962).

[32] W.H. McLeod, *Who is a Sikh: The Problem of Sikh Identity* (New York: Clarendon Press, 1989), p. 70; Madhu Kishwar, 'Arya Samaj and Women's Education: Kanya Mahavidyalaya, Jalandhar', *Economic and Political Weekly* 21, no. 17 (1986): WS9–WS13 and WS15–WS24.

reformers in imitative ceremonies introduced the 'conversion' of low castes to twice-born status in the case of the Aryas and to Khalsa in that of the Sabhaites. The convergence of the issues of conversion and caste in these vitiated times created a resonance on the question of caste that played itself out in sharp polemics and mimetic actions among the varied players in public life. There can be little doubt that Ditt Singh the polemicist must have been painfully aware of his own origins at such a time.

The fact that there is no unanimity even on the date of birth of Ditt Singh is a reflection of the paucity of personal information on him. While different authors agree that he was born on 21 April, the year of his birth is proffered variously as 1850, 1852, or 1853.[33] However, all his biographers agree on a few basic facts of his life. His father was 'Sant' Diwan Singh, a Ravidasi weaver, religious minded and an admirer (or member) of the Gulabdasi sect, well versed in the philosophies of Nyaya and Vedanta. It seems Diwan Singh's own religious inclinations influenced the choices he made for his son, whom he first taught himself and then around the age of —eight or nine sent to the village Tiur, in the Ambala district, to be educated by Sant Gurbakhsh Singh, a Gulabdasi, who instructed him in Gurmukhi, prosody, Niti-Shastra, and Vedanta. Additionally, one Lala Dayanand of the same village taught him Urdu and Persian. At the age of sixteen–seventeen, Ditta Ram moved into the main establishment of the Gulabdasis at Chathianwala, near Lahore, where Sant Desa Singh was his preceptor.[34]

Information on the religious life of his father and his own precocious career is also available in Ditt Singh's controversial booklet *Sādhū Dayānaṅd Nāl Merā Sambād (My Conversations with Sadhu Dayanand)* on

---

[33] Shamsher Singh Ashok in his preface to Ditta Ram's *Shirin Farhad* proffers 1850 as the year of Singh's birth based on oral information. He also suggests that he was born in the village Jhalian Kalan, rather than Anandpur Kalaur, Patiala, that the rest agree on. See Sant Ditta Ram (Giani Ditt Singh), *Shirin Farhad* (Ludhiana: Punjabi Sahit Academy, n.d). The year 1852 is suggested by Amar Singh in *Jiwan Chariter* and Narinder Singh Kapoor in *Giani Ditt Singh: Jiwan te Rachna* (Patiala: Punjabi University, 1987). The year 1853 is noted by Harbans Singh, *The Encyclopaedia of Sikhism*, vol. 1, (Patiala: Punjabi University, 1996), pp. 589–90; Kenneth W. Jones, *Arya Dharm: Hindu Consciousness in Nineteenth Century Punjab* (New Delhi: Manohar, 1989), p. 329; and P. Singh, *Panth Ratan*.

[34] If this information was correct, it would indicate that Ditta Ram arrived at Chathianwala in the lifetime of the founder of the sect Gulabdas (d. 1873). His first piece of writing, the qissa of *Shirin Farhad* was dedicated to Gulabdas.

his putative discussions with Swami Dayanand Sarasvati, the founder of the Arya Samaj, when the latter visited Punjab in 1877 and established a Samaj there.[35] Here, Ditt Singh writes: 'I was born in the house of a sant who preached/So from a young age I too began to settle disputations.'[36]

The Gulabdasi background of Ditt Singh is significant for many reasons. It is important to note that his father was influenced by the teachings and the philosophical leanings of the Gulabdasis, their non-dualist philosophy theoretically granting an equal status to all irrespective of the caste one had been born into. And so they repeatedly spoke against the tyrannies of varnashramadharma, writing against its practice. The Gulabdasis were indubitably one of the most exciting sects of the middle years of the nineteenth century, as Chapter 1 shows, revelling in flouting rules, but also literary in orientation and so opening to all avenues for acquiring knowledge—theoretically a monopoly of the highest castes. Not only were they willing to impart knowledge to one willing to receive it, they were fond of debate, discussion, and controversy, putting forth their points of view in an unequivocal and provocative manner.

The radical, intellectually stimulating, and the uninhibited lifestyle of the Gulabdasis must have appealed to Diwan Singh. As noted, Diwan Singh came from the upwardly mobile section of the Chamar community, the Ravidasis, who had taken to weaving, a clean profession, giving up the impurity associated with leather. According to Denzil Ibbetson, the colonialist administrator-ethnographer of Punjab, in the eastern districts of Punjab, where Ditt Singh's birth and early upbringing occurred, most of the Julahas or weavers had origins among the Chamars. However, the 'Julaha does not work in impure leather, he eats no carrion, he touches no carcasses.... In a word, the Chamar is a menial, the Julaha an artisan'.[37] For a spiritually inclined person like Diwan Singh, the Gulabdasis opened up opportunities for further learning and better status for himself and his son, without necessarily having to undertake the onerous asceticism associated with say the Udasis. The fact that Gulabdas's followers came from different castes, including Jats, Khatris, Kumhars, and Ravidasis, must have added to their appeal, offering interaction unencumbered by

---

[35] *Sadhu Dayanand Nal Mera Sambad* in G. Singh, *Giani Ditt Singh*, pp. 43–82. In this, Ditt Singh sketchily mentions his early life. It is important to remember the polemical nature of this work, and his words should not be taken at face value, as some writers have done.

[36] G. Singh, *Giani Ditt Singh*, p. 45.

[37] Ibbetson, *Panjab Castes*, p. 302.

the strictures of caste. For example, Jawahir Singh Kapoor—a Khatri 'guru bhai' of Ditt Singh, whose career paralleled his own and who was the likely inspiration in the latter's move from the Gulabdasi establishment to the Arya Samaj and then the Singh Sabha—was a lifelong friend.[38]

Furthermore, the Gulabdasis offered a genuine environment of intellectual creativity in the early years of colonial rule before the vitiations of public life marred the end of the century with communal diatribes. Besides Guru Gulabdas, a prolific writer, almost all his disciples wrote, as mentioned in Chapter 1. Ditta Ram started his writing career by writing in the most popular Punjabi literary genres. His first work was the qissa of *Shirin Farhad* (1872), and the second was verses on wiles and vices of women, *Abla Nind* (1876).[39] Ditta Ram captures the stimulating atmosphere of the Gulabdasi dera in his closing verses of *Shirīn Farhād*, the moment in traditional writing when the author re-enters his narrative after the initial invocatory verse, having earlier ended the tale being related. Here he calls himself Ditta Ram 'faqir' (mendicant), who sat in the *bārādarī* (airy pavilion) of Satguru Das Gulab, while around him friends were engrossed in various activities. Though we do not have to read these lines literally, they do capture the ambience of the dera and its literati rather well.

Koī kosh te kavī nuṅ paṛhan baiṭhe, koī baiṭh ramāiyṇāṅ gān belī
koī ṭib te bāb nuṅ dekhde je, koī gauṇe te jor pauṇ belī
paṛhan ik tauhīd nuṅ shauq belī, baiṭhe ulfatāṅ nāl sunauṇ belī ...
koī āshqāṅ dī gal tor deṅda, khol qissyāṅ de varqāṅ belī
mahārāj farjaṅd dilbaṅd āhā, vaḍe Tegh Bahādur jān belī.

Some sit to read lexicon or poetry, some sing the Ramayan friends
Some see chapters of unani medicine, some put energy in singing friends
Some read of the unity of God with interest, relating it with love to friends
Some start to speak of lovers, turning pages of qissas friends
The beloved son of maharaj the great Tegh Bahadur my life, friends.[40]

---

[38] On Jawahir Singh Kapoor, see H. Singh, *The Encyclopaedia of Sikhism*, pp. 372–3.

[39] H. Singh, *The Encyclopaedia of Sikhism*, pp. 229–30. Three of Ditta Ram's writings, *Shirin Farhad*, *Abla Nind*, and *Mansambodhan* are attributed to his pre-Sabha phase.

[40] P. Singh, *Panth Ratan*, vol. 1, p. 54. Tegh Bahadur was the son of Hari Gobind, the successor of Gulabdas, and in turn his successor and should not be confused with the ninth Guru of the Sikhs. Ditta Ram was Tegh Bahadur's preceptor.

FIGURE 6.1 Picture of Ditta Ram available in the handwritten manuscript of his *Shirin Farhad*. According to Ashok, it depicts the author at age twenty-one. Note that he is seated on a *gaddi* with cushions, in clothes of the traditional style, and in a *baradari*, an airy pavilion, which he described as the Gulabdasi establishment in his own early writings. His name Dittaramji is inscribed just above his turban.
Source: Shamsher Singh Ashok, ed., *Shirin Farhad* (Ludhiana: Punjabi Sahit Academy, n.d.).

A similar mention of Chathe Nagar (Chathianwala), the main establishment of the Gulabdasi sect, baradari, and *tālāb* (pond) is also made in the closing verses of his *Abla Nind*.[41]

What is apparent from the above is that Ditta Ram participated fully in the cultural atmosphere of the Gulabdasi establishment. He imbibed their monist philosophy, here mentioned as *ik tauhīd*, or the Unity of Being, and was immersed in their world of learning and imparting knowledge: revelling in composing poetry, indulging in Punjabi popular literary practices, absorbing bhakti and Sufi ethos, and engaging in religious discourses and disputations. Yet, even as he seemed firmly ensconced in this pluralist space, he opted out, becoming embroiled with the Arya Samaj and the new politics that came in its wake. Why did this happen?

The reasons for such a move are easy to discern. The death of the charismatic founder of the dera in 1873 may have left it bereft of a personality who could keep all disciples together. Many left soon after to create local centres of their own,[42] and

[41] P. Singh, *Panth Ratan*, vol. 1, p. 101. I visited Chathianwala, now in Pakistan, on 25 May 2008. An elderly person corroborated the architectural details of the dera. While the tomb where Gulabdas and Piro lie buried is now dilapidated, he told me of the earlier existence of a beautiful pond (*sarovar*) with a bridge across it, now destroyed.

[42] Gian Inder Sewak, '*Gulabdasi Sampradya: Rachna Ate Vichar*' (PhD diss., Guru Nanak Dev University [GNDU], 1984), p. 115. Sewak speaks of centres

others' literary careers took wing, though many remained loyal to the dera and to Gulabdas's memory. However, the more significant reason must be seen to be the effect of Swami Dayanand's visit to Punjab. Kenneth Jones speaks of his fifteen-month stay in Punjab, from April 1877 to July 1878, as one of sensational lectures, debates, and controversies. A number of Arya Samajs were established in various parts of Punjab, and the younger generation was inspired by his teachings that emphasized the need to reform society.[43] Among the new ideas promulgated by Dayanand was an insistence on the reconfiguration of caste. He envisaged a society where education, talent, and the virtues of a person would determine caste, rather than birth.[44] Though this idea is unevenly present in his opus *Satyārth Prakāsh*, it had the potential for genuine transformation, despite the notion of hierarchy remaining entrenched.[45] Among the arguments proffered by Dayanand to make his case was that of the need to change caste if a person demonstrated commensurate abilities: 'Even if a lowborn man were to possess qualifications ... of a superior class, he should be recognized as such; and if a man highborn though he be, were to act like a man of inferior class, he should be relegated to it'.[46] Dayanand reinforced his logic by giving mythological examples of caste mobility: sage Javal of an unknown caste became a Brahmin; Matang, an outcaste, became a Brahmin; and Vishvamitra changed his Kshatriya status for that of a Brahmin.[47]

We can only guess of the effect such remarkable ideas had on an 'outcaste' like Ditt Singh, though this point cannot be overstretched. His fellow Gulabdasi, Jawahir Singh Kapoor, a high caste, too was attracted to

---

opening up in Ferozepur, Patiala, Ropar, Ambala, Jullunder, Karnal, Amritsar, Kasur, Pothohar, Sialkot, Sindh, and Balochistan.

[43] Jones, *Arya Dharm*, pp. 36–7.

[44] Jones, *Arya Dharm*, p. 33.

[45] Dayanand's vacillation between caste by birth and by talent is examined in Anshu Malhotra, 'The Body as a Metaphor for the Nation: Caste, Masculinity and Femininity in the *Satyarth Prakash* of Dayanand Sarasvati', in *Rhetoric and Reality: Gender and the Colonial Experience in South Asia*, edited by Avril A. Powell and Siobhan Lambert-Hurley (New Delhi: Oxford University Press, 2006), pp. 121–53.

[46] Malhotra, 'The Body as a Metaphor', p. 135. This quotation is from second edition of Charanjiva Bharadwaja's translation of the *Satyarth Prakash* called *Light of Truth* (United Provinces: Arya Pratinidhi Sabha, 1915), p. 98.

[47] Malhotra, 'The Body as a Metaphor', p. 135.

the Arya Samaj and the new associational politics it represented, serving it as a secretary for some years. Yet, it is important to underline the manner in which Singh absorbed and repeatedly deployed the logic of caste status worked out by Dayanand. It had obvious echoes for him: a learned 'outcaste', who embarked early in life on a career of writing and lecturing, but had to battle the prejudices of society. Even though he moved out of the Arya Samaj, he never gave up the potentially revolutionary aspect of Dayanand's argument. It is also true that the Arya Samaj soon kick-started a programme of shuddhi using Dayanand's logic, at least intermittently, to justify its conversions of low castes who had found succour in religious traditions other than that of Hinduism. Thus, the argument worked out by Dayanand stayed in public life to an important extent. Ditt Singh's disquisition on caste from various perspectives is available in his *Nakli Sikh Prabodh* (*The Awakening of False Sikh/s*), produced in his Singh Sabha days and published in 1893. At one point in the work he endorses caste as an institution as it had existed in the 'early' days. Having established that the four varnas were based on the occupations, he states:

> The system benefited the Hindu *qaum* because every qaum or *varan* stood firm in their task. The reason for progress was also that if a Brahman did the work of a Chhatri, he was called a Chhatri, if he did the work of a Vaish he was called a Vaish, of a Shudar, he was called a Shudar, *and if the Shudar did the job of a Brahman, he became a Brahman.* So Krishnaji in Gita had called one's *karam* one's varan. Like Ved Vyas though born of the stomach of a fisherwoman was called a Pandit Brahman, Vashisht born of a prostitute was called a Brahman and Vishvamitra though born a Brahman, because he kept weapons was called a Chhatri royal sage.[48]

To give another example of the use of the same logic to register his frustration at the persistence of caste in society, Ditt Singh writes in the *Khalsa Akhbar* of 15 July 1898, a newspaper he edited over a number of years: 'An illiterate man who calls his caste Brahman, is addressed as Panditji, but if a man of another varan, however well-versed in Shastras is never seen as a Pandit, but people are bothered by the question that a Vaish or a Shudar does not have the right to hear the Veda.'[49]

The strength of this argument that accounted for the years Ditt Singh spent in gathering and disseminating knowledge can be gauged for

---

[48] Ditt Singh, *Nakali Sikh Prabodh*, in P. Singh, *Panth Ratan*, p. 146 (emphasis added).

[49] Quoted in Kapoor, *Giani Ditt Singh*, p. 114.

him if we also take a look at the nature of caste prejudice he faced and the public humiliations he had to swallow. We know, for instance, that when Bhai Takht Singh, the founder of the Sikh Kanya Mahavidyalaya, Ferozepur, invited Singh to this school set up in 1893 to educate Sikh girls, the local Singh Sabha refused to share their meal with him because of his caste. Takht Singh, who personally found Singh inspirational, had to take him to his house and serve him a meal there.[50] A similar bias was displayed by the priests of the Golden Temple who would not open the precincts of the temple to outcaste devotees till later in the afternoon, well after all others had left. The consecrated food, *karah prasād*, prepared by the lower castes was also not accepted at the temple. It seems people like Ditt Singh were also not exempt from such treatment.[51]

Thus, while the Gulabdasis created an enclave where caste affiliations were rejected, the Gulabdasis were increasingly relegated into a marginal community devoted to philosophical questions and intellectual pursuits by the end of the 1870s. The new public life began to engage the emerging elite on issues that now had a wider resonance in society. What the Arya Samaj offered to Ditt Singh was a bold restatement on caste that could be carried into public life, not just a flouting of established customs to be practised within a small arena among people devoted to esoteric values. The new argument was debated with force and conviction in the new fora of the public sphere—newspapers, journals, associations, and public lectures.

Ditt Singh's break with the Arya Samaj only occurred in 1888, over the vocal critiques of the Sikh gurus by the Arya leaders.[52] In the meanwhile, Ditt Singh had probably already joined or come to be associated with the Lahore Singh Sabha, set up in 1879 under the leadership of Gurmukh Singh. His new associates encouraged him to clear the Punjabi language 'Giani' examination in 1886 and he subsequently joined the Oriental College, Lahore, as a professor of Punjabi.[53] His membership of both

---

[50] M.M. Amol, *Bhai Takht Singh da Jiwan te Panth Seva* (handwritten MS), 1938, pp. 12–15. I thank Mahima Manchanda for this reference.

[51] A. Singh, *Jiwan Chariter*, pp. 74–5; Kapoor, *Giani Ditt Singh*, p. 17.

[52] Jones, *Arya Dharm*, pp. 135–9.

[53] See H. Singh, *Encyclopaedia of Sikhism*, pp. 589–90. The honorific 'Giani' before Ditt Singh's name may not signify his passing this examination. According to Ditt Singh, he was called Giani because he started preaching at a young age. *Sadhu Dayanand Nal Mera Sambad*, p. 45.

the organizations simultaneously was neither contradictory nor controversial as Ditt Singh went about creating a niche for himself in public life.
So long as Sikhism was viewed as reformed Hinduism, it did not lead to
problems—only when the Arya leaders began to condemn Sikhism as
idolatrous, and began attacking the Sikh gurus, that the situation became
intolerable, and the break came.[54] This point might be worth reiterating
because some of Ditt Singh's biographers, for instance Amar Singh, try
to prove that he was never a member of the Arya Samaj.[55] Others, following Ditt Singh's polemical *Sadhu Dayanand Nal Mera Sambad*, where he
describes three disputations between the Swami and himself—in each
of which apparently the Swami was worsted by Singh's better knowledge
of the Vedas and the Indian philosophical traditions—have dated the
pamphlet to 1877. This was the year that the Swami was in Lahore, thus
effectively showing the break of Singh with the Arya Samaj in the year of
its establishment.[56] This pamphlet, in my opinion, ought to be dated after
the break, for it would have been impossible for Ditt Singh to continue
within the Samaj after the ridicule he poured on the Swami, considering
the Swami's status within the establishment.

The mid-1880s was a time of turmoil for Ditt Singh, a period that
pushed him into clarifying his positions on a number of issues. On the
Singh Sabha front, this was the time when the Lahore group threw
a challenge to the Amritsar 'conservatives', condemning their *sanatani*
beliefs. The practice of worshipping living gurus came to be critiqued
along with the question of maintaining caste rules. The Amritsar group's
approval of an exegesis of the Granth that endorsed the *sanatani* worldview was also disapproved of.[57] The excommunication of Gurmukh
Singh from Sikhism under the seal of the Golden Temple followed at
the behest of the Amritsar group.[58] Ditt Singh also had to face a court
case for his farce, *Supan Nāṭak* (*Dream Drama*), that he published in the
Khalsa Akhbar, which lampooned the Amritsar group.[59] The issue of

[54] Jones, *Arya Dharm*, pp. 135–9.

[55] A. Singh, *Jiwan Chariter*, p. 54.

[56] The 'defeat' of the Swami is underlined by G. Singh, *Giani Ditt Singh*, p. 4.
Ashok also dates the pamphlet to 1877, *Shirin Farhad*, p. 8.

[57] A. Singh, *Jiwan Chariter*, pp. 61–9. Oberoi, *Construction of Religious Boundaries*.

[58] See the note on Gurmukh Singh in H. Singh, *Encyclopaedia of Sikhism*,
vol. 2, pp. 185–7.

[59] See the note on Ditt Singh in H. Singh, *Encyclopaedia of Sikhism*, vol. I,
pp. 589–90.

caste was covertly present in these proceedings. Gurmukh Singh, though a Chandar Jat, was seen as a son of a *langarī*, a cook, and Ditt Singh was an 'outcaste'.[60] The attacks of the Aryas on Sikhs also began to be vociferous around this time.

Simultaneously, it seems the Gulabdasis took out a 'notice' against Ditt Singh, the man who attacked 'gurudom', for being a guru to villagers in Abhaipur, Ambala, where he apparently maintained a small hermitage. The notice ran as follows:

> We've heard that Bhai Ditt Singh, when a faqir of the Gulabdasi persuasion for a long time, in Abhaipur of tehsil Kharar, zila Ambala, had built [is building?] a hut and a small garden, and calls himself a guru in the villages of the Lamba-Chhamba, and gets himself worshipped and accepts votive offerings of the people.[61]

Though none of his biographers mention when this particular *nindyā patar* (defamation letter) of the Gulabdasis came out, the question it raises points to the controversy around the tradition of living gurus. Ditt Singh did not deny the charge, explaining the charge of 'his brothers' as proving how respected he was from a young age in many towns and villages of Punjab! Singh seems to suggest that this occurred in days of his early career, at a time prior to his going to Chathianwala. He further shows that his preaching in those days was against the worship of idols, graves, pirs, superstitions, and generally in line with his ideology as a Sabhaite. However, Ditt Singh's defence of his actions still does not answer when this charge was made against him, nor is it a convincing argument. Though the Gulabdasis were advocates of Vedantic monism, the worship of graves and tombs did become an aspect of their sect, as a tomb was built on the graves of Gulabdas and Piro at Chathianwala that became an important site of Gulabdasi piety.[62] Ditt Singh was restrained in his response to the Gulabdasi 'brothers' with whom he may have maintained cordial relations. However, he used this occasion to ridicule the Arya Samajis, taking a dig at the Swami. He observed that while he was

[60] A. Singh, *Jiwan Chariter*, p. 59.

[61] G. Singh, *Giani Ditt Singh*, p. 46. According to Amar Singh, Ditt Singh in his Gulabdasi days practised Udasi/Gulabdasi asceticism that required him to smear his body with ashes and meditate in graveyards and cremation grounds, practices that later became the target of his wrath. See *Jiwan Chariter*, p. 15.

[62] Giani Gian Singh, *Sri Guru Panth Prakash* (Patiala: Bhasha Vibhag, 1970, first published 1880), p. 1293.

FIGURE **6.2**   Ditt Singh at the time of
his appointment as a Professor in
Punjabi at the Oriental College, Lahore.
While the style of turban is similar to
that portrayed in the earlier picture, he
wears a formal Western-style graduating
gown, and has a fuller flowing beard.
Source: Shamsher Singh Ashok, ed.,
Shirin Farhad (Ludhiana: Punjabi Sahit
Academy, n.d.).

already a respected preacher,
Dayanand was still looking for
an intellectual tradition to follow,
referring to Dayanand's early
experiments with different ascetic
and spiritual practices.[63]

The convergence of all these
issues indicates overlapping
affiliations that Ditt Singh concurrently maintained, even till
the mid-1880s—Gulabdasi, Arya
Samaji, and Sabhaite. However,
the turn of events from the second half of the 1880s forced his
hand to choose one of the groups
he was associated with, and he
chose the Khalsa identity being
worked out by the Lahore group
over others. However, the point
that needs to be underscored is

that it was possible till then, even for a man in the colonial public sphere,
to belong to and appropriate more than one tradition.

Perhaps, this was easier for someone like Ditt Singh, who received an
orthodox education and was introduced to Western institutions somewhat
later in life.[64] The rigid compartmentalization of religious communities
and their essential beliefs was something he learnt later. And if he did
manage to tutor himself in divisive communal politics, he never deployed
that lesson in totality. Ditt Singh displayed changeable stances in works
that ostensibly presented an unencumbered ideology of the Singh Sabha,
as the next section will show. In some ways, this early grooming in multiple intellectual and religious traditions stood Ditt Singh in good stead
even as an advocate of the Singh Sabha reforms, for he used his vast
knowledge to refute charges, make accusations, and take on the role of

[63] On Dayanand's life and thought, see J.T.F. Jordens, *Dayananda Saraswati:
His Life and Ideas* (New Delhi: Oxford University Press, 1978).

[64] The point about interaction with Western education and institutions of
the Lahore reformers is made too blithely. McLeod, for example, writes about
the Lahore Sabhaites that they 'essentially thought in western terms'. *Sikhs of the
Khalsa*, p. 159.

an untiring scribe and spokesman of the Lahore Sabha. By the time of his early death in September 1901, Singh was seen as a vigorous ideologue for the reformed Khalsa identity, and continues to be regarded as such. What such straitjacketing hides are the multilayered facets of his personality. This section has followed his life trajectory, demonstrating the personal conflicts he faced as he negotiated caste prejudices. Yet, there was no straightforward rejection of caste in Ditt Singh's writing. What one finds instead is an endorsement of the institution at times, and its rejection at others, or its persistence in reworked forms. The next section will look at some of Singh's writing to highlight his complex position on caste and understand its implications.

CASTE IN DITT SINGH'S WRITINGS

The eclectic career of Ditt Singh was reflected in the literature he produced. His writing spanned forays into popular Punjabi literary culture, to his polemical diatribes against 'other' religious communities and caste practices. He wrote biographies of Sikh gurus and martyrs, and condemned practices unbecoming of the Khalsa.[65] His contribution to Punjabi journalism was noteworthy as the editor of *Khalsa Akhbar*, a position he occupied from virtually its inception in the mid-1880s till his death, with a gap of a few years when it was discontinued. Ditt Singh was adept at writing verse, a tribute to his Gulabdasi days, though he used prose particularly in his journalistic writings. Though Singh wrote mostly in Punjabi—the language in Gurmukhi script to be appropriated by Sikhs as theirs—he was equally at home in Braj (the language of Sikh literature in the eighteenth and early nineteenth centuries), Urdu, and Farsi, choosing the language appropriate to the subject at hand.[66] The multiple innovations in the use of language in Punjab of the nineteenth century will not detain us here;[67] however, Ditt Singh's choice of language

---

[65] Ditt Singh is credited with more than forty books/pamphlets.

[66] Kapoor makes the point that Ditt Singh used Braj for philosophical issues and Punjabi for his exhortative works. *Giani Ditt Singh*, pp. 131–2. Ashok also comments on Singh's use of Bhasha (Braj) in works such as *Supan Natak*, *Abla Nind*, *Guru Nanak Prabodh*, and *Mansambodhan*, and notes his comfort with Persian and Urdu in qissas. *Shirin Farhad*, p. 9.

[67] On the politics of language in Punjab, see Farina Mir, *The Social Space of Language: Vernacular Culture in British Colonial Punjab* (Ranikhet: Permanent Black, 2010).

and genres point to his comfort with the literary and pluralistic cultures of precolonial Punjab. His discerning use of language also reveals his engagement with the agendas of reform—questions of language, caste, and the definition of religious communities—and the appropriate vehicle to carry these forward. It is for this reason that Ditt Singh is sometimes seen as a forerunner to Bhai Vir Singh,[68] in his unflagging endeavour for reforms through the medium of writing, and in his use of history and language in defining the Khalsa identity. In a sense, the trials, errors, and successes of Ditt Singh initiated a more cogent Sikh reform that followed. Here I will show how caste appeared in various forms in his writings and the different ways in which he understood the institution. The variable use of caste reflected both the deep-rooted nature of the institution in society, and the difficulties experienced in working out a theoretical argument against its prevalence among the Sikhs. Arguing for the irrelevance of caste from a Gulabdasi enclave where varnashramadharma could be disregarded, to taking the idea to a larger social arena was a task imbricated in contradictions and pitfalls, as revealed by Singh's shifting stands on the question.

To explicate Singh's protean stances on caste I will use two of his substantial pamphlets. These are the *Nakli Sikh Prabodh* mentioned earlier and *Sultān Puāṛā (Trouble over Sultan)*.[69] Both were published in the 1890s and were reprinted a number of times—*Nakli Sikh* at least thrice in the lifetime of Ditt Singh,[70] and *Sultan Puara* remained popular even after his death, his son reprinting it. *Nakli Sikh* was probably written first, as Ditt Singh later elaborated in separate pamphlets—*Sultan Puara*, *Guggā Gapauṛā*, and *Mirāṅ Manaut*, (against the worship of Sakhi Sarwar, Gugga Pir, and Miran Pir respectively)—some of the themes lampooning popular cultural practices of Punjabi Sikhs (and Hindus) that he introduces here. *Nakli Sikh* is more complex of the two because of the number of issues he tackles in its pages. Ditt Singh wrote this pamphlet to establish the separate identity of the Sikh religion and community, asserting that from the time of the early gurus onwards, their conscious effort was to create a distinct religion in Punjab: *sab toṅ judā jhaṅḍā gaḍan dā sī* (to plant a separate banner).[71] Insidiously, Singh conflates Sikh religion

---

[68] Kapoor, *Giani Ditt Singh*, p. 145.

[69] Bhai Ditt Singh Giani, *Sultan Puara*, 6th edition (n.p., n.d.) For *Nakli Sikh*, see the first footnote of this chapter.

[70] P. Singh, *Panth Ratan*, Vol. 8, p. 98.

[71] *Nakli Sikh*, p. 133.

with its Khalsa variant from the time of Nanak, the first guru, thereby pushing back in time the Sabha disapprobation of sahajdhari identity, though he later wrote about the tenth guru initiating the Khalsa in Anandpur. However, the referents in his language remain impregnated with multiple possibilities—note the use of the term 'avatar' (incarnation) to describe Nanak, alluding to the Pauranic mythological significations: 'He accepted suffering on his body/Within the Khalsa Panth was guru Nanak, the avtar'.[72]

In this tract, Ditt Singh tells Sikhs that they could learn from other religious communities, that is, Hindus, Muslims, and Christians, of how distinct identities can flourish. Simultaneously, he attempts to create separate rituals for the Sikhs, critiquing the myriad 'Hindu' practices that the Sikhs apparently followed—birth and death rituals, wearing Hindu garments (*dhotī* instead of *kachhehrā* or drawers), and keeping Hindu somatic symbols like the sacred thread (janeu), and the topknot (*choti*), instead of unshorn hair and the turban. Ditt Singh also initiates weaning the Sikhs away from popular practices like visiting the tombs of Sufi pirs. In this conscious step at culling out a Sikh identity from a mélange of practices, Singh also discusses caste, both in a conscious and 'correct' manner, according to the new Sabhaite insistence on its irrelevance in Sikhism, but also in an unconscious and complex way that assumes caste to be endemic in society. Though there were other pamphlets that Singh wrote to pronounce on Sikh traditions—*Gurmat Ārtī Prabodh, Durgā Prabodh, Darpok Singh Daler Singh*—none match in the plethora of issues he picks here, making this booklet something of a torchbearer in laying the blueprint for Sikh reform.

In *Sultan Puara*, Singh has a more straightforward task—to demonstrate to Sikhs the foolhardiness of worshipping a 'Muslim' saint, Sakhi Sarwar. In the spirit of competitive one-upmanship between popular religion and Sikh practices, Singh trivializes the miracle-making powers of Sarwar, and offers as consolation for giving up Sarwar the parallel myths and rituals of the Sikh religion. Though Singh speaks of the glory of the Khalsa religion, the pamphlet is clearly addressed to both Hindus and Sikhs, and seeks to remove them both from the reach of a Muslim pir.[73]

---

[72] Ditt Singh, *Nakli Sikh*, p. 122.

[73] *Dharamsāl te ṭhākurdwāre pichhe kīte sāre, pauṇ muṇḍiaṅ de jā janeu sarwar de darbāre* (Dharamsalas and temples have been abandoned, boys are made to wear the sacred thread in the court of Sarwar). Ditt Singh, *Sultan Puara*, p. 2.

The 'othering' of Muslims is rather crude, a far cry from the embarrassment with the excesses of anti-Muslim tirade of the eighteenth-century
rahitnamas that McLeod has discerned in the writings of the Sabhaites.[74]

The pamphlet is also important for the subregional identities within
Punjab which Singh alludes to, identifying people with their local customs. This is significant for it uncovers a manner of apprehending people
through other than their religious or caste identities. In the process Singh
underlines the appeal of Sarwar across Punjab, but also unveils the ambition of the reformist agenda for a pan regional adherence. Most of all, the
pamphlet is of interest for addressing people of different castes to abjure
the worship of Sarwar, in the first instance by recuperating their
caste identities, lost in the melee of Sarwar fairs, and the medley of beliefs
and rituals that form the core piety towards the pir. In other words, in
Sultan Puara Ditt Singh adopts a circuitous path via caste to the Khalsa ideal
of 'castelessness'. The intermingling of castes in the cultic practices of
Sarwar, and the belief that the pir disapproved of the custom of untouchability (*chhut*) were in fact raised to condemn Sarwar—'the pir does not
approve of untouchability, we go like brothers'.[75] This liminal state of
castelessness during the pilgrimage of the saint is shown to be repugnant precisely because it violates codes of caste behaviour:

> *Pīr bhāī ban ke eh sāre chale sarwar de darbāre*
> *zāt pāt nuṅ khū dubaiyā bharāī nuṅ chā pīr banaiyā*

> Becoming pir brothers they all go to the court of Sarwar
> Sinking caste in the well they have made the (Muslim) *bharai* their pir. [76]

Caste was then to be recovered and reinstated as the ideal state, and it
remains ambiguous here to what extent it could be discarded after adopting Khalsa practices.

It might be useful at this juncture to see where Ditt Singh iterates
the position that in Sikhism there was no caste. Two points need to be
emphasized here. First, the statement against the practice of caste invariably occurs when he speaks of the gurus and the importance they placed
on this matter, that is, at a moment when he was consciously stating a
theoretical position on Sikhism. Second, the idea of caste incorporated

---

[74] McLeod, *Who is a Sikh*, p. 50; *Sikhs of the Khalsa*, p. 170.

[75] Ditt Singh, *Sultan Puara*, p. 6.

[76] Ditt Singh, *Sultan Puara*, p. 3. Bharais were the 'priests' of Sarwar, and took
parties of pilgrims to the shrine at Nigaha in northwest Punjab. Ibbetson, *Panjab
Castes*, p. 229.

both the notion of varna (*baran*), the classical four castes of Brahminical Hinduism, and the idea of untouchability (*chhūt-chhāt*) associated with everyday social behaviour. The notions of purity/pollution pertained to the complex of cooking (*chaunka*) and the rules of commensality. Speaking of the erasing of caste by the tenth guru, Singh writes: *chār baran ik baran sajāye amrit chakh sabh bhrāt banāye* (four varnas were constituted as one, they were made brothers by tasting amrit). He further notes about the Khalsa thus created: *chhūt-chhāt kī rasam na karte, nahiṅ kahu se ranchak ḍarte* (they do not follow the rituals of un/touchability, nor are they afraid of anyone).[77] Earlier he had made a similar observation for the third guru, Amar Das, who advised his followers to give up the rigid principles of untouchability.[78]

Ditt Singh's most important and oft-quoted statement, because of its lyrical style, was made in *Nakli Sikh*, where he addresses the different occupational castes of Punjab and admonishes them for adhering to their traditional caste statuses despite taking amrit, or initiation into the Khalsa. Illuminating the significance of initiation, Singh elaborates on how this ceremony incorporates a person in the qualities of the tenth guru: he should now say that he is born in Patnasahib as the guru was; lives in Anandpur, like the guru did; that the tenth guru is his father, the guru's (youngest) wife—Sahib Kaur—his mother; and that their caste is Singh or Khalsa. However, people in disregard of such injunctions continued with their old names, ways, and castes:

Kaun Sikh hunde ho bhāī? Maiṅ Arorā ih hai Nāī.
Terī Sikhā kī hai jāt? Nāmā bansī Chhimbā bhrāt.
Terā dudh kaun hai pyāre? Asī Singh hāṅ Jat karāre.
Terā janam kinā de ghar dā? Maiṅ hāṅ Mihrā pānī bhardā.

What manner of a Sikh are you brother? I am Arora, and he a Nai.
What is your caste Sikh? I am from the clan of Nama, of Chhimba brotherhood.
What [manner] of milk is yours? We Singhs are distinct Jats.
Whose house have you been born? I am a Mihra who supplies water.[79]

In this mien Ditt Singh speaks about various castes/occupational and endogamous groups—Aroras, Chhimbas, Jats, Mihras, Ahluwalias, Tarkhans, Brahmins, Khatris, Sahnis, Rangretas, Ravidasis, Suniaras,

---

[77] Ditt Singh, *Nakli Sikh*, pp. 164–5.
[78] Ditt Singh, *Nakli Sikh*, p. 125.
[79] Ditt Singh, *Nakli Sikh*, pp. 172–4.

Rahtias, Lubhanas, Bhallas, Trehans, and Bedis. It is noteworthy that
he addresses the higher castes of Brahmins, Khatris, and Aroras, along
with the 'untouchables', Ravidasis and Rahtias, various artisan castes,
and other service providers, along with the Khatri castes of the first three
gurus—Bedis, Bhallas, and Trehans—the Bawas who sought to defend
their caste and status privileges against the onslaughts of the Lahore
Sabhaites. This was, perhaps, his most comprehensive statement that
endorsed if not a casteless position, the advocacy of one caste for all
Khalsa, and hence equality of status. However, Ditt Singh was far from
consistent in maintaining this position.

Having noted Ditt Singh's statements abrogating caste, it is important to review the many occasions when he evokes caste and associates
it with either duties that were required of a specific group, or appeared
intrinsic to its somatic–social make-up. Speaking of the Hindus, and the
lessons the Sikhs could learn from them via the epic Ramayana, namely
that despite the personal quest of Ram to get Sita back from her abductor
Ravan, an undertaking in which no benefit was to accrue to them, the
Hindus still make it a point to remember their god. They periodically
perform his story, or greet each other with a respectful 'Ram Ram', unlike
Sikhs who have forgotten all the good their gurus had done. Singh also
notes that Ravan was a good Brahmin, not a base person, and that Ram
had to fight him in order to fulfil the duties of a Kshatriya king (*Chhatrī
rājā*).[80] Similarly in the Mahabharata, Krishna taught Arjun his Chhatri
dharam by encouraging him to take up arms.[81] In relating these tales,
Singh assumes a moral righteousness associated with following appropriate caste prescriptions. The idea of taking the morally right path, a
duty to which one is born, or one that circumstances place a person in,
was a favourite of Singh, on which he sermonizes again in his pamphlet
Pratigyā Pālan (Fulfilling Vows).[82] Since the notion explored was one of
ensuring one's dharmic duties, he uses the rich mythology of the epics
and the Puranas along with tales from the lives of the gurus and other
exemplary figures, including celebrated Sufi sheikhs. In this anecdotal
and mythological performative mode, Singh puts to use his training as a
Gulabdasi discourser, and its pluralist cultural ethos constantly surfaced
and exceeded the brief required for fashioning a Tat Khalsa identity.

---

[80] Ditt Singh, *Nakli Sikh*, pp. 105–8.

[81] Ditt Singh, *Nakli Sikh*, p. 109.

[82] Bhai Ditt Singh Giani, *Pratigya Palan* (Lahore: Khalsa Press, 1896).

If the idea that castes are bound to specific moral duties is seen above, what emerges in *Sultan Puara* are castes tied to their occupational duties, and to pride related to birth status. It is interesting to note that Ditt Singh speaks of broad jatis in the sense of local occupational groups. Singh remonstrates through the character of a reformed Sikh (*guru kā Singh*) reminding the various castes who go for Sarwar's pilgrimage that their association with Muslims was making them break/defile their caste taboos. So a Brahmin/*misar* is reminded of his priestly duties, the value of Hindu places of pilgrimage (Ganga, Parag), of Hindu gods (Ram, Laxman, Krishandev), and symbols (janeu).[83] A Jat as a landlord is told of his high status in the village (*nambardār*) or as a leader (*sardār*) and how unbecoming it is for him to keep the company of Muslims and Chamars. Turning to a Chamar (*Chamiār*), Singh makes fun of his desire to mimic the Brahmin and the Jat in joining the pilgrimage: *bhedāṅ nuṅ bhī lage zukām, jiste kardā nahiṅ ārām* (do sheep, too, catch a cold and that is why you not rest?)[84] Unlike the higher castes, the Chamar has to earn his livelihood (presumably through manual work), or else his wife and family would go hungry and curse him. At other places, Singh addresses a Khatri—reminding him of his high status—a Mihiriya (water-carrier), and a Tarkhan (carpenter), dissuading all from joining the pilgrimage. He is particularly harsh on Kirars (moneylenders), whom he criticizes for dressing in 'Muslim' clothes, and even conducting their religious ceremonies at Nigaha (the shrine of Sarwar in western Punjab), forgetting about their temples and pilgrimage centres.

The attractions of visiting Sufi shrines were to be countered by placing people more firmly within 'their' specific religious and social practices. What is also surprising in Ditt Singh's advice to various castes is the manner in which he seeks to 'retrieve' and pin caste and community prejudice in relation to Chamars and Muslims. Here the notion of caste as organic in nature that marks and differentiates the somatic substances of different bodies is at play, the extension of which is the idea of chhua-chhut. Significantly, the Muslim is made the target of this bodily repugnance along with the Chamar, both within and outside an overarching caste hierarchy.

This cluster of ideas again comes through when the reformer Singh attempts to unravel the myths associated with Sarwar, one of which

---

[83] Ditt Singh, *Sultan Puara*, pp. 10–11.
[84] Ditt Singh, *Sultan Puara*, p. 16.

relates to Sarwar protecting cattle (*dangar*) from a tiger's attack by a single swish of his sword. To show the ordinariness of this saintly miracle, the reformer Singh relates an incident when a Chamar/Chamreta accomplished a similar feat. The followers of Sarwar are portrayed as horrified at this comparison between a highborn saint, a Sayyid, and a Chamreta. However, the reformer Singh turns their argument on its head by asking the Brahmin if he was 'higher' than a Muslim in the caste hierarchy. And then going on to speak of the revulsion inherent in worshipping a Muslim saint:

> *Musalmān malechh kahāve, kad bahman usde ghar khāve*
> *jo khāve soī hatyārā, dharam karam te gayā nikārā*
> *uh chamiār gau nahiṅ māre, marī hoī da cham utāre*
> *tāṅte nīch asī us kehṅde, jis de pās mūl na behṅde*
> *par eh musalmān hatiyāre, gau jiṅvdī nuṅ faṛ māre*
> *jiste eh saḍe han vairī, inde nāl mile nahiṅ khairī.*

The Musalman is called a *malechh*, when does a Brahmin eat at his house?
And if he does he should be called a murderer, who has forsaken his dharma and *karma*
The Chamar does not kill a cow, but takes the skin off a dead one
We still call him low, and don't even sit near him
But these Musalman butchers kill a living cow
So they are our enemies, we will never benefit in associating with them.[85]

How does one disaggregate a tangle of prejudices embedded in these lines? A striking reversal of cultural role assigned to the saint is transforming him from a Krishna-like cow protector to a universal Muslim cow slayer, and, therefore, the recipient of the odious title 'malechh' rather than being recognized as a Saiyyad.[86] The word 'malechh' was clearly encrusted with prejudices that othered Muslims, placing them outside the charmed circle of varna categories. Indeed, one is reminded of Piro's use of the term when distancing herself from her erstwhile brethren.[87] The Saiyyad saint, with his benefactions to animals and humans, and his

---

[85] Ditt Singh, *Sultan Puara*, pp. 9–10.

[86] There were other myths that associated Sarwar with 'Hindu' deities Bhairon and Hanuman, also discussed in Ditt Singh's pamphlet. On the cultural reach of Sarwar in colonial Punjab, see Harjot Oberoi, 'The Worship of Sakhi Sarvar: Illness, Healing and Popular Culture in the Punjab', *Studies in History* 3, no. 1 (1987): 29–55.

[87] See Chapter 2.

rich mythology of bringing the dead alive,[88] is reduced in Singh's literalist writing to not only an ordinary mortal, but to one who represents the othered Muslim, the target here of unabashed hate. In this pamphlet, Singh uses the term *miyāṅ*[89] even more than 'malechh' to show contempt towards Muslims, again reminiscent of Piro's use of the word when referring to the mullahs. While the term 'malechh' ostensibly places the Muslim outside the framework of the Brahminical caste system, its use in this instance, however, seems to fix him as the lowest in the graded hierarchy of the caste system with the same logic that puts the untouchable outside caste, *but only in relation to it.* Thus, there is the simultaneous incorporation/expropriation of the Muslim in a framework of hierarchy, the same that includes/excludes the untouchable. Moreover, here clearly the rules of chhua-chhut are followed by the Khalsa, the reforming Singh, who distinguishes himself from the Sarwar pilgrims precisely through the maintenance of this aspect of caste practice. If the Khalsa in other situations are expected to give up caste praxis, here its regimen must apply even more sharply to them when in contact with a Muslim: *maiṅ hāṅ Singh āp tu miyāṅ, tere baiṭhe nīr na pīyāṅ* (I am a Singh and you a miyan, I cannot drink water in your presence).[90] However, unlike the Chamar, who is also dissuaded from joining the Sarwar pilgrimage, and is, therefore, seen as part and parcel of the Hindu–Sikh 'community', the Muslim is clearly identified as the enemy (*vairī*). In *Nakli Sikh*, too, he reiterates the same point.[91] Or even when Ditt Singh takes on the various pirs of Punjab who were popular among women, for example, Miran, a favourite with women, he says the same: 'What colours are abloom, a miyan in the house of Sikhs!'[92]

---

[88] The saint was said to have brought his dead mare, Bakki, alive—another myth Singh tried to demystify. The saint was also supplicated for boons of sons, and is said to have restored to life the dead son of Dani Jatti. Ditt Singh advertised in this pamphlet and in *Khalsa Akhbar* that Dani's progeny gave up the worship of Sarwar at the behest of Singh Sabha preaching. For a discussion on this episode, see Malhotra, *Gender, Caste and Religious Identities*, p. 176.

[89] Though the term 'malechh' has received scholarly attention, the term 'miyan' has received less. When this term becomes opprobrious is difficult to say. I have noticed its usage in the writing of the Gulabdasi Piro. Ditt Singh also uses the terms 'Turak' and 'Musalman' for Muslims.

[90] Ditt Singh, *Sultan Puara*, p. 46.

[91] Ditt Singh, *Nakli Sikh*, pp. 167–9.

[92] Ditt Singh, *Nakli Sikh*, p. 188.

However, it must be emphasized that in other contexts and on a different register, Ditt Singh could also consciously 'own' Muslims as belonging
to the culture of 'Hindustan', or on many occasions the religious identity
of a person did not come into play. In a changed context, the Muslims
appeared intrinsically a part of the Indian landscape, naturally a part of its
culture. This underscores the effort that was required to disentangle and
mark as 'Hindu' or 'Muslim' a common heritage, even though the idea
of religiously etched identities was not completely novel in Punjab. Thus,
in *Nakli Sikh* Ditt Singh at one juncture sees the Christian doctrines and
traditions as the 'other', which did not belong to a North Indian ethos.
Speaking of the 'conditions of the Christians' (*Isaīāṅ dā Hāl*), Singh
says that according to the Gospels (*anjil*) Jesus was extremely restless
and unhappy before his impending execution. He speaks of Jesus being
hanged rather than crucified, perhaps pointing to his limited interaction
with the missionaries. However, he contrasts what he sees as the pitiable
state of Jesus with that of Mansur, who in popular Punjabi parlance went
to the gallows smiling, and Shams Tabrez, who evidently did not utter
a cry when his skin was torn off him and filled with hay by the king
of Multan, or indeed the ninth guru Tegh Bahadur, who bravely faced
his beheading on the orders of the Mughal emperor Aurangzeb.[93] The
appearance of the Sikh guru on the same register of personal valour as
the 'martyr of love' Mansur, and Shams Tabrez is noteworthy. Even more
intriguing is the Punjabi ownership of Mansur-al-Hallaj, a ninth-century
mystic of Baghdad, whose cry of an'al haq was particularly evocative for
the Gulabdasis, as discussed in Chapter 1. Mansur is said to have travelled to northwest India in his peregrinations and remained popular
there as did Shams Tabrez, said to be the preceptor of Jalaludin Rumi,
the thirteenth-century mystic from Turkey. Both these figures appear
repeatedly in the folklore of Punjab, in localized myths, and Ditt Singh
in *Pratigya Palan*, too, made an exemplum of their lives, elaborating on
the martyrdom associated with both.[94]

What also appears perplexing, considering his own caste background,
is Ditt Singh's derision of the Chamars. Not only does he advise the
Brahmins and Jats from staying aloof from them, he also evokes norms of
untouchability to underscore the pollution encountered in such contact.
And these instances discussed by him of distancing from the low castes
can be multiplied. A particularly interesting example is his ridiculing of

[93] Ditt Singh, *Nakli Sikh*, pp. 114–15.
[94] Ditt Singh, *Pratigya Palan*, pp. 33–7.

the Bhands and Mirasis, actors of local farces (*swāṅgs*), who entertained their patrons occasionally by dressing in different caste costumes. The Mirasis were otherwise also the genealogists, musicians, and bards of Punjab. Noting how they often turned out sartorially as rich Khatris (*sahukārs*), wearing turbans, dhotis, caste marks (tilak), and carrying pens and account books (*bahīs*), and when the performance was over they reverted to their traditional base status—*maṅgte Mirāsī* (beggar Mirasis)— he underlined that the inherent nature of a person did not change, that is, in reality a Dum-Mirasi stayed as such, and did not or could not become a high caste.[95] The point here was about the constancy of the inherited caste status, for Ditt Singh uses the same nomenclature—Dum and Mirasis—as the Hindu and Muslim bards, terms often used in unison in Punjab, which underplayed the significance of 'religious' identity, emphasizing one of caste.[96] In *Sultan Puara* again, when the reforming Sikh offers to all castes the possibility of becoming a Khalsa and so giving up their caste status, he makes a special case for the Chuhras and Chamars, that *even they* can become Singhs.[97]

How does one square this with either a theoretical position that Sikhs, particularly the Khalsa, disapproved of caste, or with Ditt Singh's own Ravidasi upbringing? We can argue that caste prejudices were so deeply internalized that despite the rationale against caste practices provided by the Gulabdasis, the Arya Samajis, or the Singh Sabhaites, and his own careful statements on the issue, Ditt Singh still spoke in caste terms, and imbibed and perpetuated oppressive and humiliating behaviour towards the low castes. Alternatively, we can suggest that Ditt Singh homed in on to the best way to create a cleavage between the Hindus and Sikhs on the one hand, and the Muslims on the other, by re-invoking and refocusing caste prejudices by projecting them to the Muslims, though this strategy had deleterious repercussions on the low castes as well. By recouping caste identities he could attempt to break practices like saint worship that were unacceptable to the Sabhaites. A third possibility is, however, suggested by Ditt Singh himself at various times in his pamphlets. This was the miraculous transmutation that occurred on becoming a Khalsa. The initiation into the Khalsa, which was now projected by the Sabhaites as the normative Sikh identity, ensured that everyone attained the caste status of the guru, a Chhatri/Khatri/Kshatriya. Incidentally, this also

---

[95] Ditt Singh, *Nakli Sikh*, p. 171.

[96] Ibbetson, *Panjab Castes*, p. 234.

[97] Ditt Singh, *Sultan Puara*, p. 72.

shows that in Punjab the Khatris, otherwise a caste associated with shopkeeping, trading, and the professions, were regularly conflated with the
Kshatriya status as we will see. Thus, Khalsa initiation became both the
simplest route to upward mobility and its advocacy could be the surest
way to make this identity attractive to all Sikhs. Ditt Singh on initiation
had given up his earlier status, he could assert, and such a transformation was available to all. Singh subtly enunciates such an interpretation
of the initiation ceremony, the taking of amrit, in both the tracts under
discussion.

In *Sultan Puara* he invites all to take the amrit, give up previous caste
and become a brave Chhatri:

> The power of this amrit let me tell you of it
> On tasting it all become brothers, giving up their old castes
> You become a brave Singh, Chhatri son of the guru
> Breaking with (worshipping of) graves, cremation grounds, Gugga, Miran
> and pirs.[98]

A similar sentiment is expressed in *Nakli Sikh*, where Singh explicates
the meaning of taking on a Khalsa identity as becoming brave Chhatris.[99]

It can be argued that Ditt Singh was advocating a metaphorical
transition to 'Chhatriness', the imbibing of the martial qualities of the
Kshatriya, rather than any literal transformation of the caste of a person.
In every instance where he speaks of becoming a Chhatri, he does so
while delineating military values of valour and prowess in war. In *Sultan
Puara*, he even brings in the contemporary participation of the Sikhs in
the British Indian army that apparently fought bravely in China, Burma,
Kabul, Qandahar, and Egypt, to draw attention to the power of amrit
and appropriate these victories to the cause of the Khalsa identity.[100] Of
course, there was a significant congruence between the British attempts
at recruiting Khalsa Sikhs in the army, their admiration of the warrior
qualities of the Khalsa, and the Sabha endeavour to render Sikhs Khalsa
and martial.[101]

Two further points may be made in relation to this martial transmutation. First, a note must be made of the idiom of miracle in which the

---

[98] Ditt Singh, *Sultan Puara*, p. 72.

[99] Ditt Singh, *Nakli Sikh*, pp. 148, 158.

[100] Ditt Singh, *Sultan Puara*, p. 71.

[101] Richard G. Fox, *Lions of the Punjab: Culture in the Making* (Berkeley:
University of California Press, 1985).

initiation into the Khalsa was invariably presented in the nineteenth-century Sabha literature. One only has to read Bhai Vir Singh's *Sundrī* to appreciate the projection of the miraculous power of the initiation amrit, instantaneously transforming individuals into paragons of valour. In a period when the miraculous was purportedly unravelling under the assault of the rational and the humdrum, as Ditt Singh himself undertook in relation to Sarwar's magical powers, the miracle of the amrit remained an exception in Sikh literature. So while the Chuhras, Chamars, or Mirasis must remain as such, those who turned Khalsa could hope for change. The message was not about a society without the framework of caste, as one of elevating one's position within it by becoming Khalsa. This worked, unsurprisingly, in tandem with Arya Samaj's notion of caste in proportion to talent. The reformers of the time dared not imagine a society without the institution of caste.

Second, Ditt Singh was not alone in understanding Khalsa initiation as ushering a change of status. In fact, he may have been endorsing a view that had a wider and an older currency. His contemporary, Giani Gian Singh, a prolific scholar discussed in Chapter 1, wrote in his authoritative *Tawārīkh Guru Khālsā* about the meaning of initiation: 'From today you belong to the Sodhi lineage of the Khatri caste[102] of the Khalsa. Your name is Singh and your abode Anandpur.'[103] In other words, entering the ranks of the Khalsa was often depicted as bringing one in proximity to the tenth guru, and an incorporation within his caste. Also, it was the Khatris, with their purported Kshatriya antecedents, who were ascribed the militaristic values, and imbibed by the Khalsa. Despite suffering humiliations for his caste in his personal life, it is possible that Ditt Singh held fast to the belief that his initiation into the Khalsa changed his status, and this may explain at least in some small measure his contempt for the low castes.

Yet another manner in which the issue of caste cropped up was on the question of the *birādarī*, caste brotherhoods/lineages, which played an important role in life-cycle ceremonies, and defined at the local level the social status of families. The question was a tangled one, for if marriages were endogamous, that is, took place within prescribed caste categories, then the issue of caste and biradari took precedence over that of the Sikh identity. This problem also then linked up with the relationship between

---

[102] Sodhi was the lineage of all the gurus from the fourth guru onwards.
[103] Gian Singh quoted in McLeod, *Sikhs of the Khalsa*, p. 45.

the Sikh 'community' and the Hindu 'community'. Ditt Singh was cognizant of the problem, and made an effort to tackle it. For instance, the Singh Sabha reformers urged the Khalsa Sikhs to marry their daughters to Khalsas, theoretically of any caste, but realized that this wasn't always possible and caste norms were invariably followed. The response to this dilemma was the advice to make 'Singh' sons-in-law:

> Get engaged to each other, and become the true brothers of the community
> Do not give a daughter to one not Singh, don't do this for any reason
> On giving a daughter make a Singh, and increase the *panth* of the guru.[104]

But the problem was more recalcitrant as it was impossible to disentangle the community affiliation between friends, relatives, and caste brotherhoods. Singh, in a fairly perceptive moment, hit the nub of the problem when he had the *nakli* Sikh proclaim:

> Commensality and relations, are tangled with each other
> There is no enmity between us, so why should we make a separate qaum
> The Hindu religion is dear to us, it is our great support.[105]

Ditt Singh, in response to how Sikhs should define their relationship with the Hindus, once again gives contradictory prescriptions and ties himself up in knots. On the one hand, he tells his readers to look at the relationship between the Hindus and the Sikhs as that between Judaism and Christianity—the one having originated from the other (*apne āp nuṅ Hindu qaum vichoṅ hī banyā hoyā samajh*),[106] but conscious of differences and having established itself as separate.[107] Guru Gobind Singh must then be seen as the true avatar, and the *Guru Granth* as their separate book. In this spirit, Singh seemingly concedes the popular assumption that the Sikh *Granth* was no more than an exegesis of the Vedas, put in a simple language because of the difficulty of understanding Sanskrit, and that he had no intention of turning the Sikhs away from either Hinduism or the Vedas: *Hindu dharam ar ved nuṅ samjho apni ḍhāl* (view the Hindu religion and Vedas as your shield).[108] On the other hand, within the space of two pages, he changes his approach and declares that the Hindu and Sikh faiths were mutually destructive—*ik duje de ghātī*.[109] Relying on the

---

[104] Ditt Singh, *Nakli Sikh*, p. 164.

[105] Ditt Singh, *Nakli Sikh*, p. 212.

[106] Ditt Singh, *Nakli Sikh*, p. 210.

[107] Ditt Singh, *Nakli Sikh*, pp. 208–10.

[108] Ditt Singh, *Nakli Sikh*, p. 208.

[109] Ditt Singh, *Nakli Sikh*, p. 213.

significance of the five bodily symbols that increasingly for the Sabhaites defined the essence of the Khalsa, Ditt Singh gives the scenario of a Khalsa going to Gaya (in Bihar) to undertake rituals related to appeasing deceased ancestors (*pind bharān*) who was likely to shed all his bodily symbols to fulfil these. Similarly, a Hindu would have to give up his top-knot, dhoti, and the sacred thread on becoming a Khalsa. In other words, it was best to see the Sikhs as a third panth or community different from the Hindus and the Turaks.[110]

The last quarter of the nineteenth century in Punjab was a time of transition. In hindsight we tend to assume the pace of change to be faster than it was and progressing in a more linear trajectory than it probably occurred. There were people, institutions, and cultures that were caught in the middle, at times uncomprehending of change, at others midwives ushering in a new era. Ditt Singh combined in his person both an agency of change and a welter of cultural practices he sought to later shed from his person and from the community whose separate identity he discursively tried to produce. The constitution of public life, the meaning, performance, and reception of religious discourses, the very stuff of religious controversies and debates transformed in these years. Having been at the forefront of controversies and debates as a Gulabdasi preacher—whether on the message of the Vedanta and the sagacity of varnashramadharma—or in the popular eye because of his participation as a young *qissākār* (storyteller) in the effervescent charm of the love of Shirin and Farhad, 'Sant' Ditta Ram or Ditta Ram 'Faqir' enjoyed a place in the public life of colonial Punjab, but one that carried the flavour of an older Punjab.

As he found his feet in the late 1880s as 'Giani' Ditt Singh, the controversies and debates around him changed, and he participated in the new environment. After almost a decade or more of staying within overlapping associations and identities, he threw his weight behind the Lahore Singh Sabha's attempt at forging a sharper and a clearer Sikh/Khalsa identity. This required him and other pioneers of his ilk to undertake the labyrinthine and difficult task of fitting cultures to the merits of the identities being constructed. It would be wrong to assume that this self-fashioning emerged out of a vacuum. Yet, it is also clear that enormous

---

[110] Ditt Singh, *Nakli Sikh*, p. 221.

sifting and defining of cultures had to be undertaken in order to 'plant the banner of Sikhism', to use Singh's words, as a distinct community. This meant commenting on who the Hindus, Muslims, and Sikhs were. This was not easy, and Ditt Singh sometimes grouped Hindus and Sikhs together, othering the Muslims, and at other places tried to spell out the differences between the Hindus and the Sikhs.

A rethinking on the question of caste was the order of the day and the Sabhaites and the Arya Samajis, both in their own ways, initiated this process. Ditt Singh's Ravidasi background perhaps invested his contribution to this effort with an urgency and edge that other stalwarts' writing on the matter may not have experienced. But to assume that it also gave him clarity on the issue would be wrong. The deep-rooted nature of the institution, a plethora of available interpretations, the attractions of upward mobility, and the strategy of using its divisive and derisive power to make cleavages between communities, could all be exploited at different points of time depending on the need of the occasion. Thus, in the corpus of Singh's writing, we find ambiguity, vacillation, and fickleness in maintaining a single, coherent line of reform. Perhaps Ditt Singh's belonging to the time he did—with its changeability and instability—may explain partially his protean stances. It is plausible that the rich and pluralistic cultural ambience he had imbibed early in his life as a Gulabdasi disciple gave him an intellectual and cultural breadth that was difficult to shed or narrow down to the extent the creation of the new identity required. Nevertheless, he sowed the seeds of many a line of argument that would be later developed by his acolytes.

Ditt Singh's niche in history will also be determined by what his followers attribute to him, and he is being resurrected today as a Dalit hero who condemned the idea of caste. Those among the Dalits who are specifically seeking out Singh's legacy are more keen to portray the personal obstacles he may have surmounted to reach a position of public leadership and respectability. Careful calibrations of his shifting stands on caste would interest them a little less. However, given the continuing frisson on the question of caste and its relevance to identity politics in the Indian Punjab, we may wish to understand Ditt Singh's equivocation on the issue. We might reflect on why despite many banishments and mutations, the institution of caste remains alive within Sikhism.

7 Theatre of the Past

Re-presenting the Past in Different Genres

Historians today are more aware than ever before of the elusive nature of the past, of the dynamic ways in which it is represented and used in the present, or the manner in which memory is constructed.[1] The professional historian is no longer the purveyor of 'the past as it happened', but rather recognizes her limited and contested corner to espouse one among the many possible discourses about the past. In academia inflected with the postmodernist derision of a single perspective—the monological utterance—what is the historian's task?[2] Speaking of his use of oral history and his invaluable reflections on it, Alessandro Portelli endorsed the historian's aspiration towards 'reality' and 'truth' not to establish positivistic 'fact', but for greater attention to 'subjective truths'.[3] The making of memory, the recounting of tales with their 'creative errors', was less about events as they happened, according to Portelli, and more about their 'meanings' for those reflecting on them and processing them through

---

[1] For the reconstruction of an event, its metaphorical use by nationalists, and its memory in the locality of its occurrence, see Shahid Amin, *Event, Metaphor, Memory: Chauri-Chaura 1922–1992* (New Delhi: Oxford University Press, 1995).

[2] On 'monological utterance', the notion that texts have an essence, see Ronald Inden, 'Introduction: From Philological to Dialogical Texts', in *Querying the Medieval: Texts and the History of Practices in South Asia*, by Ronald Inden, Jonathan Walters and Daud Ali (New York: Oxford University Press, 2000), pp. 3–28.

[3] Alessandro Portelli, *The Death of Luigi Trastulli and Other Stories: Form and Meaning in Oral History* (Albany: State University of New York Press, 1991), p. ix.

their own lives and for posterity.[4] Between subjective truths and popular memory-making deeply charged with meaning in the present[5] and the apparently disinterested academic historian delving in the archives to reconstruct events, are vast contested spaces inhabited by multiple forms and genres—vernacular histories, if you will—all in the business of drawing from and redrawing the past.[6]

In this chapter, I will look at some of the 'popular' forms in which Piro's story, which has caught the imagination of the Punjabi people at this contemporary moment, is being circulated among them.[7] Piro's story, though not entirely unknown among Punjabi academics, received a fillip when Santokh Singh or Shahryar (his nom de plume) first discovered a rather tattered handwritten manuscript of her verses, and having become fascinated with her story wrote a play on her, *Pīro Premaṇ*, in Punjabi.[8] In fact, he first wrote a script for a telefilm in Hindi, which never got made, and later wrote a play, as he tells us in his preface to the play. A few years later another play was penned in Punjabi by a literary policeman, Swarajbir, called *Shairī*[9] (Poetry), which has been performed on stage by the theatre group Manch Rang Manch in Amritsar and by the Ajoka Theatre Group of Lahore in Pakistani Punjab.[10] More recently, looking at

---

[4] Portelli, *The Death of Luigi Trastulli*, p. 50.

[5] See the comments of Pierre Nora on memory being a phenomenon of the present and history as a representation of the past in Partha Chatterjee's 'Introduction: History and the Present', in *History and the Present*, edited by Partha Chatterjee and Anjan Ghosh (London: Anthem Press, 2006), p. 10.

[6] Partha Chatterjee, 'Introduction: History in the Vernacular', in *History in the Vernacular*, edited by Raziuddin Aquil and Partha Chatterjee (Ranikhet: Permanent Black, 2008), pp. 1–24.

[7] When I speak of the Punjabi people here, I am invoking the concept of Punjabiyat, an attachment to the idea of Punjab and Punjabi culture that works across religious, caste, and class divisions, and in this case national boundaries as well. See Anshu Malhotra and Farina Mir, 'Punjab in History and Historiography: An Introduction', in *Punjab Reconsidered: History, Culture and Practice*, edited by Anshu Malhotra and Farina Mir (New Delhi: Oxford University Press, 2012), pp. xv–lviii.

[8] Shahryar, *Piro Preman* (Amritsar: Rawal Prakashan, 1999).

[9] Swarajbir, *Shairi* (Ludhiana: Chetna Prakashan, 2004).

[10] The cast of the play and its performance by Manch Rang Manch is mentioned in the play *Shairi*, pp. 198–9. I briefly met Madiha Gauhar of Ajoka in Delhi when they performed their play on Bulleh Shah in Delhi in 2012. The play on Piro was called *Piro Preman* but the performance was based on Swarajbir's script.

her growing popularity and the academic interest in her writings, Vijender Das of the Gulabdasi dera, Hansi, Haryana, has compiled all the writings of Piro, transliterated in the Devanagari script, in a volume called *Saṅt Kavyitrī Mā Pīro* (Saint Poetess Mother Piro). Das not only does an exegesis of her verses in the book but has also written an extensive introduction, whose burden is not only to tell the readers about her life, but more importantly to guide us in perceiving her in an appropriate way.[11] A compilation of her writings in Punjabi, with a very brief introduction, has also been brought out by Veer Vahab, who completed her MPhil degree on Piro's life and writing and who lives in the town of Fazilka in Punjab.[12] The question that I ask here is that in this welter of voices and forms—drama and literature in the devotional métier—is the historian's voice distinctive? I will argue that the circulation of varied discourses in the mundane world, the heteroglossia of utterances that impinge on us every day in multiple ways, plays a role in shaping what we choose to study or write about. That is to say, one's own present impacts the way in which we study the past. However, the methods and forms we adopt to lay forth our thoughts or peddle our ideas are different, and so do lend themselves to distinct tones. The historian's voice is one among many competing to speak and be heard, though the privilege of being situated in the academia, and as connoisseurs of the past, historians might be keener than others to show that 'their explanations are better than competing explanations'.[13]

HISTORY, FICTION, AND THE AUTOBIOGRAPHICAL

The question about the distinctiveness of the historian's oeuvre has become more complex since history's 'narrative' and 'fictive' qualities have been pointed out. History is seen as a species of the genus 'Story', which is told retrospectively. It is the historical narrative that like a metaphor creates meaning rather than any 'facts', in themselves selected from among a plethora that speaks in an unmediated way. Hayden White went so far as to suggest that historical narration is primarily an act of telling, and not of discovery, and that historical narratives are like 'verbal fictions',

[11] Sant Vijender Das, ed., *Sant Kavyitri Ma Piro* (Panchkula: Satluj Prakashan, 2011).

[12] Veer Vahab, ed., *Piro Kahe Saheliyo* (Jalandhar: R.B. Printing Press, 2012).

[13] Raymond Martin quoted in Geoffrey Roberts, 'Introduction: The History and Narrative Debate, 1960–2000', in *The History and Narrative Reader*, edited by Geoffrey Roberts (London: Routledge, 2001), p. 8.

with literary qualities. White's notion of 'emplotment', the plot structure chosen by the historian to narrate the story, derives from pre-existing narrative strategies and generic story patterns.[14]

Historians have protested what many consider to be an undermining of their profession, for by the 'application of conventional historians' criteria regarding accuracy, adequacy, facticity, evidentiality, plausibility, and so on' they can arrive at a good approximate of a historical truth.[15] However, the consensus at present seems to be a mix of agreement that historians do deploy narrative inventiveness to tell their stories, but also that their stories are tightly controlled by the sources at their command. Thus, while they accept that narratives are 'invented' by them, 'in the sense that they are made', they, however, insist that that 'does not mean they are made-up in the fictional sense',[16] or that their narrative might be seen to add meaning to the past, but that does not make the narrative inaccurate. As Partha Chatterjee has argued, distinguishing between history-writing and fiction-writing, that 'the conditions of plausibility remain entirely different in the two genres' as do the protocols that bind the writer and the reader.[17] The historian's method—of deploying a variety of sources, of the use of the archives, of verification and referencing (the reader may ask how a historian knows), and of authenticating facts based on the protocols of their profession and its (albeit changing) practices and values—sets them apart from literary productions. The past for the historian is, therefore, not a 'promiscuous past', in the manner described in a sexualized metaphor by Robert Jenkins, one that will go with any-body, ready to be moulded in any way a writer may wish. Rather, the historian aspires to some sort of a historical 'truth' based on the sources, which may themselves be selective, interpretive, and literary, but nevertheless impact what a historian can say, even as she is conscious of the narrative quality of her writing.[18] Ann Curthoys and John Docker speak of this oscillation of history between its literary qualities (narrative of the historian) and its close scrutiny of sources (its professional grounding)

---

[14] Roberts, 'Introduction', pp. 1–21. Also see Hayden White, 'The Historical Text as Literary Artifact', in Roberts, *The History and Narrative Reader*, pp. 221–36.

[15] Roberts, 'Introduction', p. 14.

[16] Noel Carroll quoted in Roberts, 'Introduction', p. 10.

[17] Chatterjee, 'Introduction' in *History and the Present*, p. 9.

[18] Robert Jenkins discussed in Ann Curthoys and John Docker, 'Introduction', in *Is History Fiction?*, edited by Ann Curthoys and John Docker (Sydney: University of New South Wales, 2010), pp. 1–11.

as the 'doubleness' of history, one that encourages self-reflexivity. In their words, this doubleness is 'the secret of history's cunning practice, an inventive, self-transforming discipline'.[19]

In the present case, as partially discussed in Chapter 2, the problem of sifting truth from fiction and fiction from history, is more complex because among our sources of information on Piro, the single-most important one are her own autobiographical verses, the *160 Kafis*. The reliance on the life narrative further complicates the historian's task of attempting to reach the tangible, a 'fact' that did happen in history, and the environment in which it could happen, from the autobiographer's subjective truth.

The autobiographical narrative, retrospective in nature, as shown earlier, is deeply implicated in the politics of self-identity/identities. A text where the self is both the subject of discourse and the object of inquiry, it pushes towards the formulation of subjective truths, themselves based upon contingent circumstances of the present. The rhetorical nature of writing the self, often justificatory and legitimizing, explicatory of a life, event, or a relationship, is weighted with many reasons other than merely recounting what happened. Thus, transparency in relating a life is not the autobiography's forte as life is refracted through the autobiographer's experience. Sidonie Smith and Julia Watson have noted that to 'reduce autobiographical narration to facticity is to strip it of the densities of rhetorical, literary, ethical, political, and cultural dimensions'.[20] It is for this reason, too, that the autobiographical can be seen to be dialogical, composed with an audience in mind, what Smith and Watson call its 'intersubjective' dimensions, its 'refractive interplay' based upon an imaginary exchange with a putative audience.[21] To use a performance metaphor, an autobiographical narrative, that is, its arrival at particular meanings, is in an active concert with an audience in mind, including the self as a spectator. As Ronald Inden has noted of texts in general, but in this case applicable to the autobiographical, is that they are 'articulative', an intervention on the part of an agent in the world.[22]

The autobiographical narrative is also based upon memory, again, as noted, always constructed from the present, and so imbricated in

[19] Curthoys and Docker, 'Introduction', p. 11.

[20] Sidonie Smith and Julia Watson, *Reading Autobiography: A Guide to Interpreting Life Narratives* (Minneapolis: University of Minnesota Press, 2010), p. 13.

[21] Smith and Watson, *Reading Autobiography*, p. 16.

[22] Inden, 'Introduction', p. 13.

meaning-making than in recollecting a past in an unmediated way. The telescoping of time, the conflating of past occurrences, the memorializing of particular events, and forgetfulness and silences are all aspects of this presentist perspective, one that makes life meaningful to the narrator as to the its reader/listener. Moreover, in many cultures, for example, the Indian bardic tradition, memory-making may be an activity in the hands of the specialists, and so their generic methods may influence its particular form or reification, as in genealogical histories. Among such tropes may be that of, for instance, life connected through rebirths,[23] of lives meaningful only in relational terms rather than through individual characteristics,[24] or, as in the case at hand, life understood and organized through mythological models, for example, Piro presenting herself as a putative Sita in her verses, the paragon of womanly virtues. All this can make the autobiographical narrative, ostensibly the very stuff that defines an individual, a collective, or an intensely relational endeavour. Indeed, modelling a life on 'cultural scripts', the swirling of ideal lives in the discursive realm is not a peculiarity of South Asia, and is available for imitation in virtually all cultures.[25]

The relational and intersubjective aspects of the life narrative also make it inherently performative. The term 'performative' is used here both in the sense of its meaning in drama—the performing of a character according to a script, here authored by oneself—and in the way in which the philosopher Judith Butler has used it, to indicate the reification of gendered roles through bodily disciplinary regulation and reiteration in social life.[26] On the one hand, the (re)enacting of one's life through a self-constructed script, which is the autobiography, makes it at its core theatrical, as already noted, in this case on page rather than stage.[27]

---

[23] See the discussion on Bahinabai's *Atmanivedina* in Chapter 5.

[24] See the discussion on relational lives in South Asia and the West in Kathryn Hansen, 'Self and Subjectivity in Autobiographical Criticism', in her *Stages of Life: Indian Theatre Autobiographies* (Ranikhet: Permanent Black, 2011), pp. 299–314.

[25] Jill Ker Conway, *When Memory Speaks: Exploring the Art of Autobiography* (New York: Vintage Books, 1999), pp. 6–7.

[26] Judith Butler, *Bodies that Matter: On the Discursive Limits of Sex* (New York: Routledge, 1993).

[27] The expression stage/page is taken from Sherrill Grace, 'Theatre and the Autobiographical Pact: An Introduction', in *Theatre and Autobiography: Writing and Performing Lives in Theory and Practice*, edited by Sherrill Grace and Jerry Wasserman (Vancouver: Talon books, 2006), p. 13.

The script-drama, if drama is a specialized kind of script, makes the autobiographical life theatrical, when theatre is a specialized kind of performance; only in this case, the mise en scène is not on stage, but is created every time someone reads/listens to the narrative voice of the autobiographer.[28]

The naturalization of gender roles in society that Butler speaks of, on the other hand, that constructs woman or the feminine in certain ways— for example, as deferential, silent, or veiled in many cultures—means that the autobiographer has to negotiate societal expectations in certain ways. This can, of course, mean adhering to those expectations; but the recourse to speech when society expects silence can often be read as a statement of defiance, of 'talking back', as in the case of Piro.[29] It is for this reason that the life narrative is seen to be especially deployed by women and the oppressed, like Dalits in the Indian case.[30] This performative talking back occurs, one may suggest, despite what is often an overwhelming societal concern for ideal behaviour. For Butler, it is the non-alignment of the different expectations of society from a person which creates the ruptures for individual expression and agency, for defiant speech.[31] However, between the force of societal ideals, gendered discourses, and individual concerns, the autobiographical performance may present the self in a variety of ways, sometimes conforming and compliant, at others confrontational and contumacious.

Speaking about the distinctive quality of autobiography from fiction, Philippe Lejeune had proffered the idea of an 'autobiographical pact' between the autobiographer and the reader.[32] By affixing a name to the related narrative, the autobiographer sealed the pact, so to speak, with his/her truth, underscoring that the events narrated in fact happened in history. This idea is similar to that about history-writing and the protocols

[28] Richard Schechner, 'Drama, Script, Theater, and Performance', in his *Performance Theory* (London: Routledge, 2003 [1988]), pp. 66–111.

[29] Patricia Hart and Karen Weatherman with Susan H. Armitage, eds, *Women Writing Women: The Frontiers Reader* (Lincoln: University of Nebraska Press, 2006), p. 3.

[30] Sharmila Rege, *Writing Caste/Writing Gender: Narrating Dalit Women's Testimonios* (New Delhi: Zubaan, 2006).

[31] Sidonie Smith, 'Performativity, Autobiographical Practice, Resistance', in *Women, Autobiography, Theory: A Reader*, edited by Sidonie Smith and Julia Watson (Madison: The University of Wisconsin Press, 1998), pp. 108–15. See Chapter 5.

[32] See Chapter 2.

that bind the historian and the reader—that the narrative of the historian, in fact, speaks of a historical occurrence. Between truth-telling and a rehearsed performance, subjective truths and objective facts, the autobiographer (as the historian) inhabits a space in close proximity to fiction and its charms.

DRAMATIZING A THEATRICAL LIFE: NARRATIVES ON PIRO

In this section, I will refer readers to the summary of Piro's *160 Kafis* in Chapter 2, not repeated here, but imperative to understand the construction of the two dramas based on her supposed life and a third hagiographical account of a Gulabdasi devotee and head of its Hansi branch. Two points need to be borne in mind. First, Piro's repertoire of writings, as discussed at various points in this book, is larger than this autobiographical text, the others being more spiritually inclined verses, and our authors dip into them mostly without distinguishing between her different works, using them as uncomplicated factual sources to narrate her life. Second, the few significant though fragmentary sources on the Gulabdasis, discussed in Chapter 1, and the information available in them is used in the plays to construct Piro's life, along with a generous dollop of imagination. The specificities of the sources that were written in the late nineteenth and the early twentieth centuries and their internal dynamics are of little concern to our authors, though a sharp historical consciousness informs their writing, in particular in the preface, afterword, and introduction used by our three authors to address their audience. There are thus clear intentions of plotting their stories in the ways they do, and in addressing their audiences/readers, instructing them to read in specific ways.

This brief discussion will form the background for the next part of the paper where I will take up some common themes that appear in all accounts, including what the historian is drawn to, and bring out the nuances of the different treatments of these in the various scripts. This will also provide an occasion to show how these authors develop Piro's story. While the differences between what a historian can possibly say and the volubility of the fictionalized genres will be brought out, the endeavour will also be towards unpacking and teasing out the 'meanings' of these differences, and the concerns which become visible particularly in storytelling, and their significance in contemporary times. Historians have sometimes used fiction and the (auto)biographical genres to illuminate an age, particularly when other sources are scanty, or when fiction is insightful of an age.[33] However, the question remains as to what extent and in what manner may 'auto-fiction' or 'faction'—if we see the autobiographical as a performative mix of fact and fiction—be used to tell us of Piro's times, and ours.[34]

Shahryar's *Piro Preman*, Swarajbir's *Shairi*, and Vijender Das' *Sant Kavyitri Ma Piro*

Broadly following Piro's *160 Kafis*, Shahryar's play scripted in Punjabi (Gurmukhi script) is significantly invested in unearthing, indeed, exhuming Piro from the metaphorical coffin (*tabūt*) in which she lay buried. Having himself discovered her poetry by chance, Shahryar is keen to bring her poetry to an audience who can now take pride in the fact that Punjab produced a woman poet in the nineteenth century. As will be discussed in some detail later, the author and his protagonist share this quest of salvaging her poetry: the play develops around Piro's own consciousness of rescuing her poetry and poetic talent, which attracts her to her guru Gulabdas—the magnificent poet and philosopher of his age (*dhurander shāyar aur phalsāphī*). So great is Piro's poetic flair that the relationship between the guru and the disciple overturns in Shahryar's drama, the guru acknowledging her poetic faculty as superior to his own. While Shahryar follows the broad events in Piro's *Kafis*, including her abduction, the play's central theme is that of poetic recuperation: recuperating Piro's poetry and her status as a poet. As the foreword to the play says of her and the objective of the play, it is *bebāk kāvik virse dī shanākhat* (recognition of a fearless poetic heritage).[35] A second theme that emerges strongly is that of the presence of a woman, Piro in what should ostensibly have been a monastic order sans women, an all-male enclave. How her presence leads to friction within the

---

[33] Jonathan Spence liberally uses the fiction of a seventeenth-century writer, P'u Sung-ling, to tell us, among other things, about women's and widows' lives and womanly ideals in Chinese society. Natalie Davis uses among her various sources the personal reminiscences of a character, Jean de Coras, of the court case he handled in her recounting of the life of Martin Guerre, a work that combined in her words the features of a 'legal text and a literary tale'. See Jonathan D. Spence, *The Death of Woman Wang* (New York: Penguin Books, 1978). Natalie Z. Davis, *The Return of Martin Guerre* (Cambridge: Harvard University Press, 1983).

[34] See Smith and Watson for the use of these terms.

[35] Shahryar, *Piro Preman*, p. 11.

members of the dera is explored in the play. Through this theme, the historically negative attitudes towards women—their sexuality and their capability—are dramatized and an attempt is made to establish her subjectivity and agency.

Swarajbir's *Shairi* also follows this formula of Piro as a self-conscious poet, quite determined to write and recite her poetry. However, the playwright creates a far more complex plot than Shahryar's rather straightforward one, teeming with characters. Not only does he give a wholly imaginary background story to Piro—a family and caste background—but also puts Piro on a double quest, for saving her poetic talent, along with that of finding a true lover. The two goals are intertwined in the play, for the one who would love her truly would also love her poetry and so would not impose societal expectations of ideal womanly behaviour on her, defined by, among other ways, negatively as having nothing to do with pen and paper or poetic ambitions. In a convoluted plot that unfolds in six acts, each of several scenes, Swarajbir takes Piro through four lovers, three of her own choosing and one not, as her first lover gifts (sells?) her to her second, a powerful social and professional superior of the first. It is only when she reaches Gulabdas that her journey, her search for true love and support, and also for an aficionado of her poetry, ends. Her guru/murshid and lover is excessively appreciative of her poetry, in fact, enamoured of it as of her, much like Shahryar's Gulabdas.

Again, as in Shahryar's play, the presence of a woman in the guru's dera, the monastic establishment, creates a stir, the rumblings of a revolt among some disciples who feel their guru is treading the wrong path, having abandoned the right conduct becoming of a guru of his stature. However, the role this incipient rebellion plays in Swarajbir's *Shairi* is far more corrosive than in Shahryar's *Piro Preman*. In *Shairi*, the disciples hatch a plot to get rid of Piro, having persuaded a loyal eunuch and servant (*sevādār*) of Gulabdas to poison her, a person who had been made responsible by Gulabdas for serving and protecting her. However, just as the protector of Piro turns her killer, so does the disciples' own conspiracy backfire on them as their guru also drinks the poisoned milk partaken by Piro, and dies, unable or unwilling to contemplate life without her. The disciples then end up not saving/rescuing their guru, but actually abetting/hastening his downfall/end. Irony and paradox are piled up to effect and enhance the dramatic elements in the play.

Moreover, the trope of dying together in each other's arms, or more saliently, being buried in a common tomb or even a grave, plays to the 'cultural script', imbibed from the Punjabi qissa tradition, one of the most important literary traditions of Punjab.[36] The romantic characters of these qissas are not only part of common parlance in Punjab, but have also been used by poets, including Punjabi Sufis, as ideals of maddened love (a love metaphorically for god, *ishq haqīqī*, rather than the more personal love, *ishq majāzī*) or as self-sacrificing lovers necessarily doomed in a cruel and uncomprehending world. Most romantic Punjabi qissas, whether Hir–Ranjha (to which *Shairi* makes overt references as Piro is compared to *Hīr saletī* (Hir of Sials) for her beauty and her ability to speak for herself) or others like Sohni–Mahival, Mirza–Sahiban, Shirin–Farhad, Sassi–Punnun, or Layla–Majnun, revolve around the travails of an impossible love. For a variety of reasons, ranging from caste mismatch, debasing of self through following a degraded profession (for the pursuit of a lover), and the troubling womanly sexuality when outside of parental control, lovers are doomed to failure in Punjabi qissas. Indeed, they are condemned to death; death signifying both a punishment for defying societal norms, as well as having the power of redemption. By making the ultimate sacrifice of life, the lovers are redeemed, idealized, and made icons of true love unafraid of death, a love that achieves the divine. By having Gulabdas and Piro die together in each other's arms, Swarajbir invokes as he fulfils the audience/readers' empathy/expectations towards a given cultural palimpsest. The notional idea of divine love is underscored in materiality, because the two, Piro and Gulabdas, did in fact share a common tomb, reminiscent of the qissa lovers like Sassi–Punnun or Sohni–Mahival.[37] One may even suggest that a true romance in the Punjabi literary context must not be allowed to end in any other way. Thus, the inconvenient historical 'truth' that Gulabdas died eight months after Piro in 1873, and both died of natural causes rather than unnatural ones, or that the two lived for many years together without any serious disciple revolt or tension, does not suit Swarajbir's particular mode of storytelling.[38] As the play closes, through the device of *sutradhār* or storyteller, literally one who is

---

[36] See the discussion in Shemeem Burney Abbas, 'Female Myths in Sufism' in her *Female Voice in Sufi Ritual: Devotional Practices of Pakistan and India* (Karachi: Oxford University Press, 2003), pp. 85–107. For the popularity of the qissa tradition, see Farina Mir, *The Social Space of Language: Vernacular Culture in British Colonial Punjab* (Ranikhet: Permanent Black, 2010).

[37] Abbas, *Female Voice*.

[38] Ditt Singh's verse, discussed in Chapter 1, is interpreted as a revolt by disciples. However, as I have discussed in Chapter 6, Ditt Singh never slandered the Gulabdasis and remained loyal to the guru in the latter's lifetime.

tying the disparate threads of the story together, Swarajbir does mention the eight-month hiatus between the two deaths, but says that Gulabdas figuratively died with Piro, which can be interpreted as signifying that his life after her death was akin to a living death: *Khojī dasde han ki Pīro jī dī maut to aṭh mahīne bād Gulābdās vī akāl chalāṇā kar gayā. Par sāḍa khiyāl haī ki Gulābdās vī tadoṅ mar giyā sī, jad Pīro dī maut hoī* (Researchers tell us that Gulabdas died after eight months of Piro's death. But we believe that Gulabdas died when Piro died).[39]

While Shahryar in his play kept the eight-month gap between the two deaths, he did invoke the qissa tradition by having Gulabdas die while carrying a lamp towards her grave (*mazār*). He conjured up the image of worship on a Sufi saint's grave, having Piro's devotee prostitutes sing her verses as *qawwālī*s (singing associated with Sufi *samā* or environment) while Gulabdas, as her most worshipful devotee, carried the lamp, falling dead on her grave, where he too wished to be buried. The irony that Shahryar wished to underscore was that this guru/pir, this philosopher of his age, ended up being nothing more than a devotee of Piro. Shahryar put it thus: *Oh sanyāsī banyā, udāsī banyā, vedāntī banyā, vām mārgī banyā, te shāyad kuj vī na ban sakiyā.... Oh kamyāb pīr sī lekin Pīro da ban ke reh gayā* (He became an ascetic, an udasi, vedanti, vam margi,[40] but perhaps he could not become anything. He was a successful pir but he ended up becoming Piro's).[41] The play on the words Pir/Piro, a Sufi adept and his lover/disciple Piro, was very much a part of Swarajbir's play as well, where his protagonist is called Ayesha, but who gives herself the name Piro when she makes Gulabdas her pir, murshid, or guru. Among the very many possibilities her name conjured, she could have been Peeranditti or Pirunissa as all our authors speculate, the most romantic version seemed the punning Pir/Piro combination, latched on by our two playwrights.

That two of the texts under discussion are plays, dramas scripted for performance as for readership, needs further elucidation. As mentioned

---

[39] Swarajbir, *Shairi*, p. 184.

[40] 'Udasi' refers to followers of Sirichand, the elder son of Guru Nanak. 'Vedanti' refers to Gulabdas's belief in advaita or non-dualism derived from the Vedanta. 'Vam Margi' refers to followers of tantra, here evoking sexual practices, normally seen as forbidden to ascetics. Shahryar believes that Gulabdas was a follower of the hedonistic and materialist Charvak tradition.

[41] Shahryar, *Piro Preman*, p. 62.

before, at least two theatre groups have performed Swarajbir's play, the more dramatic of the two plays, with its many twists and turns. It is in *Shairi* that Piro struggles to articulate her poetry as a right, tries to find in various lovers her true friend and benefactor, and, in a nascent fashion, tries to locate her own agency and voice, even as the world at many levels conspires to strangulate her incipient revolt against given feminine conduct. The narration of Piro's story through a drama does a few things: it plays with, enhances, and amplifies the dramatic elements present in Piro's own theatrical *160 Kafis*, even if this is done by introducing many fictional characters and situations not present in her verses; by invoking certain cultural scripts, it creates an environment of empathy to which the audience responds; and it attempts to reach out to large audiences, those who can read the script as a story, and those who can watch the story unfold on the stage.

The fragmentary nature of Piro's *160 Kafis* that obsesses about her travails—her focus on her arrival at the guru's establishment, her going back to Lahore because of the appeals of her kin/wards, her confrontation with religious authorities, her abduction, her rescue—can be seen as the unfolding of an elaborate melodrama, stage-managed by her. Drama available as a script and as a play, the doubled effect of 'stage and page', would supposedly reach out to more people, who the playwrights feel ought to be familiar with Piro's tale. And that is the nub—as I will discuss further in the next section—of Piro's story, as the discovery of her *160 Kafis* and other texts are themselves such dramatic and important events that her having happened in history becomes a compelling reason to celebrate her with as large an audience, of viewers and readers, as possible. Once again, it is Swarajbir's play that uses many tools of drama that can be enacted to envisage the possibility of, in fact, staging it. Through the device of a sutradhar, the storyteller who links and takes forward the story—or the *gāyak maṅdlī*, a singing group, which also performs a similar task of explaining a situation, emotion, or pushing the tale to the next stage—the playwright envisions the mise en scène, conjuring the proscenium where the story can be told, history brought alive, and performed for those so far ignorant of its particular treasure, that is, Piro. Within the performative context when a tale unfolds built on a story thread that has cultural precursors, in this instance the qissa tradition among other themes, the performers and singers can involve the audience in a uniquely empathetic atmosphere in that moment. This is similar to the creating of sama or environment, for example, that Abbas speaks of when her performers sing about Sufi poetics deeply entrenched among the audience for whom they perform.[42]

Vijender Das' *Sant Kavyitri Ma Piro*, as the title suggests, is a completely different text. Hagiographical and devotional in make-up, it sets out to correct the misapprehensions people may have of Piro, indeed to undo to some extent the canard of multiple lovers, rebellious disciples, or the taint of prostitution as a profession that may be seen to stigmatize Piro. Piro is addressed as *Mā* or *Mātā*, a mother, underlining her respected maternal status among the Gulabdasi heirs, not to mention as one shorn of a sexualized attitude associated with a former prostitute. Vijender Das adopts at least two strategies to overcome the debilities that afflict the perception of Piro. Though mostly relying on the same material as the two dramatists, he accrues greater authority for his voice by assuming for it the role of an insider within the Gulabdasi tradition. He attributes knowledge about Piro's background from not only the historical sources and academic discussion around her, of which he is acutely aware, but also from an old and venerated Gulabdasi with an impeccable lineage within the sect to whom only he has access. Introducing the chapter on her character and her guru, he writes: *Mātā Pīrojī ke janamkāl ke vishay mein Gulābdāsī Sāmpradāye ke vridh sant Milkhīshāh shishya Budheshāh shishya Gulābdāsjī ne is prakār varṇan kiya haī ...* (On the subject of Mother Piro's birth, the old saint of the Gulabdasi sect Milkhishah, the disciple of Budheshah, who was the disciple of Gulabdas, has described it thus ...).[43] The second, a corollary to the first, is to speak with an authoritative demeanour. The tone adopted by Vijenderji has little place for ambiguity, speculation, or hearsay at most junctures, though may pander to an academic discussion at times. As noted, our two dramatists at various points in the texts of their plays bring in the element of their own speculation and fictionalized depiction. The 'Afterword' of Swarajbir's *Shairi*, for instance, begins by frankly admitting that the play is not a description of the life of Piro or Gulabdas, but rather picks up some known episodes of their lives, whose sequence he has manipulated (*main inā ghatnāvān nun age pichhe kar ke vartiyā haī*—I have used these episodes in my own sequencing).[44] By adopting a voice of certainty, Vijender Das dismisses any doubt about the devotion-worthy status of Piro as of Gulabdas, because devotion, by its

---

[42] Abbas, *Female Voice*, pp. 93, 100.

[43] Das, *Sant Kavyitri*, p. 20.

[44] Swarajbir, *Shairi*, p. 185.

very nature, must be based on absolute faith. However, being aware of the academic debate around her, Vijenderji is keen to give his work academic acceptability, carefully footnoting and using other professional devices to adduce it academic authority. He may begin his discussion by conceding that a variety of opinions prevail over an issue, but as he proceeds, this multiplicity of utterances is abandoned, and a single voice emerges—heteroglossia is replaced by monologue. This can be demonstrated through the example about Piro's origins as discussed by him.

Swarajbir in his Afterword begins by voicing the opinion of various sources and scholars on Piro's origins. These range from her birth in the Gujranwala province of Punjab to her birth in the *bar*/jungle area, her parents supposedly being small landholders. He goes on to say that all scholars and sources are agreed on one aspect of her life, which is that she ends up as a prostitute plying her trade in Lahore (*sāre vidvānāṅ dī sāṅjhī rae iho bandī hai ki Pīro kaṅjrī/raṅdī sī, te Lahore vich peshā kardī sī*).[45] Vijenderji starts by discussing these prevailing opinions on the place of Piro's birth, and by mentioning that her parents were small landholders, but then goes on to speak with certainty about her early education with *maulvī*s in Islam and the Arabic language, thereby perhaps explaining her ability to compose poetry.[46] He then goes on to speak about the misfortunes of her early life (discussed in a speculative voice by others as well, that she may have run away with an itinerant religious man). However, how she lands up in a brothel of Lahore, ambiguous in other accounts, is explained with complete authority by Das, even though it overturns his earlier statement of her parents' landholding origins. Das informs, having become an orphan, and later, after the death of the religious man, a sadhu, who sheltered her, Piro, is pushed into prostitution by her father's brother (chacha). Indeed, Vijenderji avoids using the term 'prostitution', preferring to say that her chacha pushes her into performing mujra, the dance form associated with prostitutes. Thus, despite the speculation of landholding origins, this endorses a statement he had made earlier of her birth in a low-caste Mirasi/Dom family. Piro's tale in Vijender Das' recounting has a tone of pathos, and she emerges as a poor orphan, a helpless innocent woman, forced into a profession because of destitution

---

45 Swarajbir, *Shairi*, p. 185.

46 A mere hint in one of Piro's verses of having been taught with mullahs is interpreted in this authoritative way. The contradiction that all her poetry comes to us in manuscripts written in the Gurmukhi script, and not the Perso-Arabic that must have been taught in schools attached to mosques, is never brought up.

(*bholī bhālī abalā Pīro*—innocent helpless Piro).[47] The question of Piro's
agency is an important one and I have in Chapter 5 discussed it as significantly visible and asserted in her *160 Kafis*. Depicting her as helpless and
a victim of fate, in the face of Piro's voluble speech as seen in her verses,
her 'talking back' is done to diminish the disapprobation associated with
her career. For victimhood is the opposite of purposive choice (though
we have no source that can tell us how she comes to be in a brothel), and
showing Piro as a victim of sexual predators works better as a 'cultural
script' that expects women's sexuality to be under control rather than
women as sexually in charge of their own lives. Brought up in an environment where her parents apparently kept company of various holy men,
Vijenderji tells us that even in the brothel she not only constantly tried
to find a way out of her misery, but also sang Sufi compositions, for that
was the poetry she wrote. And so he can vouch for a stainless character
of Piro, an assertion that brooks no alternative opinion: *Charitra kī uktā
kasauṭī par mātā Pīro kā jīvan purṇatā pavitra evam nikhrā hua pratīt hotā
haī* (On the touchstone of character mother Piro's complete life seems
pure and bright).[48]

Finally, the broad contours of Piro's story, not just as told by her but as
gathered from her and other Gulabdasi sources and oral accounts can be
summarized as built around these issues and events: her birth and parental
occupation, her becoming an orphan, her running away/abduction by a
holy man, her plying customers in a Lahore brothel, her wish for a release
from her sleazy environ, her getting to know of Gulabdas's establishment
and its openness towards all castes, her reaching Gulabdas and his attraction
towards her and her poetry (for Vijenderji there was no physical side
to their relationship), the incipient rebellion among his disciples, and
her living out the rest of her life with him in Chathianwala. These were
picked and fictionalized by Shahryar and Swarajbir, both playing on the
qissa romance of her life, and sanitized and made into a morality play by
Vijender Das, demonstrating how if one's devotion and spiritual quest is
strong enough, redemption is bound to follow.

Interestingly, all the story-building elements described above were,
in fact, present in the first academic short article published on her by a
scholar of Punjabi literature, Devinder Singh 'Vidyarthi' in 1974.[49] One

[47] Das, *Sant Kavyitri*, p. 22.

[48] Das, *Sant Kavyitri*, p. 23.

[49] Devinder Singh 'Vidyarthi', 'Punjabi di Paheli Istri Kavi', *Khoj Darpan* 1,
no. 2 (July 1974): 89–95.

may suggest that he created the master template that became the basis for subsequent representations of Piro. His article was based on his early research on Punjabi women poets in the 1940s in a still undivided Punjab, and a few sources on the Gulabdasis compiled around the fin de siècle. His conversations with scholars familiar with Punjabi literary traditions, both before and after 1947, and with those like Shamsher Singh Ashok, responsible for collating handwritten manuscripts for the government of the Indian Punjab, were an important source for him. However, what Vidyarthi did not write about was Piro's abduction and escape from Wazirabad, which is available in her own *160 Kafis*, which he may not have known about or read in its entirety or dismissed as imaginary, but which became an important part of subsequent narratives. The important point here is about the persistence of a representational template once it is patterned and patented. To use the concept of White, the story of Piro was organized in a particular 'plot', a reworked Punjabi romance if you will. However, the details of the romance—which in themselves were borrowed from available cultural scripts, for example, the qissas or devotional hagiography where a budding saint finds her guru/god fighting all social odds—were worked out by individual authors who represented her story with a lilt of tragedy or a tilt towards morality. How far might any of these elements also be seen in the script developed by a historian? There were some themes that were systematically worked into these accounts. In the next section, particular themes and their treatment and representation by various authors will be discussed.

REPRESENTING PIRO: SOME THEMES

A Woman Poet and a Feminist Quest

The most significant aspect of Piro's life that Shahryar and Swarajbir, even Vijender Das, set out to represent to the world is the fact that she was a poet. She is presented as a poetess par excellence, the first Punjabi woman poet, self-conscious of her talent, and keen to preserve it. The titles of all the authors highlight this aspect of her life. Shahryar calls his play *Piro Preman*, basing it on what was apparently her nom de plume, Preman, though I have not come across it in her manuscripts. Swarajbir calls his play *Shairi* (*Poetry*) and casts Piro as a proud poet, conscious of her talent and confident of her ability to leave a mark on history. Swarajbir underlines the fact that she is a woman poet by noting his surprise when he realizes that the poet he had been reading was a woman and not a man writing as a woman, referring to the trope of masquerading in a feminine persona common in Sufi and bhakti poetry of male poets addressing a masculine god.[50] The title of Vijender Das' book simply points to the saint-poet Piro.

In the view of all our authors, Piro's poetic outpourings also put her among the women bhakti (and Sufi) poets in these plays, and thereby place Punjab on the map of women bhaktas who sang their songs. It may be pointed out that while many parts of India produced women saints whose songs and poems are remembered to this day,[51] Punjabi society and culture did not throw up any such poet, despite the emergence of Sikh gurus influenced by bhakti ideas. In the face of contemporary discourse about gender relations and women's place in society, wherein Punjab emerges as an especially patriarchal society, the discovery of Piro's poetry may be seen as refreshing good news.[52] For popularizing Piro allows Punjab a modicum of reprieve from its status as a culture inhospitable for women, making a beginning towards redressing its society's egregious gender imbalance. All our authors are, therefore, keen to put her on the map of women bhaktas of India. Vijender Das, for example, inducts Piro in an impressive all-India list: 'In Rajasthani and Hindi literature Mira, in Gujarati literature Ganga Sati, Marathi ... Janabai, Bangla ... Chandravati, Oriya ... Madhavidasi, Kashmiri ... Lal Dei, Tamil ... Andal and Telugu ... Vaikamma ... the same honoured place in Punjabi literature indubitably belongs to Piroji.'[53]

Shahryar's play is dedicated to Lalleshwari—Lal Ded—the famous fourteenth-century woman mystic of Kashmir, whose *vākhs* or sayings are still popular there.[54] He clarifies this allusion to Lalla in his preface, underlining the close resemblance between Piro and her: Lalla was the

---

[50] Swarajbir, *Shairi*, p. 7. On the trope of a feminine persona of male poets see Carla Petievich, *When Men Speak as Women: Vocal Masquerade in Indo-Muslim Poetry* (New Delhi: Oxford University Press, 2007).

[51] Some of these have been discussed by Susie Tharu and K. Lalita in their *Women Writing in India*, vol. I, *600 BC to the Twentieth Century* (New Delhi: Oxford University Press, 1991). Also see A.K. Ramanujan, 'On Women Saints', in *The Divine Consort: Radha and the Goddesses of India*, edited by J.S. Hawley and D.M. Wulff (New Delhi: Oxford University Press, 1999), pp. 316–24.

[52] Anshu Malhotra, 'The Importance of Being Piro in Punjab', *The Tribune*, Chandigarh, 6 December 2012.

[53] Das, *Sant Kavyitri*, p. 11.

[54] Ranjit Hoskote, *I, Lalla: The Poems of Lal Ded* (New Delhi: Penguin, 2011).

Hindu disciple of a Muslim pir according to Shahryar; and Piro was a Muslim disciple of a Hindu pir.[55] This is a reference to the popular belief that Lalla, with her Kashmiri Shaiva antecedents, discarded these and became a wandering ascetic seeking god. In popular understanding she is also meant to have been a mentor to the famous Nuruddin Rishi (and not he as her pir, though for Shahryar perhaps it was more poetical to make a more straightforward relationship of inversion between Hindu/ Muslim guru/disciple) who in one apocryphal account is said to have refused to be breastfed by his mother, Lalla nursing him instead.[56]

Our authors also make a reference to Mirabai, by far the most popular of women bhaktas of north India, and Piro is presented as her worthy successor, who, like Mira, surmounted many social constraints to follow her heart.[57] In fact, in Piro's entire poetic repertoire there are only two allusions to Mira's poetry, and Mirabai herself is never mentioned. However, one reference is clear enough—*Pīro pī pyālṛā matvāri hoī* (on drinking from the cup Piro became intoxicated),[58] invoking the taking of the poisoned cup sent to Mira by those embarrassed of her flouting social norms, though it turned to ambrosia on her drinking from it. This reference emerges in verses that explored Piro's mystical awakening, and spoke of the intoxication of the mystical experience. In the *160 Kafis*, and some of her other poetry, Piro compares herself to low-caste Pauranic women characters like Bhilni, Kubjan, or Karmabai, who were all emancipated by Vishnu despite their base backgrounds, rather than place herself among women bhaktas as such. As discussed in Chapter 4,

[55] Shahryar, *Piro Preman*, p. 9.

[56] http://en.wikipedia.org/wiki/Lalleshwari, last accessed 6 March 2014. Scholars, however, look at Lal Ded as a contemporary of the great Sufis Saiyid Husain Simnani and Mir Saiyid Ali Hamadani of the Kubrawiyya order. Her close association with these Sufis is so strong that she is often remembered as a Muslim saint, and an apostle of Islam in Kashmir. See Mohammad Ishaq Khan, *Biographical Dictionary of Sufism in South Asia* (New Delhi: Manohar, 2009), pp. 189–90. According to Hoskote, Lalla was appropriated by the Hindus as Lalleshvari and Lalla Yogini, and Muslims as Lal-'arifa. The more communally neutral terms for her were Lal-Ded ('Grandmother Lal', or 'Lal the Womb'). She was also affectionately called Lalla. Hoskote, *I, Lalla*.

[57] For a short succinct account of Mira, see J.S. Hawley and M. Juergensmeyer, *Songs of the Saints of India* (New Delhi: Oxford University Press, 2008 [2004]), pp. 119–42. Also see Chapters 4 and 5.

[58] *S3*: 18.

she refers to low-caste male bhaktas like Kabir, Sadhna, or Saina. However, our authors evoke Mira as the archetype of a north Indian woman bhakta many times. Shahryar refers to Mira in his preface as representing social revolt, as does Piro in his understanding, a social overturning so radical that even twentieth-century society could not bear to see Mira's story, alluding to a television programme on Mira that was apparently withdrawn after protest.[59] Vijender Das, besides making direct references to various women bhaktas, also anachronistically says that had Piro's poetry been recognized in her own time, she would have found reference in Nabhadas' *Bhaktamāl* and James Tod's work, besides being discussed by various well-known contemporary scholarly figures who have studied bhakti poets![60] In the desire to promote Piro as one worthy of the company of those like Mira, Vijenderji quite misses that Nabhadas' biographical sketches of bhakti saints belongs to the early seventeenth century, and that Piro would have been a contemporary of Colonel Tod's later life, a colonial scholar who worked on Rajasthan (Mira's region) rather than Punjab.

It is in Swarajbir's play that the self-conscious poet Piro is put on an almost feminist quest. At the heart of his play is his protagonist Piro/ Ayesha on a voyage of expressing her poetic talent (not of discovering it for she already knows she has it), and the playwright throughout the script uses both Piro's own compositions, and his own penmanship to give her verses to recite and say. The play traces her search for a lover who would appreciate her talent. While there are moments in the play when Swarajbir attempts to give Piro unfettered agency, for instance, after her sojourn with her third lover, she vows to live by herself, but this comes to nothing as she soon finds herself in the company of Gulabdas, her last lover and guru. To be fair to the playwright, he does depict her taking many decisions on her own, running away with her first lover, a horseman in Ranjit Singh's army, or her third, an itinerant holy man, but despite the playwright's feminist awareness, he cannot quite imagine Piro/Ayesha alone. Such a situation in the play perhaps emerges from circumstances that do not allow a woman to live by herself, nor earn her livelihood, except as a prostitute, though it might also be the playwright's imaginative limitations. And so it seems Piro needs a man who will give her support so she may fully realize her poetic potential. However,

---

[59] Shahryar, *Piro Preman*, p. 9.
[60] Das, *Sant Kavyitri*, p. 14.

Swarajbir wishes to emphasize her agential self through the assertion of her poetic skills, a facility that includes and exceeds her other identities of caste and gender. He put these words in her mouth: *maiṅ kanjrī vī āṅ te shāirā vī ... shāirā vī āṅ te tīvīṅ vī* (I am a prostitute and a poetess ... a poetess and a woman).[61]

This acceptance of her multiple identities by Piro in Swarajbir's play is an aspect of her embracing all women as (akin to) herself. The notion of a Punjabi sisterhood or womanhood that emerges is also given the hue of a Punjabi romance, making Piro the quintessential heroine of Punjabi qissas referred to earlier. In a small scene introduced solely to emphasize poetic exchange and dialogue (*sawāl–javāb*) between Gulabdas and Piro, representing their joint verses or *Sanjhi Siharfi*, the two discuss the nature of a woman.[62] While the guru offers the more traditional reading of women—as responsible for making beggars of men, for starting wars, or as embodying desire, maternal affection, love, and hatred—Piro replies by claiming to be all (qissa) women. Her reply, *Ayesha, Pīro, Hīr te Sahibāṅ, sab diyāṅ iko bātāṅ* (Ayesha is Piro, Hir, and Sahiban, they are all the same), referring to the heroines of the qissas Hir–Ranjha and Mirza–Sahiban, is based on the belief that she represents them all.[63] When the guru further tries to distinguish between good and bad women, Ichhran and Loona, the good and the bad mothers of another popular qissa *Puran Bhagat*, rewritten in this period by the poet Qadir Yar in Ranjit Singh's court, Piro, once again, encompasses these women in herself.[64] *Ichhrāṅ, Loonā, Sundrāṅ, Sohnī, iko chole vasan* (Ichhran, Loona, Sundran, and Sohni wear the same garment/body), Piro replies, emphasizing her embodying them all, trying to wipe out artificial differences men and circumstances weave into their lives.[65] By claiming to be these women, Piro gives them a voice through her own speech and verses. Thus, the playwright celebrates that a woman, Ayesha/Piro, has initiated a poetic conclave—a *majlis*—drawing attention to its novelty as a cultural institution for women, and through it signalling an unstoppable cultural change where women will speak up for themselves and for other women.

---

[61] Swarajbir, *Shairi*, p. 91.

[62] This is not the actual content of their *Sanjhi Siharfi* in which Gulabdas explicates the advaita doctrine, imbibed and elaborated by Piro.

[63] Swarajbir, *Shairi*, p. 127.

[64] See Chapter 8 for further comments on *Puran Bhagat*.

[65] Swarajbir, *Shairi*, p. 127. Sundran nurtured unrequited love for Puran in the qissa *Puran Bhagat*. Sohni is the heroine of the qissa Sohni–Mahiwal.

That Swarajbir puts his heroine in the feminist mould, even while indicating that feminism may be a ruse to categorize women who do not fit into culturally sanctioned roles, can be seen from his epigraphs—a verse from Piro's spiritual poem, and a quotation from the early suffragette, journalist, literary figure, and feminist of the twentieth century, Rebecca West, who says she is labelled a feminist because she doesn't fit into the roles of a doormat or a prostitute.[66] Swarajbir implies that men look at women as fitting only into these two roles, and at many points in his play, he alludes to both the cultural attitudes towards women, and Piro's determination to break and overturn these norms. Her first two lovers in the play are shown to be repeatedly irritated by her insistence on pursuing poetry, asking her to leave this to men, and do what women do—look after homes, and at the most sing women's songs.[67] Her second lover, Ilahi Bakhsh, a powerful general in Maharaja Ranjit Singh's army, becomes angry when she expresses her desire to meet Hashim Shah, a poet in the Maharaja's court. This exchange between them on the one hand portrays her notion of her place in society, in the company of other poets, and on the other, becomes a reason for the playwright to introduce societal attitudes that see women as inferior to men. The latter is done by the 'paratextual'[68] intervention of the gayak mandli, or the singing troupe that vocalizes social attitude: *Ih duniyā mardāṅ dī duniyā ... tīvīṅ tāṅ hai nīvīṅ* (This world belongs to men, women are inferior). To this Piro/Ayesha replies that neither is a woman inferior, nor will she remain silent, but will claim her speech—*hun bolegī tīvīṅ*—now a woman will speak. Again, making an oblique reference to Mira and her inebriation on the poisoned cup, the playwright makes her assert that she will drink the poisoned cup of poetry, and revel in its intoxication: *Sukhan piyālā vish dā jāna, ghuṭ ghuṭ kar ke pīvāṅ; luṅ luṅ de vich nashā jo hove, us nashe vich jīvāṅ* (I know poetry to be the poisoned cup, and I'll

---

[66] 'I myself have never been able to find out precisely what feminism is. I only know that people call me a feminist whenever I express sentiments that differentiate me from a doormat or a prostitute.' (Swarajbir, *Shairi*, p. 8.)

[67] Swarajbir, *Shairi*, p. 31.

[68] This refers to the text that is outside the narrative proper; here, it is the playwright's use of the singing troupe to push the story forward, or to explain a situation or an attitude. I am borrowing from the discussion in the 'Introduction' of Tony K. Stewart, *Fabulous Females and Peerless Pirs: Tales of Mad Adventure in Old Bengal* (New York: Oxford University Press, 2004), p. 9.

drink it sip by sip; and the resulting intoxication in my every pore, I'll live by that inebriation).[69]

For all our authors, Piro also carried forward the Sufi poetical tradition as represented by the renowned Sufi mystic Rabia of Baghdad, Swarajbir proffering before Piro/Ayesha the role models of Rabia and Mira in the same breath, as women who by following asceticism had the doors of knowledge (*ilm*) opened for them.[70] Swarajbir, in particular, by imitating certain well-known phrases, what one can even call the imprint of the poetry of the Sufis beloved of Punjabis, made her implicitly an inheritor of that legacy as well. By using the words 'lun lun', for example, in the line quoted above, he made a reference to the poetry of Sultan Bahu, a seventeenth-century mystic of Punjab. Later, Bulleh Shah is alluded to when the gayak mandali comments on the poetic exchange between Gulabdas and Piro using the phrase *nach nach yār manāyā Pīro'* (Piro danced and placated her friend/ murshid),[71] reminiscent of Bulleh's *tere ishq nachāyā kar ke thaīyā thaīyā* (your love made me dance on a beat) and in popular understanding his mad dancing to please his murshid Shah Inayat.[72]

At other places, our authors make references to Punjabi women poets whose names begin to appear in some nineteenth-century treatises, for instance, the little known Sahib Devi 'Arorī' (mentioned in Ganesh Das's *Chār Bagh-i-Panjāb*),[73] and Piro's contemporary Nurang Devi, who, like Piro, wrote poetry living in the sect of Wazir Singh, and like her too wrote jointly with her guru the *Sanjhi Siharfi*.[74] Through this compact

---

[69] Swarajbir, *Shairi*, pp. 54–5. Significantly, the use of '*luṅ luṅ*', or bodily pores/ hairs, is reminiscent of the poetry of Sultan Bahu, the seventeenth-century Punjabi Sufi, whose Punjabi kafis remain very popular to this day: *luṅ luṅ de muṛ lakh lakh chashmā*—in every pore lakhs of eyes (to admire and look at the master). This makes denser the signification embedded in the words Swarajbir gives to Piro. For Bahu's verse, see Jamal J. Elias, translated and introduced, *Death before Dying: The Sufi Poems of Sultan Bahu* (Berkeley: University of California Press, 1998), p. 25.

[70] Swarajbir, *Shairi*, pp. 69–70.

[71] Swarajbir, *Shairi*, p. 137.

[72] Namvar Singh, ed., *Bulleh Shah ki Kafiyan* (New Delhi: National Institute of Punjab Studies, 2003), pp. 152–3.

[73] J.S. Grewal and Indu Banga, translated and edited, *Early Nineteenth Century Panjab: From Gunesh Das's Char Bagh-i-Panjab* (Amritsar: Guru Nanak Dev University, 1975), p. 31.

[74] Shamsher S. Ashok, *Siharfian Sadhu Wazir Singh Kian* (Patiala: Punjabi University, 1988).

intertextuality that evokes Punjabi qissas, Sufis, and even little-known women poets, Piro was not only made the inheritor of this diverse and loved legacy, but also her worthiness, as deserving of canonization, was underscored by these linkages. Thus, in Swarajbir's play when Piro cries out her pain that the world looks at her as a prostitute and a low caste, the playwright through the words of Gulabdas reassures her that she will be remembered by posterity as she is the first woman poet of the five waters/rivers of Punjab and its language—*panjān panīyān dī zabān dī pehlī aurat shāyar*.[75] As Shahryar put it, she is no longer to remain buried and forgotten in a coffin, but is to be respected and celebrated.

Though Piro was a skilled poet able to compose in some popular poetic forms of the period such as the kafi and the siharfi, much more could be said on the form of her *160 Kafis*, an autobiographical fragment that did not really belong to a set poetic genre even though she called it kafis. Though the verses rhymed, the autobiographical content gave it a uniqueness that is surprising as it is innovative. The *160 Kafis* is indicative of her inventiveness, perhaps a necessity for those like Piro who were clawing their way in a world not presented to them on a platter. The bending of the rules of prosody as the *160 Kafis* indicate, along with perhaps the mending of her life, a process of healing and recovery, which may have initiated its writing, does show a relatively tentative poetic journey for Piro.

It is in this context that the portrayal of Gulabdas by Shahryar and Swarajbir as a mawkish figure totally smitten by Piro and her poetry seems rather excessive. For Shahryar there is a reversal of roles of the murshid and the murid, the guru and his disciple, for after encountering Piro and her poetry, Gulabdas acknowledges her to be his guru, ready to beat the drum (*tablā*) to the singing of her verse.[76] After her kidnapping, he is shown to pine for her, and after her death, his empty life finds meaning only in being buried in her grave. Swarajbir, too, depicts Gulabdas as being awestruck by Piro and her poetic talent. After her coming back to his dera in the aftermath of her abduction, he longs to hear her recite her verses, wishing that till his last breath she should sing and he listen.[77] In complete divergence from the playwrights, Vijender Das invests in showing Gulabdas as a powerful, miracle-making saint, a Gnostic of his

---

[75] Swarajbir, *Shairi*, p. 134.

[76] Shahryar, *Piro Preman*, pp. 13–15.

[77] Swarajbir, *Shairi*, p. 161.

age who lived in excess of 150 years.[78] As an incumbent on the Gulabdasi seat at Hansi, Haryana, it was important for Vijenderji to present himself as an inheritor of the legacy of a powerful saint. At the same time, being conscious of the need to present historical facts, Vijenderji gives a long list of around forty-seven available writings and manuscripts of Gulabdas with his sect. As discussed in Chapter 1, there is no doubt that Gulabdas was both a prolific writer and a powerful guru.

Though a significant part of the poetic oeuvre of Piro is available, it is very small in comparison to the writings of Gulabdas. Its importance is also attributable to who she was, her writing and talent developing despite her many social and gendered disabilities. Far from the maudlin figure our playwrights sketch, Gulabdas is consistently portrayed in Piro's poetry as a powerful, miracle-working saint, in whose presence Piro deprecatorily, even if in a formulaic fashion, refers to herself as a slave. Almost all her poetic repertoire consistently speaks of him in awe-inspiring terms, the multiple references to his puissance emphasized in her verses. In the face of this, one can only conclude that his sappy portrayal in these plays is a deliberate foil to highlight Piro's poetical achievement.

Piro the Prostitute

Though Piro calls herself a vesva or prostitute once in her *160 Kafis*, it is our other sources on the Gulabdasis that make this point rather strongly, using multiple terms including 'kasbi', 'randi', 'besya', and 'kanchani' to underline her background in prostitution, and those of her ilk who apparently became the disciples of Gulabdas.[79] However, there is no information about her years in prostitution, or how she came to be a part of this profession, though there has been plenty of speculation. There are also references to dancing girls in another of her works, the *Rag Sagar*, composed of songs set to ragas which describe the celebration of the Holi festivities in her guru's establishment, including the performances of dancing girls.[80] Any reference to her early years then falls in the realm of speculation, hearsay, and imputation, beginning with Vidyarthi as noted earlier. The suggestion that Piro had a suitor in one Ilahi Bakhsh—a

---

[78] Das, *Sant Kavyitri*, p. 35.

[79] Giani Gian Singh, *Sri Guru Panth Prakash* [hereinafter *PP*] (Patiala: Bhasha Vibhag, 1970, first published 1880), p. 1294.

[80] *Rag Sagar* in Das, *Sant Kavyitri*, pp. 212–39.

FIGURE 7.1   This is a contemporary coloured picture of the older print of
Gulabdas and Piro in black and white. In an interesting accumulation of symbols,
a bird (*bāj*—falcon/hawk?), associated with the tenth guru Gobind Singh, is placed
before Gulabdas, who himself carries a *gulāb*, a rose, symbolizing his name.
Source: Courtesy of Vijender Das.

gunner and a general in the army of Ranjit Singh—comes from a later,
but an important, source.[81] However, Piro's *160 Kafis* does harp on
conflict around her person, and the possibility that a powerful person
such as Ilahi Bakhsh sponsored her professional guardians who created
the trouble she mentions cannot be ruled out.

In the face of a lack of adequate information, how do our authors construct the character of a prostitute, and specifically Piro as one? Vijender
Das' insistence upon seeing Piro as a victim of circumstances that propel
her towards a brothel in order to survive has already been discussed. Her
spiritual awakening, and her consistent efforts to leave her surroundings
make an important part of his story of her redemption, for like a lotus she
blooms in the mud, he has told me on many occasions.[82] Shahryar, too,
hints at her years in the profession to be marked by misery, the need to
nurture her poetry keeping her going. He also depicts her as having run

[81] Mahant Ganesha Singh, *Bharat Mat Darpan* (Amritsar: Vaidak Bhandar,
1926), pp. 127–30.

[82] I have been in touch with Vijenderji since 2006. See the Chapter 8.

away from home with an elderly sadhu who died after a few years, leaving her to fend for herself, after which she turned to prostitution.

Swarajbir, in his fictional rendering of Piro's life, constructs the term 'prostitute' a little differently. In his drama, as shown, a restless Piro runs away from home in order to discover herself, nurture her poetry, and find true love. It is a woman who over the course of a few years ends up with a quartet of lovers that makes her a kanjari, a prostitute, in Swarajbir's rendition, rather than any association with a brothel. When a woman decides to run away from home, it is understood by all the characters in the play that she becomes a woman easily available, and so a target of predatory men. She has, therefore, wilfully foregone the safety of her parental house without acquiring the security of a husband's home, a deliberate forsaking of male sexual surveillance. Swarajbir also underscores the physical nature of Ayesha/Piro's relationship with all her lovers, the lovers' lust, their physical 'thirst' (*treh*) underscores a woman falling out of line as her sexuality finds expression outside marriage. Thus, after describing Ayesha/Piro and her first lover's physical hunger for each other, the gayak mandli highlights the ambiguity of her sexual–social status: *na viāhī na kuwārī* (neither married nor a virgin).[83] And so the friends—Visakha and Murad—of her first lover Rehmat Ali, ask him to share his sugar candy (*gur*) with them since he has managed to get a kanjari for his pleasures.[84] Piro's defiant statement, referred to earlier, where she calls herself a kanjari (prostitute), shayra (poet), and a tivin (woman), while a cultural challenge that demands acceptance of her multifaceted personality, at the same time also inadvertently accepts society's branding of her as a loose, unchaste woman.

All our authors construct Piro as a victim of predacious men (*deh ke saudāgar*—traders of flesh)[85] or remark on her own ability to attract men by presenting her as very beautiful and in the peak of youth. Piro's own writings do not speak of her looks, and the available iconic representations of Piro are neither realistic nor explicit to settle the matter. In the plays, however, men target her because of her inordinate beauty. The implicit message that emerges in this archetypal construction of the sexually desirable according to the male gaze is that the sexuality of a pretty woman is more vulnerable than that of a homely one. In the

[83] Swarajbir, *Shairi*, pp. 18–19.
[84] Swarajbir, *Shairi*, p. 33.
[85] Das, *Sant Kavyitri*, p. 8.

very first account of the Gulabdasis of the late nineteenth century, Piro is presented as having great beauty (*rūp baḍ*).[86] Again, it is in Swarajbir's play that his fictionalized Ayesha/Piro is presented as a sexually charged beauty, as gorgeous as the mythical Hir, a 'mistress of beauty' (*husn dī malikā*).[87] One of the men from her village describes Ayesha/Piro as having bright eyes like lamps lit at night, and her body nearly bursting from her bodice.[88] Interestingly, in the prefatory notes of Veer Vahab, a young scholar who is clearly obliged to all our authors discussed here, she refers to Piro's beauty as an established fact: *Pīro mātā dī sohṇi sūrat nuṅ rab ne rījhāṅ nāl ghaṛiyā* (Piro mother's beautiful face was chiselled by god with great affection).[89]

Significantly, Vijender Das and Swarajbir, taking a cue from Vidyarthi, quote one of her own verses as proving the point about men's voluptuous desire centring upon her, and her rejection of their uncontrollable libido. For Vijenderji and Vidyarthi, this verse represents her victimization by men's rapacity proving her need to become free of her circumstances and as an example of her spiritual yearning. For Swarajbir, it shows both her ability to choose her own sexual partners, and her rejection of unwanted attentions. However, they all unequivocally take it as representative of Piro speaking of her past in prostitution:

Thiriyāṅ hoiyāṅ de pās na baiṭhīye jī, tishnā apnī kaḍ sunāvde nī
Pīro pare dhakeliye paṅbarāṅ nuṅ, jale āp te aurāṅ jalānde nī.

Let's not sit with stragglers, they tell you of their desire,
Piro says shove away such lowly, they burn themselves and make others burn.[90]

It is, of course, possible that Piro meant just what she is attributed to her by our authors—a past in Lahore's brothels, in retrospect seen as time spent with despicable and base men. Indeed, Piro's various verses undoubtedly carry a flavour of her life as she lives it or had lived it. While the *160 Kafis* relate an incident, a period in her life, her siharfis are collections of stray thoughts (some of which are autobiographical in nature), spiritual inclinations, and her sect's attitudes towards social institutions

---

[86] Giani Gian Singh, *PP*, p. 1293.

[87] Swarajbir, *Shairi*, p. 36.

[88] Swarajbir, *Shairi*, p. 15.

[89] Vahab, *Piro Kahe Saheliyon*, p. 9.

[90] Piro's siharfi in Das, *Sant Kavyitri*, p. 97.

whether of caste or religion, strung together by the genre's need of composing a verse on a given letter. The diverse topics thus discussed cannot
be seen by the historian as indicative of any one thematic development.
The first part of this verse, for example, speaks of running after shadows
like material goods, and it is not necessary that desire here must necessarily speak of a bodily one, though it might. The certainty of a fictive or a
moral tale, then, is not the mien a historian can adopt.

An interesting twist in both the plays under discussion is the projection of a rebellion in the establishment of the guru with the arrival of a
prostitute in their midst. An ascetic's camp ought to nurture celibates,
Gulabdas's disciples explain, and it should not have a place for a former
prostitute. A verse of Gulabdas's disciple, Ditt Singh, which castigates
a holy person for 'keeping' a prostitute, is the reason for introducing
this dramatic element in these plays: *raṇḍī aur faqīr kā sadā anādī vair,
jab āye ghar sādh ke, kahāṅ gujāre khair* (a prostitute and an ascetic are
enemies forever, when can there be well-being when she arrives in the
home of a holy man).[91] While Shahryar merely hints at the brewing of
such a rebellion, suggesting Piro would win this conflict, in Swarajbir's
play, as discussed earlier, it becomes its theatrical denouement. Vijender
Das, on the other hand, is at pains to show the acceptance of Piro by
the Gulabdasis, indeed, the respect they accord her by putting her on the
pedestal as a mother.[92] I have suggested in Chapter 1 that though the
verse in question does indeed hint at a disapproval of such a relationship
between an ascetic and a whore, Ditt Singh could not have been with
Gulabdas in Chathianwala until the very last years of the latter's life, by
which time any scandal associated with the coming of Piro to Gulabdas
was probably long dead, and any tensions smoothened out. Moreover,
these lines appeared in a set of verses, conventional in nature, which are
meant to see women's sexuality as dangerous, leading men astray. Thus,
what the hinging of the dramatic element in the plays on the arrival of
a prostitute in the dera does is to compress time, impute meanings not
necessarily present in Piro's lifetime, or not present in the way they have
been dramatized here. The theatrical rebellion in these plays underlines
the changed priorities of Gulabdas—from a teacher to his disciples to

---

[91] See Chapter 1.

[92] Das has a section where he gives the verses of some disciples of Gulabdas
in praise (*upma*) of mother Piro, for example, Sant Attar Singh. Das, *Sant Kavyitri*,
p. 56.

a lover of Piro—reducing his life and work to his relationship with her. The playwrights, it seems, work to illuminate Piro's poetic talent by diminishing both Gulabdas's poetic skills, as well as his stature among his disciples.

Piro, a Low Caste

In the *160 Kafis*, Piro repeatedly calls herself a low-caste woman (sudar nari). The self-representation as a low—sudar—woman is a multifaceted expression, with metaphoric and literal connotations. To be a prostitute in Punjab is to be in the ranks of the kanjars or the low caste associated with pimps and prostitutes, whether one is born into the caste or inducted into it at a later date. Thus, calling herself a sudar underscores the liter-ally low-status position she occupies in a stratified society. Moreover, the term 'sudar' carried with it the metaphoric understanding of a 'woman' who—across castes—was akin to a sudra of the dharmashastras, denied a high status. Additionally, to call oneself base in relation to one's guru was entirely appropriate. Within both the bhakti and Sufi traditions, disciples often had to efface, even humiliate themselves, in the presence of the sheikh or the guru to show the suppression of the ego, a sense of the self, which would initiate the novice's commencement on the spiritual path. Further, the use of the bhakti trope by Piro—of being one among the low-caste saints like Kabir or Saina—made possible this fluid connotative multiplicity of the word sudar to come through. Similarly, Piro deliber-ately compares herself to low-born women of the Pauranic literature on whom god showered favour.

Vijender Das interprets this overloaded sudar of Piro in the most literal sense—she is born in the house of Mirasis, and her uncle forces her to perform their traditional function, dancing the mujra. In Shahryar's play, both the literal and the allegorical meanings of being sudar are tapped. However, he is at pains to show how Gulabdas's 'golden self' (*swaran hau*), referring to his higher caste and social status as he was a Jat, bows before the ostensibly base self of Piro.[93] His chastised ego recognizes the superior poetic and spiritual talent of Piro.

Swarajbir follows Shahryar in making Gulabdas recognize Piro's innate superiority, but makes this recognition more dramatic by making her belong fictionally to a low-caste family of oil-pressers (*teli*). Swarajbir

---

[93] Shahryar, *Piro Preman*, p. 9.

makes Piro aware of her low caste, as she is shown to initiate a dialogue over caste with Rehmat Ali, her first lover and a Jat, whom at that point she hoped to marry. She speaks of the caste mismatch between them, a possible problem in marriage, as alike castes are meant to marry each other, evoking the rule of endogamy. Ali acknowledges his own caste of a Jat, while at the same time mouthing the theoretical position that there is no caste among the Muslims. Ayesha/Piro, however, enumerates the many Muslims in her village who claimed to be Saiyads, Jats, Rajputs, Chamars, Arains, Telis, and Musalis, and that Telis are often called sudars. As noted, this reference to her low social status is perhaps meant to highlight the degree of her poetical achievement. At the same time, her reference to Bhagtu Chamar of her village who sang the songs of Raidas or Bhagat Ravidas, a 'guru of Chamars', and so aired the pain and grievance of being born in his caste, must be seen as a comment by the playwright on the politics of caste in contemporary Punjab.[94] The self-assertion of Dalit communities, particularly the former Chamars, and the elevation of the status of Guru Ravidas as their saint, with separate places of worship established by them, is a significant innovation of a more recent past.[95] Importantly, there is much in Piro's poetry that rejects varnashramadharma, the structure of caste and stages of life central to Brahminical society, making explicit her sect's acceptance of all castes, and offering redemption to all. However, Swarajbir makes little reference to this aspect of her writing or quotes her works directly here. Rather, his stand on caste is seemingly driven by the present Dalit politics in a state that has the largest percentage of Dalits in it (over 28 per cent).[96]

It is in this context that we must see his deliberate construction of the establishment of Gulabdas and his dera as antithetical to the traditional norms of caste and status. The dera of Gulabdas in Chathianwala is presented as a deliberate attempt on his part to create a 'court' (*darbār*) inverting that of Ranjit Singh in Lahore, after his clash with Ilahi Bakhsh in the play and after Ranjit Singh's men order him to vacate Lahore. This initiates a conflict—*hākam te faqīr dī larāī*—a battle between a governor and a mendicant, we are told. So instead of an abode of soldiers

---

[94] Swarajbir, *Shairi*, pp. 26–7.

[95] Mark Juergensmeyer, *Religious Rebels in the Punjab: The Social Vision of the Untouchables* (New Delhi: Ajanta Publications, 1988).

[96] K.S. Singh, ed., *People of India*, vol. 37, *Punjab* (New Delhi: Manohar, 2003), pp. xxvi, xliv.

and courtiers, Chathianwala is set up as a place of saints and disciples, where in the place of the high castes, the low castes dwell (*nīviaṅ jātāṅ*). Further outlining the differences, Swarajbir brings in an element of indigenousness in Gulabdas's ostensible court. Unlike Lahore, where Persian is the official language and is patronized, Punjabi is spoken in Chathianwala, and, moreover, written in the Gurmukhi script as against the Perso-Arabic one of the court.[97] This recourse to an autochthonous culture is significant and will receive further comment later, though for the moment it is worth making a note of what is owned (saints, low castes, Punjabi, Gurmukhi) and what is shown as alien (courtiers, high castes, Persian, Perso-Arabic script).

While working out these binary oppositions, Swarajbir focuses on the many low-caste disciples of Gulabdas, including Ditt Singh, though he does not delve into details about his relatively higher-caste followers. Thus, a place is made for a woman—Ayesha/Piro—in his court as a woman is one amongst the low, a sudra. When some of his disciples reject her presence in the dera, calling her a woman, a prostitute, a Muslim, and a low caste, Gulabdas reminds them of his monist philosophy, the advaita principle of non-dualism he adheres to, where all beings—animate and inanimate—are made of the same divine substance: *raṅḍī, chaṅḍī, jīv, ātmā, parmātmā, ādmī, mīṭṭī, havā, ag, ākāsh, pashu, paṅchhī ... ih sab iko tat haī* (prostitute, goddess, life, soul, god, man, soil, wind, fire, sky, animals, birds ... are the same substance/essence).[98] In his afterword, where he writes with a historical perspective, Swarajbir makes the point about how in many ways Gulabdas was ahead of his times. The seeds of feminist (*narīvādī*) thinking, and of the place of Dalits in society (*Dalit chintan*), in his opinion, can be traced to his dera, and other like-minded gurus of the time,[99] for in these establishments low castes and women were respected. Calling his establishment an independent-minded one, Swarajbir emphasizes its rebellious nature against the courtly courtesies of the time. He is appreciative of the poetic talent of many poets like Maiyya Das, Shamdas Arif, and Kishan Singh Arif in the dera of Gulabdas, and makes the point that these intellectuals of his time were attracted to Gulabdas because of this element of revolt and independence in the latter's thinking. While there is no doubt that the Gulabdasi establishment

---

[97] Swarajbir, *Shairi*, p. 97.

[98] Swarajbir, *Shairi*, pp. 102–3.

[99] Swarajbir, *Shairi*, p. 196.

espoused some of the more radical ideas of this age, it may be a touch anachronistic to call it feminist or Dalit-oriented. The diatribes against varnashramadharma and the social salience of a mixed-caste community did throw a social challenge, but as Wendy Doniger has discussed, these could also coexist in pockets with otherwise socially conservative norms. In other words, alternative societies that ignored caste rules were formed, but to what extent they could challenge or change caste norms remains debatable.[100]

Religion and Identity

The question of religious identity, of apostasy and conversion, in many ways drives Piro's *160 Kafis*. Piro's 'conversion narrative' revolves around her entry into the establishment of a guru, who belongs to a broad Hindu–Sikh ascetic tradition, and the problems this creates for her.[101] Her confrontation with Islamic religious and judicial authorities, her subsequent abduction on refusing to be reincorporated into Islam, and her escape from captivity to get back to her guru and sect, form the crux of her *160 Kafis*. Though there are other salient questions that emerge in a relatively muted fashion, for instance, the question of the treatment of daughters, Piro foregrounds her angst in the religious idiom. It is the crossing of the threshold of religion, then, that brings on a train of events that cause her to suffer. These events also present her with an opportunity to prove her mettle before her guru—her steadfast loyalty towards him in the face of mental agony and physical confinement. To justify her place next to her guru as his consort, Piro uses Hindu mythology to give examples of godly couples that belong together, speaking of Ram/Sita, Krishna/Radha, or Shiva/Parvati as her role models. In her *160 Kafis* and other writings outward religiosity is also rejected as a meaningless carapace in relation to inner awakening as achieved by bhakti saints. Using sharp words, as did Punjabi Sufis, to lampoon religious figures—Islamic and Hindu—she revels in her guru and sect, who see the Hindu and Muslim, high and low caste, man and woman with equal eyes.

For both Shahryar and Swarajbir, the question of conversion or of the resultant conflict never assumes a centrality that it has in Piro's own telling of events. In many ways, Piro, who was born a Muslim, stays as

---

[100] Wendy Doniger, *On Hinduism* (New Delhi: Aleph, 2013), p. 489.

[101] See Chapters 2 and 3.

such in their depiction, despite her sojourn and stay at Chathianwala with the Gulabdasis. It is the thwarting of the pride and will of the powerful Ilahi Bakhsh, who is portrayed in Swarajbir's play as her second lover, which initiates her problems: her abduction in Shahryar's play, and a confrontation between Gulabdas and Ilahi Bakhsh in Swarajbir's drama. It is in Vijender Das' writing that the question comes up, and though he does not refer to her conversion as such, he hints at it, mentioning her getting *dīkshā*, an initiation into discipleship, by being given a mantra and a name to chant. In his narration, the dwelling of a Muslim woman in a non-Muslim establishment (*gair Muslimoṅ ke ḍere*) does create a conflictual situation, handled by Ilahi Bakhsh by calling a panchayat or a council of important Islamic religious authorities of Lahore. They ask for Piro to be sent away from Gulabdas's establishment, for otherwise this would result, in Vijenderji's words, in *mazhabī jhagṛe* (religious confrontation/riots). It is only once Piro leaves the Gulabdasi dera that she is asked to reconvert (*use mazhabī shikshā lene ko kehte haiṅ*—they ask her to take religious education) and marry Ilahi Bakhsh. On this Piro replies that she is already married to her god-guru (*isht guru*) Gulabdas.[102] Whether Das here is referring to an actual or a metaphorical marriage remains unclear. Significantly, later Vijender Das defends what he calls 'real' Islam by saying that in it there is no place for using force in religious matters (*dhārmik kaṭṭartā*, literally, religious bigotry) referring to the forceful abduction of Piro. Interestingly, he later refers to Piro displaying the qualities of a 'true Muslim', for in the face of the fanaticism of those who wanted her to revert to Islam, she remains calm and peaceful. In her Gulabdasi avatar, it follows, the differences between Hindus and Muslims have ended or become meaningless.[103] Das goes on to speak of the Gulabdasi faith in Vedantic philosophy which is free of communal differences (*sāmpradāyik matbhed*).[104]

Vijender Das' narrative is thus cautious in the handling of a crisis in Piro's life that emanated from her crossing religious boundaries. He can be said to be writing with the awareness of the contemporary problem of religious conflict between Hindus and Muslims, as seen in his use of terms like 'sampradayik matbhed', and also contemporary sensitivities on religious questions. Despite Piro becoming a Gulabdasi after having

---

[102] Das, *Sant Kavyitri*, pp. 8–9.
[103] Das, *Sant Kavyitri*, p. 15.
[104] Das, *Sant Kavyitri*, p. 16.

forsaken Islam, he very carefully suggests that true Islam is not bigoted. He goes on to speak of the Gulabdasi sect being open to Hindus and Muslims, where religious differences are immaterial. At the same time, Das may be seen to be subtly 'Hinduizing' the Gulabdasi historical bequest when he describes Gulabdas's and Piro's graves, lying parallel in a tomb in Chathianwala, not as graves, *kabr* or *gor*, but samadhi, connoting the Hindu practice of interring ashes of holy persons.

As noted earlier, for Swarajbir, Piro remains a Muslim, even when with Gulabdas in his dera, as, for example, when she starts calling herself Piro, referring to her Muslim background where their holy men are called pir. Throughout the play, Swarajbir uses various devices, sometimes subtle, and at others consciously articulated, to underline Piro's 'Muslimness'. He gives her the name Ayesha, her namesake being the young, favourite, educated, and politically conscious wife of the Prophet, perhaps hinting at the same qualities in his heroine. She is shown to wear a veil (*naqāb*) in the opening scene, is presented as offering namaz five times a day, her worship inevitably referred to as *bandagī*, a Persian-derived word indicating in this context a Muslim practice.[105] The question of language and the signifiers it releases and constructs is an important one, as I have already indicated when speaking of Swarajbir's comparison between the apparently wholly indigenous Punjabi/Gurmukhi of Gulabdas's court and the Persian/Urdu of the Maharaja's. The ownership of Punjabi as the language of the people is important, but when it gets to be associated with only the Gurmukhi script, it acquires communal overtones. Historically, Punjabi was written in at least three scripts—Perso-Arabic, Gurmukhi, and Devanagari. The promotion of Punjabi in Gurmukhi conjointly as the language of the Sikhs began only in the late nineteenth century and is promoted as a policy in the Indian Punjab today, though Gurmukhi did develop with the sacred Sikh literature.[106] The Islamizing signifiers, particularly when associated with Piro, work as a subtext, because at an overt level, Swarajbir consciously attempts to create a secular outlook. This can be seen in the linking of Piro with the Punjabi Sufi poetic tradition as represented by Bulleh Shah and Shah Hussain, as well as the qissa tradition with her comparison to Hir. She is also shown to imbibe in the Gulabdasi mien the disregard for religious differences between the Hindus and Muslims, without necessarily giving up her own cultural

[105] Swarajbir, *Shairi*, p. 14.

[106] Malhotra and Mir, 'Punjab in History and Historiography', p. xxix. However, it is also true that all Sikh sacred literature was written in the Gurmukhi script.

inheritance.[107] One may, therefore, surmise that a subliminal tension pre-
vails in *Shairi* between the 'owning' and the 'othering' of the Indo-Islamic
legacy. At the same time, by overplaying Piro's Islamic upbringing he can
make us marvel at the secularity of Gulabdasi history.

In many ways Shahryar, too, continues to emphasize Piro as a Muslim,
particularly in his preface where he mentions this Muslim woman's
murshid being a Hindu, as discussed earlier. The most theatrical statement of Piro's Islamic patrimony comes in his description of Gulabdas's
death, eight months after Piro's. Shahryar tells us that this Hindu man,
forgoing cremation, the practice among Hindus, left instructions to be
buried in the same grave as Piro—*Pīro dī kabar khol ke mainu us diyāṅ
haḍḍiyāṅ de nāl hī kabar vich utār ke pher donāṅ dī miṭṭī nu vī ik banā
denā* (opening Piro's grave place me with her bones in the grave and then
mix the earth)—at once evoking the Muslim custom of burial and the
Punjabi romance of dying/lying together.[108] From one of our sources on
the Gulabdasis we know that Gulabdas died eight months after Piro in
1873 and that they were buried in a single tomb (*makbarā*), the remains of
which are still extant (though barely so) in Chathianwala in Pakistan.[109] A
single tomb is transformed into a single grave in Shahryar's imagination
(even Swarajbir mentions the same grave/kabr),[110] enhancing the effect
of a romance that supposedly defied boundaries of religion. Defying religious rituals sharpens the appeal of romantic love as it introduces the
element of rebellion, of thwarting the norm. However, in the process it
also gestures to the 'normal', that the ordinary must follow, the ascriptive
identities that define the lives of the less exalted.

The Miraculous and the Enchanted World

The literary imagination of Piro relies on allusion and allegory that
relates to the epics, Pauranic stories, and legends, including the miracle-
working powers of bhakti saints. This is not only important to the manner in which her narrative moves forward, but also pivotal to how she
constructs characters, more specifically her own. By assuming the role of
Sita, for instance, she allows Sita's characteristic devotion to her husband

[107] Swarajbir, *Shairi*, p. 145.
[108] Shahryar, *Piro Preman*, p. 8.
[109] Giani Gian Singh, *PP*, p. 1293.
[110] Swarajbir, *Shairi*, p. 184.

to be impressed upon her in relation to her guru Gulabdas, or use Sita's righteousness to condemn those who perpetrate Piro's abduction. In the same vein, she attributes miraculous powers to her guru Gulabdas at the time of her rescue from her incarceration in Wazirabad, powers that enhance his saintly credentials in a worldview where the saints announce their elevated status by performing such feats.[111] The relationship of holy persons to a higher consciousness, their near-godly status, needed to be displayed in order to establish their superiority among mere mortals. In the early modern period, this could often mean competitive miracles, as holy men of different hues might use miraculous deeds to enhance their status and that of their sect.[112] Among the many epithets Piro uses to describe her guru, she calls him *jānī-jāno* and *antaryāmī*, both connoting him as all-knowing, *abnāsī*, indestructible, and limitless (*bihad*), all attributes that extol his extraordinary status. The guru himself is shown to be aware of his powers in her *160 Kafis*. When he sends his two disciples to engineer her escape from Wazirabad, he tells them that her rescue is preordained, but that they will earn credit for it by actually performing the task. Thus in Piro's recounting of the story of her rescue, the locks in the room where she is imprisoned fall away on their own, the sentinels keeping vigil outside her room are blinded even as they open the doors and she walks away. Later, as Piro and her two rescuers make their way out of the city gates, the guards there, too, are blinded, and the chase of the three disciples is initiated only when they are well out of the city. All these wonderful occurrences Piro clearly says are because of her guru, a miracle-working perfect man.

Vijender Das comes closest to acknowledging the guru's miracle-working powers, as is appropriate in his devotional account, but is still constrained enough to speak of some of the unusual occurrences in ways that can be at least explicated. Thus, the blinding of the guards is explained both as a result of a dark, black, stormy wind, and because the guards fall asleep: *tabhī achānak kālī syah āndhī chal paṛī ... bandigrah maiṅ jab pravesh kiyā to kehte haiṅ pehredār so gaye* (suddenly a dark black stormy wind blew ... when they entered the prison, they say the guards fell asleep).[113] The insertion of 'they say' is an interesting

---

[111] See Chapter 5.

[112] Simon Digby, trans., *Wonder-Tales of South Asia* (Jersey: Orient Monographs, 2000).

[113] Das, *Sant Kavyitri*, p. 9.

stratagem for giving this particular recounting a quality of hearsay, quite contrary to his normally authoritative tone. This allows him both a rational distance from what he relates while maintaining the extraordinary status of his guru.

Miracles have no place in the telling of Piro's story by either Shahryar or Swarajbir. Shahryar, who follows the broad outline of Piro's story in his drama, does speak of the two disciples going to rescue her. However, exactly how Piro is released from her captivity is not portrayed, for the next scene shows her having reached Chathianwala and Gulabdas. Swarajbir's fictionalized story has no place for either the abduction as recounted by Piro, nor her release, and so there is no dilemma of explaining miracles or the impossibility of their occurrence. In plays typically addressed to 'disenchanted' twenty-first century audiences, the playwrights do not presumably wish to get caught in situations that seem wholly irrational and impossible to elucidate. The central episode of Piro's *160 Kafis*, her kidnapping, enforced imprisonment, and miraculous release, one may suggest, gets a short shrift, as modernity and its need for rational explanation demands a rescinding of an aspect of the event as represented by Piro. But what about the historian? Groomed in a discipline that has repeatedly made a distinction between faith and reason, what is the meaning of Piro's guru's miracle as it intervenes in and changes her life?[114] I have in Chapter 5 discussed Piro's representation of this miracle in terms of her establishing her agency, in the specific context of bhakti devotion as she experiences it in the mid-nineteenth century. However, the subjective nature of specific 'meaning-making', an idea this paper began with, needs to be borne in mind along with disciplinary constraints.

STORYING A STORY—HISTORIANS AND OTHERS

'To tell a story is to take arms against the threat of time, to resist time, or to harness time', wrote Portelli, highlighting some significant aspects of orality and how memory is constituted by cultures.[115] In another context, A.K. Ramanujan spoke of the salience of transmitting stories in cultures: if you have a tale and do not tell it, then it will make you

---

[114] For a recent statement discussing the distinctness of faith and scholarship, the latter based on logic and rationality, see Romila Thapar, 'Good Times are Gone', *Outlook*, 24 March 2014, pp. 70–2.

[115] Portelli, *The Death of Luigi Trastulli*, p. 59.

miserable until you find a way to relate it.[116] The transmission of stories in cultures is linked to both resisting the erasure by time, of perpetuating cultural values, of harnessing old, past stories to transfuse them to new generations, and also oft times to transmute them to newer forms. The questions of transfusion and transmutation are important as these emphasize a dialogical relationship with texts/stories. When we interact with texts from the past we engage 'in a process of criticism, appropriation, repetition, refutation, amplification, abbreviation, and so on', that is, an active process of 'supplementation' that underscores our engagement from the present.[117]

Piro told her own story. Rather, she told one story, among the many stories of her life that she could possibly tell. To her, in retrospect, it may have been the most important story of her life, so she worked carefully on crafting it. Epic characters, bhakti saints, Sufi poetics, and Pauranic women became the templates she used as she filled it with characters— her mighty guru with his marvellous powers, some disciples who pitched in for her rescue, her antagonists and religious authorities, her friends and source of succour. She legitimized the place she came to occupy next to her guru.

Piro's lost story when rediscovered excited those who heard/read it. Here was a woman's story, told in her own words, from a time when women's subjectivity hardly ever found expression in the written word, particularly in Punjab, not to speak of being preserved in historical records where women's voice was rarely available. Moreover, here was a woman vociferous and voluble, not mincing words when it came to speaking against her agonistic interlocutors, deeply respectful when it came to her guru, and remarkably steeped in and able to bring out the nuances of her sect's learning and her own varied cultural heritage. This 'wow' moment of finding Piro, the recuperation of her voice, therefore, set off many to recount her tale—from her own story, and from what could be gathered from the frugal sources at their command. This chapter has, therefore, been about the retelling of Piro's tale. The tale that Piro fabricated, the warp and weft of her life that she chose to memorialize,

---

[116] See Ramanujan's discussion on the folktale 'Tell It to the Walls' in A.K. Ramanujan, 'Towards a Counter-System: Women's Tales', 'Telling Tales', and 'Tell it to the Walls: On Folktales in Indian Culture', in *The Collected Essays of A.K. Ramanujan*, ed. Vinay Dharwadker (New Delhi: Oxford University Press, 2013 [1999]), pp. 429–84.

[117] Inden, 'Introduction', p. 10.

and the memories being created today of her life and times is examined here. The questions that drive this chapter focus on who says (can say) what, how and why?

Narratives embedded in the historian's oeuvre have been increasingly brought to the fore in recent times. The knitting of the narrative and the unfolding of the plot—'the way in which the story materials are arranged by narrators in order to tell the story',[118] or the design and intention of the narrative[119]—are perhaps common to fiction writers and historians. In other words, whatever the form or the medium of relating it—the genre— the story imbricated in it is recognizable.[120] However, as the chapter has discussed, historians are tightly controlled by their sources—they may say some things with certainty, suggest and hint at others, even indulge in informed speculation on some questions, but cannot do more than that, though they may arrange their materials in a way that itself may follow a plot, say a story. The protocols of their discipline keep a leash on the historians, even making them tentative when sources are fragmentary. In Piro's case, the plausibility of Piro's story, the contexts of her writing, and the stories available in other sources, can only hint at a fascinating story of her remarkable adventure, but say little with certainty.

The writing of fiction or fictionalized 'true' stories (to work with an oxymoron)[121]—the histrionics of the dramas and the pathos of the devotional account—is comparable to the genre of oral history in at least one way, the fictional plots that develop with free play to imagination have much to do with meaning-making. The way we recall a story or the way we wish to relate it and how we wish others to recollect it has a lot to do with what sense we make of it. Fiction, much like oral narration, can mix up historical, poetical, and legendary narratives.[122] In the fictionalized accounts of Piro's story, the density of her own allegories come doubly packed with cultural materials that can lend themselves to her tale, the 'supplementarity' that opens it up to a variety of meaning-making.

---

[118] Portelli, *The Death of Luigi Trastulli*, p. 50.

[119] Peter Brooks, *Reading for the Plot: Design and Intention in Narrative* (Oxford: Clarendon Press, 1984), p. xi. Meaning, temporality, and transmission are the other important aspects of a narrative plot that Brooks discusses. See the chapter, 'Reading for the Plot', pp. 3–36.

[120] Brooks, 'Reading for the Plot', p. 4.

[121] Shahryar, for example, is consciously writing from what he calls Piro's autobiography (*swajīvangāthā*). *Piro Preman*, p. 10.

[122] Portelli, *The Death of Luigi Trastulli*, p. 49.

Further, our present sensibilities—whether feminist, Dalit, secularist, or whatever else—also shape our stories, our meaning-making. We are attracted to particular stories of the past. The cultural past we have inherited, at the same time, imposes its own limitations. We cannot make the past say more than it yields, unless we fictionalize it. But what Portelli calls 'shuttlework', the telling of a story with the present in mind, perhaps is common to all raconteurs, including the historian.[123] The recuperative nature of the historian's as well as the litterateurs' projects here are a case in point. For the feminist historian as for the others, the thrill of a newly discovered woman's voice acts to energize new creativity. Further, the same aspects of Piro's life—her acknowledging a past in prostitution, her allusions to her low caste, and to her womanly self in the establishment of an ascetic—draw attention and are commented on. Yet, the constraints working on a historian—the use of various sources, their verifiability, and their acceptance in the academic world and among peers—perhaps are different from those that might curb the litterateur.

The fictional accounts here amplify and work with prefabricated cultural frames. The steeping of Piro's story in qissa romance, the placing of Piro with women bhaktas, the patriarchal notion of women's sexuality, or the understanding of the tragic transactions of prostitution, for example, are made to work because they play with familiar cultural sensibilities. But Piro's own account needs to be fictionalized so that specific meanings may come forth. Piro's *160 Kafis* do not speak of her life as a qissa romance, though she may be seen to make oblique references to Hir when she confronts religious authorities. Piro finds more in common with low-caste women in bhakti legends than she finds with legendary women bhaktas. She does not chafe against all patriarchal authority as a modern feminist, but only that of her guardians who kidnap her. At the same time, she does not portray herself as a helpless woman, an abala, but confronts her abductors with equanimity and guile, rejecting the sordid transactions that may have been made on her behalf. The 'velocity' of narration, what gets amplified and what gets a short shrift is then somewhat different for historians and others.[124]

Writing of the postmodern turn within history, and the loss of innocence it has entailed, Patrick Finney notes 'that we have no access to the past

---

[123] Portelli, *The Death of Luigi Trastulli*, p. 65.

[124] On the concept of velocity in oral narration, see Portelli, *The Death of Luigi Trastulli*, p. 49.

except through the sedimented layers of the previous textualisations'.[125] This is true of how fictional accounts may work with cultural legacies and how historians may work with historical accounts, including the sources with which they deal. A woman's subjectivity as communicated through a serried autobiographical fragment allows for many textualizations, each working with its own cultural signifiers. All, however, contribute to the discursive life of a subject. In this plethora of voices, historians, even when dependent on previous textualizations, must remain alert to the principles of their own discipline.

The fictional accounts discussed in this chapter re-story Piro's narrative working with cultural palimpsests that make stories appealing and meaningful. The next chapter, easing the historian in the role of the ethnographer, investigates the reworking of Gulabdasi rituals, making the sect meaningful for present adherents.

---

[125] Patrick Finney quoted in Roberts, 'Introduction', p. 15.

8 Fantasticating Fables, Sacralizing Spaces, and Remaking Rituals

The Gulabdasis at a Contemporary Moment

In this chapter, I will look at how the Gulabdasis are faring in contemporary north India by studying one of its multiple branches in Hansi, Haryana, and by understanding the activities and concerns of the head of this dera, Shri Vijender Das. In the first part of this chapter, I will describe the attempts made by Vijenderji to mythologize events from the life of Gulabdas in order to create around him an aura of an extraordinary person. He does this through narrating 'fictional' stories and performing 'invented' rituals and festivals, and by sacralizing spaces hitherto not a part of the older Gulabdasi sacred site(s). The motivation on the part of Vijenderji, as he has explained to me on several occasions, is to popularize his sect, and also to make people know about the founder of the sect, Guru Gulabdas. Gulabdas's numerous writings have formed the fount of knowledge and philosophy that inform the sect and is meant to be the basis of its praxis. While that may have always been the case, I will argue here that changed circumstances after the partition of India and the loss of the abode of the guru at Chathianwala have invested the situation with fluidity. This has evoked innovative responses to the territorial loss on the one hand and engendered contestation in terms of recognition of the guru's spiritual succession on the other. Though the branching off into local Gulabdasi centres headed by prominent disciples of Gulabdas may have been initiated in the lifetime of the guru himself, the dissensus noted here develops around claims to the spiritual inheritance of the guru. The thrust of the argument, however, is to unfold the reach of local religiosities and rituals, the performative negotiation with the followers, and emphasize the innovation and replenishment of cultural proclivities and stories.

The second part will examine how the Gulabdasi understanding and practice of caste and gender relations have changed or remained the same from the late nineteenth century, and how mainstream religions have or have not influenced its liturgical, ritual, and other practices today. I will argue for a historical openness in the sect on issues of caste and the inclusion of women, though important changes too have occurred since the time of Gulabdas. I will also show how the dera run by Vijenderji has appropriated and been influenced by practices associated with Hinduism, Sikhism, and Islam, but has at the same time managed to maintain its distinction. Another way to understand such eclecticism, as it has been argued in this book, is to recognize that one can have affiliation to a sect while retaining one's membership or identity of one of the three dominant religions of Punjab, as it seems to be the case for some Gulabdasis. Finally, I will briefly comment on how in the present jostling for space among the many deras that attract followers in Haryana and Punjab, most catering to an increasingly assertive Dalit constituency, the Gulabdasis might look at their future.

STORIES AND PERFORMANCES

In his classic essay, 'Notes on the Balinese Cockfight', Clifford Geertz sees in the cockfight a microcosm of Balinese society, a reflection of its most cherished values, norms, and hierarchies, and famously pronounces that it was a 'story they tell themselves about themselves'.[1] Taking a cue from Geertz, I will recapitulate two among the many stories in the repertoire of Vijenderji, by narrating which he not only tells his Gulabdasi followers stories about themselves, for example, how to express and organize their devotion, but also relates these to a wider world. Among the latter are the villagers in whose lands Gulabdasi sacred sites are being 'constructed', both literally and metaphorically, but also a wider world out there which may be interested in the life

---

[1] Clifford Geertz, 'Deep Play: Notes on the Balinese Cockfight', *Daedalus* 10, no. 1 (Winter 1972): 1–37.

of Guru Gulabdas and his many followers, particularly the erudite and literary ones in the guru's immediate circle.

There are many stories Vijenderji narrates about Gulabdas, each story's numinous impact enhanced by the substories woven around the central one, creating a mythical lore around Gulabdas's persona. I use the term 'fictional' to describe them in the sense in which Natalie Davis uses it in her reading of the supplication accounts of the condemned for kingly pardon and remission in sixteenth-century France, giving attention 'to their forming, shaping, and moulding elements: the crafting of a narrative'. Davis notes that 'the artifice of fiction did not necessarily lend falsity to an account', and 'nor did the shaping and embellishing of a history necessarily mean forgery'.[2] In the stories Vijenderji narrates of the birth and death of Gulabdas that I will analyse here, there are grains of historical facts; however, what is of interest is the manner in which he moulds his account, embellishing some known aspects of his life with the fantastic and the miraculous. I have argued in Chapter 5 that in the enchanted world of the saintly exemplars in the Indian context, their association with miracle-making and the fantastic was very important to give them a stature of holiness, making them a manifestation and an instrument of the divine on earth. Here I wish to contend that it is these embroidered elements, the trimmings to the bare cloth of birth and death, that allow the mythologizing of Gulabdas's life, and of linking it to holy lives lived earlier, a dialogic relationship with those A.K. Ramanujan called the 'relevant others'.[3] These relevant others were, on the one hand, the mythological figures whose lives in some ways reflected on that of Gulabdas, and on the other, the people who would hear and consume the stories being told about him. Ramanujan also spoke about the peculiar quality of Indian folklore. Unlike the classical Sanskritic tradition, which was unique in many respects, India's folkloric tradition participated in an international network of motifs, genres, types, and structures, using them 'to say something particular, local, and unique'.[4] The motif of saintly lives is, in many ways, both pan-Indian and universal, especially in a world still open to the lure of the magical and the enchanting. However, we will see

---

[2] Natalie Zemon Davis, *Fiction in the Archives: Pardon Tales and Their Tellers in Sixteenth Century France* (Stanford: Stanford University Press, 1987), pp. 3–4.

[3] A.K. Ramanujan, 'Who Needs Folklore', in *The Collected Essays of A.K. Ramanujan*, edited by Vinay Dharwadker (New Delhi: Oxford University Press, 1999), p. 536.

[4] Ramanujan, 'Who Needs Folklore', p. 537.

that in the particular tales about Gulabdas's life woven by Vijenderji, in their symbolic imaging and their referential field, the local north Indian and specifically Punjabi popular cultural traits are noticeable, much as in Ramanujan's folkloric examples.

Vijenderji has 'invented' traditions and rituals that revolve around a two-day festival held on 27 and 28 August every year; 28 August being celebrated as the birth anniversary of Gulabdas. This occasion is celebrated in and around the village of his birth, Ratol, in the Tarn Taran district of the Indian Punjab, partly observed by me in 2013.[5] Eric Hobsbawm has defined invented traditions as those that are relatively recent in origin, often traceable to a dateable period, which however evoke a relationship of continuity with the past.[6] All these elements are characteristic of the new festivities initiated by Vijenderji in the very recent past—from about the year 2000. As discussed earlier, the major festival of the Gulabdasis during the lifetime of the guru was Holi, celebrated over a few days in the month of Phagun (March), in the main establishment of the Gulabdasis in Chathianwala, district Kasur, now in the Pakistani Punjab.[7] It may be underscored that the necessity of creating new traditions and sacred spaces occurred at least partially because of the irreversible loss of the old Gulabdasi establishment in Chathianwala due to the partition of India in 1947, more particularly the site of the tomb where Gulabdas and his foremost disciple, Piro, lay buried. This loss of a spatial–sacral centre that housed a tomb, the source in Sufi lexicon (to which the Gulabdasis were open) of continuous manifestation of the saint's *baraka*, his blessings and munificence, was indeed a severe loss. The multiple Gulabdasi branches in Punjab and Sindh, whose sacred centre was Chathianwala, had to shift base after

---

[5] This chapter is partly based on my notes taken during the celebration of this festival on 27 August 2013, and when I was informed of and asked to partici-pate in the early morning (4 a.m.) ritual planned for the next day (which I could not do). I have also attended a festive occasion observed by Vijenderji's own dera in Hansi on 28 March 2007. I have met and made notes in Vijenderji's house in Sonepat, Haryana on 10 June 2010. I have met and had telephonic conversations with Vijenderji and his wife Saroj over many years now, starting in 2006.

[6] Eric Hobsbawm, 'Introduction', in *The Invention of Tradition*, edited by Eric Hobsbawm and Terence Ranger (Cambridge: Cambridge University Press, 1983), p. 1.

[7] Anshu Malhotra, 'Bhakti and the Gendered Self: A Courtesan and a Consort in Mid-Nineteenth Century Punjab', *Modern Asian Studies* 46, no. 6 (2012): 1506–39.

the Partition to north India, including Punjab, Haryana, and Rajasthan. Furthermore, the sheer enormity of the psychological, social, and cultural impact of the cleaving of the country was partly mitigated by spawning new discourses, practices, and memories. Anna Bigelow, for example, notes the profound change in the stories about the Sufi Haidar Sheikh of Malerkotla after Partition. From narratives legitimating the saint's lineage, the focus shifted to those legitimating interreligious cohabitation. Bigelow also speaks of mobilizing memories of the past that give a community its identity, allowing old values and truths to metamorphose into shapes that are appropriate in new contexts.[8] Thus, the delicate task of propagating the past and a community's sense of itself, in new ways suitable to a changed context, creating new memories that build on older ones is what Vijenderji sets out to perform. Vijenderji's inventiveness can also be attributed to the need to find a focal point for the otherwise dispersed branches of the sect, and the revisiting of places associated with the guru provide the binding factor that brings them together, though some of its branches have kept in touch over the years. Moreover, one may detect the presence of an abrasive competition between the ambitions of Vijenderji to popularize the sect and become the node around whom the new festivities would revolve and the descendants of the line from Hargobind, the successor of Gulabdas in Chathianwala, installed on the gaddi (seat) by the guru himself, at least as the historical records show.[9] The latter have a dera in the Titookhera village, Sirsa district, Haryana, and probably make the claim to being the original branch of the sect. While paying due respect to the Titookhera branch, it is quite apparent that Vijenderji is in the process of burnishing his own credentials as a dynamic and outgoing guru taking the sect forward in comparison to the more inward-looking branch at Titookhera.[10]

[8] Anna Bigelow, *Sharing the Sacred: Practicing Pluralism in Muslim North India* (New York: Oxford University Press, 2010), pp. 36–7.

[9] Giani Gian Singh, *Sri Guru Panth Prakash* [hereinafter *PP*] (Patiala: Bhasha Vibhag, 1970, first published 1880), p. 1295.

[10] That succession to the seat of a guru and inheriting his mantle may often lead to conflict and to the setting up of new branches has been discussed by scholars. Daniel Gold, *The Lord as Guru: Hindi Sants in North Indian Tradition* (New York: Oxford University Press, 1987), pp. 79–86. Also his 'Continuities as Gurus Change', in *The Guru in South Asia: New Interdisciplinary Perspectives*, edited by Jacob Copeman and Aya Ikegame (London: Routledge, 2012), pp. 241–54.

Every year since around 2000, when Vijenderji goes to Ratol and the nearby Rajoki village with his band of followers—he performs rituals, sings bhajans and songs, distributes consecrated food (*prashād*) and otherwise shares food with them, interacts with them, 'plays' with them, and often relaxes with them—he performs to a theatrical script conceived by him. As Richard Schechner has aptly described, 'By performing in special places or places made special by performing in them', this time is marked as 'non-ordinary' and 'for special use only'.[11] Further, Schechner writes, what is performed is 'encoded' in 'special kinds of communication' here between himself and his audience, which includes his followers, his family, but also other villagers and hangers-on, including an occasional academic like myself.[12] Performances by their very nature are 'processual'—in the making and constantly drawing their audiences into a constellation of staged and other activities—'transporting' them at least temporarily to the world created by the performer and binding them to the accumulation of meanings and significations as they unfold. In this instance, people are invited into the world of their gurus, Gulabdas and Vijenderji, and are reminded of what it means to be a Gulabdasi. Performance, as Schechner notes, is 'twice behaved behavior' pointing to the 'rehearsals' that may go into it, in this case a repetitiousness born of yearly performance, as of the ritualistic activity.[13] However, every performance is also unique, a 'liminal' domain, not only because of the improvisations that may go into it, but also because of the inability to do exactly as before, making each occasion a special one. The rituals enacted by Vijenderji during these festivities, by their repetitive nature and the solemnity around them, sanctify both the time and space of their performance. The participation of the audience is crucial in making the ritual efficacious. By taking part in it and by partaking of its symbolic polyphony and the affect produced, the audience in effect allows its making. The festivities that 'play' over two days (and in fact begin earlier when the preparation for them starts) are also poised on the continuum between efficacy and entertainment, the 'braided structure' that is intrinsic to performances. While the ritual and other markers employed by Vijenderji constructs the sacred, the duration

---

[11] Richard Schechner, *Performative Circumstances: From the Avant Garde to Ramlila* (Calcutta: Seagull Books, 1983), p. 90.

[12] Schechner, *Performative Circumstances*, p. 90.

[13] Ritual is described as 'a formalized, collective, institutionalized kind of repetitive action', whether sacred or profane. See Edward Muir, *Ritual in Early Modern Europe* (Cambridge: Cambridge University Press, 1997), p. 3.

of the festivities with many a variegated moment is also a part of the profane world of leisure and entertainment.[14] These cohere to give the occasion its special features, making it out of the ordinary—a quality, to use Victor Turner's descriptor of communitas, emphasizing a period free of differentiating structure.[15]

Vijenderji, shorn of the traditional sacred site of his sect as already noted, goes about creating a new sacred topography in and around the places associated with Gulabdas. Commenting on the 'locative' nature of the Hindu world view on the interface between geography and myths, Diana Eck writes that 'landscape is relational, and it evokes emotion and attachment'.[16] By treading on the land traversed by Gulabdas, Vijenderji attempts to rebuild an emotional connect with certain sites—Ratol, where Gulabdas was born, and Rajoki, where he had an orchard and which, moreover, houses in a tomb-like structure the two tumuli/projections (*thambū*) commemorating the place where two of Gulabdas's disciples died very soon after Gulabdas's own death (at least in Vijenderji's story)—a part of a new sacred 'map' that would anchor these festivities. The loss of the tomb of Gulabdas and Piro in Chathianwala— to the woes of Partition, and soon even its material remains to complete neglect[17]—though a grievous loss to be mourned is in many ways not an irreplaceable one.[18] As Eck notes of the propensities of Hinduism, 'The critical rule of thumb is this: those things that are deeply important are to be widely repeated.' And further that landscape is characterized 'not by exclusivity and uniqueness, but by polycentricity, pluralism, and duplication'. Thus, Vijenderji seeks to pluralize and make available to his present followers the sacredness springing from the very life of Gulabdas. He has sought to 'duplicate' the Chathianwala religious

[14] Muir, *Ritual in Early Modern* Europe, p. 139.

[15] Victor Turner, *Dramas, Fields, and Metaphors: Symbolic Action in Human Society* (Ithaca: Cornell University Press, 1974), pp. 166–7.

[16] Diana Eck, *India: A Sacred Geography* (New York: Harmony Books, 2012), pp. 11, 51.

[17] I visited the tomb in Chathianwala in Pakistan on 26 May 2008. It is in a dilapidated condition, used as a buffalo shed by the local villagers; it is unlikely to survive for very long.

[18] On my visit to the tomb I managed to 'steal' a small piece of a brick from the tomb for Vijenderji, something he had asked for, against my better judgement and despite the fear of Pakistani immigration. He accepted this 'gift' with gratitude and kept it in a silken cloth with great reverence.

experience in Ratol and Rajoki, the latter having the added advantage of being a village on the border with Pakistan, like Chathianwala, and from a particular place and position overlooking the original tomb. The simultaneous 'darshan' of, or the gazing at the new and the old sites in one sweep, one may assume, doubles the merit in partaking of the holy site/sight. Eck also perceptively speaks of the clusters or circles of sacred places whose circumambulation forms an essential aspect of a pilgrimage. The clustering of the above mentioned places and the festivities that involve in visiting them and performing rituals there are then a part of a sacred annual pilgrimage initiated by Vijenderji.

I may also briefly note my role as an amateur ethnographer, a historian, and a privileged academic interlocutor with Vijenderji here, and the polyvalent power dynamic that my presence in his entourage creates in the proceedings. Ethnographic encounters, as James Clifford notes, are contingent and power laden, not transparent, as the earlier academic 'writing cultures' assumed.[19] Clifford refers to them as 'partial truths', or ethnographic 'fictions', or even the oxymoron 'true fictions', to emphasize a range of strategies including those of 'ellipsis, concealment, and partial disclosure' that make up the ambiguity of these encounters. Equally important in his view is the writing itself—whether making notes in the field as I have done, or transcribing taped interviews/conversations, or the later writing up. The implications of this textuality and the narrative strategies of representation, therefore, have to be borne in mind. However, the recounting of 'fictional' stories of Vijenderji in an ethnographic 'fictional' mode of the academic—fiction squared in a manner of speaking—should not freeze the writing pen from attempting representation, but caution towards its partial view. Rather than looking at writing as transparent, it would be more profitable to make the entanglements of power in the ethnographic encounter pellucid.

I submit to the greedy voraciousness of my writing hand, the observing eye, and the listening ear in my various meetings, interviews, and telephonic conversations with Vijenderji. Equally, I wish to point to the appropriation of my presence amidst his followers by Vijenderji to enhance his power, and the prestige of his self-created mission. Having been a rather striking observer from Delhi University on two festive occasions in 2007 in Hansi and 2013 in Ratol, in terms of class and educational

---

[19] James Clifford, 'Introduction: Partial Truths', in *Writing Culture: The Poetics and Politics of Ethnography*, edited by James Clifford and George E. Marcus (New Delhi: Oxford University Press, 1990), pp. 1–26.

advantage I had over his followers, Vijenderji exploited my presence each time to showcase the importance of what he was doing by implicitly stressing 'look who is interested in what I'm doing'. I was invited to the mike and the stage on the first occasion, and after a very brief encomium that I sang to Piro, I quickly vacated my elevated seat in undignified panic as I soon became a recipient of fervent and respectful feet-touching by Vijenderji's followers, along with him and his sister Rajenderji. I realized very quickly that I did not wish to be seen as a guru or rather in my case an 'urug' of any sort.[20] On the second occasion, not only was I the cynosure of curious eyes, I was introduced, and then the importance of my research with its highly exaggerated impact in the world was impressively mentioned.[21] I was suitably presented with a *saropā* (literally, head [*sar*] to feet [*pā*] shawl, a length of saffron cloth) along with Vijenderji and his wife Sarojji at Rajoki.

The privilege of my position also gave me a place along with Vijenderji's family on our pilgrimage journey around the villages of the Punjabi countryside on 27 August 2013. I was graciously bundled into an air-conditioned Innova car along with Sarojji, their son Honey, Sarojji's sister and her family, and Vijenderji for a part of the journey, while his *saṅgat* (followers) were piled into two buses that had been hired for the occasion. This situation gave me access to what Erving Goffman, to use a drama metaphor again, has called the 'backstage'.[22] This is a space where one drops one's guard or mask, a mask worn in public performances. While in their public appearance, not only Vijenderji but his family would be expected to maintain a certain dignified decorum, this could at least partially be dropped in the private intimacy of the vehicle. As this chapter will show, I have used my backstage presence to draw inference and insight into the proceedings/performances as they unfolded, a position that I might be said to have exploited to my advantage.

[20] Kirin Narayan describes the comings and goings of many old and new age gurus, the latter referred to as *urugs* (perhaps suggesting that they were the opposite of gurus) by her father, in their bohemian Bombay home in the 1960s and 70s: 'At the reflecting edge between cultures, a guru's teaching ended and an *urug's* discipleship began.' See her *My Family and Other Saints* (Chicago: University of Chicago Press, 2007), p. 1.

[21] This happened in Patti, part of the itinerary in 2013.

[22] Erving Goffman, *The Presentation of Self in Everyday Life* (New York: Anchor Books, 1959).

SHRI VIJENDER DAS

Vijenderji, as the above section would have shown, is a dynamic personality among the contemporary Gulabdasis, the driving force guiding the new desire for popularity and a larger following. His background and life will, therefore, give us a glimpse of a contemporary guru, and a sense of the energetic pursuance of his self-created goals.

Vijenderji was not born into a Gulabdasi family but was adopted into one at a very early age. He was born in Bawana, Haryana, in a weaver caste (Julaha); his father Ramkala was a freedom fighter. His adoptive family comes from the line of a disciple of Gulabdas, Sant Seva Singh, from Zira in Ferozepur, Punjab. Vijenderji's grandfather, Sant Bishan Das 'Arif' (son of Sardar Ram Singh Gill of Jagravan village, Rumi Pind, in Ludhiana, Punjab) was a disciple of Seva Singh. His own son, Nirbhay Singh Gill, took over his gaddi or seat in Hansi, who, in turn along with his wife Krishna Rani, adopted Vijenderji, leaving him his gaddi. While we can see how gradually the gaddi came to be in the patrilineal family, the Hansi seat is significant for a strong presence of women in it as well. An Istri Sabha (Women's Association) was set up in Hansi by the wife of Bishan Das, Jamna Devi—a woman, according to Vijenderji, of a forceful character (he used the word 'hard' [*sakht*] to describe her, as against her 'kind' [*dayālu*] and 'soft and polite' [*vinamr*] husband). Indeed, to the present day, many older women followers of Jamna Devi come for the annual function (*samāgam*) in Hansi, as I witnessed on 28 March 2007. The daughter of Sant Nirbhay Singh and Krishna Rani, Rajenderji, was also present on that occasion and was clearly seen as a guru and a guide by the women. Throughout the function she sat on an elevated seat along with Vijenderji, and was made offerings by the congregation. One of the important qualities of the sect described by Vijenderji to me is that it is in favour of independence (*swatantratā*) for women. At the same time it may be speculated that the lack of a male progeny may have encouraged Sant Nirbhay to adopt a son to take over his spiritual inheritance. This became clearer when Vijenderji told me that he had been initiated into the sect (*nām dān le liyā*, literally 'taking the gift of the name') at the early age of six or seven from Maharaj Brahm Das of Rohtak, Haryana, who had a dera in Saharanpur,[23] and that he became the inheritor of the Hansi legacy in 1989.

[23] The initiation involved listening to 'Amar Katha' (the immortal story) from the *Updesh Vilas*, a work on delivering the 'message' by Gulabdas, based on

It is important to remember that Vijenderji has a life outside the dera and the responsibilities it entails. He leads a middle-class lifestyle, living with his wife and two children in Sonepat, Haryana.[24] He pursues a career with the Home Guards, and his calling card introduces him as Vijender Kumar, a District Commandant in Sonepat, with the additional charge of Panipat, who has been twice awarded the president's medal for excellence of service.[25] His children, a son and a daughter, are pursuing their studies and hope for regular jobs when they finish education. His wife, Saroj, is vivacious, and certainly enjoys her middle-class life with its associated luxuries. However, all three do participate in Vijenderji's religious activities, particularly Saroj, who has to take her place next to him as his spouse, on many occasions. However, she has confessed to me at least twice that while her husband has *junoon* (unbounded passion) for Gulabdas and the dera, she herself is not very religious.[26] It is her marriage to Vijenderji that has made her accept religious responsibilities as his spouse, because women are expected to 'adjust' to their husbands' needs after marriage. However, Saroj is exceptionally skilled at playing her 'role' as a partner to her spiritually inclined husband. She does this with élan, mixing especially amongst his female following, accepting their respect, but also joking with them, and putting them at ease. She also helps out Vijenderji in his passion for preserving the literary legacy of his sect by often transcribing the Gurmukhi script for him into Devanagari, or reading it out, as he does not know the former, and almost all the older manuscripts of his sect are in the Gurmukhi script. She is also very ambitious for him. She encouraged him to buy the land around Gulabdas's birthplace in Ratol, and hopes that someday he will be able to build a grand temple there. She also once told me that the story of Piro was fascinating, and that a film should be made on her, as it has enough twists and turns in it which are ideal for cinema. Thus, in many ways she

---

Vedanta philosophy according to Vijenderji. Brahm Das was said to have had a very long life (1870–1972). The motif of long life is an important one for Vijenderji. See Chapter 1.

[24] There are both married and unmarried followers and heads of deras among the Gulabdasis, as Vijenderji has told me.

[25] This he has conveyed to me through WhatsApp, on which he sends me regular updates about the sect, particularly the manuscripts he collects. More recently, he sends me pictures of functions held or simple 'good morning' messages.

[26] Sarojji said this to me in 2007 and 2013.

is a true partner to Vijenderji, matching his enthusiasm for the propaga-
tion of the Gulabdasi sect with her own vision for its grand future.

However, the fulcrum of the Gulabdasis in their bid for increasing
their popularity and following is Vijenderji. He is responsible for germi-
nating and nurturing this ambition. He describes himself as a person
crazy or besotted (*diwānā*) with his guru Gulabdas, a passion described
in his words as that between a lover and his beloved (*āshiq aur māshūq*).[27]
He is a person with both charisma and drive. Having trained to take on
the leadership of his community, he commands the respect and reverence of his followers. He is comfortable speaking in front of crowds of
his followers, and his speeches to them are often punctuated with singing
verses from Gulabdas's writings, or from among the writings of other
disciples of Gulabdas. These have been memorized by him over the years,
and quite literally are 'in his throat' (*kaṇṭhastha*), any word or emotion
triggering the 'flow'.[28] I use 'flow' in the manner in which Schechner
describes an actor carried away by a performance, so engrossed does
Vijenderji become in his role of a guru that that role has transformed him
into living his part, blurring the line between the 'role' and the 'real'.[29]
He uses such verses liberally whenever explaining a point to any one,
often unconsciously. In other situations, as I will show later, he may quote
verses 'reflexively' as well, that is knowingly using them for effect on an
audience. Having taken it upon himself to make more people know and
engage with his sect, he does this with a sense of mission. For example,
when he came to know from an early scholar of Piro that I was working
on her as well, he got in touch with me, and over the years ensured that
I would remain in touch.[30] When he realized that there are other scholars
interested in the writings of Piro, he collected them himself, and had
them published in the Devanagari script that he could follow himself and
which would be more convenient for many others. He has, over the years
that I have known him, become obsessive about collecting and archiving,
either in the original or in photocopies, manuscripts produced by the
various disciples of Gulabdas, including the more controversial ones

[27] The relationship between God and devotee is often represented in this way
in Sufi imagery.

[28] Ramanujan, 'Who Needs Folklore', p. 539.

[29] Schechner discusses the idea of 'flow' in a performance and of 'transformation' because of it. See his 'Performers and Spectators Transported and
Transformed', in his *Performative Circumstances*, pp. 90–123.

[30] In time I ensured that as well as this chapter indicates.

like Ditt Singh, or those like Kishan Singh 'Arif' who wrote for a more popular market in late nineteenth-century Punjab. He has built himself a mini archive of the various writings of the Gulabdasis, which he proudly showed me when I visited him in Sonepat in 2010. The following episode, where I accompanied him, will highlight his extraordinary energy towards this endeavour.

On 27 August 2013, when I spent the whole day with him, his family, and followers as they went about celebrating the festivities organized around Gulabdas's birth anniversary, we made a last stop in late evening at the city of Tarn Taran, after a day that started at 7:30 in the morning for me, but probably much earlier for Vijenderji. After a quick visit to the large gurdwara dedicated to Guru Arjan Dev, the fifth guru of the Sikhs, while the rest of his followers relaxed there and his wife went shopping with her sister, I went along with Vijenderji and a few other men in what seemed to me to be quite an important reason for him to come to Tarn Taran.[31] Vijenderji was on a quest to acquire a manuscript of one Hira Singh, a Gulabdasi, about whom he had heard from another scholar who had earlier worked on the Gulabdasis. Manjit Singh, a resident of this city, he had heard, was in possession of the manuscript. To get to him we first went to a small electrical goods shop, whose owner knew Manjit Singh, and who was the contact for Vijenderji. This shopkeeper in turn took us to a larger shop of electrical goods run by the son of Manjit Singh, Navjot Singh. Manjit Singh, we were told, had had a bypass heart surgery and it was not possible to meet him. Vijenderji, in his characteristic way, impressed upon Navjot his great devotion to Gulabdas, by once again freely quoting from his verses, and persuading him of the urgency of his quest for the manuscript. Navjot promised to speak to his father, who apparently in his youth had contemplated writing a dissertation on the Gulabdasis, but had subsequently abandoned the idea. In the conversation that ensued in Navjot Singh's shop, where a few others were also present, Vijenderji got to know about an old Gulabdasi dera in a nearby village of Arsa. I am quite sure that in the future Vijenderji will not only pursue Hira Singh's text, but also find out more about the Arsa people, and if possible have them participate in the Gulabdasi festivities![32]

---

[31] Another important reason was that he could feed his two busloads of congregation a meal in the free kitchen run by the gurdwara, the institution of *langar* that is an integral part of almost all Sikh temples.

[32] I am happy to report that he managed to get hold of Hira Singh's manuscript.

FIGURE 8.1   Vijender Das (in white) with local villagers and Gulabdasi followers
in Ratol in August 2013.
Source: Courtesy of the author.

Vijenderji thus combines in his person the qualities of a devotee and a
self-trained scholar, a guru and a family man, an anchor for his people,
and a conduit for spreading the Gulabdasi legacy. He wears his many
hats with ease, never getting flustered, and told me quite categorically on
being asked if any of his roles clashed that he managed them with ease.
Above all, it is his organizational ability and exceptional energy that drive
his junoon (intoxication, craze), his *diwanāpan* (frenzy) for Gulabdas,
'Mata' Piro, and the Gulabdasi future.

STORIES AND THEIR PERFORMATIVE AFFECT

In this section I will relate two among the many stories in Vijenderji's
repertoire to highlight his inventive use of 'fictional' narratives for new
organizational and devotional ends. These relate to Gulabdas's birth and
death around which Vijenderji has choreographed the new festive occasion of the Gulabdasis. Birth and death, the beginning and the end of a
life cycle, are liminal events, 'transitional periods betwixt and between

the state of being and the state of not-yet or no-longer being'.[33] Anette Pankratz and Claus-Ulrich Viol see these periods as saturated with liminality, power, and performance in most cultures, marked by rituals and represented in multiple narratives. The threshold nature of birth and death imbues them with peculiar vulnerability, threatened by forces beyond human control, and, at the same time, immense power, as they open up in the human world a communicative event with the great unknown. In Hindu metaphysics, birth and death are linked to the cycle of rebirths (and re-deaths), and, therefore, these events allow a maw, an opening as it were, into the long saga of existence. The ritual and other (for example, medical) high priests of these events wield power that comes both from their liminal status and also from their representational and performative potential. It is the powerful imperative of birth and death then that Vijenderji seeks to harness, even as he refashions Gulabdasi narratives. The rituals that he builds around these moments work as ritual symbols do in Turner's analysis, condensing many references and uniting them in a single cognitive and affective field, but the one that I particularly wish to emphasize is the creation of communitas.[34]

THE STORY OF GULABDAS'S BIRTH

The first story I will relate here, which I have heard from Vijenderji, is regarding the birth of Gulabdas. The story is as follows.

'Mata' Desan and Amira Jat, the parents of Gulabdas, were childless for many years. Mata Desan prayed to the holy *Granthsahib*[35] in which she had great faith. Thanks to the grace of the Granth, a son was born to her—Gulabdas.[36]

---

[33] Anette Pankratz and Claus-Ulrich Viol, 'Introduction: Liminality, Power and Performance', in *Birth and Death in British Culture: Liminality, Power and Performance*, edited by Anette Pankratz, Claus-Ulrich Viol, and Ariane de Waal (Newcastle upon Tyne: Cambridge Scholars, 2012), p. 1.

[34] Victor Turner, 'Social Dramas and Ritual Metaphors', in his *Dramas, Fields, and Metaphors*, pp. 23–59.

[35] Granthsahib refers to the Adigranth of the Sikhs that was compiled in the early seventeenth century and has the teachings and hymns of the gurus.

[36] It is interesting that here a text is granted power to produce changes in human life rather than a saint or a guru.

Gulabdas was born smiling (*hanste hue*), and the excited *dāī* (midwife) ran off
to announce that some sant (saint) or avtār (reincarnation of god, typically
Vishnu) was born. He could also sit from birth. The child was from the very
beginning of a spiritual bent. Once when quite young, around seven years old,
while walking with his father, a *bhrol* (dust storm) carried him away, throwing
him in a *khū* (well). No one could find him for a long time. The mother, once
again, prayed to the Granth, taking the vow that she would let her son become
a sant if only he was located.[37] He was found deep in meditation in the well.
He asked his mother if he should become a sant now. The mother couldn't
bear the thought of parting from him and said 'no'. However, he left home and
family by the age of ten and embarked upon the path of sainthood.

Though this rather brief account of Gulabdas's birth and early childhood ends here, it has an afterlife, a postscript in our times. Sometime
around the year 2000, when Vijenderji started visiting Rajoki, he also felt
the urge to go to Ratol, the village of Gulabdas's birth. Joginder Singh
Bhatia, whose father, Sant Pyara Singh, was a close friend of Sant Bishan
Das, Vijenderji's grandfather, facilitated this quest. Both older men had
lived in Lyallpur (now Faislabad in Pakistani Punjab) before the partition of the country. Pyara Singh was a disciple of Dharamdas, another
follower of Gulabdas. On my sojourn with Vijenderji on 27 August 2013,
we had left Ratol to first visit Joginder Singh Bhatia's upper middle-class
home in the town of Patti, where Vijenderji's whole sangat (following)
of about two hundred people had been fed by Bhatiaji's household, a
custom this affluent shopkeeper of readymade garments has been following since 2000. On my quizzing Mrs Bhatia about their Gulabdasi
background, she informed me that her in-laws were Gulabdasi as her
father-in-law was such, and that she has seen them keeping in touch
with other Gulabdasis for over thirty years. Patti is about a forty-five
minute drive from Ratol, and Joginderji took Vijenderji there on
his request.

On that memorable day in Ratol when Vijenderji went there for the
first time, he informed me that he went straight to the site of Gulabdas's

---

[37] The making of the child into a sant is akin to a reciprocal bargain with god/
Granth; a 'gifting' back of the child for spiritual purposes or the work of god in return
for the 'gift' of (locating) the child.

birth. The place is a dump yard now as nothing would grow or prosper there, for instance, houses erected would fall, and the villagers used the space to throw garbage, though they were aware that it was Gulabdas's birthplace. Vijenderji stood on the heap of garbage and addressed the villagers for three hours. With tears streaming from his eyes, and in a 'flow', he begged the villagers to make this place one of remembrance for Gulabdas. The woman who owned this plot of land had a daughter-in-law who was two months pregnant, and was not keeping well. She asked for Vijenderji's help. Vijenderji just told her that from that day onwards she would be well and give birth to a son. This came to be. (Vijenderji told me as an aside that the Gulabdasis do not believe in superstitions, or in ghost and spirits—*bhūt-pret*—but at the same time informed me that Gulabdas too had helped many women conceive.) The woman then sold that plot of land to Vijenderji, who has gone on to erect an unpretentious house with an open courtyard, where he holds his annual function. In the future he hopes to make a more magnificent 'temple' for Gulabdas here.

FIGURE 8.2   Vijender Das and followers in the space marked for a temple in Ratol venerating the picture of Gulabdas.
Source: Courtesy of the author.

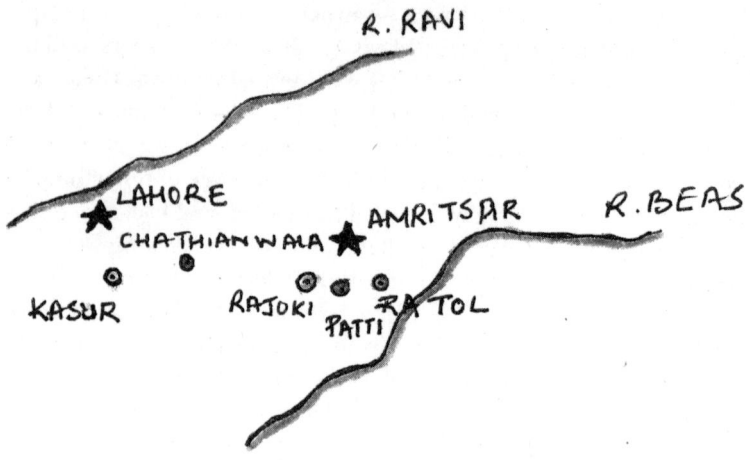

FIGURE 8.3 Map showing the sites in and around Amritsar, including the villages Ratol and Rajoki (the latter close to Chathianwala across the border) that are traversed annually by Vijender Das as part of the circumambulation of Gulabdasi sacred sites (map not to scale).
Source: Courtesy of Aditi Kodesia.

The rather recent sacralization of this site and the 'continuing' emana- tion of the fabulous here (no house built would stand), in what can now be seen as the combined preternatural power of Gulabdas and Vijenderji, has yet another episode. The descendants in this village of Gulabdas through the woman Dudhi (Darshan Kaur),[38] married to Sukhdev Singh, and her two sons were, to begin with, not quite enthused with Vijenderji's fervour for Gulabdas. However, when I visited Ratol on 27 August 2013, the home of this family was where Vijenderji and his family were stay- ing (despite having bought another house for themselves in this village), where I was offered refreshments, and this family was bearing some of the cost of the unfolding festivities. This change of heart, Sarojji informed me, was because ever since Gulabdas's birth festivities were initiated in the village, the family's business of selling milk to large companies like Amul had grown manifold, and concomitantly, so had their belief. Now they not only participated wholeheartedly, but also bore some costs on

---

[38] Vijenderji has explained the *vanshāvalī* (genealogy) of Gulabdas as the Ratol land being settled by Jaichand (the land, therefore, being referred to as *Jaichand kī paṭṭī*), whose son was Amira, the father of Gulabdas.

the occasion, Sukhdev accompanying Vijenderji in his peregrinations to other holy sites. Vijenderji has in fact made many converts in the village to the Gulabdasi cause who also as a part of his entourage (sangat) travel with him as he first visits Patti from Ratol and then Rajoki.[39] The main event that occurs on the morning of 28 August, celebrated as the day of Gulabdas's birth, when the Gulabdasi *darbārsāhib*[40] with its collection of the writings of Gulabdas and Piro is carried on the heads of the villagers, would not be possible if the whole village did not participate in these festivities. They wake at dawn, do a *prabhāt pherī*[41] (morning round) with the book on their heads, and congratulate each other on the 'birth' of Gulabdas.[42] This simple ceremony ensures the participation of the whole village in owning and claiming the Gulabdasi legacy.

Going back to the story of Gulabdas's birth, two strands stand out in that succinct account among others. The first is the one of his mother's inability to conceive, and her eventual success because of her extraordinary faith in the Sikh Granth. The second is that of the auspicious auguries that accompanied the birth of the child—he was born sitting and smiling for example, a developmental precocity and beatitude indexing the spiritual career that followed.[43] A third strand—of the child falling in the well at an early age is reminiscent of the saga of Puran Bhagat—a particularly multivalent motif that is able to combine and re-present the first two strands of the story, rendering them more meaningful.

The qissa of Puran Bhagat, a popular tale in Punjab, in brief is as follows: The strapping twelve-year-old Puran, son of the legendary king Salvan of Sialkot from his first wife Ichhran, was kept in a dark dungeon for the first twelve years of his life because of an adverse

---

[39] In 2013, when I accompanied Vijenderji and his family as they visited various Gulabdasi sites, there was another family that was making this trip for the first time. This was Saroj's sister, Madhu, her husband, and two children. Though this family had no faith as such in Gulabdas and knew little about him, they were here for therapeutic reasons. Madhu had not been keeping well, and they hoped that this 'pilgrimage' might help her get Gulabdas's blessing.

[40] Darbarsahib is how the Sikh Guru Granth is respectfully called, the text given a royal, courtly salutation. The Gulabdasis imitate the same gesture for their text.

[41] A ritual of walking through the village at dawn singing praises of Gulabdas.

[42] I did not witness this event but was informed of how Gulabdas's birth is celebrated bringing the festivities to an end.

[43] Auspicious events and auguries around the birth and death of holy figures is a common motif in India. See Chapter 5.

astrological prediction.[44] Salvan's young (and low-caste) second wife
Luna falls in love with him on seeing him and when Puran resists
her advances, Salvan, on the behest of Luna, orders his execution.
However, the executioner instead of killing him has his limbs chopped
off and thrown into a well. Puran stays meditating in the well for
another twelve years. When the legendary jogi Gorakhnath happens
to pass by the well, he has Puran taken out and restores his limbs by
sprinkling water on them. Puran spends the next twelve years with the
jogis, going back to his father's kingdom after that, but not before the
beautiful queen Sundran falls in love with him and later kills herself
because Puran does not wish to be tied down to worldly bonds. In
Sialkot, his true identity is revealed, and his father, childless all these
years and now repentant, begs Puran to stay and become the king.
Puran refuses, but grants a boon to the childless Luna that she would
bear a son, the legendary future Raja Rasalu.

The emotions and semiotics that the *Qissā Pūran Bhagat* explores are
myriad to which a short outline here cannot do justice. For instance, the
story is a Punjabi cultural example of the tale of Potiphar's wife, that is,
of a mother figure attracted to a son figure.[45] It is also about unrequited
love (of Luna and of the beautiful Sundran for Puran) and inappropriate
sexuality, as it is about the connection between the Punjabi landscape and
culture with the ubiquitous Nathpanthis or jogis, ever present in their
stories and accounts.[46] The initiation of Puran, and his incorporation
into the Nathpanthi way of life is presented in the qissa as a rebirth, as a
limbless, fetus-like Puran is re-birthed. Puran re-enters the world from
a womb-like well after what one may call an onerously long gestation of
twenty-four years, divided into twelve-year periods of tribulations.[47]

---

[44] The qissa of Puran Bhagat was a popular tale from Punjab. Its best exponent
was Qadir Yar (1802–1892), in Ranjit Singh's court. So pleased was the Maharaja with
this rendition that Qadir Yar was given a grant of land (*jāgīr*) with a well in it! Kartar
Singh Duggal, *Maharaja Ranjit Singh: The Last to Lay Arms* (New Delhi: Abhinav
Publications, 2001), p. 122. The legend was also collected by British folklorists
from oral performers of the qissa, among them Richard Temple, *The Legends of the
Punjab*, vol. 2 (Patiala: Language Department Punjab, 1988 [1884]), pp. 375–456.

[45] For a discussion on Oedipal themes in the South Asian context, see A.K.
Ramanujan, 'The Indian Oedipus', in Dharwadker, *The Collected Essays*, pp. 377–97.

[46] See the Introduction.

[47] Twelve years is a recurring motif in some legends. An ascetic, for instance, is
meant to visit his home after twelve years to confirm detachment from the family.

However, the dominant emotion which Vijenderji's narrative is attentive to is that of the excessive love of a mother for a son. The inability of
Ichhran to be with her son in the first twelve years of his life and then
his ostensible execution, and finally her joyous meeting him after she
has gone blind, literally crying her eyes out for her absent son, are deeply
emotional events which were played out in the renditions of Puran's
qissa.[48] The mother–son relationship has enormous traction in Punjab
and is a theme that is repeatedly encountered in its culture (and so the
revilement of Luna's taboo sexuality, as the elevation of Ichhran's pure
love)—whether the need to have a son to affirm a woman's place among
her affines, or the suffering of a mother (Ichhran) at the loss of a son
(Puran).[49] Vijenderji's narrative weaves rather skilfully this overwhelming
desire of Punjabi mothers for sons, as that of Gulabdas's mother or that
of the woman whose daughter-in-law's pregnancy matured and led to
the birth of a son in accordance with Vijenderji's blessing. Women who
traditionally took recourse (and still do) to holy men and visited various
sites for achieving reproductive success, whether a pir's mazar or a well,
is the leitmotif on which Vijenderji moulds his narrative. Puran Bhagat's
khuee, or the well of Puran Bhagat, in the village Chaprar, Sialkot, in
Pakistani Punjab, still attracts women who go to bathe in its waters to fulfil their desire for children, as does Luna's *baolī* or step-well in the village
Chamiari, near Ajnala, in the Indian Punjab.[50] Significantly, Vijenderji

[48] My mother, who had memorized parts of the qissa as a child, would often
render Ichhran's laments for her lost son with tears in her eyes and a catch in
her voice: *Maiṅ vī lae āwāṅ dārū akhiyāṅ dā, Pūran chaḍ nā gayā savād koī; akhāṅ
hovaṇ te put lab lavāṅ, bolī valoṅ maiṅ put sanjānyaī* (I too would get medicine for
the eyes, Puran has left me without taste; if I had eyes I would have found my son,
I have recognized him from his speech).

[49] The example of Dani Jatti is one such where she brings back a dead son to
life through the grace of pir Sakhi Sarvar. For a discussion on this example, and
for the culture of visiting saints' graves for boons of sons, see Anshu Malhotra,
Gender, Caste and Religious Identities: Restructuring Class in Colonial Punjab
(New Delhi: Oxford University Press, 2002), pp. 176–9. The obverse side of this
son-preference culture is the adverse sex ratio in Punjab. See Anshu Malhotra,
'Shameful Continuities: The Practice of Female Infanticide in Colonial Punjab', in
Sikhism and Women: History, Texts and Experience (New Delhi: Oxford University
Press, 2010), pp. 83–114.

[50] On the Chaprar village, see Muhammad Hassan Miraj, 'Pooran Bhagat',
available at http://www.dawn.com/news/755152/pooran-bhagat/2. On Chamiarai,
see http://www.Kartarpur/Arch/Chamiari.htm, last accessed on 8 November 2013.

FIGURE 8.4   The well in Ratol where Gulabdas is said to have fallen. It is now covered, cleaned, and marked as a Gulabdasi site.
Source: Courtesy of the author.

has 'located' in Ratol the well where Gulabdas fell, and has had it cleaned, its sides painted, and its mouth covered with a wire mesh, part of his attentive marking of sacred Gulabdasi sites (see Figure 8.4).

Thus his narrative, by playing with familiar themes and symbols—mothers and sons, holy men (and books) and reproduction, wells and spirituality—builds on a cultural palimpsest on which many a story has been written or orally transmitted in Punjab. It is not the veracity of the story that is the question here. As I have discussed in Chapter 1, there are other more 'historical' accounts of Gulabdas's birth and early career. Nor is there any reason to call it a 'forgery', as Davis notes, as its apocryphal artifice adorns bare facts with mythical possibilities, which indeed is the point. It is the moulding of the story, narrating and performing it to a

---

In the Indian Punjab, women also go to the Vaishnav establishment in Dhianpur, Gurdaspur district, near the city of Batala, which has a step-well where they bathe and look for boons of children. I know of two female relatives who have 'bathed' here and attributed subsequent successful pregnancies to this.

culture's unique predilection that is important. Its performative affect draws spectators from varied perspectives, families and followers, other Gulabdasi participants, villagers and hangers-on, and those scattered about, close to the site and into an enchanted circle, living Gulabdasi religiosity in that special time.[51]

THE STORY OF GULABDAS'S DEATH

In the following story, Vijenderji ties up Gulabdas's death (*jyotī jyot*, literally the merging of flames, divine and human) with that of two of his followers Gurmukh Das and Jawahir Singh. The story is as follows.

Gulabdas knew of his death seven days before it occurred, and rode on his mare to his orchard in Rajoki to meet his two loyal disciples/servants (*sevak*s) Gurmukh Das and Jawahir Singh. The two disciples had selflessly served the master. Gurmukh Das, the eldest among his disciples, was in charge of running the kitchen in the dera at Chathianwala, and so Gulabdas addressed him fondly as his *betī* (daughter). Jawahir Singh was responsible for keeping accounts (*māyā*, here money). When the time of his death came, Gulabdas stepped close to his own grave next to Piro's (who had died a year earlier), and gave his turban/*mukuṭ* (crown) to Gurmukh Das, he being the eldest.[52] Gurmukh Das, in turn, placed the turban/crown on the head of Hargobind (Gulabdas's adopted son and his chosen successor). Both disciples also expressed their desire to die with Gulabdas. Gulabdas told them to take *samādhī* at Rajoki, which they did. The two disciples' samadhis, represented as two protruding circular juttings on the floor—tumuli (*thambū*)—are in a tomb-like structure in Rajoki—Gurmukh Das' on the right (*daiṅ*) and Jawahir Singh's on the left (*baiṅ*).

<hr>

[51] For different perspectives of the viewers, depending on from where they may be viewing the spectacle of Ramnagar Ramlila as it unfolds, see Richard Schechner, 'Ramlila of Ramnagar: An Introduction', in Schechner, *Performative Circumstances*, pp. 238–88.

[52] In 2010 Vijenderji spoke of a turban (*pagrī*) while in 2013 he called it a crown (*mukuṭ*).

There are four aspects of this rather sketchy story that are of particular interest. The first is the ambiguity about where the incidents described were occurring—Chathianwala or Rajoki. Did Gulabdas 'give up' his life in Rajoki, where the two tumuli are present or in Chathianwala, where Piro and Gulabdas are buried? While writing the story down I had to consult my notes constantly, as I was not quite sure of what Vijenderji had told me on two different occasions, 2010 and 2013, and I may have created greater clarity in my re-rendition of the story than in fact existed in Vijenderji's account. It is as if the proximity of the two places, and ironically the great chasm between the two due to the Partition, has also made them interchangeable. It is an ambiguity, I will suggest, that is deliberately built into the story. The slippage between Chathianwala just across the border, and Rajoki accessible here and now (however, without the guru's grave or tomb) can be said to allow for transferring the charisma of that place here. The lack of the guru's remains in Rajoki, one may suggest, is compensated for by the mention of the guru's visit, the reference to his orchard, and ultimately to the advice to his two disciples to take samadhi here. As Eck has suggested, what is deeply desired and spiritually significant can be duplicated, and Vijenderji certainly attempts to duplicate partly the Chathianwala effect in Rajoki (see Figure 8.5).

A second aspect further underscores the point about interchangeability on the one hand, but also brings in the question of displacement on the other. While the tomb in Chathianwala is a testament to the close relations between Gulabdas and Piro, the guru and his foremost disciple buried side by side, the samadhis at Rajoki can be said to displace Piro as

FIGURE 8.5 The tomb at Rajoki under repair that houses the *samadhis* of the two Gulabdasi disciples Gurmukh Das and Jawahir Singh.
Source: Courtesy of the author.

his closest disciple, and confer that honour to Gurmukh Das and Jawahir Singh. Of course, what is at stake in Gulabdas's death, in Chathianwala or Rajoki, is its ability to sacralize the space where he died, or more accurately in the case of Rajoki, where he advised his two loyal sevaks to take samadhi.

Piro's loss as the foremost disciple can be said to be the gain of Gurmukh Das and Jawahir Singh to that elevated status. That Piro's background in prostitution has been a source of continual embarrassment to the sect is important to remember, as I have discussed in the last chapter. Vijenderji acknowledges her past in prostitution, but glosses it as born out of helplessness and compensates for it by emphasizing her inherent spiritual tendencies. According to Vijenderji, the Titookhera branch descendants of Gulabdas, through his adopted son Hargobind, do not speak about her because of her disreputable profession and her *chhotī jātī* (low caste). Condemning their thinking as petty, Vijenderji projects himself as a person who is respectful of her, reveres her as his mother, transforming her sexually ambiguous status to a normalized maternal one in the sect. In 2007, when I had met Vijenderji's saintly sister Rajenderji in Hansi, on learning about my work on Piro, she had told me to write all that is 'correct', and not write the 'wrong stuff', which perhaps meant that I was not to mention either Piro's past profession or her relationship with the guru. Today, many of the Gulabdasis often do not know about Piro, or not know much, and one can say that the displacement of the central sacred site from Chathianwala to Ratol/Rajoki has meant her relative eclipse from Gulabdasi memory.

A third noteworthy aspect is the deliberate play with the word 'samadhi'. The semantic range of the word moves from meditation/concentration/contemplation to a mystical experience of trance. It also refers to self-immolation, especially through entombment of an ascetic, to the place where such an entombment, cremation, or a burial may have taken place, or the ashes of a saintly figure may lie buried.[53] Vijenderji's narrative combines these meanings, but in his telling, death is self-willed, without any external aid, not only of guru Gulabdas but also of the disciples. It is the holiest of the saints who can predict when they will leave their mortal body, and all the more holy, who do it at will. The saintliness of Gulabdas, in Vijenderji's telling, grants even the disciples the power to die because

[53] R.S. McGregor, *The Oxford Hindi–English Dictionary* (New Delhi: Oxford University Press, 2004 [1993]); *Punjabi University Punjabi–English Dictionary* (Patiala: Publications Bureau Punjabi University, 1994).

the guru wills so. The samadhis of the disciples, marked by a couple of protuberances on the floor of a tomb in Rajoki, have to then perform the task of the absent grave of the guru.

Finally, we need to pay attention to the symbolic significance of Gulabdas first putting his turban/crown on Gurmukh Das, through which he transferred his authority to him, who in turn passed it on to Hargobind, the central action in the story as it were.[54] This depicts Gurmukh—as the oldest disciple of the guru—as the rightful claimant of his seat/gaddi. We can also read this as Gurmukh being the first successor to Gulabdas, and Hargobind as the second. Vijenderji's narrative does not question the credentials of Hargobind; he did after all succeed to the Chathianwala gaddi. The attempt is to give commensurate importance to Gurmukh, who emerges as the chosen successor to Gulabdas at the time of the latter's death, chosen in appreciation of the selfless service he performed for his guru. While Vijenderji on his own steam can hardly rival the superior claims of the Titookhera branch to being the most 'authentic' successor to Gulabdas (Gulabdas had after all adopted Hargobind), Gurmukh's story can, in the least, lend legitimacy to Rajoki, making it a place of Gulabdasi significance.[55] Since the salience of Rajoki has been recognized and celebrated only by Vijenderji, it establishes an important relationship between the two. That the Titookhera people are not entirely convinced or enthused by Vijenderji's activities, as he has confessed to me, comes out clearly in their ostensible accusation of Vijenderji taking away their livelihood and 'business'. That the 'business' of spirituality breeds rivalries today is an incontestable inference drawn from this story, especially as multiple gurus seek to increase their following from among similar constituencies.

As in Ratol, another process worth tracking here is Vijenderji's relations with the villagers of Rajoki, and, more importantly, of his ability to persuade them to participate in this Gulabdasi festival with fervour. In 2013 when I visited Rajoki with Vijenderji and his entourage, we were welcomed very warmly by the locals in this border village, who had also organized for Vijenderji's convenience the space around the central shrine for people to sit around, and for the ceremonies to unfold.

---

[54] There are many parallels between kingly authority and that of a saint, including similar symbolic insignia of power. The moment of succession—the passing on of the seat of power, whether spiritual or temporal—is the liminal moment that can be conflict ridden. See footnote xx.

[55] *PP* mentions Gulabdas's adoption of Hargobind from the potters' caste.

On the dusty space inside the tomb, and around the central shrine, they had spread some freshly cut grass on top of which *darīs* (thick cotton carpets) were laid out for the sangat to sit on. There was a mike in the space between the two thambus, and various paraphernalia had been provided for the rituals. After recalling the story of the two disciples, Vijenderji had exhorted his followers to make liberal donations so this tomb structure, which was under repair, could be brought back to its pristine glory. The ritual consisted of washing the thambus with half a bucket of milk by Vijenderji and other Gulabdasi heads from various centres and lighting incense, followed by a *parīkramā* (going around the sanctum) (see Figure 8.6).

After this the audience could come to 'touch their foreheads' (*mathā teknā*) here, paying traditional obeisance, give a little money, and receive prashad. Singing of bhajans accompanied these ceremonies, with particularly one young Gulabdasi from Ratauli who is a part of Vijenderji's entourage singing on his own for a fairly long time while playing the *dholak* drum. Thus, these various rituals were able to draw in not only his sangat, but also almost the entire village—men, women, and children— into the celebrations. Many places in the village resembled various sites of performance and festivity, separate and yet collectively braided together in the Gulabdasi fair. These rituals resembled the ones in Ratol, where in the morning people had come to Gulabdas's birthplace for matha tekna, make offerings, sing songs, and receive prashad. Later, the congregation of Vijenderji was fed at a langar by the young men of Rajoki, a meal that consisted of sweet rice, *rotī* (bread), and *dāl* (lentils).

FIGURE 8.6   Inside the tomb in Rajoki, Vijender Das and another Gulabdasi perform the ritual cleaning of the *thambūs*. Locals and other Gulabdasi followers can be seen in the background.
Source: Courtesy of the author.

How did the predominantly Sikh Rajoki villagers, where Vijenderji first came only in 2000, come to participate so wholeheartedly in this Gulabdasi ceremony? Vijenderji had told me earlier in 2010 that the Rajoki villagers treated this space as a gurdwara, a Sikh temple, and when he had gone there in 2000, they had to lift up their holy Granth for him to locate the two thambus, which they now do every year to facilitate the ceremonies. That year when he had washed them with milk, the tumuli had turned red, affirming the momentousness of the occasion and the sacredness of the space. Apparently, the villagers have founded some kind of a 'society' that is now undertaking the repair of the site, and their source of income is a seven-acre cultivated plot of land around this area that was once Gulabdas's orchard. Vijenderji took me around the area, marking the theatrical site of his performance I suggest, showing me a well from the old times, and Gulabdas's stable, where he told me that the guru had kept his favourite mares, Lakhi and Lado. The villagers have also discovered in this structure under repair twenty-four kilos of gold that came from the pillars (as an ornamentation that was melted?) and are now determined to put it back (as decoration?) when the tomb is fully repaired.[56] I was also introduced to an old Sikh who remembered this site as a Gulabdasi one before the Partition, and who recalled an incident from the time of Jagjit Bahadur (the great grandson of Hargobind) when the roof of this edifice (*imārat*) had fallen during a fair (*melā*).[57]

Again, it is not important to know if Gulabdas had in fact visited this area just before he died, or the likely apocryphal nature of his interaction with Gurmukh and Jawahir, considering the guru had nominated Hargobind as his successor. The Rajoki story of Gulabdas's demise, howsoever fabulous, is built upon an existing edifice, the 'fiction' resting upon the solid materiality of a tomb. It beckons through Vijenderji's performative skill and devotional fervour those willing to be drawn into its magic, and it seems there are many who are happy to be led into the enchanted world of the Gulabdasi sacred.

[56] Vijenderji told me another story of how this gold was taken to a goldsmith (*sunār*) who on seeing so much gold became greedy (*nīyat kharāb ho gaī*, his intentions became bad) and told the villagers it was brass (*pital*), but then later retracted and told them the truth. The fact that he could not sustain the lie is seen as an example of Gulabdas's grace in this place.

[57] Jagjit Bahadur (b. 1914) had lost a daughter in this episode though his wife had been saved.

RELIGION, CASTE, AND GENDERED IMAGININGS TODAY

Dominant Religions and Gulabdasi Appropriations

So far in this chapter we have seen the Gulabdasi re-imaginings of the sacred, the attempt to anchor its sacred to certain spaces—and vocalize it through stories—that are meaningful in the present. The link with the past is created through reworked myths, rituals, and histories, and re-presented and performed in ways that make sense to the leaders and followers today. In Vijenderji's narrative, historical and mythological memories coalesce to beget the Gulabdasi present and a vision of the future, a future that seems to hold the hope for greater participation and more spectacular presence among the peoples of north India. However, at this moment of euphoria for the future, it may be pertinent to see how the Gulabdasis can be seen against what were in the past their salient characteristics, what had set them apart from the ordinary and the commonplace life. By looking at its present religious, caste, and gendered imaginings, as I have observed at different occasions, I hope to comment on its changed outlook, along with what appear as significant continuities with the past.

As discussed in previous chapters, philosophically the Gulabdasis adhered to advaita vedanta's idea of the oneness of Brahman and Jiva, the divine and human, imbibed through Gulabdas's early years under Udasi and Nirmala teachers. When Gulabdas called himself Brahm, he also envisioned the possibility of all humanity being one with god, an important reason for opening their dera to people from all religions and castes. The emotional appeal, as, for instance, in Piro's writings, was in tune with bhakti devotion, which she enhanced for her own reasons through the openings that the Gulabdasis developed in their piety. She directed her devotion towards the guru, the conduit in her cosmos between god and the human world. Historically, as Piro emphasized in her many writings, the bhakti saints came from all castes, but many were from the lowest, making the Gulabdasi sect a multi-caste entity. Thus, the theological, philosophical, and social systems imbibed by the Gulabdasis made them socially radical, a point they chose to highlight by speaking of their opposing the varnashramadharma. At the same time, in the cultural world of the mid-nineteenth century, the Gulabdasis were seen as inheritors of certain legacies identified with Sikh sects, whether the Udasis or the Nirmalas, and in many ways as part of a more accommodative 'Hindu' identity. I will now briefly comment on the forms of religiosity, as viewed in relation to the commonly understood attributes of Hindu, Sikh, and Islamic identities, and see how the Gulabdasis have interacted and appropriated from them while maintaining their distinction.

Let me start with Gulabdasi relations with Islam, both because Piro was Muslim in her early life and because she wrote of conflict with the Muslims, even if her wider spiritual message was inclusive. Indeed, perceived conflict with Muslims and Islam in contemporary India has a cultural ubiquity that belies the actual presence of Muslims as a minority in the country, though a substantial minority in sheer numbers. In Punjab, particularly as a result of the contentious history of Partition that involved dividing the state between India and Pakistan, the sanguinary riots that accompanied it, and because of the appeal of the rhetoric of the Hindu Right, Islam is often presented as the other of Sikhs and Hindus.[58] Historically too Sikh identity, particularly as worked out in the rahit literature, seemingly built itself against and in conflict with Islam, though there were multiple other possibilities and mitigating factors on the ground, among them demotic interaction, shared devotional traditions that venerated Sufi pirs, popular performative traditions, sects like the Gulabdasis that embraced all, and much more. The dominant visual representations of Sikh history—as, for instance, in the gurdwara at Tarn Taran dedicated to the fifth guru Arjan Dev that I visited during Gulabdasi festivities, which has a museum studded with paintings—work on the emotional frame of torture of Sikh martyrs by the then Muslim rulers of Punjab.[59] Of course, from the late nineteenth century some Sikhs worked more consciously towards separating their identity from that of the Hindus, and more so in the late twentieth century, an issue to be discussed later.

Privileged as I was to be a member of the 'backstage' of Vijenderji's family as they traversed over Gulabdasi sacred sites, anti-Islamism raised its head on a number of occasions. Here, I will give two examples to indicate a sense of its commonplace pervasiveness. It must be remembered

---

[58] The ruling Shiromani Akali Dal (SAD) is an ally of the Hindu Right wing Bhartiya Janata Party (BJP), now in power at the center since 2014 with an overwhelming mandate.

[59] Similar themes, particularly in the context of Sis Ganj Gurudwara in Delhi, were discussed by Kanika Singh in her paper 'Representation of Heritage in Museums on Sikh History' in the conference on *New Perspectives on Punjab Studies: Rethinking Historiography* held at the Nehru Memorial Museum and Library, New Delhi, on 29–30 April 2015.

that Rajoki is a border village, and as you approach it, you begin to encounter bunkers set up by the Indian army and barbed wire fence on the border, making you aware of the 'enemy' beyond a few kilometres. Early in the month of August in a border violation in Kashmir, the Indian army had accused its Pakistani counterpart of killing five of its soldiers, exacerbating the tension palpably felt at the border when I visited the area.[60] It is also pertinent to mention that Vijenderji's sangat, including his family, had the previous evening witnessed with great touristy enthusiasm the rather nasty but popular histrionics played out daily at the Wagah border, staged by the Indian and Pakistani army in practiced patriotic unison.[61] On our way from Patti to Rajoki (Vijenderji was not in the hired Innova with us) the conversation turned to Pakistan and its Muslim population. It started with Vijenderji's son showing on his phone a particular Facebook post on the lionizing of Nathuram Godse, Mahatama Gandhi's assassin.[62] The driver of the Innova at this instance interrupted with what is an oft-used Hindu Right rhetoric that all the Muslims of India should have gone to Pakistan, and someone voiced another rhetorical gem, that 'Muhammadans' had been left behind to increase their population in India. My intervention at this instant that such propaganda sat ill with their Gulabdasi inheritance had the salutary effect of bringing the unsavoury conversation to a close. However, on our way back from Rajoki (this time with Vijenderji in the vehicle) the theme

[60] Available at http://timesofindia.indiatimes.com/India/Indian-soldiers-were-sitting-ducks-in-August-6-ambush-due-to-tactical-lapses/articleshow/21983927. cms, last accessed on 20 November 2013. I re-read this part of the chapter on 28 July 2015, the day after three terrorists entered the town of Dinanagar in the Punjab border district of Gurdaspur and killed at least three civilians and three police personnel. More recently still, on 2 January 2016, the Pathankot Air Force Station was attacked by terrorists in which six security personnel died. It is as if relations between the two Punjabs, Indian and Pakistani, are caught in an eerie time warp.

[61] On the Wagah drama see Virender S. Kalra and Navtej K. Purewal, 'The Strut of the Peacocks: Partition, Travel and the Indo–Pak Border', in *Travel Worlds: Journeys in Contemporary Cultural Politics*, edited by Raminder Kaur and John Hutnyk (London: Zed Books, 1999), pp. 54–67.

[62] Since this was written in 2013 and after the BJP government came into power at the centre in May 2014, there have been concerted efforts by the 'fringe elements' of the Sangh *parivār*, the Hindu right wing 'family', to build Godse busts and declare him a patriot. See, for example, http://timesof india.indiatimes.com/city/meerut/UP-BJP-Hindu-Mahasabha-fight-over-Godse-busts/articleshow/456171233.cms, last accessed on 26 January 2015.

was picked up again. Someone said that the villagers had complained that even if their buffaloes stray into Pakistani territory their soldiers do not spare them. Apparently, the black colour of the buffaloes reminded someone of the black dresses of the Pakistani soldiers in the Wagah performance, and that the colour did not look nice. Sarojji then commented that the Muslims kept their women in black *burqās* (veils), so why not men in black uniforms? The inanity of the comment that evoked mild titters and a brush off from Vijenderji shows the pervasiveness of marking out Muslims as the others.

Ironically, we were headed towards Lakhna village, just a couple of kilometres from Rajoki, to visit the mazar (the shrine around the site of a grave) of Muhammad Shah, a Muslim disciple of Gulabdas, while the rest of the sangat headed for Tarn Taran and the Sikh gurdwara. This short detour Vijenderji organized for my benefit for he knew I would be keen to look around this village, as I was aware of Muhammad Shah's Gulabdasi background, and I think also because he wished to assert that his dera was open to people from all religions and castes. What I encountered in Lakhna took me by surprise, because this was an active religious place, eclectic in its collection of godly figures. In the centre of a square room was Mohammad Shah's grave, over it a decorated roof, the grave covered respectfully with green sheets, reminiscent of Sufi sheikhs (see Figure 8.7).

FIGURE 8.7   The *mazār* of Mohammad Shah with the pir's slippers kept respectfully and the pictures of gods and goddesses on a ledge.
Source: Courtesy of the author.

There was also a smaller grave, towards a corner of the room, and at a lower level, which was that of Mir Shah, presumably a devoted disciple. Remarkably, Sufi pirs, Hindu gods and goddesses, Sikh gurus, in pictures and posters, stuck on the wall and kept on ledges, surrounded this shrine to Muhammad Shah. One door to the shrine had the celebrated Hindu godly couple Shiv and Parvati painted on it (see Figure 8.8); another had an etching of Muhammad Shah and Mir Shah (see Figure 8.9). There was also a copy of the Quran, and a pair of *khadāoṅs* (wooden slippers) of the pir. A picture of Gulabdas, commonly available in Gulabdasi functions, was also present. Another picture, Vijenderji insisted, was that of Gulabdas shown with a beard in the 'Muslim fashion'. The keeper of this motley shrine, a Sikh, dressed as a Sufi in black clothes and a green turban, gave us a little prashad of puffed rice and sugar candy. Then he took

FIGURE 8.8   A door panel with Shiva and Parvati carved on it.
Source: Courtesy of the author.

FIGURE 8.9 A panel on the door in Lakhna village with the image of Mohammad Shah. Inscribed over it is 'Pir Baba Mohammad Shah Ji'.
Source: Courtesy of the author.

us to another smaller room just outside the shrine where there was *dhūnī* or a fire pit with some iron rods in it, and a large *nagāṛā* drum hung on the wall. On my asking him if there were any Muslims in the village at all, he told me that this was a totally Sikh village, but that the villagers looked after this place, a recurring trend in contemporary Punjab.[63]

[63] In recent years a desire to preserve mosques and other abandoned religious spaces has been noticed in Punjab. See Anshu Malhotra and Farina Mir, 'Punjab in History and Historiography: An Introduction', in *Punjab Reconsidered: History, Culture and Practice*, eds Anshu Malhotra and Farina Mir (New Delhi: Oxford University Press, 2012), pp. xlviii–xlix. Also see Anna Bigelow, 'Post-Partition Pluralism: Placing Punjab in Indian Punjab', in *Punjab Reconsidered*, pp. 409–34. Anna Bigelow also comments on how most Sufi shrines in Punjab today are managed by non-Muslims, Malerkotla being an exception. See Bigelow, *Sharing the Sacred*, p. viii. The scholar Yogesh Snehi has studied multiple Sufi shrines in the Indian Punjab maintained and run by non-Muslims.

Three points need to be made about this extraordinary shrine at Lakhna. First, one can assume that the villagers may have converted a Sufi shrine of 'Pir Baba' Muhammad Shah since independence to its present eclectic state with its assortment of gods, goddesses, and gurus. This recasting as a temple/shrine complex may be more meaningful to them, one to which they could relate, especially in the absence of any Muslims who could facilitate their interaction with the mazar. That they actively maintained this place is apparent in its clean ambience and shiny pictures, and in the distribution of food offerings. Second, Muhammad Shah, however close he may have been to Gulabdas (Lakhna, Rajoki, and Chathianwala are adjacent villages), must have run this place as an independent establishment. Perhaps, he was one of the many followers of Gulabdas who set up his independent establishment.

Third, and significantly, Muhammad Shah's grave-shrine fits in rather well with the Gulabdasi tradition of making tombs on the grave sites or cremation platforms of their gurus and favoured disciples, as with that of Gulabdas and Piro at Chathianwala, and Gurmukh Das and Jawahir Singh at Rajoki. Gulabdas and Piro preferred to be buried rather than cremated, showing their affinity to the Sufi practices of Punjab, leaving their disciples with a permanent structure they could revere subsequently, as our historical records show. In an odd way, the syncretism at display in Lakhna at Muhammad Shah's shrine, howsoever bewildering to an outsider in today's Indian Punjab, may be said to capture a broad inclusive spirit of the Gulabdasis.

Importantly, Vijenderji has attributed both the stories discussed in this chapter, of Gulabdas's birth in Ratol, and his disciples' samadhis at Rajoki, and in fact even the oral recounting of Piro's early life, to a low-caste and Muslim Mirasi follower of Gulabdas called Milkhi Das/ Milkhi Shah. According to Vijenderji, Milkhi Shah had his own *takia* (seat) at village Kandola Kalan, near Nurmahal, close to Jalandhar. He is said to have been born in 1884, a little over a decade after the death of Gulabdas, and is said to have died only in 1989, at the age of 105. The author of a work called *Hidāyat Nāmā*, a compendium of advice, Vijenderji quite literally attributes to him a repertoire of advice stories that have allowed him to refashion Gulabdasi religiosity. One may, therefore, say that asserting openness towards Muslims and an inclusivity that reaches out to all peoples remains saliently an ideology of the sect that Vijenderji wishes to propagate despite some of his people absorbing aspects of the prevalent divisive rhetoric ubiquitous in north India.

Gulabdasis may be said to be at home with both Sikhism and Hinduism, as their philosophical inclinations and devotional métier emerges from within the commodious pluralism that defined these collectivities in the early nineteenth century.[64] However, as discussed in this book, for Piro, a broad 'Hindu' identity included most Sikhs within its ambit, excluding the Khalsa. Though most of Vijenderji's followers, and indeed the sangat that had assembled from places like Alwar in Rajasthan and Yamunanagar, Hansi, and Hissar in Harayana, were non-Sikhs, they mixed easily with the Sikhs of Ratol, Rajoki, and Patti. This is worth pointing out because Vijenderji had told me in 2010 that Ratol had a reputation of being sympathetic to the idea of a separate Sikh homeland (he used the term *garam daliye*—supporters of the hot or radical group—to describe them), when the movement for Khalistan had been at its peak in the late 1970s and the 1980s.[65] Indeed, the countryside in and around the cities of Tarn Taran and Amritsar in this border area is dotted with Sikh gurdwaras, dedicated to various Sikh gurus and martyrs, so that the dominant Sikh religious affiliation in the Indian Punjab is visually evident everywhere. However, none of this stopped the many villagers of Ratol and Rajoki from participating in Gulabdasi ceremonies wholeheartedly. In Rajoki, one may recall that what for the villagers is a functioning gurdwara is temporarily vacated for Gulabdasi rituals. I also saw serious young men bearing the five symbols of the Khalsa sit gravely through the ceremonies conducted by Vijenderji in Rajoki.[66] This comfort with eclectic religiosity is in a fundamental sense a part of South Asian popular culture. As Farina Mir has argued in relation to worship at Sufi shrines by tracking its popular literary representation in the colonial period, this was an aspect of Punjabi life across all religious communities, a reflection of piety that did not detract from other religious affiliations.[67] Specifically

---

[64] Speaking about the difficulty in defining what might be called Hinduism, essentially a reflection of its diversity, Doniger writes that it may be compared to a 'Zen' diagram that has no central ring, as against a Venn diagram. See Wendy Doniger, *The Hindus: An Alternative History* (New Delhi: Penguin/Viking, 2009), pp. 28–9.

[65] On the Khalistan movement, see Giorgio Shani, *Sikh Nationalism and Identity in a Global Age* (New York: Routledge, 2008), pp. 40–99.

[66] On the Five Ks and the evolution of these Khalsa symbols over time, see W.H. McLeod, 'The Five Ks', in his *Essays in Sikh History, Tradition, and Society* (New Delhi: Oxford University Press, 2007), pp. 115–23.

[67] Mir, 'Genre and Devotion in Punjabi Popular Narratives: Rethinking Cultural and Religious Syncretism', in Malhotra and Mir, *Punjab Reconsidered*, pp. 221–60.

in this case the easy acceptance of Gulabdasi ceremonials is only partly because Gulabdas was seen to be from a Sikh lineage, though Vijenderji is quite clearly a non-Sikh. It is because people are empathetic to varied and mystical manifestations of the divine presence among humans that works, though familiarity with certain rituals and material instruments of faith helps. There are some similarities of the Gulabdasi symbolic world with that of Sikhism. For example, the book that has some of the writings of Gulabdas and Piro is given by the Gulabdasis the status of their own holy book (carried on their heads when announcing the birth of Gulabdas) and is called the *Darbar Sahib* in imitation of Sikh reference to the *Adi Granth*. It is kept in folds of silken cloth like the Sikh book. It may also be mentioned that the repudiation of venerating living gurus among the Sikhs is a modern phenomenon, polemically argued by the Lahore Singh Sabha only in the last decade of the nineteenth century.[68] That there were then many Sikhs ranged against it, and continue to be so, must also be remembered.[69]

Finally, the Gulabdasi world in many ways may be defined as 'Hindu', if we understand Hinduism as what its adherents believe it is. Wendy Doniger has sought to explain 'alternative Hinduisms' by insisting that 'different Hindus not only lived different Hinduisms but privileged different aspects of Hinduism'.[70] The Gulabdasis may be said to privilege the guru, and his Vedantic philosophy, into which Vijenderji was initiated at a young age. According to Vijenderji, the Gulabdasis ultimately aim towards self-realization, the residing of Brahma(n) within them. It is only when this realization occurs (*bodh hone ke bād*) that the difference between a guru and a disciple disappears, but presumably till then the guru remains the guiding beacon. However, the devotion that Vijenderji displays towards the founder-guru Gulabdas resembles that which one may have for a godly being. The rituals conducted by Vijenderji at Ratol or Rajoki, the veneration of the pictures of Gulabdas, the burning of incense, the singing of devotional songs or the distribution of consecrated food is very similar to popular Hinduism that one witnesses in temples and homes. I suggest that Vijenderji's ritualistic practices smack of popular Hinduism more than might be present in some other Gulabdasi deras.

---

[68] See Chapter 6.

[69] Prominent among these groups are the Nirankaris, Namdharis, and the many Dalit deras.

[70] Doniger, *The Hindus*, p. 32.

I have witnessed groups from other deras—Alwar, Yamunanagar—perform in both 2007 and 2013. The use of simple instruments, the single-stringed ektara and a water pot (*maṭkā*) with rubber stretched over its mouth were used by them to sing songs in a gentle manner that emphasized the immortality of the soul and the happiness to be had in the company of the guru.

> *Satguru ke des baso nirmohī*
> *Yahāṅ base sukh hoī*
> O deathless one, live in the country of the guru
> To dwell here is to be happy.

Or even the more reverential:

> *Āj mhāre raṅg barse*
> *Satgurujī āye mhāre pāvanā.*
>
> Colour rains here today
> Satguru has come to my place.[71]

These can be contrasted to those sung more often by women on the dholak, from among the core group of Vijenderji's followers, where satguru is praised as divine, and women sing loudly together. In my notes I had written of it as 'visually psychedelic religiosity', comparable to the proliferating *bhajan maṇḍalīs* (devotional song groups) that one encounters everywhere in middle-class Hindu religiosity.

An interesting example of 'Hinduization' is seen in the *Ārtī mātā Pirojī kī* that Vijenderji has appended to his collection of her writings.[72] Arti involves devotional hymns sung to a god/goddess at the end of a ritual, and is usually accompanied with lit lamps waved around idols of gods. The most popular arti in north India is sung to Jagdish, the lord of the world, and Vijenderji's arti to 'Mother Piro' resembles in parts this hymn.

> *Jai Pīro mātā, satguru jaī Pīro mātā*
> *Tumko jo jan dhyāve, ichhit phala pātā.*
>
> Victory to mother Piro, satguru, Victory to mother Piro
> Whoever meditates on your name, receive the desires of their heart.[73]

---

[71] These devotional songs were heard and noted by the author in 2013.

[72] Sant Vijender Das, ed, *Sant Kavyitri Ma Piro* (Panchkula: Satluj Prakashan, 2011), p. 240.

[73] Das, *Sant Kavyitri Ma Piro*, p. 240

These resemble the words of *Om jai jagdīsh hare ... jo dhyāve phala pāve* (Victory to the lord of the world ... whoever meditates on you receives their desires).

I wish to emphasize that whatever the relations and interactions of the Gulabdasis with the dominant Indian religions of north India might be, and these are bound to have traction when people at various points of time forefront different identities, they have nevertheless maintained a distinctive identity that comes from their core devotion to Gulabdas and his ideas. The eclecticism that seems to be at display at various Gulabdasi celebrations should not take away from a desire to propagate a Gulabdasi identity, in ways that can make sense to its growing number of adherents. By leaning on popular Hinduism, Sikhism, or Islam, and indeed by accepting a Gulabdasi identity that did not negate other identities one may possess, the Gulabdasis may be seen to be appropriating aspects of these religions that work in tandem with their ideas, which are foregrounded as the core ones that make a person a Gulabdasi.

Caste Composition and Gendered Imaginings

As argued in earlier chapters, a fundamental way in which the Gulabdasis characterized themselves was in their opposition to the varnashrama-dharma. Philosophically, the potential of all beings to be a part of the divine, envisaged in advaita monism, could theoretically make all equal, though this may not be seen in practice in all sects that followed advaita. At various times, tensions could manifest between the polydox tendencies (tolerance of multiplicity of ideas), as Doniger calls it, and orthopraxy (intolerance of multiplicity of behaviour).[74] The Gulabdasis, however, as their dera in Chathianwala made evident, had followers from among the high castes and the low, and allowed a great degree of flexibility in what one chose to be, an openness that the guru encouraged, making them what one may call 'poly-prax'. The eclectic religiosity of the Gulabdasis was matched by their assorted caste composition, with Jat, Khatri, Chamar, Muslim, and Mirasi disciples in the dera. That this may not have banished completely from among them notions of embodied hierarchy can be seen from the emphasis Piro put in her bhakti-laden poetry on the importance of making soteriological openings for the low caste. However, the fact that she succeeded and did become the disciple who shared tomb space with the guru himself speaks of the caste inclusivity

[74] Doniger, *The Hindus*, p. 46.

of the Gulabdasis. So does the choice of a Kumhar (potter) caste successor Hargobind, to the Jat guru Gulabdas, made by the guru. At the
same time, one may bear in mind that though there were many groups
throughout Indian history that renounced caste, Doniger makes the point
that they took the form of establishing alternative societies, where caste
was ignored, and perhaps Gulabdasis in their initial years may be said to
be one such group.[75] In other words, the potential radicalism available in
such groupings, though salient by their very existence and by the written
and oral circulation of their ideas, was somewhat blunted by their opting
out of 'normality' into their own particular life.

From the late nineteenth century in Punjab, as elsewhere, rethinking
on caste and what it may mean to community identities or the nation in
the making made it an issue of polemics and politics. More recently still,
the former low castes have begun to assert themselves socially and politically and take pride in their Dalit identity, signalling more interesting
times qualitatively different from the earlier exclusive existence.[76] The
Gulabdasis in this new ambience can embrace both their histories and
their present with enthusiasm, and perhaps parade their intrinsic 'difference' with pride, that is, revel in their incorporative values that kept them
open to all castes. It is this present, with some of its contradictions, that
invites comment.

On the two occasions that I have interacted closely with Vijenderji's
followers, in 2007 and 2013, it was evident that most of them were poor
and were of relatively low castes. In 2013, on asking Vijenderji about the
caste composition of his followers, he told me that they came from all
'varnas'. On my specific question, that if many were Dalits, he affirmed,
saying that many were from *mazhabī* background. The word 'mazhabī'
is a polite euphemism generally used for low-caste Chuhras, or the
scavenger caste, acquired through conversion to Sikhism, while most
Hindu Chuhras today might prefer the nomenclature of Balmiki.[77] The

---

[75] Doniger, *The Hindus*, p. 39.

[76] On the Ad Dharm movement of the early twentieth century among the
Ravidasis of Punjab, see Mark Juergensmeyer, *Religious Rebels in the Punjab: The
Social Vision of the Untouchables* (New Delhi: Ajanta Publications, 1988). On the more
recent Dalit mobilization and identity in Punjab, see Ronki Ram, 'Beyond Conversion
and Sanskritization: Articulating an Alternative Dalit Agenda in East Punjab',
Modern Asian Studies 46, no. 3 (2012): 539–702.

[77] See Swaran Singh, 'Mazhabī' and 'Balmiki' in I.J.S. Bansal and Swaran
Singh, eds, *People of India*, vol. 37, *Punjab*, Anthropological Survey of India

Gulabdasi dera in Hansi is quite close to Balmiki Chowk, with its statue of sage Valmiki, the sage–author of the Ramayana, said to be a low-caste dacoit in his early life; and to Vishwakarma Chowk as well, the figure venerated by artisanal and labouring groups as the divine architect.[78] Vijenderji further informed me that he also had disciples from among the Kanjar caste in his dera, and also the Sirkiband, who make products like mats from elephant grass called *sarkaṇḍā*.[79] Found on the outskirts of Delhi, Vijenderji attributed their absorption into the Gulabdasi dera by Sant Sahib Das of Rohtak, Haryana, in the 1890s.

According to Vijenderji, there were many high-caste Gulabdasis as well. The Istri Sabha that was established by his grandmother Jamnaji had mostly high-caste women followers. While his grandfather Sant Nirbhay was a Jat, his grandmother Jamnaji, was from an Arora, Batra background, a higher caste in Punjab associated with trading and shopkeeping, and her women disciples, who came formerly from areas in Multan and Sindh, were mostly high caste. According to Vijenderji, almost ninety per cent of his followers in Hansi were from higher castes. However, my impression was of a number of poor and low-caste followers. The point of significance is that of a mixed caste following, Vijenderji himself being from a weaver caste and his wife Saroj from a higher-caste Radhasoami background.[80]

The class/caste differentiation between Vijenderji and his family—middle class, higher caste, and educated—and his follower disciples became very evident, once again, as I shared the 'backstage' with them in the vehicle ferrying us around the countryside of Punjab in August 2013. As one of the buses carrying the Gulabdasi sangat on the way from Ratol

---

(New Delhi: Manohar, 2003), p. 316 and p. 59 respectively. Also see H.A. Rose, *A Glossary of the Tribes and Castes of the Punjab and North West Frontier Province*, vol. 2 (Patiala: Languages Department, Punjab, 1990 [1883]), p. 41.

[78] For a description of Vishwakarma and his worship see Narayan, *My Family and Other Saints*, p. 33.

[79] Swaran Singh, 'Sirkiband' in *People of India: Punjab*, p. 418. On Kanjars, see Rose, *Tribes and Castes*, pp. 474–5. Though in Punjab proper the term 'Kanjar' is used for pimps and prostitutes, in and around Delhi, they are a wandering caste, also associated like the Sirkiband with rope-making.

[80] Radhasoamis are the followers of Swami Shiv Dayal, and mostly come from a middle-class background. See Mark Juergensmeyer, 'The Social Significance of Radhasoami', in *Bhakti Religion in North India: Community Identity and Political Action*, edited by David N. Lorenzen (New Delhi: Manohar, 1996), pp. 67–93.

to Patti stopped so that the second bus could catch up and we stopped with them, the passengers of the Innova started cracking jokes about Vijenderji's followers. As they scattered in the fields on both sides, trying to find places to relieve themselves, Sarojji laughingly commented on their propensity to wander, uncaring of time, and Vijenderji's disciplining them into a schedule. The same occurred at Rajoki, when the curiosity of the sangat to go closer to the border with Pakistan aroused titters among the family group. Sarojji excused their behaviour by speaking of their first ever visit to Punjab, and the resultant excitement.

Despite private jokes it is important to understand that this mixed caste following of Vijenderji is absolutely vital for him to cultivate and patronize. The careful organization of this trip to Punjab—hiring of buses, working out boarding and lodging, incorporating leisure time, coordinating with various heads and followers from different parts of Haryana, Punjab, and Rajasthan—planned and executed by Vijenderji, is a testimony to how seriously he takes his duties towards his followers. Whether Vijenderji places any particular emphasis on the Dalit identity of his sangat is difficult to say, but the fact remains that this conglomeration of castes makes him a guru of importance, perhaps even making him a political player in charged electoral battles where caste identities surface and are exploited by politicians.[81] In any case, the grandiose vision of the Gulabdasi future that Vijenderji has is dependent on the assemblage and loyalty of his followers, and Vijenderji is always solicitous and concerned about their well-being.

How would one perceive the place of women among Vijenderji's followers? This question is important not only because the Gulabdasi past had a very prominent woman—Piro—among its ranks, who wrote powerful poetry and became the premier disciple of the guru, but also because gender equality has a resonance today that just cannot be ignored by those seeking positions of leadership. Conscious as Vijenderji is of presenting the right image of the Gulabdasis to the world, this is an issue he must have somewhat reflected on.

His inheritance on the gender question, however, is uneven. While Piro was prominent, she did remain subordinate to the guru and very consciously so, as her poetry showed. That in her lifetime the guru had already appointed a successor, Hargobind, indicates both a patrimonial

---

[81] A brother of Vijenderji from his original family is a local politician in Haryana.

principle at work in the dera, and also perhaps the difficulty, if not the impossibility, of exceeding some liabilities that came with embodied gender imaginings. That Piro's agential pushing of the envelope of such gender imaginations was an important aspect of her life has been argued. And perhaps it is significant to stress that she must have continued to exercise inordinate power even after death as long as the tomb in which she lay buried alongside the guru remained an object of veneration among the Gulabdasis. But how did gender equations and relations change as the tomb became abandoned post-Partition and various contemporary concerns impinged upon evolving Gulabdasi identity?

It is striking that many of the contemporary followers of Vijenderji do not know much about Piro. I have already mentioned how my presence among his entourage impacts on the importance of the sect, and its followers. Both in Hansi in 2007 and in Ratol, Patti, and Rajoki in 2013, Vijenderji makes it a point to introduce me as someone working on his 'mataji' Piro. But this is followed by a few explanatory words on who she was and her importance to the sect, though my efforts are praised unequivocally and I am made responsible for spreading Piro's name in far-off places. Clearly, distance from Chathianwala has also bred amnesia about her. More significantly, the liturgical and ritual practices of the Gulabdasis, not to mention their effort at propaganda, have not seen fit to perpetuate her name or her close association with the guru. Though Vijenderji has owned her as his mother, bringing out an edition of her writings, there does seem to be a distance between the intellectual world in which he keenly participates, and the ritual and everyday world where her presence does not seem to be required, or can be displaced by other, suitably male disciples like Gurmukh and Jawahir.

Thus, two contrasting but not necessarily contradictory tendencies are visible among the Gulabdasis. Their historical and more recent past has thrown up important women who have been literary figures and who were also in positions of leadership. Vijenderji has proffered to me the poetry of two literary figures of the sect, Gurdai and Hardai, one I have so far not taken up. Whatever the quality of their verses may be, it shows women in the sect with literacy and literary skills. I have also mentioned Jamnaji and Rajenderji in positions of leadership and power, and commanding respect of their flock. I cannot comment on Jamnaji beyond what Vijenderji has told me and in his opinion she was an eminent personality. It is apparent, however, that Rajenderji had some devoted women followers, and on ceremonial occasions Jamnaji occupied an elevated place at par with Vijenderji. Though I have suggested the establishment of a patrilineal principle with the succession of Vijenderji, this may also have occurred because of the celibate status of Rajenderji, and the need to find a successor to the Hansi gaddi.

At another level, the relatively subordinate position of women in the sect is also apparent. Visiting leaders of various Gulabdasi branches are always men, and they sit on elevated seats as compared to women and other men who sit on the floor. This was clear in Joginder Singh Bhatia's house in Patti, where a handful of men sat on sofas in their drawing room while women sat on the floor. Segregation between men and women in seating arrangements is also always maintained, where men sit on one side and women on another, much like it is practiced within Sikh gurd-waras. I suggest that ritual elevation of a few women may not undo the more entrenched gender biases present in society at large, and so among the contemporary Gulabdasis the presence of ordinary women, among a few exceptional ones.

It is difficult to foretell what the future of the various branches of the Gulabdasis will be, or more particularly that of the Hansi branch. Certainly driven by the ambition and leadership of Vijenderji, they are set to increase their numbers, make a ritualistic presence felt in the country-side of Punjab and Haryana, and give competition to the Dalit deras that seem to proliferate in these two states. History is a great resource for the Gulabdasis, and Vijenderji has a bagful of stories about their past that can be unearthed, reworked, and retold to recoup a more egalitarian society in terms of caste and gender.

Recent scholarly writing on Indian gurus has drawn attention to the diversity, variety, and prolificacy of the gurus, what is termed as their 'uncontainability'.[82] This is a pointer to not only their range, or the variety of situations and places where one may find them, but also to the 'polyvalent meanings of the gurus themselves and their unusual capacity to accrue resonances'.[83] Copeman and Ikegame also speak of the 'domaining effects' of gurus, when 'the logic of an idea associated with one domain

---

[82] Jacob Copeman and Aya Ikegame, 'The Multifarious Guru: An Introduction', in *The Guru in South Asia: New Interdisciplinary Perspectives*, edited by Jacob Copeman and Aya Ikegame (London: Routledge, 2012), pp. 1–45.

[83] Copeman and Ikegame, 'The Multifarious Guru', p. 3.

is transferred to another'.[84] Vijenderji may be seen as one such fructuous guru, who carries the mantle of his guruship to link the domain of Gulabdasi past to its present. He does this artfully, linking an evanescent past with its ephemeral territorial materiality with a refashioned materially tangible present, all the while evoking resonances that make the past speak to the present. The connections he makes, the linkages he articulates, and the rituals he designs speak of an inventive guru. Moreover, he is a guru refurbishing his leadership even as he endeavours to keep meaningful for his followers their attachments to the spirituality articulated by the exceptional and literary original guru, the iconoclastic Gulabdas.

Important in the performance of his guruship are the stories that Vijenderji relates, stories that provide the link to the past as they connect with the present. When A.B. Lord spoke about the performances of oral 'singers of tales' in the former Yugoslavia, he emphasized their creativity, noting their ability to compose as they performed.[85] This was a feat which was accomplished through a cultural repertoire of formulas and formulaic expression, and of themes that the oral performers of epic songs had imbibed. Though not employing formulas, mnemonic or otherwise, the cultural repertoire of Vijenderji consists of tales, formulaic insofar as repetitive of certain themes which resonate with his audience and followers. His performances are palimpsests, innovating on intimate cultural themes and familiarly new stories. This chapter has shown how the Gulabdasi past continues to enrich anew, in the process, composing stories and investing rituals and sites with meaning. That this also entails memorializing the past in new ways while displacing earlier peoples and sites is part of the effort to keep the past relevant.

---

[84] Copeman and Ikegame, 'The Multifarious Guru', p. 2.

[85] Albert B. Lord, *The Singer of Tales*, edited by S. Mitchell and G. Nagy, 2nd edition (Cambridge: Harvard University Press, 2000).

Conclusion

Devotion and dissent are both forms of asserting agency, Udaya Kumar has noted recently, even though the former invokes loyal submission and the latter an oppositional stance.[1] This work has shown that the architectures of Piro's agential self were built on both these pillars. Her rebellion against her clan and profession set her up against a powerful world, on the periphery of courtly structures of Ranjit Singh's Lahore. The consequences of her febrile dissent, including her abduction, were so traumatic that she had to write down her experience, and air her anger and resentment, but also exult in her ultimate triumph. This she did in her *160 Kafis*, an inventive, autobiographical, and versified lament that allowed the telling of her tale, in her own métier. Her verses, aesthetically rich, spoke in a metaphorical language, where Piro could be a Sita to her Ram-like guru, as she could be a Hir haranguing the fractious mullahs. Her narrative, if not outwardly, then as a subtext, also carried a sullen sense of being a daughter in a setup where she was at stake.

Her devotion, on the other hand, to her guru and sect and more saliently embedded in a bhakti tradition bestowed on her a cultural repertoire, a resource of language and imagination, which made possible the avowal of her autonomy. The alignment with the bhakti tradition made available several openings for Piro. It facilitated identification with the low caste and the marginal, the bhakti saints like Saina and Sadhna, and significantly Kabir, in whose company Piro placed herself.

---

[1] Udaya Kumar, 'Sree Narayan Guru's Idiom of the Spiritual and the Worldly', in *Devotion and Dissent in Indian History*, edited by Vijaya Ramaswamy (New Delhi: Foundation Books, 2014), pp. 370–9.

The devotional path also meant the emulation of women bhaktas. Though Piro alluded to Mira, she found particularly meaningful elusive figures with sketchy details of their lives like Kubjan, Bhilni, and Karmabai. These women with ambivalent pasts, whether in terms of caste or sexuality, were deployed by Piro to show that these attributes were not a hindrance in their soteriological choices and spiritually rich lives. By mining the emotional range of both bhakti and Punjabi Sufi traditions of challenging authority figures and repudiating bogus and flashy religiosities, Piro gained entry into the interior world of humble devotion that turned the self towards the guru and god. Both interiorized bhakti and advaita philosophy's search for the divine in the self, its solipsism, nurtured a selfhood that found expression in Piro's autobiographical outpouring. Piro's other, more spiritually inclined, verses, her siharfis, for example, were also strewn with autobiographical referencing. Piro's quest for autonomy and subjectivity, the search for selfhood then, was sought to be achieved with a constant assertion of the self: in pain, in indignity, in anger, in obsequious submission to the guru, or as a conduit of the guru's conjuring of the miraculous. Her own miracle, of escaping the clutches of her abductors, like that of her predecessor of the seventeenth century, Bahinabai, who narrated the story of a cow and its calf, was not played out on a grand scale; it was merely indicative of being the chosen one. Yet, in many ways, Piro's own life, given the odds stacked against her, was a miracle.

The demeanour of defiance that we often see in Piro was of course also a part of her peculiar circumstances. The dissonant quagmire of Hindu–Sikh/Khalsa–Muslim relations that animated her writing was both an echo of the rhetorical flourishes of bhakti and Sufi polemics against religious authorities, as it was a determination to shape her life in her own light. As a renegade Muslim in a Hindu–Sikh monastic establishment, and as a prostitute defying her destiny of sexual availability to powerful men, Piro's self and story were inextricably linked with a dissentient religious stance. It is difficult to disaggregate her saga, her inhabitation of her particular story as of constructing it, from the rhetorical standard of exterior/interior religiosity—of humble seekers of truth (haq) versus those drunk on power and bookish knowledge of self-aggrandizement—that bhakti and Sufi tales revelled in. Piro comes to us through her own performative storytelling as simultaneously defiant and deprecating, bold and bellicose at one moment, humble and effacing at another, in command of her destiny, and as a servant (dasi) of her powerful (zoravar) guru.

The guru and his Gulabdasi establishment were the enabling institutions that allowed the manifestation and affirmation of Piro's rebellion, and her selfhood. If dissent can be seen as a mode of being, a confirmation of lives imagined other than routine and regular, then, Gulabdas's dera at Chathianwala embodied the dwelling where the marginal could find abode. Not that the guru represented in his own or his disciples' imagination anything other than majestic presence and benevolent munificence. It was, however, the strength of his intellectual and spiritual explorations that sutured him and his establishment to permanent insurgence of thought: the rejecting of the norm and the normalizing mainstream of varnashramadharma and cowering before intransigent power. The unrelenting logic of his monist thought enabled the thwarting of caste hierarchy, and to an extent gender hierarchy too, giving an entry to the likes of Piro for exploring spiritual matters. At the same time, the guru himself was an aspect of the divine, the radiant sun as Piro noted, Brahm, the seeker/proclaimer of the rightful Truth (an'al haq), above ordinary mortals. The logics of this godly hierarchy should not take away from the condemnation of other hierarchies, for the mantra of soham (I am s/he) was inclusive, of potential equality. This is why his many disciples were able to set up independently. Gulabdas personally enjoyed the selfless adoration of his disciples in his lifetime, and may have even chafed at the lack of recognition from powers that were at the helm in Lahore. However, he did not genuflect to the powerful, though with the onset of the colonial rule he may have curbed the extravagance of his preaching and its spatial reach.

The coming of colonial rule in Punjab in 1849 queered the pitch, as it were, for the pace of life and caste rebellions as they existed in society. The governmentality of the colonial state—the particular institutions and techniques of rule that it deployed, including building the power–knowledge nexus based on the minute noting of the biopolitics of the populace—changed the rules of governance. Not that the insurrections of those like Gulabdas lost their relevance. In a land as iniquitous as Punjab, and as receptive to the flourishing of diverse ideas as it was, Gulabdas and his disciples continued on their contumacious path. However, the young and ambitious like Ditta Ram, wishing to make a mark in public life with its new rules guided by associational interventions and the print media, identity politics and representation in governmental institutions, and colonialism, initiated new opportunities. Perhaps Ditta, now Ditt Singh and a member of the Lahore Singh Sabha, never renounced the pelf that his Gulabdasi antecedents gave him; he was, after all accused by the Gulabdasis of maintaining a small hermitage where he was still the guru. But he did attempt to shed the Gulabdasi inheritance of a pluralistic culture.

The rethinking on religion, on specifically 'who is a Sikh' as McLeod defined the problematic, necessarily also pushed to the forefront the question of caste.[2] Caste at once became more inflexible as it came to be identified with the core of Indian social organization; and the emancipation from its shackles encouraged a leap of imagination that encompassed horizontal groupings and religion-based initiatives. Ditt Singh—while envisaging the polemics on caste outside the Gulabdasi advaita-inflected predilections of thwarting the varnashramadharma and basing it on Khalsa positioning of caste's marginality to Sikhness—didn't quite know what to do with it. For Ditt Singh, caste was necessary, as an essential aspect of social life: he found abhorrent the intermixing of castes as of religions. Caste was also abominable, the gurus having denounced it. On becoming a Khalsa, Singh argued, one did not necessarily forgo caste; however, one may now be associated with the gurus' Khatri lineage. Similarly, for Sikh and Khalsa identities to achieve equivalence, the intermixing of Hindus and Muslims, Sikhs and Hindus, must also be brought to an end. Of course, the mutability of Singh's thought on caste as on religion meant that the desire for pristine identities remained a distant dream. On the other hand, by even attempting segregation of religions and aggregation of castes, Singh turned his back on the Gulabdasi message of divine presence/essence in all. He turned away too from Piro's insistent cry of interiority that made caste redundant, or her celebration of her guru Gulabdas who openly accepted all, whether a Hindu or a Muslim, a high caste or low, a woman or a man, within his fold.

The fraught nature of Ditt Singh's project on caste as on religious identity has both found a resonance in our own times, as it has transmuted inexorably in the cacophony of our contemporary identity politics. The challenge to varnashramadharma has been replaced by relentless caste assertions. In contemporary Punjab, one manifestation of caste politics has been the effulgence of Dalit pride. In the numerous deras that have come to dot the Indian Punjab's and Haryana's countryside, with mainly though not exclusively Dalit following, the culture of the gurus flourishes. At once approachable and spiritual, connecting with the cosmic world

[2] W.H. McLeod, *Who is a Sikh: The Problem of Sikh Identity* (New York: Clarendon Press, 1989).

and providing care in this mundane one, the myriad gurus cater to the multiple needs of their legendary followings.

Gulabdas, therefore, has left a rich legacy for someone like Vijender Das to make his own. And it is Ditt Singh's Dalit identity that is as much celebrated as that of a Singh Sabha reformer, if not more so. Gulabdas was steeped in advaita theology and monist philosophy, expressing himself in poetic meters and intellectually stimulating disciples, just as he threw a social challenge to his contemporaries. While Vijender Das is neither a poet or a philosopher, nor necessarily a challenger of ascriptive identities, he is nevertheless inventive in his charismatic guruship, reviving Gulabdas's legacy and revivifying Gulabdasi followers. The cultural and territorial template on which Gulabdasi heritage is built seeks to align Gulabdasi particularities with larger cultural concerns that energize popular religiosities. Under Das' guruship, the emanation of the miraculous, the seeking of blessings, and psychedelic rituals performed to popular approbation coalesce to create a blend of what is uniquely Gulabdasi, but which also acquires a veneer of popular Hinduism. Through reinventing rituals around Gulabdas's life, especially his birth and death, Das speaks to his followers, Dalits and others, here and now. He thus compensates for the loss of the partitioned Punjab that is not available, of Kasur, Lahore, and moreover Chathianwala, the guru's domicile. The interleaving of loss and gain, the guru and his disciples, tales and rituals makes for a heady mix. The future beckons with the promise of spreading the guru's name far and wide.

And what about Piro? This work has commented on the myriad ways in which she is remembered today, the manner in which she is celebrated as a woman bhakta, particularly by some Gulabdasis like Das, but also others including influential playwrights. She has become a beacon for contemporary feminists, litterateurs, and historians who feel the need to recuperate her history, poetry, and recalcitrance in order to fabricate enabling precedents. It has been shown in this work that sometimes there are cultural grooves on which memory is etched, which make possible remembrance at all. The productive tension that makes for the interplay of memory and history, fiction and fact, autobiography and hagiography, and through them all memorialization, allows for varied remembrance. The very institutionalization of the discipline of history in India, Dipesh Chakrabarty has recently argued, was a process of negotiation between those constructing professional 'cloistered history' and those engaged in disputations that took place in its 'public life'.[3] A multiplicity, Shahid Amin has highlighted, resided in the varied memories of Ghazi Miyan, whether of his hagiographers or his rustic balladeers.[4] This tensility in the various recounting will be a condition too of Piro's life. Between the historian's effort of reconstructing an individual life from fragmentary sources, merely indicative of a rich and full life, to the effort's of Piro's playwrights of enacting a feminist and qissa heroine persona on her, to Piro's veneration as a mother and the first woman bhakta of Punjab by the Gulabdasi acolytes, the process of negotiation between academic history and the subject's public life will remain interesting. Piro is each and all: a spectre to be moulded, an incessant presence in the invocations to the self in her aesthetic poetry, and a frisson in the tactility of the manuscripts that contain her words.

---

[3] Dipesh Chakrabarty, *The Calling of History: Sir Jadunath Sarkar and His Empire of Truth* (Ranikhet: Permanent Black, 2015), p. 37.

[4] Shahid Amin, *Conquest and Community: The Afterlife of a Warrior Saint Ghazi Miyan* (New Delhi: Orient BlackSwan, 2015).

Bibliography

PRIMARY SOURCES

Giani Bhai Ditt Singh. *Sultan Puara*, 6th edition. (n.p., n.d.).

Gulabdas. *Pothi Gulab Chaman*. Lahore: Tajul Kutub, 1881.

Piro. *Ik Sau Sath Kafian*. Ms. 888. Amritsar: Bhai Gurdas Library, Guru Nanak Dev University.

Sant Bahadar Singh Ji. *Amritras Granth*. Amritsar: Yantralaya Chasmanur, 1898.

Shamdasji. *Chaupat Granth*. This manuscript was in possession of Ram Kumarji, a Gulabdasi from Tigrana, Haryana.

Singh, Bhai Ditt Giani. *Pratigya Palan*. Lahore: Khalsa Press, 1896.

SECONDARY SOURCES

Abbas, Shemeem Burney. 'Female Myths in Sufism'. In her *Female Voice in Sufi Ritual: Devotional Practices of Pakistan and India*. Karachi: Oxford University Press, 2003, pp. 85–107.

Abbott, Justin E. *Bahina Bai: A Translation of Her Autobiography and Verses*. New Delhi: Cosmo Publications, 2005.

Adcock, C.S. 'Brave Converts in the Arya Samaj: The Case of Dharam Pal'. In Malhotra and Mir, *Punjab Reconsidered*, pp. 261–86.

Ahmad, Aziz. 'Sufism and Hindu Mysticism'. In Aquil, *Sufism and Society in Medieval India*, pp. 31–51.

Amin, Shahid. 'Un Saint Guerrier: Sur la Conquete del' Inde du Nord par les Tures au xi Siecle'. *Annales—Histoire, Sciences Sociales* 6, no. 2 (March–April 2005): 262–92.

———. *Conquest and Community: The Afterlife of a Warrior Saint Ghazi Miyan*. New Delhi: Orient BlackSwan, 2015.

———. *Event, Metaphor, Memory: Chauri-Chaura 1922–1992*. New Delhi: Oxford University Press, 1995.

Amol, M.M. *Bhai Takht Singh da Jiwan te Panth Seva*. Handwritten manuscript, 1938.

Anagol, Padma. 'Agency, Periodization, and Change in the Gender and Women's History of Colonial India'. *Gender and History* 20, no. 3 (2008): 603–27.

———. 'From the Symbolic to the Open: Women's Resistance in Colonial Maharashtra'. In Ghosh, *Behind the Veil*, pp. 21–57.

Aquil, Raziuddin. 'Episodes from the Life of Shaikh Farid-ud-Din Ganj-i-Shakar'. *International Journal of Punjab Studies* 10, no. 2 (2003): 25–46.

———, ed. *Sufism and Society in Medieval India*. New Delhi: Oxford University Press, 2011.

Aquil, Raziuddin and Partha Chatterjee, eds. *History in the Vernacular*. Ranikhet: Permanent Black, 2008.

Arnold, David and Stuart Blackburn, eds. *Telling Lives in India: Biography, Autobiography and Life History*. Delhi: Permanent Black, 2004.

Asad, Talal. 'The Construction of Religion as an Anthropological Category'. In his *Genealogies of Religion: Discipline and Reasons of Power in Christianity and Islam*. Baltimore: The Johns Hopkins University Press, 1993, pp. 27–54.

Ashok, Shamsher Singh. *Siharfian Sadhu Wazir Singh Kian*. Patiala: Publications Bureau, 1988.

Assman, Jan. *Cultural Memory and Early Civilization: Writing, Remembrance, and Political Imagination*. Cambridge: Cambridge University Press, 2011.

Austin-Broos, Diane. 'The Anthropology of Conversion: An Introduction'. In *The Anthropology of Religious Conversion*, edited by Andrew Buckser and Stephen D. Glazier. Lanham: Rowman and Littlefield Publishers Inc., 2003, pp. 1–12.

Baixas, Lionel. 'The Dera Sacha Sauda Controversy and Beyond'. *Economic and Political Weekly* 42, no. 40 (2007): 4059–74.

Bal, Gurpreet. 'A 19th Century Woman Poet of Punjab: Peero'. *Indian Journal of Gender Studies* 10, no. 2 (2003): 177–203.

Ballantyne, Tony. 'Resisting the 'Boa Constrictor' of Hinduism: The Khalsa and the Raj'. *International Journal of Punjab Studies* 6, no. 2 (1999): 195–216.

———. *Between Colonialism and Diaspora: Sikh Cultural Formations in an Imperial World*. Delhi: Permanent Black, 2007.

Banarasidas. *Ardhakathanaka*. Edited and translated by Mukund Lath as *Half a Tale*. Jaipur: Rajasthan Prakrit Bharati Sansthan, 1981.

Banerjee-Dube, Ishita, ed. *Caste in History*. New Delhi: Oxford University Press, 2008.

Bayly, C.A. *Empire and Information: Intelligence Gathering and Social Communication in India, 1780–1870*. New Delhi: Cambridge University Press, 2007 (reprint).

Bayly, Susan. 'Introduction'. In her *Caste, Society and Politics in India: From the Eighteenth Century to the Modern Age*. Cambridge: Cambridge University Press, 2005 [1999], pp. 1–24.

Bharadwaja, Charanjiva, trans. *Satyarth Prakash (Light of Truth)*, 2nd edition. United Provinces, Arya Pratinidhi Sabha, 1915.

Bhatia, Ishita. 'UP BJP, Hindu Mahasabha Fight Over Godse Busts'. Available at http://timesofindia.indiatimes.com/city/meerut/UP-BJP-Hindu-Mahasabha-fight-over-Godse-busts/articleshow/45671233.cms. Accessed on 26 January 2015.

Bhattacharya, Neeladri. 'Predicaments of Secular Histories'. *Public Culture* 20, no. 1 (2008): 57–73.

Bigelow, Anna. 'Post-Partition Pluralism: Placing Islam in Indian Punjab'. In Malhotra and Mir, *Punjab Reconsidered*, pp. 409–34.

———. *Sharing the Sacred: Practicing Pluralism in Muslim North India*. New York: Oxford University Press, 2010.

Bingley, A.H. *Sikhs*. Patiala: Languages Department, 1970 [1899].

Blackburn, Stuart. 'Life Histories as Narrative Strategy: Prophecy, Song, and Truth-Telling in Tamil Tales and Legends'. In Arnold and Blackburn, *Telling Lives in India*, pp. 203–26.

Bokhari, Afshan. 'Masculine Modes of Female Subjectivity: The Case of Jahanara Begum'. In Malhotra and Lambert-Hurley, *Speaking of the Self*, pp. 165–202.

Booth, Marilyn. 'Locating Women's Autobiographical Writing in Colonial Egypt'. *Journal of Women's History* 25, no. 2 (2013): 36–60.

Bose, Mandakranta, ed. *Faces of the Feminine in Ancient, Medieval and Modern India*. New Delhi: Oxford University Press, 2000.

Breckenridge, Carol A. and Peter van der Veer, eds. *Orientalism and the Post-Colonial Predicament: Perspectives on South Asia*. Philadelphia: University of Pennsylvania Press, 1993.

Briggs, George W. *Gorakhnath and the Kanphata Jogis*. Delhi: Motilal Banarasidass, 1973 [1938].

Brooks, Peter. *Reading for the Plot: Design and Intention in Narrative*. Oxford: Clarendon Press, 1984.

Brown, Louise. *The Dancing Girls of Lahore: Selling Love and Saving Dreams in Pakistan's Pleasure District*. New York: HarperCollins, 2006.

Burke, Peter. 'History of Events and the Revival of Narrative'. In Roberts, *The History and Narrative Reader*, pp. 305–17.

Butler, Judith. *Bodies That Matter: On the Discursive Limits of "Sex"*. New York: Routledge, 1993.

Bynum, Caroline Walker. *Holy Feast and Holy Fast: The Religious Significance of Food to Medieval Women*. Berkeley: University of California Press, 1987.

Chakrabarty, Dipesh. *The Calling of History: Sir Jadunath Sarkar and His Empire of Truth*. Ranikhet: Permanent Black, 2015.

Chakravarti, Uma. 'The World of Bhaktin in South Indian Traditions: The Body and Beyond'. In her *Everyday Lives, Everyday Histories: Beyond the Kings and Brahmanas of 'Ancient' India*. New Delhi: Tulika Books, 2006, pp. 275–92.

Chambers, Samuel A. and Terrell Carver. *Judith Butler and Political Theory: Troubling Politics*. London: Routledge, 2008.

Chatterjee, Indrani and Richard M. Eaton, eds. *Slavery and South Asian History*. Bloomington: Indiana University Press, 2006.

Chatterjee, Partha. 'Introduction: History in the Vernacular'. In Aquil and Chatterjee, *History in the Vernacular*, pp. 1–24.

———. *The Nation and Its Fragments: Colonial and Postcolonial Histories*. Princeton: Princeton University Press, 1993.

Chatterjee, Partha. 'The Nation and Its Outcasts'. In his *Nation and Its Fragments*, pp. 173–99.

———. 'Women and the Nation'. In his *Nation and Its Fragments*, pp. 135–57.

Chatterjee, Partha and Anjan Ghosh, eds. *History and the Present*. London: Anthem Press, 2006.

Chattopadhyaya, Brajadulal. *Representing the Other? Sanskrit Sources and the Muslims (Eighth to Fourteenth Century)*. Delhi: Manohar, 1998.

Chhabra, G.S. *Social and Economic History of the Panjab*. New Delhi: Sterling Publishers, 1962.

Clifford, James. 'Introduction: Partial Truths'. In *Writing Culture: The Poetics and Politics of Ethnography*, edited by James Clifford and George E. Marcus. New Delhi: Oxford University Press, 1990, pp. 1–26.

Cohn, Bernard. *Colonialism and Its Forms of Knowledge: The British in India*. Princeton: Princeton University Press, 1996.

Conway, Jill Ker. *When Memory Speaks: Exploring the Art of Autobiography*. New York: Vintage Books, 1998.

Copeman, Jacob. 'The Mimetic Guru: Tracing the Real in Sikh-Dera Sacha Sauda Relations'. In Copeman and Ikegame, *Guru in South Asia*, pp. 156–80.

Copeman, Jacob and Aye Ikegame, eds. *The Guru in South Asia: New Interdisciplinary Perspectives*. London: Routledge, 2012.

———. 'The Multifarious Guru: An Introduction'. In their *Guru in South Asia*, pp. 1–45.

Curthoys Ann, and John Docker. 'Introduction'. In their *Is History Fiction?* Sydney: University of New South Wales, 2010, pp. 1–11.

Dale, Stephen. 'The Poetry and Autobiography of the *Babur-nama*'. *Journal of Asian Studies* 55, no. 3 (1996): 635–64.

Dalmia, Vasudha. 'Forging Community: The Guru in a Seventeenth-Century Hagiography'. In her *Hindu Pasts*, pp. 141–72.

———. *Hindu Pasts: Women, Religion, Histories*. Ranikhet: Permanent Black, 2015.

———. '"The Only Real Religion of the Hindus": Vaisnava Self-Representation in the Late Nineteenth Century'. In *Representing Hinduism: The Construction of Religious Traditions and National Identity*, edited by Vasudha Dalmia and H. von Stietencron. New Delhi: SAGE Publications, 1995, pp. 176–210.

———. 'Women, Duty and Sanctified Space in a Vaishnav Hagiography of the Seventeenth Century'. In her *Hindu Pasts*, pp. 173–88.

Dalmia, Vasudha and Munis D. Faruqui, eds. *Religious Interactions in Mughal India*. New Delhi: Oxford University Press, 2014.

Dalrymple, W. 'The Red Fairy'. In his *Nine Lives: In Search of the Sacred in Modern India*. London: Bloomsbury, 2009, pp. 112–45.

Darnton, Robert. 'Philosophers Trim the Tree of Knowledge: The Epistemological Strategy of the Encyclopedie'. In his *The Great Cat Massacre and Other Episodes in French Cultural History*. New York: Vintage Books, 1985, pp. 191–213.

Das, Veena. 'On Female Body and Sexuality'. *Contributions to Indian Sociology* (n.s.) 21, no. 1 (1987): 57–66.

Das, Vijender. *Sant Kavyitri Ma Piro*. Mohali: Satluj Prakashan, 2011.

Dasgupta, Shashibhushan. *Obscure Religious Cults*. Calcutta: Firma KLM Pvt. Ltd, 1976.

Davis, Natalie Z. *Fiction in the Archives: Pardon Tales and Their Tellers in Sixteenth Century France*. Stanford: Stanford University Press, 1987.

———. *The Return of Martin Guerre*. Cambridge: Harvard University Press, 1983.

———. *Trickster Travels: The Search for Leo Africanus*. New York: Faber and Faber, 2008.

———. *Women on the Margins: Three Seventeenth Century Lives*. Cambridge: Harvard University Press, 1995.

Dayton, Cornelia H. 'Rethinking Agency, Recovering Voices'. *American Historical Review* 109, no. 3 (2004): 827–43.

de Man, Paul. 'Autobiography as De-facement'. *Modern Language Notes* 94, no. 5 (1979): 919–30.

Denton, Lynn Teskey. *Female Ascetics in Hinduism*. Albany: State University of New York Press, 2004.

Deshpande, Satish, ed. *The Problem of Caste: Essays from Economic and Political Weekly*. Hyderabad: Orient BlackSwan, 2014.

Devji, Faisal F. 'Gender and the Politics of Space: The Movement for Women's Reform 1857–1900'. In *Women and Social Reform in India*, vol. 2, edited by Sumit Sarkar and Tanika Sarkar. Ranikhet: Permanent Black, 2011 [2007], pp. 99–114.

Dhavan, Purnima. *When Sparrows Became Hawks: The Making of Sikh Warrior Tradition, 1699–1799*. New York: Oxford University Press, 2011.

Digby, Simon, trans. *Wonder-Tales of South Asia*. Jersey: Orient Monographs, 2000.

Dirks, Nicholas B. 'The Textualization of Tradition: Biography of an Archive'. In his *Castes of Mind: Colonialism and the Making of Modern India*. Princeton: Princeton University Press, 2001, pp. 81–106.

Dobe, Timothy. 'Vernacular Vedanta'. In his *Hindu Christian Faqir: Modern Monks, Global Christianity and Indian Sainthood*. New York: Oxford University Press, 2015, pp. 182–3.

Doniger, Wendy. *On Hinduism*. New Delhi: Aleph, 2013.

———. *The Hindus: An Alternative History*. New Delhi: Penguin/Viking, 2009.

Duggal, Kartar Singh. *Maharaja Ranjit Singh: The Last to Lay Arms*. New Delhi: Abhinav Publications, 2001.

Dursteler, Eric R. *Renegade Women: Gender, Identity, and Boundaries in the Early Modern Mediterranean*. Baltimore: The Johns Hopkins University Press, 2011.

Eakin, Paul John. *Fictions in Autobiography: Studies in the Art of Self-Invention*. Princeton: Princeton University Press, 1985.

Eaton, Richard M. 'Sufi Folk Literature and the Expansion of Indian Islam'. In Aquil, *Sufism and Society in Medieval India*, pp. 70–81.

Eck, Diana. *India: A Sacred Geography*. New York: Harmony Books, 2012.

Eden, Emily. *Up the Country: Letters Written to Her Sister from the Upper Provinces of India*. London: Curzon Press, 1978 [1930].

Elias Jamal J., translated and Introduced. *Death before Dying: The Sufi Poems of Sultan Bahu*. Berkeley: University of California Press, 1998.

Ernst, Carl W. 'Situating Sufism and Yoga'. *Journal of the Royal Asiatic Society* 15, no. 1 (2005): 15–43.

Ewing, Katherine, ed. *Shari'at and Ambiguity in South Asian Islam*. New Delhi: Oxford University Press, 1988.

Feldhaus, Anne. 'Bahina Bai: Wife and Saint'. *Journal of American Academy of Religion* 50, no. 4 (1982): 591–604.

Fenech, Louis E. 'Conversion and Sikh Tradition'. In *Religious Conversion in India: Modes, Motivations and Meanings*, edited by Rowena Robinson and Sathianathan Clarke. New Delhi: Oxford University Press, 2003, pp. 149–80.

———. *The Darbar of the Sikh Gurus: The Court of God in the World of Men*. New Delhi: Oxford University Press, 2008.

———. *Martyrdom in the Sikh Tradition: Playing the 'Game of Love'*. New Delhi: Oxford University Press, 2000.

Flood, Finbarr. *Objects of Translation: Material Culture and Medieval "Hindu–Muslim" Encounter*. Ranikhet: Permanent Black, 2009.

Flood, Gavin. *An Introduction to Hinduism*. New Delhi: Cambridge University Press, 2009.

Fox, Richard. *Lions of the Punjab: Culture in the Making*. Berkeley: University of California Press, 1985.

Frazier, Jessica. *The Continuum Companion to Hindu Studies*. London: Continuum, 2011.

Geertz, Clifford. 'Deep Play: Notes on the Balinese Cockfight'. *Daedalus* 10, no. 1 (Winter 1972): 1–37.

Gelber, Hester Goodenough. 'A Theater of Virtue: The Exemplary World of Saint Francis of Assisi'. In *Saints and Virtues*, edited by J.S. Hawley. Berkeley: University of California Press, 1987, pp. 15–35.

Ghosh, Anindita, ed. *Behind the Veil: Resistance, Women and the Everyday in Colonial South Asia*. Ranikhet: Permanent Black, 2007.

———. 'Introduction'. In Ghosh, *Behind the Veil*, pp. 1–20.

Ginzburg, Carlo. *The Cheese and the Worms*, translated by John and Anne C. Tedeschi. London: Routledge and Kegan Paul, 1980.

———. 'Microhistory: Two or Three Things That I Know About It'. In his *Threads and Traces: True, False, Fictive*, translated by Anne C. Tedeschi and John Tedeschi. Berkeley: University of California Press, 2012, pp. 193–214.

Goffman, Erving. *The Presentation of Self in Everyday Life*. New York: Anchor Books, 1959.

Gold, Ann G. 'Sexuality, Fertility and Erotic Imagination in Rajasthani Women's Songs'. In *Listen to the Heron's Words: Reimagining Gender and Kinship in North India*, edited by Gloria G. Raheja and Anne G. Gold. California: University of California Press, 1994, pp. 30–72.

Gold, Daniel. 'Continuities as Gurus Change'. In Copeman and Ikegame, *Guru in South Asia*, pp. 241–54.

———. *The Lord as Guru: Hindi Sants in North Indian Tradition*. New York: Oxford University Press, 1987.

Goswamy, B.N. and J.S. Grewal. *The Mughals and Jogis of Jakhbar: Some Madad-i-Ma'ash and Other Documents*. Simla: Indian Institute of Advanced Study, 1967.

———. *The Mughals and Sikh Rulers and the Vaishnavas of Pindori*. Simla: Indian Institute of Advanced Study, 1969.

Grace, Sherrill. 'Theatre and the Autobiographical Pact: An Introduction'. In *Theatre and Autobiography: Writing and Performing Lives in Theory and Practice*, edited by Sherrill Grace and Jerry Wasserman. Vancouver: Talonbooks, 2006, pp. 13–29.

Grewal, J.S. 'The Shari'at and the Non-Muslims'. In his *Miscellaneous Articles*. Amritsar: Guru Nanak Dev University, 1974, pp. 118–22.

———. *Guru Tegh Bahadur and the Persian Chroniclers*. Amritsar: Guru Nanak Dev University, 1976, pp. 78–9.

———. *The Sikhs of the Punjab*. New Delhi: Cambridge University Press, 2002 (reprint).

Grewal, J.S. and Indu Banga, trans and eds. *Early Nineteenth Century Punjab: From Ganesh Das's Char Bagh-i-Panjab*. Amritsar: Guru Nanak Dev University, 1975.

Grewal, J.S. and S.S. Bal. *Guru Gobind Singh (A Biographical Study)*. Chandigarh: Punjab University, 1967.

Guha, Ranajit. 'Chandra's Death'. In his *Small Voice of History*, pp. 271–303.

———. *The Small Voice of History: Collected Essays*, edited by Partha Chatterjee. Ranikhet: Permanent Black, 2009.

———. 'The Small Voice of History'. In his *Small Voice of History*, pp. 304–17.

Gupta, Hari Ram. 'Guru Tegh Bahadur: A Biographical Study'. In *Guru Tegh Bahadur: Background and the Supreme Sacrifice: A Collection of Research Articles*, edited by Gurbachan Singh Talib. Patiala: Punjabi University, 1976, pp. 3–24.

Hans, Raj Kumar. 'Devotion and Dissent of Punjabi Dalit Sant Poets'. In Ramaswamy, *Devotion and Dissent in Indian History*, pp. 188–215.

———. 'Sant Poet Wazir Singh: A Window to Reimagining Nineteenth Century Punjab'. *Journal of Punjab Studies* 20, nos 1 and 2 (2013), 135–58.

Hans, Surjit. *A Reconstruction of Sikh History from Sikh Literature*. Jalandhar: ABS Publications, 1988.

Hansen, Kathryn. *Stages of Life: Indian Theatre Autobiographies*. Ranikhet: Permanent Black, 2011.

Hart, Patricia and Karen Weatherman with Susan H. Armitage, eds. *Women Writing Women: The Frontiers Reader*. Lincoln: University of Nebraska Press, 2006.

Hasan, Farhat. 'Presenting the Self: Norms and Emotions in *Ardhakathanaka*'. In *Biography as History: Indian Perspectives*, edited by Vijaya Ramaswamy and Yogesh Sharma. Hyderabad: Orient BlackSwan, 2009, pp. 105–22.

Hastings, James, ed. *Encyclopaedia of Religion and Ethics*, vol. 12. New York: Charles Scribner's Sons, 1958.

Hausner, Sondra L. 'Ascetic Traditions'. In Frazier, *Continuum Companion to Hindu Studies*, pp. 100–7.

Hausner, Sondra L. and Meena Khandelwal. 'Introduction: Women on their Own'. In *Nuns, Yoginis, Saints and Singers: Women's Renunciation in South Asia*, edited by Meena Khandelwal, Sondra L. Hausner, and Ann Grodzins Gold. New Delhi: Zubaan, 2007, pp. 1–47.

Hawley, J.S. 'Author and Authority'. In his *Three Bhakti Voices*, pp. 21–47.

———. 'Mirabai as Wife and Yogi'. In his *Three Bhakti Voices*, pp. 117–38.

———. 'Morality beyond Morality'. In his *Three Bhakti Voices*, pp. 48–69.

———. *A Storm of Songs: India and the Idea of Bhakti Movement*. Cambridge: Harvard University Press, 2015.

———. *Three Bhakti Voices: Mirabai, Surdas, and Kabir in Their Times and Ours*. New Delhi: Oxford University Press, 2012 [2005].

Hawley, J.S. and G.S. Mann. 'Mirabai in the Pothi Prem Ambodh'. *Journal of Punjab Studies* 15, no. 1–2 (2008): 199–223.

Hawley, J.S. and Mark Juergensmeyer. *Songs of the Saints of India*. New Delhi: Oxford University Press, 2008.

J.S. Hawley, Anshu Malhotra, and Tyler Williams, eds. *Text and Tradition in North India*. New Delhi: Oxford University Press, forthcoming.

Hayden, Robert M. 'Antagonistic Tolerance: Competitive Sharing of Religious Sites in South Asia and the Balkans'. *Current Anthropology* 43, no. 1 (2002): 205–19.

Hess, Linda. 'Kabir's Rough Rhetoric'. In Schomer and McLeod *The Sants*, pp. 143–65.

Hobsbawm, Eric and Terence Ranger. eds. *The Invention of Tradition*. Cambridge: Cambridge University Press, 1983.

Horstmann, Monika. 'Parasbhag: Bhai Addan's Translation of Al-Ghazali's Kimiya-yi sa'adat'. In *Patronage and Popularisation, Pilgrimage and Procession: Channels of Transcultural Translation and Transmission*, edited by Heidi R.M. Pauwels. Wiesabden: Harrassowitz, 2009, pp. 9–22.

Hoskote, Ranjit. *I, Lalla: The Poems of Lal Ded*. Delhi: Penguin, 2011.

Ibbetson, D.C.J. *Punjab Castes*. Patiala: Bhasha Vibhag, 2000 [1883].

Inden, Ronald, Jonathan Walters, and Daud Ali. *Querying the Medieval: Texts and the History of Practices in South Asia*. New York: Oxford University Press, 2000.

'It was Waiting to Happen'. *Hindustan Times*, 28 May 2009, New Delhi.

Jakobsh, Doris R. *Sikhism and Women: History, Texts and Experience*. New Delhi: Oxford University Press, 2010.

Jakobsh, Doris R. and Eleanor Nesbitt. 'Introduction–Sikhism and Women: Contextualizing the Issues'. In Jakobsh, *Sikhism and Women*, pp. 1–39.

Jha, Shweta Sachdeva. 'Tawa'if as Poet and Patron: Rethinking Women's Self-Representation'. In Malhotra and Lambert-Hurley, *Speaking of the Self*, pp. 141–64.

Jones, Kenneth W. *Arya Dharm: Hindu Consciousness in Nineteenth Century Punjab*. Delhi: Manohar, 1989.

Jordens, J.T.F. *Dayananda Saraswati: His Life and Ideas*. New Delhi: Oxford University Press, 1978.

Joshi, Sanjay. *Fractured Modernity: Making a Middle Class in Colonial North India*. New Delhi: Oxford University Press, 2001.

————. 'Introduction'. In his *The Middle Class in Colonial India*. New Delhi: Oxford University Press, 2010, pp. xxxix–xl.

Juergensmeyer, Mark. *Religious Rebels in the Punjab: The Social Vision of the Untouchables*. Delhi: Ajanta Publications, 1988.

————. 'The Social Significance of Radhasoami'. In *Bhakti Religion in North India: Community Identity and Political Action*, edited by David N. Lorenzen. Delhi: Manohar, 1996, pp. 67–93.

Kalra, Virender S. and Navtej K. Purewal. 'The Strut of the Peacocks: Partition, Travel and the Indo–Pak Border'. In *Travel Worlds: Journeys in Contemporary Cultural Politics*. London: Zed Books, 1999, pp. 54–67.

Kapoor, Narinder Singh. *Gyani Ditt Singh: Jiwan te Rachna*. Patiala: Punjabi University, 1987.

Kaviraj, Sudipto. 'The Invention of Private Life: A Reading of Sibnath Sastri's "Autobiography"'. In Arnold and Blackburn, *Telling Lives in India*, pp. 83–115.

Kerr, Ian. 'Sikhs and State: Troublesome Relationships and a Fundamental Continuity with Particular Reference to the Period 1849–1919'. In *Sikh Identity: Continuity and Change*, edited by Pashaura Singh and N.G. Barrier. New Delhi: Manohar, 1999, pp. 147–74.

Khan, Dominique-Sila. *Crossing the Threshold: Understanding Religious Identities in South Asia*. London: I.B. Tauris Publishers, 2004.

Khan, Mohammad Ishaq. *Biographical Dictionary of Sufism in South Asia*. Delhi: Manohar, 2009.

Kishwar, Madhu. 'Arya Samaj and Women's Education: Kanya Mahavidyalaya, Jalandhar'. *Economic and Political Weekly* 21, no. 17 (1986): WS9–WS13 and WS15–WS24.

Kugle, Scott, commentary and translation. 'Haqiqat al-Fuqara: Poetic Biography of "Madho Lal" Hussayn'. In *Same-Sex Love in India: Readings from Literature and History*, edited by Ruth Vanita and Saleem Kidwai. Delhi: Macmillan, 2000, pp. 145–56.

Kumar, Udaya. 'Autobiography as a Way of Writing History: Personal Narratives from Kerala and the Inhabitation of Modernity'. In Aquil and Chatterjee, *History in the Vernacular*, pp. 418–48.

————. 'Sree Narayan Guru's Idiom of the Spiritual and the Worldly'. In Ramaswamy, *Devotion and Dissent in Indian History*, pp. 370–9.

Lahori, Mufti Ghulam Sarwar Qureshi. *Tarikh Makhzan-i-Punjab*. Lahore: Dost Associates, 1996 (1877).

'Lalleshwari'. Wikipedia entry. Available at http://en.wikipedia.org/wiki/Lalleshwari. Accessed on 6 March 2014.

Lambert-Hurley, Siobhan. 'The Heart of a Gopi: Raihanna Tyabji's Bhakti Devotionalism as Self-Representation'. In Malhotra and Lambert-Hurley, *Speaking of the Self*, pp. 230–54.

Lawrence, Bruce B. 'The Sant Movement and North Indian Sufis'. In Schomer and McLeod, *The Sants*, pp. 359–73.

Leslie, Julia. 'The Implications of Bhakti for the Story of Valmiki'. In *The Intimate Other: Love Divine in Indic Religions*, edited by A.S. King and J. Brockington. Delhi: Orient Longman, 2005, pp. 54–77.

———. *The Perfect Wife: The Orthodox Hindu Woman According to the Stridharmapaddhati of Tryambakayajvan*. New Delhi: Oxford University Press, 1989.

Lord, Albert B. *The Singer of Tales*, edited by S. Mitchell and G. Nagy, 2nd edition. Cambridge: Harvard University Press, 2000.

Lorenzen, David N., ed. *Bhakti Religion in North India: Community, Identity and Political Action*. Delhi: Manohar, 1996.

———. *Kabir Legends and Ananta-Das's Kabir Parchai*. Albany: SUNY Press, 1991.

———. *Praises to a Formless God: Nirguni Texts from North India*. Albany: SUNY Press, 1996.

———, ed. *Religious Movements in South Asia 600–1800*. New Delhi: Oxford University Press, 2004.

———. 'Sain's Kabir-Raidas Debate'. In his *Praises to a Formless God*, pp. 169–81.

———. *Who Invented Hinduism: Essays on Religion in History*. New Delhi: Yoda Press, 2006.

———. 'Who Invented Hinduism?' In his *Who Invented Hinduism*, pp. 1–36.

Mackenzie, Catriona. 'Imagining Oneself Otherwise'. In *Self and Subjectivity*, edited with a commentary by Kim Atkins. Malden: Blackwell Publishing, 2005, pp. 284–99.

Madan T.N. *Non-Renunciation: Themes and Interpretations of Hindu Culture*. New Delhi: Oxford University Press, 2001 [1987].

Mahmood, Saba. *The Politics of Piety: The Islamic Revival and the Feminist Subject*. Princeton: Princeton University Press, 2005.

Malhotra, Anshu. 'Bhakti and the Gendered Self: A Courtesan and a Consort in Mid-Nineteenth Century Punjab'. *Modern Asian Studies* 46, no. 6 (2012): 1503–39.

———. 'The Body as a Metaphor for the Nation: Caste, Masculinity and Femininity in the *Satyarth Prakash* of Dayanand Sarasvati'. In *Rhetoric and Reality: Gender and the Colonial Experience in South Asia*, edited by Avril A. Powell and Siobhan Lambert-Hurley. New Delhi: Oxford University Press, 2006, pp. 121–53.

———. *Gender, Caste and Religious Identities: Restructuring Class in Colonial Punjab*. New Delhi: Oxford University Press, 2002.

———. 'The Importance of Being Piro in Punjab'. *The Tribune*, Chandigarh, 6 December 2012.

———. 'Killing, Gifting or Selling Daughters: The Pressures on a High Caste Identity'. In her *Gender, Caste and Religious Identities*, pp. 47–81.

Malhotra, Anshu. 'Panths and Piety in the Nineteenth Century: The Gulabdasis of Punjab'. In Malhotra and Mir, *Punjab Reconsidered*, pp. 189–220.

———. 'Print and Bazaari Literature: Jhagrras/Kissas and Gendered Reform in Early Twentieth Century Punjab'. In *Gendering Colonial India: Reforms, Print, Caste and Communalism*, edited by Charu Gupta. Hyderabad: Orient BlackSwan, 2012, pp. 159–87.

———. 'Shameful Continuities: The Practice of Female Infanticide in Colonial Punjab'. In Jakobsh, *Sikhism and Women*, pp. 83–114.

———. 'Telling Her Tale? Unravelling Life in Conflict in Piro's *Ik Sau Saṭh Kāfiaṅ*'. *The Economic and Social History Review* 46, no. 4 (2009): 541–78.

Malhotra, Anshu and Farina Mir. 'Punjab in History and Historiography: An Introduction'. In Malhotra and Mir, *Punjab Reconsidered*, pp. xxviii–xix.

———, eds. *Punjab Reconsidered: History, Culture and Practice*. New Delhi: Oxford University Press, 2012.

Malhotra, Anshu and Siobhan Lambert-Hurley. *Speaking of the Self: Gender, Performance and Autobiography in South Asia*. Durham: Duke University Press, 2015.

Malhotra, R.P. and Kuldeep Arora, eds. *Encyclopaedic Dictionary of Punjabi Literature*. Delhi: Global Vision Publishing House, 2003.

Mandair, Arvind-Pal S. *Religion and the Specter of the West: Sikhism, India, Postcoloniality, and the Politics of Translation*. New York: Columbia University Press, 2009.

———. 'Time and Religion-making in Modern Sikhism'. In Murphy, *Time, History and the Religious Imaginary*, pp. 186–202.

Mann, Gurinder Singh. 'Guru Nanak's Life and Legacy: An Appraisal'. In Malhotra and Mir, *Punjab Reconsidered*, pp. 116–60.

Marglin, Frederique A. 'Female Sexuality in the Hindu World'. In *Immaculate and Powerful: The Female in Sacred Image and Social Reality*, edited by C.W. Atkinson, C.H. Buchanan, and M.R. Miles. Boston: Beacon Press, 1985, pp. 39–60.

Marriott, McKim. 'Hindu Transactions: Diversity without Dualism'. In *Transactions and Meanings: Directions in the Anthropology of Exchange and Symbolic Behavior*, edited by B. Kapferer. Philadelphia: Institute for the Study of Human Issues, 1976, pp. 109–42.

Matringe, Denis. 'Hir Varis Shah: A Story Retold'. In *Narrative Strategies: Essays on South Asian Literature and Film*, edited by Vasudha Dalmia and Theo Damsteegt. New Delhi: Oxford University Press, 1998, pp. 19–30.

———. 'Krsnaite and Nath Elements in the Poetry of the Eighteenth Century Panjabi Sufi Bullhe Shah'. In *Devotional Literature in South Asia: Current Research 1985–1988*, edited by R.S. McGregor. Cambridge: Cambridge University Press, 1992, pp. 190–206.

McGregor, R.S. *The Oxford Hindi–English Dictionary*. New Delhi: Oxford University Press, 2004 [1993].

McLeod, W.H. *Guru Nanak and the Religion of the Sikhs*. New Delhi: Oxford University Press, 1996 [1968].

McLeod, W.H. 'Caste in the Sikh Panth'. In his *The Evolution of the Sikh Community: Five Essays*. New Delhi: Oxford University Press, 1996 [1976], pp. 83–104.

―――. *Early Sikh Tradition: A Study of the Janam-sakhis*. Oxford: Clarendon Press, 1980.

―――. *Exploring Sikhism: Aspects of Sikh Identity, Culture and Thought*. New Delhi: Oxford University Press, 2000.

―――. 'The Five Ks'. In his *Essays in Sikh History, Tradition and Society*. New Delhi: Oxford University Press, 2007, pp. 115–23.

―――. 'Sikhs and Caste'. In *Textures of the Sikh Past: New Historical Perspectives*, edited by Tony Ballantyne. New Delhi: Oxford University Press, 2007, pp. 104–31.

―――. *Sikhs of the Khalsa: A History of Khalsa Rahit*. New Delhi: Oxford University Press, 2003.

―――. *Who is a Sikh: The Problem of Sikh Identity*. New York: Clarendon Press, 1989.

Mehta, Deepak. '"Naming" Conversion: Being Muslim in Old Delhi'. In *My Favourite Levi Strauss*, edited by Dipankar Gupta. New Delhi: Yoda Press, 2011, pp. 118–44.

Metcalf, Barbara D. 'The Past in the Present: Instruction, Pleasure, and Blessing in Maulana Muhammad Zakariyya's Aap Biitii'. In Arnold and Blackburn, *Telling Lives in India*, pp. 116–43.

Minkowski, Christopher. 'Advaita Vedanta in Early Modern History'. In *Religious Cultures in Early Modern India: New Perspectives*, edited by Rosalind O'Hanlon and David Washbrook. New Delhi: Routledge, 2011, pp. 105–42.

Mir, Farina. 'Genre and Devotion in Punjabi Popular Narratives: Rethinking Cultural and Religious Syncretism'. In Malhotra and Mir, *Punjab Reconsidered*, pp. 221–60.

―――. *The Social Space of Language: Vernacular Culture in British Colonial Punjab*. Ranikhet: Permanent Black, 2010.

Mir, Mustansir. 'Teachings of Two Punjabi Sufi Poets'. In *Religions of India in Practice*, edited by Donald S. Lopez, Jr. Princeton: Princeton University Press, 1995, pp. 518–29.

Miraj Muhammad Hassan, 'Pooran Bhagat'. Available at http://www.dawn.com/news/755152/pooran-bhagat/2 and http://www.Kartarpur/Arch/Chamiari.htm. Accessed on 8 November 2013.

Morgan, Sue, ed. *The Feminist History Reader*. London: Routledge, 2006.

Muir, Edward. *Ritual in Early Modern Europe*. Cambridge: Cambridge University Press, 1997.

Mukta, Parita. *Upholding the Common Life: The Community of Mirabai*. New Delhi: Oxford University Press, 1997.

Murphy, Anne. 'An Idea of Religion: Identity, Difference and Comparison in the Gurbilas'. In Malhotra and Mir, *Punjab Reconsidered*, pp. 93–115.

―――. 'Introductory Essay'. In her *Time, History and the Religious Imaginary*, pp. 1–11.

―――, ed. *Time, History and the Religious Imaginary in South Asia*. London: Routledge, 2011.

Nabha, Kahn Singh. *Gurushabad Ratnakar Mahan Kosh: Encyclopaedia of Sikh Literature.* Patiala: Bhasha Vibhag, 1981 [1930].

Naim, C.M., trans., annotated, and introduced. *Zikr-i-Mir: The Autobiography of the Eighteenth Century Mughal Poet: Mir Muhammad Taqi 'Mir'.* New Delhi: Oxford University Press, 1999.

Nair, Janaki. 'On the Question of Agency in Indian Feminist Historiography'. *Gender and History* 6, no. 1 (1994): 82–100.

Narayan, Kirin. *My Family and Other Saints.* Chicago: University of Chicago Press, 2007.

Navratan, Kapoor. *Sadhu Gulab Das: Jivan te Rachna.* Patiala: Publications Bureau, Punjabi University, 2002.

Nayar, Aruti. 'Moran, the Mystery Woman'. *The Tribune.* 24 August 2008. Available at http://www.tribuneindia.com/2008/20080824/spectrum/main3.htm. Retrieved on 28 November 2014.

Nayar, Kamla E. and Jaswinder S. Sandhu. *Socially Involved Renunciate: Guru Nanak's Discourse to the Nath Yogis.* New York: SUNY Press, 2007.

Novetzke, Christian Lee. *History, Bhakti, and Public Memory: Namdev in Religious and Secular Traditions.* Ranikhet: Permanent Black, 2008.

Oberoi, Harjot. 'The Worship of Sakhi Sarvar: Illness, Healing and Popular Culture in the Punjab'. *Studies in History* 3, no. 1 (1987): 29–55.

———. *The Construction of Religious Boundaries: Diversity in the Sikh Tradition.* New Delhi: Oxford University Press, 1994.

Official website of Kangra district. Available at hpkangra.nic.in/abtus_history. html. Accessed on 20 December 2014.

Oldenburg, Veena Talwar. 'Lifestyle as Resistance: The Case of the Courtesans of Lucknow'. In *Contesting Power: Resistance and Everyday Social Relations in South Asia,* edited by Douglas Haynes and Gyan Prakash. Berkeley: University of California Press, 1991, pp. 23–61.

———. 'Afternoons in the Kothas of Lucknow'. In *Shaam-e-Awadh: Writings on Lucknow,* edited by Veena Oldenburg. New Delhi: Penguin, 2007, pp. 111–31.

Oman, John Campbell. *Cults, Customs and Superstitions of India.* Delhi: Vishal Publishers, 1972 (reprint).

———. *The Mystics, Ascetics, and Saints of India.* Delhi: Oriental Publishers, 1973 (reprint).

Openshaw, Jeanne. *Writing the Self: The Life and Philosophy of a Dissenting Bengali Baul Guru.* New Delhi: Oxford University Press, 2010.

Orsini, Francesca. *The Hindi Public Sphere 1920–1940: Language and Literature in the Age of Nationalism.* New Delhi: Oxford University Press, 2002.

———. 'The Reticent Autobiographer: Mahadevi Varma's Writings'. In Arnold and Blackburn, *Telling Lives in India,* pp. 54–82.

Pandit, Rajat. 'Indian soldiers were "sitting ducks" in August 6 ambush due to "tactical lapses". Available at http://timesofindia.indiatimes.com/India/Indian-soldiers-were-sitting-ducks-in-August-6-ambush-due-to-tactical-lapses/articleshow/21983927.cms. Accessed on 20 November 2013.

Pankratz, Anette, Claus-Ulrich Viol, and Ariane de Waal, eds. *Birth and Death in British Culture: Liminality, Power and Performance.* Newcastle upon Tyne: Cambridge Scholars, 2012.

Pauwels, Heidi. 'Diatribes Against Saktas in Banarasi Bazaars and Rural Rajasthan: Kabir and His Ramanandi Hagiographer'. In *Religious Interactions in Mughal India,* edited by Vasudha Dalmia and munis D. Faruqui. New Delhi: Oxford University Press, 2014, pp. 290–318.

Pechilis, Karen. 'Bhakti Traditions'. In Frazier, *Continuum Companion to Hindu Studies,* pp. 107–22.

Pennington, Brian K. *Was Hinduism Invented? Britons, Indians, and the Colonial Construction of Religion.* Oxford: Oxford University Press, 2005.

Peterson, Linda H. 'Institutionalizing Women's Autobiography: Nineteenth Century Editors and the Shaping of an Autobiographical Tradition'. In *The Culture of Autobiography: Constructions of Self-Representation,* edited by Robert Folkenflik. Stanford: Stanford University Press, 1993, pp. 80–103.

Petievich, Carla. *When Men Speak as Women: Vocal Masquerade in Indo-Muslim Poetry.* New Delhi: Oxford University Press, 2007.

Pinch, William R. *Warrior Ascetics and Indian Empires.* New Delhi: Cambridge University Press, 2006.

Pollock, Sheldon. *The Language of the Gods in the World of Men: Sanskrit, Culture and Power in Premodern India.* Delhi: Permanent Black, 2007.

———, ed. *Literary Cultures in History: Reconstructions from South Asia.* Berkeley: University of California Press, 2003.

———. 'Ramayana and Political Imagination in India'. In Lorenzen, *Religious Movements in South Asia,* pp. 153–208.

Portelli, Alessandro. *The Death of Luigi Trastulli and Other Stories: Form and Meaning in Oral History.* Albany: State University of New York Press, 1991.

Porter, Roy, ed. *Rewriting the Self: Histories from the Renaissance to the Present.* London: Routledge, 1997.

Prentiss, Karen P. *The Embodiment of Bhakti.* New York: Oxford University Press, 1999.

Punjabi University Punjabi–English Dictionary. Patiala: Publications Bureau Punjabi University, 1994.

Quigley, Declan. *The Interpretation of Caste.* Oxford: Clarendon Press, 1995.

Radhakrishnan, S. and Charles A. Moore, eds. *A Source Book in Indian Philosophy.* Princeton: University of Princeton Press, 1957.

Ram, Ronki. 'Beyond Conversion and Sanskritization: Articulating an Alternative Dalit Agenda in East Punjab'. *Modern Asian Studies* 46, no. 3 (2012): 639–702.

Ramanujan, A.K. *The Collected Essays of A.K. Ramanujan,* edited by Vinay Dharwadker. New Delhi: Oxford University Press, 1999.

———. 'The Indian Oedipus'. In *Collected Essays of A.K. Ramanujan,* pp. 377–97.

———. 'Men, Women and Saints'. In *Collected Essays of A.K. Ramanujan,* pp. 279–308.

———. 'The Ring of Memory: Remembering and Forgetting in Indian Literatures'. In *A.K. Ramanujan: Uncollected Poems and Prose,* edited by Molly

Daniels-Ramanujan and Keith Harrison. New Delhi: Oxford University Press, 2001, pp. 83–100.

Ramanujan, A.K. 'Towards a Counter-System: Women's Tales', 'Telling Tales', and 'Tell it to the Walls: On Folktales in Indian Culture'. In *Collected Essays of A.K. Ramanujan*, pp. 429–84.

———. 'Where Mirrors are Windows: Towards an Anthology of Reflections'. In *Collected Essays of A.K. Ramanujan*, pp. 6–33.

———. 'Who Needs Folklore'. In *Collected Essays of A.K. Ramanujan*, p. 536.

———. 'On Women Saints'. In *The Divine Consort: Radha and the Goddesses of India*, edited by J.S. Hawley and D.M. Wulff. New Delhi: Oxford University Press, 1999, pp. 316–24.

———. 'On Women Saints'. In *Collected Essays of A.K. Ramanujan*, pp. 270–8.

Rama Krishna, Lajwanti. *Panjabi Sufi Poets A.D. 1460–1900*. New Delhi: Ashajanak Publications, 1973.

Ramaswamy, Vijaya, ed. *Devotion and Dissent in Indian History*. New Delhi: Foundation Books, 2014.

Rao, Velcheru N. 'A Ramayan of Their Own: Women's Oral Tradition in Telugu'. In *Many Ramayanas: The Diversity of a Tradition in South Asia*, edited by Paula Richman. Delhi: Oxford University Press, 1994, pp. 67–88.

Ray, Niharranjan. *The Sikh Gurus and the Sikh Society: A Study in Social Analysis*. Patiala: Punjabi University, 1970.

Rege, Sharmila. *Writing Caste/Writing Gender: Narrating Dalit Women's Testimonios*. New Delhi: Zubaan, 2006.

Ricci, Ronit. *Islam Translated: Literature, Conversion, and the Arabic Cosmopolis of South and Southeast Asia*. Ranikhet: Permanent Black, 2011.

Rinehart, Robin. 'Interpretations of the Poetry of Bulhe Shah'. *International Journal of Punjab Studies* 3, no. 1 (1996): 45–63.

———. 'The Guru, The Goddess: The *Dasam Granth* and Its Implications for Construction of Gender in Sikhism'. In Jakobsh, *Sikhism and Women*, pp. 40–59.

Roberts, Geoffrey, ed. *The History and Narrative Reader*. London: Routledge, 2001.

Rose, R.A. *A Glossary of the Tribes and Castes of the Punjab and the North West Frontier Province*. Patiala: Languages Department, 1970 [1883].

Sangari, Kumkum. 'Mirabai and the Spiritual Economy of Bhakti'. *Economic and Political Weekly* 25, no. 27 and 28 (1990): 1464–75 and 1537–52.

'Sansar Chand'. Wikipedia entry. Available at en.wikipedia/wiki/Sansar_Chand. Accessed on 20 December 2014.

Sant Ditta Ram (*urf* Gyani Ditt Singh). *Shirin Farhad*, with an 'Introduction' by Shamsher Singh Ashok. Ludhiana: Punjabi Sahit Academy, n.d.

Sarkar, Mahua. 'Introduction: Writing Difference'. In her *Visible Histories, Disappearing Women: Producing Muslim Womanhood in Late Colonial Bengal*. New Delhi: Zubaan, 2008, pp. 1–26.

Sarkar, Tanika. 'A Book of Her Own. A Life of Her Own: Autobiography of a Nineteenth Century Woman'. In *From Myths to Markets: Essays on Gender*, edited by Kumkum Sangari and Uma Chakravarti. New Delhi: Manohar, 2001, pp. 85–124.

———. *Words to Win: The Making of Amar Jiban–A Modern Autobiography*. New Delhi: Kali for Women, 1999.

Sarna, Navtej. *The Book of Nanak*. New Delhi: Penguin/Viking, 2003.

Saunders, Leslie S. *Report on the Revised Land Revenue Settlement of the Lahore District of the Panjab 1865–69*. Lahore: Central Jail Press, 1873.

Schechner, Richard. 'Drama, Script, Theater, and Performance'. In his *Performance Theory*. London: Routledge, 2003 [1988], pp. 66–111.

———. *Performative Circumstances: From the Avant Garde to Ramlila*. Calcutta: Seagull Books, 1983.

———. 'Performers and Spectators Transported and Transformed'. In his *Performative Circumstances*, pp. 90–123.

———. 'Ramlila of Ramnagar: An Introduction'. In his *Performative Circumstances*, pp. 238–88.

Schimmel, Annemarie. *Mystical Dimensions of Islam*. Delhi: Yoda Press, 2007 [1975].

Schomer, Karine and W.H. McLeod, eds. *The Sants: Studies in a Devotional Tradition of India*. Delhi: Motilal Banarsidass, 1987.

Sekhon, Sant Singh. *A History of Punjabi Literature*, vol. 2. Patiala: Publications Bureau Punjabi University, 1993.

Sen, Nabaneeta Dev. 'Chandravati Ramayana: Feminizing the Rama Tale'. In Bose, *Faces of the Feminine*, pp. 183–91.

Sewak, Gian Inder. 'Gulabdasi Sampradya: Rachna Ate Vichar'. Unpublished PhD diss. Amritsar: Guru Nanak Dev University, 1984.

Shackle, Christopher. 'Punjabi Sufi Poetry from Farid to Farid'. In Malhotra and Mir, *Punjab Reconsidered*, pp. 3–34.

Shahryar. 'Kalaam Mata Piro ka'. *Hun* (2009): 166.

———. *Piro Preman*. Amritsar: Rawal Prakashan, 1999.

Shani, Giorgio. *Sikh Nationalism and Identity in a Global Age*. New York: Routledge, 2008.

Sharma, Radha. *Lahore Darbar*. Amritsar: Guru Nanak Dev University, 2001.

Sherma, Rita DasGupta. '"Sa Ham–I am She": Woman as Goddess'. In *Is the Goddess a Feminist: The Politics of South Asian Goddesses*, edited by Alf Hiltebeitel and Kathleen M. Erndl. Sheffield: Academic Press, 2000, pp. 24–51.

Shulman, David. 'Cowherd or King? The Sanskrit Biography of Ananda Ranga Pillai'. In Arnold and Blackburn, *Telling Lives in India*, pp. 175–202.

Singh, Bhai Vir. *Sundri*. New Delhi: Bhai Vir Singh Seva Sadan, 1983 (1898).

Singh, Giani Ditt. *Nakali Sikh Prabodh*. In *Panth Ratan Bhai Ditt Singh Giani, Rachnavali–Bhag Athvan* by Pritam Singh. Mohali: Published by the Editor, 2007.

———. *Sadhu Dayanand Nal Mera Sambad*. In *Gyani Ditt Singh: Jiwan Ate Rachna* by Gurditt Singh. Chandigarh: Dharam Prachar Committee, 1998, pp. 43–82.

———. *Sultan Puara*, 6th edition (n.p., n.d.).

Singh, Giani Gian. *Sri Guru Panth Prakash*. Patiala: Bhasha Vibhag, 1970 [1880].

Singh, Gurditt. *Gyani Ditt Singh: Jiwan Ate Rachna*. Chandigarh: Dharam Prachar Committee, 1998.

Singh, Gyani Amar. *Jiwan Chariter Singh Sabha Lehar de Ughe Sanchalak Gyani Ditt Singh Ji*. Amritsar: Gulab Singh Malak Firm, 1962.

Singh, Harbans, ed. *The Encylopaedia of Sikhism*, vol. 1. Patiala: Punjabi University, 1996.

———. *The Encyclopaedia of Sikhism*, vol. 2. Patiala: Punjabi University, 1996.

Singh, K.S., ed. *People of India*, vol. 37, *Punjab*. Delhi: Manohar, 2003.

Singh, Khushwant. *A History of the Sikhs*, vol. 2, *1839–2004*. New Delhi: Oxford University Press, 2008 [1963].

———. *Ranjit Singh: Maharajah of the Punjab*. London: George Allen and Unwin Ltd, 1962.

Singh, Mahant Ganesha. *Bharat Mat Darpan*. Amritsar: Vaidak Bhandar, 1926.

Singh, Namwar, ed. *Bulleh Shah ki Kafian*. Delhi: National Institute of Punjab Studies, 2003.

Singh, Pashaura, *The Bhagats of the Guru Granth Sahib: Sikh Self-Definition and the Bhagat Bani*. New Delhi: Oxford University Press, 2003.

Singh, Pritam. *Panth Rattan Bhai Ditt Singh Gyani—Rachnavali*, part I. Mohali: author published, 2005.

Singh, Swaran. 'Mazhabi' and 'Balmiki'. In K.S. Singh, *People of India*, p. 316 and p. 59 respectively.

———. 'Sirkiband'. In K.S. Singh, *People of India*, p. 418.

Sital, Jit Singh. *Bulleh Shah: Jivan te Rachna*. Patiala: Punjabi University, 2002.

Smith, Sidonie. 'Performativity, Autobiographical Practice, Resistance'. In *Women, Autobiography, Theory: A Reader*, edited by Sidonie Smith and Julia Watson. Madison: The University of Wisconsin Press, 1998, pp. 108–15.

Smith, Sidonie and Julia Watson, eds. *Reading Autobiography: A Guide for Interpreting Life Narratives*. Minneapolis: Minnesota University Press, 2000.

Snehi, Yogesh. 'Situating Popular Veneration'. *NMML Occasional Paper*. New Delhi: Nehru Memorial Museum and Library, 2015.

Snell, Rupert. 'Confessions of a 17th-Century Jain Merchant: The *Ardhakathanak* of Banarasidas'. *South Asia Research* 25, no. 1 (2005): 79–104.

Sobti, Krishna. *Dar se Bichhuri*. New Delhi: Rajkamal, 1984 [1958].

Sontheimer, Gunther-Dietz. 'Hinduism: The Five Components and Their Interaction'. In *Essays on Religion, Literature and Law*, edited by Heidrun Bruckner, Anne Feldhaus, and Aditya Malik. Delhi: Manohar, 2004, pp. 401–19.

Soomro, Khadim Hussain, compiled. *Seth Vishandas: A Great Philanthropist*, compiled and translated by Zafar Iqbal Mirza from Vishandas' biography *Ratanjot*. Sehwan Sharif: Sain Publishers, 1997.

Spence, Jonathan D. *The Death of Woman Wang*. New York: Penguin Books, 1978.

Sreenivasan, Ramya. Drudges, 'Dancing Girls, Concubines: Female Slaves in Rajput Polity, 1500–1850'. In Chatterjee and Eaton, *Slavery and South Asian History*, pp. 136–61.

Sreenivasan, Ramya. 'The Marriage of "Hindu" and "Turak": Medieval Rajput Histories of Jalor'. *Medieval History Journal* 7, no. 1 (2004): 87–108.

Stewart, Tony K. 'In Search of Equivalence: Conceiving Muslim–Hindu Encounter Through Translation Theory'. *History of Religions* 40, no. 3 (2001): 260–87.

———. *Fabulous Females and Peerless Pirs: Tales of Mad Adventure in Old Bengal.* New York: Oxford University Press, 2004.

Strnad, Jaroslav. 'Searching for the Source or Mapping of the Stream: Some Text-Critical Issues in the Study of Medieval Bhakti'. In Hawley, Malhotra, and Williams, *Text and Tradition in Early Modern North India.*

Swarajbir. *Shairi.* Ludhiana: Chetna Prakashan 2004.

Syan, Hardip S. *Sikh Militancy in the Seventeenth Century: Religious Violence in Mughal and Early Modern India.* London: I.B. Tauris, 2013.

Talbot, Cynthia. 'Inscribing the Other, Inscribing the Self: Hindu–Muslim Identities in Pre-Colonial India'. *Comparative Studies in Society and History* 37, no. 4 (1995): 692–721.

Temple, Richard. *The Legends of the Punjab*, vol. 2. Patiala: Language Department Punjab, 1988 [1884].

Thapar, Romila. 'Good Times are Gone'. *Outlook.* 24 March 2014, pp. 70–2.

———. *Somanatha: The Many Voices of a History.* New Delhi: Viking/Penguin Books, 2004.

Tharu, Susie and K. Lalita, eds. *Women Writing in India*, vol. 1, *600 BC to the Early Twentieth Century.* New Delhi: Oxford University Press, 2007 [1991].

Thornton, Edward. *A Gazetteer of the Territories under the Government of the East India Company and of the Native States of the Continent of India*, vol. 4. London: W.H. Allen and Company, 1954.

Turner, Victor. *Dramas, Fields, and Metaphors: Symbolic Action in Human Society.* Ithaca: Cornell University Press, 1974.

———. 'Social Dramas and Ritual Metaphors'. In his *Dramas, Fields, and Metaphors: Symbolic Action in Human Society.* Ithaca: Cornell University Press, 1974, pp. 23–59.

Vahab, Veer, ed. *Piro Kahe Saheliyon* (in Gurmukhi script). Jalandhar: R.B. Printing Press, 2012.

van der Veer, Peter. 'Syncretism, Multiculturalism and the Discourse of Tolerance'. In *Syncretism/Anti-Syncretism: The Politics of Religious Synthesis*, edited by Charles Stewart and Rosalind Shaw. London: Routledge, 1994, pp. 196–211.

Vanita, Ruth. 'I'm an Excellent Animal: Cows at Play in the Writings of Bahinabai, Rukun Advani, Suniti Namjoshi and Others'. In her *Gandhi's Tiger and Sita's Smile: Essays on Gender, Sexuality and Culture.* New Delhi: Yoda Press, 2005, pp. 290–310.

Vatuk, Sylvia. '*Hamara Daur-i-Hayat*: An Indian Muslim Woman Writes Her Life'. In Arnold and Blackburn, *Telling Lives in India*, pp. 144–74.

Vaudeville, Charlotte. 'Pandharpur, City of Saints'. In her *Myths, Saints and Legends in Medieval India.* New Delhi: Oxford University Press, 1996, pp. 199–219.

Vaudeville, Charlotte. *A Weaver Named Kabir: Selected Verses with a Detailed Biographical and Historical Introduction*. New Delhi: Oxford University Press, 2005 [1993].

Venkatachalapathy, A.R. 'Making a Modern Self in Colonial Tamil Nadu'. In *Biography as History: Indian Perspectives*, edited by Vijaya Ramaswamy and Yogesh Sharma. Hyderabad: Orient BlackSwan, 2009, pp. 30–52.

Vidyarthi, Devinder Singh. 'Punjabi di Pehli Istri Kavi'. *Khoj Darpan* 1, no. 2 (1974): 89–95.

Vishwanathan, Gauri. 'Colonialism and the Construction of Hinduism'. In *The Blackwell Companion to Hinduism*, edited by Gavin Flood. Malden: Blackwell Publishing, 2005, pp. 23–44.

Waheeduddin, Fakir Syed. *The Real Ranjit Singh*. Patiala: Publications Bureau Punjabi University, 1981.

Wakankar, Milind. *Subalternity and Religion: The Pre-History of Dalit Empowerment in South Asia*. London: Routledge, 2010.

Warner, Michael. 'Publics and Counter-Publics'. *Public Culture* 14, no. 1 (2002): 49–90.

Webster, John C.B. *Religion and Dalit Liberation: An Examination of Perspectives*. Delhi: Manohar, 2002.

Werbner, Pnina and Helene Basu. 'The Embodiment of Charisma'. In *Embodying Charisma: Modernity, Locality and the Performance of Emotion in Sufi Cults*, edited by Pnina Werbner and Helene Basu. London: Routledge, 1998, pp. 3–27.

White, David G. *The Alchemical Body: Siddha Traditions in Medieval India*. Chicago: The University of Chicago Press, 1996.

White, Hayden. 'The Historical Text as Literary Artifact'. In Roberts, *The History and Narrative Reader*, pp. 221–36.

Williams, Tyler. 'From Local to Trans-Regional Poets: Translating Texts and Traditions in the Niranjani Sampraday'. In Hawley, Malhotra, and Williams, *Text and Tradition in Early Modern North India*.

Wilson, H.H. *Hindu Religions: An Account of the Various Religious Sects of India*. Delhi: Bharatiya Book Corporation, n.d. (reprint).

Zelliot, Eleanor. 'Women Saints in Medieval Maharashtra'. In Bose, *Faces of the Feminine*, pp. 192–200.

Index

About the Author

Anshu Malhotra teaches at the Department of History, Faculty of Social Sciences, University of Delhi, India. She holds a PhD from the School of Oriental and African Studies (SOAS), University of London. She has been a Fellow at the Nehru Memorial Museum and Library, New Delhi (2013–15), and the Hughes Fellow at the University of Michigan, Ann Arbor, USA (2008). She has written extensively on gender issues over the past two decades. She is also the author of *Gender, Caste, and Religious Identities: Restructuring Class in Colonial Punjab* (2002). Her other previous publications include the edited volumes *Speaking of the Self: Gender, Performance, and Autobiography in South Asia* (2015) with Siobhan Lambert-Hurley and *Punjab Reconsidered: History, Culture, and Practice* (2012) with Farina Mir.